Visual Information Communication

Mao Lin Huang · Quang Vinh Nguyen ·
Kang Zhang

Editors

Visual Information Communication

Editors

Mao Lin Huang
Faculty of Engineering and
    Information Technology
University of Technology, Sydney
PO BOX 123
Broadway, NSW 2007
Australia
maolin@it.uts.edu.au

Quang Vinh Nguyen
School of Computing and
    Mathematics
University of Western Sydney
Locked Bag 1797
South Penrith DC, NSW 1797
Australia
vinh@scm.uws.edu.au

Kang Zhang
Department of Computer Science
University of Texas at Dallas
800 West Campbell Road
Richardson, TX 75080
USA
kzhang@utd.edu

ISBN 978-1-4899-8390-9   ISBN 978-1-4419-0312-9 (eBook)
DOI 10.1007/978-1-4419-0312-9
Springer New York Dordrecht Heidelberg London

Springer is part of Springer Science+Business Media (www.springer.com)

Table of Contents

Preface

Visual communication through graphical and sign languages has long been conducted among human beings of different backgrounds and cultures, and in recent decades between human and machine. In today's digital world, visual information is typically encoded with various metaphors commonly used in daily life to facilitate rapid comprehension and easy analysis during the communication process. Visual information communication generally encompasses information visualization, graphical user-interfaces, visual analytics, visual languages and multi-media processing. It has been successfully employed in knowledge discovery, end-user programming, modeling, rapid systems prototyping, education, and design activities by people of many disciplines including architects, artists, children, engineers, and scientists. In addition, visual information is increasingly being used to facilitate human-human communication through the Internet and Web technology, and electronic mobile devices.

This manuscript provides the cutting-edge techniques, approaches and the latest ongoing researches in the context of visual information communication. It is a collection of 24 chapters selected from more than 60 submissions to the VINCI'09 - 2009 Visual Information Communications International Conference, that is held in Sydney Australia, September 2009. These chapters were selected through a stringent review process to ensure their high standard in quality, significance and relevance. Each chapter was reviewed by at least two international Program Committee members of VINCI'09.

The book covers a broad range of contents in five key sub-areas of visual information communication, including.

1) The Arts of Visual Layout, Presentation & Exploration: focuses on the design and development of optimized techniques and algorithms for improving the readability of visual objects and structures, in terms of their geometrical layouts, graphical displays and exploration views. Readability can be expressed by means of aesthetic rules, such as the minimization of edge crossings, display of symmetries and optimized design of color and shape schemes.

2) The Design of Visual Attributes, Symbols & Languages: visual communication is similar to network and human-to-human communications that need a set of predefined rules (or languages) for information transmissions. In network communication, the talk between network devices is based on a set of communication protocols, such as HTTP and FTP, while the huaman-to-human communication is based on a variety of languages derived from different cultures. In the design of visual languages for human-machine or human-human communications, we need to address the languages' expressiveness and intuitiveness. The visual languages should be easy to learn and to use; and avoid ambiguity, syntax and semantic errors. This section focus on the above issues in the design of primitive visual properties, such as graphic attributes, symbols and grammars for visual communication.

3) Methods for Visual Analytics & Knowledge Discovery: visual analytics is the integration of interactive visualization with automated analysis techniques to answer a growing range of questions in science, business, and analysis. Visual analytics encompasses topics in computer graphics, interaction, visualization, analytics, perception, and cognition. This section focuses on the proposal of new methods and technologies in this area.

4) Systems, Interfaces and Applications of Visualization: this section focuses on the latest development of new applications, such as advanced tools, software and user interfaces that can be used to facilitate visual communication for a variety of objectives.

5) Methods for Multi-media Data Recognition & Processing: In recent years we have witnessed an increasing role of multi-media data, in the form of still pictures, graphics, 3D models, audio, speech, video or their combination in the real world. This has led to a demand for automatic generation and extraction of both low and high levels of features from multi-source data in order to enhance their potential for computational interpretation, feature detection and processing. This section focuses on the proposal of novel methods that can be used to effectively and efficiently process the multi-media data.

The book offers a systematic presentation of the state of the art in the related fields. With this, the book is very significant and valuable as a reference or a professional book for researchers as well as senior and post-graduate computer science and engineering students.

The manuscript cannot be completed without the helps of many peoples. We would like to thank all the authors for their contribution to the book and their effort in addressing reviewers' and editorial feedback. Thanks also go to the VINCI'09 program committee members and the reviewers for their thorough reviews and constructive comments. Our appreciation also goes to Hung Nguyen, Doan Hoang and organization committee members for their invaluable support. Finally, we would like to thank Susan Lagerstrom-Fife and Jennifer Maurer at Springer USA for their assistance in publishing this manuscript in a timely fashion.

Mao Lin Huang
Quang Vinh Nguyen
Kang Zhang

July 2009

The Physical Visualization of Information: Designing Data Sculptures in an Educational Context

Andrew Vande Moere and Stephanie Patel

Design Lab, Faculty of Architecture, Design and Planning
The University of Sydney, Australia
{andrew;stephie}@arch.usyd.edu.au

Abstract. This paper is a qualitative case study analysis of the issues involved in designing and implementing data sculptures, the physical "embodiment" of data in a tangible presence, shape or form, within the context of an undergraduate design studio. It demonstrates how approaches and theories from the field of data visualization can form a rich contextual resource and motivational tool for teaching principles of creative design. A relatively short, two-week assignment challenged students to investigate and convey a meaningful data-driven insight through a tangible representation. In this paper, we analyze the resulting collection of physical artifacts developed by the students to reveal notable design approaches of embodying abstract information. We present a novel classification of data sculptures based on a semiotic taxonomy (symbolic, iconic, or indexical) and consider the qualities of representational fidelity and narrative formulation, for instance when the unfolding of the data-driven narrative is seen as a process, rather than an outcome. In addition, we investigate how the introduction of digital fabrication techniques influenced the design strategies chosen by the students versus hand-made approaches.

Keywords: design, education, data visualization, information aesthetics, data sculpture, digital fabrication.

1 Introduction

Information visualization (*infovis*) is traditionally viewed as a means to understand and analyze complex data sets. Its main tasks typically include: the accurate detection of data patterns, the facilitation of decision making based on data trends, and the communication of data-driven information and knowledge. With of its deep roots in scientific reasoning, research into information visualization has mainly focused on supporting scientific goals and optimizing analytic tasks. As a result, visualization is traditionally considered a tool that is neutral, dispassionate and objective, as it caters for the solutions to well-defined and specialized task of its expert users.

In recent years, there has been a tendency to "democratize" the practice of data visualization, which is characterized by (1) the ability to develop visualizations through free, open and well-supported software development platforms by computer

M.L. Huang et al. (eds.), *Visual Information Communication*,
DOI 10.1007/978-1-4419-0312-9_1, © Springer Science+Business Media, LLC 2010

novices, (2) the increasing number of freely available, large, complex and interesting data sets from government, science and business sources, and (3) the refocusing of traditional data visualization goals towards including the education of a large, lay audience about data-supported insights. In the context of this last point, the fields of arts, design, media and sciences have a common interest in utilizing innovative forms of visualization to represent the knowledge, relevance and meaning hidden within complex information structures. By articulating the common interests and goals of visualization across these academic fields, shared problems are addressed in a multi-perceptual space and a broader cultural context [1, 2, 3].

Several new visualization taxonomies have been proposed that incorporate the increasing *artistic* tendencies in the practice of data visualization. For instance, Warren Sack [4] has noticed how the "anti-sublime" information visualization has outgrown science and engineering and has ultimately become embraced by conceptual art. He proposes looking beyond whether such visualizations are pretty, beautiful, or easy to use, and instead recognize their *aesthetics of governance* – the interpretation and articulation of meaning, rather than just the purity of the information being represented, as a creative response to visual forms of contemporary art. Pousman et al. [5] coined the term *casual visualization* as conveying an "increased focus on activities that are less task driven, data sets that are personally meaningful, and built for a wider set of audiences". Viegas and Wattenberg [6] use the term *artistic data visualization* for those data depictions that embody a forceful point of view by recognizing the power of visualization as a potential communication medium. In turn, we defined *information aesthetic* visualization to denote the interlocking combination of aesthetics and design (e.g. visual style, user experience), a shift in focus, away from conveying patterns and trends towards narrating meaning and underlying principles, and finally, a tendency towards more fluid user interaction and user participation (e.g. flow, user feedback) [7]. The term information "aesthetics" here refers to the degree of involvement and engagement it facilitates, rather than denote a subjective measure for visual appeal or even the quality of the work. Similarly, the term *database aesthetics* has been used in the field of Design and Media Arts to denote a new aesthetic approach undertaken by a collection of artists who use the vast amounts of available information as their medium of expression [8] [8]. At this extreme of what some might doubt can still be called "visualization", the visual ordering and organization of information has become an artistic choice, a choice motivated by the intent to influence and critique the digitization of daily life.

This rich spectrum of approaches shows the importance of design and creativity in the visualization field. To explore the potential of design and of data visualization as a communication medium in its own right, the main author has coordinated and taught an undergraduate Design Studio at the University of Sydney. In particular, the studio course aimed to combine the fields of design, new forms of digital technology and data visualization as a platform for research-led teaching in design education. As such, one of its assignments comprised of the design and the implementation of a "data sculpture". The main aim of this paper is to report on the design strategies and experimentation by the students within the context of this assignment. It will present a novel classification of data sculptures based on a semiotic taxonomy (symbolic, iconic, or indexical) and the qualities of representational fidelity and narrative formulation.

2 Designing a Data Sculpture

We define *data sculpture* as the physical "embodiment" of data in a tangible presence, shape or form [9]. That is, a data sculpture is a direct externalization of the data it represents: except of its aesthetic expression that might relate to its perceivable or tangible features, it possesses no additional direct functionality other than conveying meaning to its onlookers. This meaning is often based on quantitative data, which directly determines its visual characteristics such as its shape, color or size. However, data sculptures could even aim to reveal more qualitative measures, such as emotion, context or background that relate to the circumstances around dataset or the insight shown. The "raison d'être" (reason for being or existence) for a data sculpture is thus communicating insight, which might range from a scientifically founded causal correlation, over simple visual similarities in time-based trends, to an emotion based on a consequence of a data pattern. Its design is often motivated by exploiting physical qualities to capture the attention of lay people to data-related issues that would be otherwise disregarded if shown as factual descriptions, journalistic articles, infographic illustrations or data graphics. The novelty and aesthetic of its sculptural form and its physical affordances often drive the interest of people to attempt to decipher the content.

2.1 Physical Qualities

Although humans are well experienced in navigating, interpreting and interacting with physicality in everyday life, designing (and implementing) a tangible artifact that allows for abstract meaning to be gathered through physical form is not an obvious task. In particular, we believe that a useful data sculpture requires a strong design rationale underlying its perceived physical qualities, including: *embodiment*, *metaphorical distance*, *multi-modality*, *interaction*, *affordance* and *physicality*.

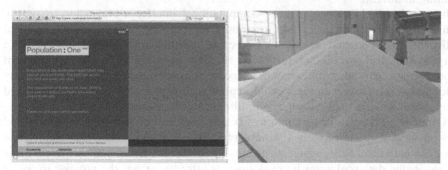

Fig. 1. Screen-based versus physical data representation of an identical dataset. *Left*: World Population One [10]. One person is one *pixel*: the world's population represented as a large, scrollable image. *Right*: Of All the People in all the World [11]. One person is one *rice grain*: here, the population of the US as a one heap of rice.

Embodiment. We define *embodiment* as the expression of data through the process of *data mapping*, which in turn describes the use of a *metaphor* to translate (inherently non-physical) data values into a perceivable form [9]. While determining a useful and useable data mapping is already a well-known consideration in the design of a data visualization technique, we believe that the physical character of a data sculpture has the potential to significantly influence the sense-making process of its users who interpret its meaning. For example, as shown in Figure 1, the experience of seeing a population represented as a collection of data pixels [10] versus a heap of rice [11] seems to be significantly different. While the first instance resembles that of scrolling through a huge digital image file, the unanticipated magnitude and unfamiliar shape conveyed by a huge rice heap leads to a stark and memorable experience that has the ability to surprise and intrigue onlookers.

Metaphorical Distance. The design of a data sculpture touches the issue of *metaphorical distance*, the distance between the chosen metaphor and the data itself, and between the metaphor and the perceived reality [9]. In other words, while most screen-based depictions are of abstract or iconic quality due to the limited available bandwidth for representation, reality offers the freedom to simulate meaning closer to our mental image, preconceptions and expectations, and provides for a broader contextual interpretation. A data sculpture, seen as a whole, combines two metaphorical depictions: that of the meaning it reveals when seen as a physical depiction of an object with all its connotations (e.g. rice, food, mountain), and that of a shape that is determined by data (e.g. size and height convey a meaning).

Multi-Modality. It is still an open question as to what aspects of the huge vocabulary of non-visual representation could be used for the effective communication of information in data sculptures. Some early experimentation has lead to advancements in the field of *ambient display*, which proposed to turn everyday architectural spaces into "interfaces" by changing the state of the physical matter, solids, liquids and gases that they contain by well-chosen data-driven values [12]. However, while such multi-modal "rendering" of information might increase the perceivable bandwidth of a user while providing for a memorably experience, it also highlights the question of our ability to inverse the stimulation of our senses into a meaningful insight.

Interaction. While contemporary computational interfaces are mainly based on mouse and touch-screen interaction metaphors, representing information as a physical reality has the potential to use our inherent experience of interacting with the everyday physical world that surrounds us. The exploration of our environment through grasping, poking, caressing or squeezing has been encouraged since our early childhood years. Data sculptures could exploit such exploratory playful actions (and many more) as ways to overview, zoom, filter or select information.

Affordance. Next to its metaphorical connotation, information can also be carried by a physical shape through its *affordance(s)*, the externally perceivable quality that allows an individual to recognize its potential to perform a specific action. We believe that designing data sculptures by exploiting its affordances has the promise to reveal powerful perceptual cues for accurately and intuitively deciphering the information that is embodied in a particular physical form. Similar to the use of visual cues in traditional visualization, affordances could have the capacity to be learned and interpreted in a functional way, thereby conveying informational meaning and foregoing higher-level visual abstraction. However, even in reality, most affordances are learnt through past experience, education or trial-and-error actions, and porting everyday physical usage scenarios to the most abstract issue of communicating information is complex.

Physical Properties. Since most data visualization techniques have been specifically designed to be presented on two-dimensional media such as paper or computer screens, a different design approach required when developing "equivalent" representations in the physical realm. The most obvious challenge is to withhold reverting back to pixel-based graphics or simply "giving depth" to already known data visualization metaphors such as scatter plots, line graphs or pie charts. In fact, besides the high degree of resolution of pixel-based representations, there is no real compelling reason why physical displays should mimic purely computer-based visual languages. What a "pixel-less" display might loose in resolution, it could make up in a richer experience that may also include aspects of multi-modality in form of touch (e.g. texture, granularity), sound (e.g. shaking noise) or even smell (e.g. from material). The design of such a physical artifact needs to take into account various considerations, of which *ergonomics* (e.g. dimensionality, use), *materiality* (e.g. appropriateness, tangible quality), *robustness* (e.g. for long-time interaction), *sustainability* and *cost* are just a few.

2.2 Digital Fabrication

Early versions of the data sculpture assignment deliberately left open any constraints in terms of fabrication. As a result, most students chose for hand-made constructions based on cheap, of-the-shelf parts. In the last year, however, the assignment was integrated within the context of *digital fabrication*, or the use of *rapid prototyping* machines such as a laser cutter, a milling machine and a 3D plotter. The aim of this integration was two-sided: firstly, to allow students to learn how to integrate digital technology within the process of designing physical artifacts; and secondly, to encourage a more sophisticated form-finding design process, for instance allowing large quantities of data values to be exactly matched to physical measurements.

The *laser cutter* facilitates the accurate production of highly complex 2D design work by enabling the cutting or engraving of sheet material. A wide range of materials can be cut, including paper, fabric, card, thin plywood, acrylic sheet or Perspex. Despite being solely capable of producing 2D shapes, complex and visually appealing 3D structures can be constructed using these forms as interlocking modules of the overall structure. While being a quick and relatively cheap method, the main design challenge moves towards how these modules fit together and how material properties influence the overall aesthetic and structural integrity of the produced form. The *milling machine* has the capability of cutting 2D and 2.5D objects from digital height data. More specifically, it can produce 2.5D objects using 3D model form information as well as 2.5D relief surfaces. A typical milling machine can mill a range of medium and low-density materials such as hardboards, plywood, resin board and Styrofoam. The *3D printer* (plotter) is able to produce complex 3D forms with internal and external structures from 3D CAD data, using a process by which thin 2D layers are sequentially built up on top of each other. 3D forms can also be developed as molds for ceramic and metal casting, as well as creating models that can be sanded, drilled, tapped, painted and electroplated (depending on the material powder composite used for the printing).

As a result, the student works discussed hereafter will show either hand-made or digital fabricated artifacts, depending on the year the assignment was given. In Section 3.4, we will discuss some general qualitative differences in perceived design approaches between the two fabrication methods.

3 Designing Data Sculptures

The qualitative case study analysis described below is based on a collection of student works created during a design studio assignment provided to 3rd year Design Computing undergraduate students at the University of Sydney, taught between 2005 and 2009. With an average student number of 28, the total collection of data sculptures consists of about 140 works. The small subset of pieces mentioned in this paper were chosen for their quality and documentary value, although we claim that the proposed design strategy model can be applied to all student works. The data sculpture assignment was of an intensive nature, as students were only provided with two (sometimes three) weeks from initial design brief to final submission. Intermediate presentations focused on the chosen data insights and the design of the sculptures themselves. Although one might note that the limited time aspect restricts the degree of design experimentation and the sophistication of the execution, the primary focus of the assignment was to teach students to use creative design as a means for explorative research and lateral thinking. The focus of the main design assignment of this particular course unit has been described in a previous paper [13].

3.1 Educational Context

Students were asked to establish a remarkable or worthwhile insight that underlies a specific, potential data pattern they were personally interested in (e.g. local traffic patterns). They had then to find two different and freely available datasets that contained the probable proof for this particular pattern to occur (e.g. weather, car traffic data). A minimum of three different data attributes between the two chosen datasets had to be selected (e.g. time, ambient temperature, car counts), and at least one appealing data trend or pattern between them had to be identified (e.g. less cars travel through the city when it rains). The main challenge of this assignment focused on designing a data mapping technique that represents the finding in a physical form in an understandable way, whilst also demonstrating aesthetic qualities that would encourage lay people to spend time to learn and experience it.

Next to the learning involved in discovering, retrieving, handling, and analyzing obscure datasets, one of the most practical learning outcomes of this assignment was to encourage students to consider the communication of information beyond the traditional computer screen, and to experiment with metaphorical storytelling when representing data outside of the virtual realm. They had to design and implement an "information artifact", of which the form was as much as possible "determined" by quantitative data. The resulting object should be decorative, inquisitive and informative, while exploiting the unique qualities of physicality to communicate meaning without the need for separate or extensive labels, captions or legends. In other words, the sculpture should be sufficiently beautiful and mesmerizing to be exhibited in a typical living room. But it should also be able to reveal a compelling (data-supported) insight when visitors accidentally discover it, and curiously ponder, look closer, or interact with it.

3.2 Preliminary Data Sculpture Design Taxonomy

We propose two conceptual design dimensions that capture the rich and broad design space explored by the students: *representational fidelity* and *storytelling formulation*. These dimensions were chosen to highlight the relationships between data-mapping metaphor, expressed physical form, offered interaction affordance and the generation of form as a means of facilitating insight through tangible and visual discovery.

Representational Fidelity refers to the design rationale behind the *embodiment* of data to convey underlying data patterns through the physical aesthetic form of a data sculpture. It encompasses both the chosen data-mapping metaphor and its *metaphorical distance* to the data that it represents. This metaphorical distance or rather, the level of abstraction, can be described in the language of semiotics, the field of philosophy that studies the use or interpretation of signs and symbols. A semiotic *sign* is comprised of three properties [14]: the *signified*, the *signifier* and the *sense*. An object, the signified, stands in place of a physical thing or idea. Representing the object is a signifier, which aims to create the same sense that an observer can understand by experiencing or seeing the signified. Signs can describe a notion in a *symbolic, iconic* or *indexical* term, which we chose as the basis for classifying the representational fidelity of a data sculpture. A symbolic representation is an embodiment in which the signifier bears no resemblance to the signified. The relationship between the two must be learned using a defined convention in order to understand it. An indexical representation is one in which the signifier bears a direct relationship (either physically or causally) with the signified. It is through this direct relationship on which an understanding is formulated. An iconic representation lies somewhere between the two, in which the signifier bears some resemblance to the signified through a defined metaphorical relationship. The metaphor facilitates understanding between the signifier and the signified by transporting knowledge from the source domain to the target domain [15], for instance by analogy in emotional tone, theme or functionality. As will be shown, representational fidelity greatly influences how narrative is generated through the underlying data patterns that are captured by a data-mapping algorithm, metaphorical translation or causal outcome.

Narrative Formulation describes how a data sculpture facilitates the discovery of information through its external *physical form* and any *interactive affordances* it provides. Physical properties provides for a multi-sensory interpretation using the visual aesthetics, sound qualities and tangible features of a sculpture. The use of form proposes a largely passive behavior, solely based on the visual and tangible perception by the user. Affordance and interactivity, on the other hand, suggests a more proactive attitude where the conveying of meaning relies on the active discovery of insights through actively handling components of the data sculpture by the user. This category highlights how the intuitive or learned manipulation of physical affordances of a data sculpture has the potential to augment insight discovery and sense making as a form of sequential storytelling.

3.3   Representational Fidelity

This section discusses the different forms of design rationale that were observed in the student works in the context of representational fidelity, amongst both the digitally fabricated sculptures and hand-made sculptures. As mentioned before, works can be described as being symbolic, indexical or iconic reflections of the signified.

Symbolic. We define symbolic representations to be works characterized by a form-finding approach that employs a so-called *arbitrary* data-mapping approach, that is it has no meaningful conceptual connection to the data. Even when arbitrary, the used mapping must always be deterministic, so that data fidelity is always retained, and values can be retrieved back from the form and vice-versa. However, we have recognized that "arbitrary" can be split into two different types: *graph-like* and *abstract*. A graph-like approach applies an algorithmic-based mapping convention that mostly strongly resembles a conventional 2D or 3D data visualization method. The sculptural form creation method ranges from simply giving "depth" to a two-dimensional chart or graph, to the creation of a series of three-dimensional elements that collectively make up a unique three-dimensional shape (see Figure 2).

Fig. 2. Graph-like symbolic data sculptures. *Left*: dataLix. Comparison of unemployment rate between males and females in Australia (1978-2005). The (male and female) helix revolutions are indicative of the number of people looking for work, while creases in the ribbon accentuate the rate of data change. (Student: Andrew Wallace) *Center:* Crime Association Cluster. Balls are colored to indicate the different associations victims have with the crime committed against them, with volume equivalent to the number of occurrences. (Student: Mitchell Page). *Right*: Money Fire. Two adjacent surfaces made up by ribbons compare the industry performance of large versus small companies over time. The size of data variances is mapped as color brightness to result in a holistic destructive flame. (Student: Jenny Song)

Arbitrary *abstract* approaches, as shown in Figure 3, do not resemble chart or graph aesthetics, and instead focus on more sculptural qualities. However, all external dimensions are fully determined by exact data values. That is, all data elements are translated into separate visual elements, while the data values determine their visual properties, such as position, size, direction or color. Here, the design approach resembles that of an ("information") architect, in which data is used as a ground material to be sculpted into a free form. As will be discussed later, this category in particular was more easily explored using digital modeling and fabrication techniques.

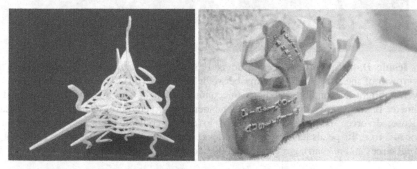

Fig. 3. Abstract symbolic data sculptures *Left*: Out of Sight, Out of Mind. Comparison between water usage and the media coverage of the water shortage issue in Australia, over time. The triad-shaped layers are determined by the number of media articles versus the vertical supports that convey water usage. (Student: Beth Green) *Right*: Aviation and Bird Strikes. Each "arm" represents an Australian state, with length indicative of the number of air strikes, and color to reflect the different environmental characteristics of the air strike incidents. (Student: Julia Tang)

Iconic. Iconic representations bear resemblance to the signified by means of a well-chosen *metaphor*. Metaphors are culturally defined, arbitrary, conventional representations that derive expressive power from the extent to which its context is understood [16]. Hence, the effectiveness of their associated expression is dependent on how well the metaphor has been learned. The most effective metaphorical representations are those that utilize an appropriate mapping model to capture the *relational structure* of the signified object, rather than just its features [15]. This particular concept is highlighted in the two contrasting data sculptures, show in Figure 4, in which an identical metaphor (i.e. flower) has been used. In the first example, a flower's natural association with "growth" has been used to convey the underlying pattern of economic growth in Australia. The governmental expenditure is mapped to the radius of each of the flower's three-layered sets of twelve petals, with each layer representing one year, and each petal one month. As shown in the adjacent Figure, the flower metaphor can also be conveyed to reveal connotations of "love", alluding to the beauty of love through petal formation, sensuality through its scent, and heartbreak with thorns. The relative amount of fallen rose petals stand in place of failed marriages in Australia, some of which have been pierced by the thorns, each of which represent a re-marriage.

Fig. 4. Iconic Data Sculptures. *Left*: Budget Flower. Three layers of 12 petals show the relative growth of the Australian economy between 1979 and 1981. The explicit imbalance of the flower highlights a monthly periodicity in economic growth, with revenue being mapped to the perimeter of the petals while width is dependent on expenditure. (Student: Andrea Lau) *Right:* Rose, divorce, marriage. Hardships of love are iconically represented through the metaphor of a rose. Its petals have been plucked and pierced to represent the relative amount of recorded divorces and re-marriages between 2000 and 2002. (Student: Ellis Lum Mow)

Indexical. Representations that bear a *direct* relationship (either physically or causally) with the signified are defined as being indexical. In Figure 5, one artifact shows how different sorts of electronic, electric, headphone, phone, coaxial and networking cables can be twisted and interweaved to represent a physical timeline of a single person's typical activities during an average day that uses cabling in some way. Here, samples of real cabling are used to directly denote the use of cabling. Approaching the form-finding task from a more abstract perspective, another student explored the danger of wearing thongs (Figure 5). Several thongs have been deformed from their original, functional condition, into something devoid of purpose other than (data) sculptural, to highlight the particular motivations behind people's uses of them as footwear. In both these examples, the students established a meaning that underlies the context of the data through a direct, indexical embodiment.

Fig. 5. Indexical Data Sculptures. *Left*: Daily Networking. Different types of network cables are interweaved amongst each other to reflect the relative length of time spent using particular network technologies during an average day. (Student: Nikash Singh) *Right*: Thongs. The dangers associated with wearing thongs are reflected by a series of physical thongs that have been pierced with a nail for every thousand thong-related injury requiring hospitalization. (Student: Rebecca Young)

3.4 Conceptual Movements in Representational Fidelity

Next to data sculptures that clearly show qualities of only one of the three semantic categories, we have also observed conceptual movements from one to another.

Symbolic → Iconic. Initially, most students grappled with making a conceptual transition from presenting information on screen-based media towards the physical realm. They had difficulties with exploiting the potential design space physicality offers beyond copying already known representation techniques. Having been schooled for several years in computer-based topics such as web design, 3D modeling and software programming, a typical student's first reaction was to (literally) give "depth" to well-known data visualization techniques such as line and bar graphs, pie charts or scatter plots. Although most students attempted to avoid reaching the typical scientific aesthetic of a graph, many opted to "add" some "beautifications" in a way that still retained the typical high fidelity and high resolution of a traditional graph. This particular design approach was chosen with varied intentions in mind. As shown in Figure 6, one student highlighted the remarkable "spikiness" of daily sales data around the yearly Christmas periods by designing the sculpture to resemble an abstract, iconic representation of a (spiky) Christmas tree. While the external form was determined by a circular line graph (i.e. symbolic), the sculpture resembled the cross-section of a Christmas tree, whilst the green color further enhanced this metaphor (i.e. iconic). Here, the traditional data visualization technique (i.e. circular line graph) was augmented to provide an intuitive clue and to reinforce the meaning behind the observed data pattern. Another project used the shape and form of a spinal backbone to compare and contrast the number of departures and arrivals of visitors in and to Australia, during times of economic growth and decline. The iconic representation of a spinal shape was chosen to consider tourism as a strong but fragile backbone for the general economy, but also to dramatically highlight the formal

characteristic of the data trend that was discovered (i.e. the sharp drop in tourists due
to the recent economic downturn), which visually resembled a human spine. Both
design approaches contrast the broad metaphorical spectrum for merging the
representation of abstract data with meaning.

Fig. 6. Symbolic to Iconic. *Left*: Data Spikes. Australian retail sales between 1982 and 2009.
The sharp retail "spikes" around Christmas were metaphorically linked to the color and external
characteristics of a (sliced) Christmas tree. (Student: Drew Cosgrove) *Right*: Economic impact
on the tourism industry in Australia (2005-2009). Monthly tourism arrivals have steadily
increased, yet experienced an abrupt fall due to the recent economic downturn. The curvature
of a spinal backbone metaphorically enhances the curvature of this data trend. (Student: Lucy
Ro)

Iconic → Symbolic. Other data sculptures demonstrate a conceptually opposite
approach, as they started from a purely iconic representation that was specifically
designed to manifest the meaning underlying the data. That is, these sculptures aimed
to reflect a well-recognized object that somehow linked back to the concepts behind
the data through an interpretative or metaphorical relationship. Then, in a move
towards a symbolic approach, its external form, such as its color, size and proportion,
was directly modified according to an "arbitrary" mapping. For instance, using a
sporting trophy as an iconic starting point (see Figure 7), one student developed an
algorithm-based depiction of each rugby team's seasonal results within the league,
applying a mathematical algorithm (i.e. symbolic) that creates an organic form.
Similarly, the DNA double-helix model is algorithmically modified (i.e. symbolic) to
narrate the story of Karma – what goes around comes around – with the two strands
representing US crime rates and US natural disaster occurrences respectively.
Karma's notion of the eternal existence and relationship between actions and
consequences are metaphorically represented through the natural intertwining of DNA
strands, concentrated in areas along the length of the strands where similar rates of
change in the data values are evident. In another example, an ikebana display makes
up a metaphor of an almost religious altar devoted to prosperity, while the
arrangement, lengths and direction of all the flowers specifically reflect the data
values of Australian retail turnover (1995-2005). These works thus rely on the
viewer's preconceived understandings of the connotations underlying the used
metaphor to intuitively understand the shown datasets. While the external measures
can be interpreted as data graphs, these examples demonstrate how the viewer can be
encouraged to unpack meaning through understanding the metaphorical message.

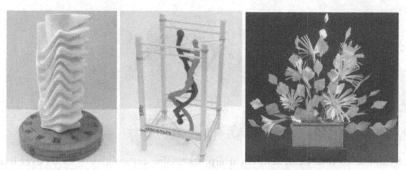

Fig. 7. Iconic to Symbolic. *Left*: NRL Trophy. Yearly rugby team performances are contrasted between each other, with the radii of the waves measured proportional to crowd attendance and thickness to ranking. (Student: Ali Malla) *Center*: Karma. Comparison between murder rates (1997-2007) and occurrence of natural disasters in the United States (1998-2008). The strands represent each dataset, and are intertwined more tightly together as the two reflect equivalent rates of change. (Student: Jean Viengkhou) *Right*: Ikebana. Prosperity of the Australian economy is measurable by the different plant types, their directional placement and relative lengths. (Student: Joyce Wong)

Symbolic → Indexical. Almost unique in its characteristics of movement within the representational fidelity domain, sculptures of the nature symbolic → indexical are distinctive in that the visualization is a "direct" physical consequence of the data sculpture, which in turn is determined by a data-driven algorithm. For example, data values describing the technological advancements and calculating power in CPU computer chips were determinant in the design of the shape of a music harp's outer frame (see Figure 8). By plucking on the tensioned nylon strings (i.e. symbolic) users are able to physically experience (i.e. indexical) the data. Similarly, data values describing the influential effects of alcohol on the human body were used as a basis for developing a series of textile color patterns with different granularities (i.e. symbolic), based on a series of dripping experiments with a set of data-driven, laser-cut filters (see Figure 8). Insight discovery into this "represented" data was only unfolded by a process of active participation in experimenting in mixing and layering colored inks, leaving a perceivable pattern of decay (i.e. indexical) as the liquid (i.e. data) drips through the perforated meshes (i.e. data filters, data querying). As such, these sculptures epitomize the very potential of a data sculpture's physicality to be exploited as a *tool* that allows for a more active user experimentation rather than a static object, and the discovery of meaning as a *process* rather than a design outcome.

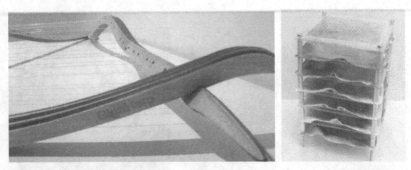

Fig. 8. Symbolic to Indexical. *Left*: GigaHarp. Increasing capabilities of CPUs over time are reflected by the tones generated by the plucking of the harp strings. The frame is derived from the gradient increase in computer processing speeds, with the strings tuned to each other to create a reverberation relative of transistor size. (Student: Kevin Chen) *Right*: Alcohol's Filtered Influence. Each filter is comprised of a matrix of holes that allows water to filter through each layer in a timeframe reflective of the delayed effect of alcohol. (Student: Trent Robinson)

Indexical → Symbolic. Some student design strategies initiated from an indexical representation by starting from the object depicted by the data itself. As shown in Figure 9, one student conveyed the usage of individual keys of a computer keyboard by deforming the components of an existing keyboard (i.e. indexical), here raising the keys to exact heights to reflect the frequency of their use (i.e. symbolic). Developing a highly complex and intricate sculpture, another student focused on the issues associated with gambling addiction by building differing playing card-based (i.e. indexical) structures to represent varying aspects retrieved from data statistics (i.e. symbolic), such as the revenue generated at each of the card-gaming tables at a Sydney casino. Both data sculptures underline how direct, indexical representations radiate easily perceivable and intuitive cues as to the context of the represented data, despite modifying the original form through an abstract mapping approach. It can be observed, however, that this approach is particularly complex, as data-driven changes need to still retain the overall form of the existing object.

Fig. 9. Indexical to Symbolic. *Left.* Keyboards. A keyboard is modified to reflect the usage of the keyboard as an input device. Individual keys are raised at a height measurable to the average number of times they have been pressed over time. (Student: Alex Duckmanton) *Right:* Playing Cards. Packs of playing cards are modeled into a series of abstract components. Flower blossom-shaped cards create a visual appeal akin to the luring effect of gambling, which surround a tower of cards reflective the revenue generated by typical card-gaming tables. (Student: Andrew Morrisson)

Iconic → Indexical. Only a few data sculptures exhibited a direct, indexical representation that grew from a metaphorical, iconic depiction. Conveying a narrative about the cause of fire-related deaths, one data sculpture featured in Figure 10 utilizes matches as a metaphor for fire. However, by lighting (an exact relative amount of) the matches, the student transformed what initially was a metaphor into a causal relationship with fire (i.e. indexical). Another student took a metaphor as a starting point and instead created a direct physical representation through the physical weight of one of the sculpture's elements, here representing the amount of pesticides (1 kilogram) required to generate 100 grams of cotton. Comprising of four layered artifacts that, when brought together, visually depicts the form of a cotton plant flower (i.e. iconic), the student conveyed the physical representation of the data values by various means, including the relative difference in physical weight (i.e. indexical). Both these examples show how the design rationale that underpins the indexical approaches of these works highlight the designer's intent to initiate a narrative process in which the user is compelled to explore both conceptually as well as physically.

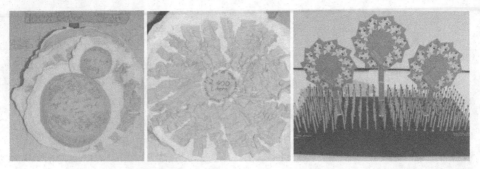

Fig. 10. Iconic to Indexical. *Left and Middle:* 100% Cotton. The sculpture shows the implications on the environment resulting from the water usage requirements for creating a 100g cotton singlet. Individual components iconically represent separate statistics, which brought together, form the structure of a cotton plant flower. (Student: Jessie Heppel). *Right:* Redheads. Each fire match is representative of the number of trees killed per day to meet the demand for matchstick production. Of those matches that are extinguished, each is representative of a human death. (Student: Madeline Reader).

Indexical → Iconic. Due to the abstract nature of most of the used datasets, indexical representations were relatively scarce. Of those that were digitally fabricated, one data sculpture demonstrated how computational tools required for rapid prototyping techniques could be used to generate an indexical representation. As shown in Figure 11, the impact of human conflicts was mapped geographically (a map is indexical in that it points to the locations of things) as etched concentric rings, resembling ripples or shockwaves, on to a series of layered Perspex sheets. Another data sculpture demonstrated how indexical representations can be iconized by using components in a simple electronic circuit. Representing relative energy consumption, the sculpture incorporated a series of ten light bulbs, several of which were lit to symbolically represent a percentage value reflecting energy usage. In this way, both examples illustrate that the iconic representations bear a single degree of separation to the signified as a means of reiterating the context of the represented data.

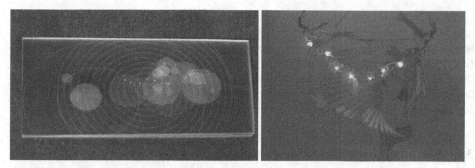

Fig. 11. Indexical to Iconic. Left: Ripples of Conflict. Layers of Perspex sheets are stacked on top of one another to reveal a geographic mapping of concentric circles equivalent to the number of human deaths associated with global conflicts. (Student: Martha Gouniai) *Right*: Clothes Pegs. A series of light globes reflect the percentage of total energy saved when line-drying clothes as oppose to using a clothes dryer. (Student: Stephanie Patel)

Representation Fidelity by Fabrication. The distribution of design approaches across the representational fidelity domain differed substantially between the two different manufacturing approaches: hand-made and digitally fabricated. Data sculptures created using digital fabrication techniques reflected works across the entirety of the representational fidelity domain (i.e. iconic/symbolic/indexical), whereas data sculptures that were hand-made reflected a more limited spectrum that hovered between symbolic and iconic representation. The variance between the modes of fabrication is probably a consequence of the fact that the former technique requires the creation of a new data-driven artifact, while the latter approaches the task by deriving a form by means of modifying already existing objects. As such, hand-made projects often began with indexical or iconic representations of the data they were embodying, whereas there is little virtue in simulating an existing object through rapid prototyping. The hand-made sculptures demonstrated that the integration of the object, or a metaphorical connotation to it, into a sculpture's form provides for a more intuitive context to understanding the represented data insight. At the same time, it contributes to the difficulty in generating physical forms that accurately represented data values, which in turn seems to be the reason for the greater occurrence of exploration into interpretive symbolic representational forms, rather than algorithm-based representational forms.

Digital fabrication, on the other hand, facilitated students with the familiarity of computation and 3D modeling through the use of digital tools and software, enabling them to retain the full integrity and high resolution of quantitative data values. Consequently, algorithmic symbolic representations were prevalent examples among the digitally fabricated sculptures, in particular algorithmic mappings in the form of charts and graphs. In comparison with the hand-made charts and graphs, the digitally fabricated sculptures illustrated far more precise and accurate mathematically-driven forms, which even reached a theoretical dimensional resolution of 0.1mm. This in turn obviously produced sculptures of a higher finished quality, but often lacked the level of artistic quality exemplified by the hand-made sculptures. Hence, many digitally fabricated pieces relied on an iconic or indexical influence in order to provide the necessary context or clues to understand the embodied data.

The capability for producing higher resolution sculptures could also be the reason behind the greater range of interactive pieces amongst the digitally fabricated sculptures. A higher resolution provides for a greater control for sculpting physical form, allowing concepts like puzzles and interlocking modules as a tool for narrative discovery and open exploration. In turn, very few hand-made sculptures displayed both intricate and accurate data value representations through the narrative formulation.

3.4 Narrative Formulation Fidelity Among Student Works

Some of the data sculptures aimed to facilitate the discovery of information through the inclusion of affordance properties and interactive features that unfold the narrative of the underlying data as a process, rather than an outcome. Students approached developing an integrated narrative formulation from differing perspectives, with some sculptures conveying insights largely through *physical properties* and *affordances* of the sculpture's form, while others relied solely on the use of *interactive features*.

Physical Properties and Affordances. Such design approaches highlighted a prominent but often overlooked aspect of data sculptures – the potential for *emergent* physical forms. Emergence can be characterized as the consequence of an unanticipated result. The stark appearance of forms generated by emergent properties not only draws attention to itself, but also acts as a potential research method for the designer and a catalyst for questioning into the reasoning that underlies the emergent property. A prime example that illustrates this aspect is a two-sided data-driven surface that explored trends in the extinction of species around the world (Figure 12). By embodying the trends in extinction from two different datasets through a topographic landscape curved out from two opposite sides of the same object, some unanticipated holes appeared which potentially have a meaning that can be traced back to time-equivalent intersections within the original datasets. In this case, the datasets consisted of levels in threatened vertebrate species and threatened plants.

Fig. 12. Emergence in Fabrication. Threatened Species. A surface topography is created by mapping the rise and fall of threatened plant species on the top side, and the rise and fall of threatened vertebrate species on the bottom side. The unanticipated, emergent holes in the resulting surface draws focus and can be considered indicative of the major extinctions in Earth's history regardless of species at particular points in time. (Student: Kristian Tasevski).

Interaction. Some students designed affordances that give prominence to the interactive usage of the sculptures, encouraging users to grab, push, or rotate it. For instance, the selectively cut holes in the data sculpture shown in Figure 13 enables the user to peer through the holes and make direct comparisons between the height of the color-matched segments above and below the surface. Having used the laser cutter to develop a series of complex interconnecting cogs, another student developed an object that required its users to turn a specially-made key in order to a series of etched markings on two circular Perspex plates. An emergent pattern underlying the dataset becomes visually apparent upon successfully lining up the two plates.

Fig. 13. Interactive data sculptures. *Left*: Data Mirror Wheel. Recurring trends in retail turnover versus average household expenditure are represented as a mirrored pattern on the top and bottom of a board. The board is strategically cut in such a way that observers can peer through and compare segment heights. (Student: Sheila Tan) *Right*: Rainfall and Babies. Rainfall rates and birth rates are mapped along the circumferences of two Perspex sheets. Users will see a correlation between the number of babies being born and increase in recorded rainfall when the two sheets are lined up accordingly. (Student: Andrew Kurniawan)

Other data sculptures consisted of separate parts of which, when put together, the whole revealed more than the parts alone. Separating the sculpture in this way allows for a process of *data-driven narrative formulation*, by engaging users to take it apart and gradually learn more detailed insights into the data through exploring its interactive features. One example includes the separate data facts behind cotton-based clothing manufacturing (see Figure 10), separated in four separate modules that all together make up the external shape of the cotton plant. Interaction begins with two balls symbolic of cotton balls – both are weighted specific to the 1kg of pesticides required to grow enough cotton for the 100g cotton-made singlet, as direct physical comparisons to the data they represent. One student developed an interactive Venn diagram formed by a tower of interlocking puzzle blocks (see Figure 14, left). Each of the mutually exclusive areas is representative of the overall mood of a single diary entry, and interlock together to reflect the order in which the entries are written. Narrative underlying the data is hence conveyed as the sculptures are taken apart into its many components and then connected together to form a cohesive artifact.

Fig. 14. Interactivity and Play. *Left*: Diary Entries. A set of puzzle blocks are shaped and colored to reflect the semantic analysis and overall mood of each diary entry. Each block is uniquely shaped and parameterized, while interlocking together as an historical timeline of entries. (Student: Mandy Leung) *Right*: Social Behavior Pyramid. The facing sides of the pyramid are inversed to each other, reflecting the stark opposites in behaviors observed among train commuters with and without MP3 players. Users are encouraged to unfold the sculpture into diverse shapes, to compare all possible pairs of opposing sides. (Student: Georgie Pope)

Play. A number of students even produced data sculptures that aimed for interaction as the sole and primary means for communicating information. Proactive engagement and actively exploring a data sculpture has a high potential to augment the learning experience with that of play and joy. Of these works, the majority seemed to be characterized by puzzle-based interaction as the avenue for narrative development. Moreover, some modification of the data sculpture (namely, the arrangement of discrete components in a set order) produces a derivative form that subsequently has the capacity to reveal different data patterns that were originally envisioned. For instance, one student work invites users to take apart the different layers, each of which represent a different Tetris level, and compare the relative sizes of the six blocks that sit in designated slots on each layer (see Figure 15). Much like the Tetris stack in terms of its layered stack composition, a rotational spherical orb requires its users to play with the object, rotating its circular discs around until they eventually line-up according to a series of etched markings. Another student developed a sculpture based on the outer form of a pyramid. Users are encouraged to interact with the sculpture by literally "unzipping" it along the edges laying the net flat out, or zipping up the edge to explore the sculpture in its pyramid form, and recognizing the insights by looking through the layered depictions on its sides (Figure 14, right). The decision to focus on interaction as an integral element requires much thought into building robustness into the sculptural form. Each of the works reflect playful design approaches that facilitate a tangible exploration through puzzle-based engagement allowing them to gain a more detailed insight into the underlying data after ordering the puzzle-pieces accordingly.

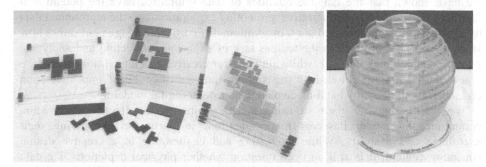

Fig. 15. Interactivity and Play. *Left*: Tetris Stack. Each physical layer represents a level within a Tetris game, comprising of six designated slots for each of the typical Tetris blocks, their sizes relative to the number of times they appeared in the level. (Student: Christine Lam) *Right*: Economy and Shark Attacks. The orbital shape of the sculpture brings together a contrasting relationship between the state of the economy and the number of shark attacks. It affords users to easily turn and rotate any of the discs to line up. (Student: Chloe Yeung)

4 Conclusion

In this paper, we have discussed the value of data sculptures in the current information aesthetics movement as a potential way to engage lay people in understanding complex data insights. We also presented over twenty different data sculpture examples and discussed the most remarkable design strategies followed by our undergraduate design students. In addition, the paper described the aspects of physical properties, affordances, interactivity and play, and analyzed the most important differences in design rationales between digitally fabricated and hand-made pieces.

The design principal is an important question to many data visualization projects. Very often, a successful visualization approach comes from the design stage. However, little research has focused on the design process of visualizations. In an attempt to capture the range of design strategies followed by the students, we have defined a simple semiotic model based on three categories – symbolic, indexical, and iconic. The proposed model can be used as a resource for inspiration for other design educators or future data sculpture designers, and even has the potential to be used to inform the design rationales of traditional, screen-based data visualizations. In particular, the model could be used to refine teaching strategies, or recognize the qualitative differences between the fields of data visualization, information aesthetics and data art. The proposed model thus illustrates the rich metaphorical spectrum of design approaches that might range from mapping data in fully abstract or arbitrary ways, over metaphorical constructions, to more process-driven causal effects. It also illuminates the true qualities of a data sculpture as a potential effective tool through which (data-supported) meaning can be conveyed, for instance in an educational context, advertising campaign, or public exhibition or museum settings. Furthermore, we have shown that the tangible qualities of data sculptures have the potential to facilitate the formulation of narrative, promoting exploration into the represented data by a process of interaction and play. In addition, this particular assignment shows how students can be motivated in the tedious task of exploring, collecting and analyzing obscure and complex datasets, while allowing for creative and lateral thinking. More practical students are allowed on focusing on the sophistication of implementation and fabrication, either by hand-made manufacturing or digital modeling.

We realize that the claim of using a data sculptures as effective information communication media deserves more attention, in particular in proving their usefulness and usability. While interesting and challenging in a creative design education context, it is still an open question whether physical depictions like data sculptures are indeed effective or efficient in conveying information in a more enjoyable or memorable way than traditional screen-based media. Developing and executing appropriate evaluation studies that respect the unique qualities of physicality should therefore be the focus of future research.

Acknowledgements

We would like to thank all the students, tutors and teaching assistants who took part in the past infostudio courses, and in particular Justin Clayden, Sucharita Patra, Nick Cawthon, Monika Hoinkis, Andrea Lau, Martin Tomitsch and Gabriele Ulacco.

References

1. Bertelsen, O. W., Pold, S.: Criticism as an Approach to Interface Aesthetics. In: Nordic conference on Human-Computer Interaction, Tampere, Finland, pp. 23-32. ACM (2004)
2. Judelman, G.: Aesthetics and Inspiration for Visualization Design: Bridging the Gap between Art and Science. In: International Conference on Information Visualisation (IV'04), pp. 245-250. IEEE (2004)
3. Vande Moere, A.: Form follows Data: the Symbiosis between Design and Information Visualization. In: International Conference on Computer-Aided Architectural Design (CAADfutures'05), pp. 31-40. Vienna, Austria, OKK Verlag (2005).
4. Sack, W.: Aesthetics of Information Visualization. In: Context Providers. C. Paul, V. Vesna and M. Lovejoy (eds.). Boston, MIT Press (2006)
5. Pousman, Z., Stasko, J., Mateas, M.: Casual Information Visualization: Depictions of Data in Everyday Life. In: IEEE Transactions on Visualization and Computer Graphics 13(6): 1145-1152. IEEE Press (2007)

6. Viegas, F. B., Wattenberg M.: Artistic Data Visualization: Beyond Visual Analytic. In: Lecture Notes in Computer Science 4564(15): 182-191. (2007)
7. Lau, A., Vande Moere A.: Towards a Model of Information Aesthetic Visualization. In: International Conference on Information Visualisation (IV'07), Zurich, Switzerland, pp.87-92. IEEE (2007)
8. Vesna, V.: Database Aesthetics - Art in the Age of Information Overflow, University of Minnesota (2007).
9. Zhao, J., Vande Moere A.: Embodiment in Data Sculpture: A Model of the Physical Visualization of Information. In: Conference on Digital Interactive Media in Entertainment and Arts (DIMEA'08), Athens, Greece, pp. 343-350. ACM (2008)
10. Mautner,   B.:   Population   One   -   One   Person   is   One   Pixel,   URL, http://www.royalsapien.com/pop1/ (2006)
11. Cafe,   S.:   Stan's   Cafe,   Of   All   the   People   in   All   the   World,   URL, http://www.stanscafe.co.uk/ofallthepeople/ (2008)
12. Wisneski, C., Ishii, H., Dahley A., Gorbet, M., Brave, S., Ullmer B., Yarin, P.: Ambient Displays: Turning Architectural Space into an Interface between People and Digital Information. In: International Workshop on Cooperative Buildings (CoBuild '98), pp. 22-32. Springer (1998)
13. Vande Moere, A.: infostudio: Teaching Ambient Display Design using Home Automation. In: Conference of the Australian Computer-Human Interaction (OZCHI'05), Canberra, ACM (2005)
14. Ogden, C. K., Richards, I. A.: The Meaning of Meaning." 8th Ed. New York, Harcourt, Brace & World, Inc. (1923)
15. Johnson-Laird, P. N.: Analogy and the exercise of Creativity. In: Vosniadou, S and Ortony, A. (eds.) Similarity and Analogical Reasoning, pp 313—331. Cambridge University Press, New York (1989)
16. Ware, C.: Information Visualization: Perception for Design. Morgan Kaufmann, San Francisco (2000)

Visual Analysis of History of World Cup: A Dynamic Network with Dynamic Hierarchy and Geographic Clustering

Adel Ahmed[1], Xiaoyan Fu[2], Seok-Hee Hong[3], Quan Hoang Nguyen[4], Kai Xu[5]

[1] King Fahad University of Petroleum and Minerals, Saudi Arabia
adel.f.ahmed@gmail.com
[2] National ICT Australia, Australia
xiaoyan.fu@nicta.com.au
[3] University of Sydney, Australia
shhong@it.usyd.edu.au
[4] University of New South Wales, Australia
quanhn@cse.unsw.edu.au
[5] ICT Center, CSIRO, Australia
kai.xu@csiro.au

Abstract. In this paper, we present new visual analysis methods for history of the FIFA World Cup competition data, a social network from Graph Drawing 2006 Competition. Our methods are based on the use of network analysis method, and new visualization methods for dynamic graphs with dynamic hierarchy and geographic clustering. More specifically, we derive a dynamic network with geographic clustering from the history of the FIFA World Cup competition data, based on who-beats-whom relationship. Combined with the *centrality* analysis (which defines dynamic hierarchy) and the use of the *union of graphs* (which determines the overall layout topology), we present three new visualization methods for dynamic graphs with dynamic hierarchy and geographic clustering: wheel layout, radial layout and hierarchical layout. Our experimental results show that our visual analysis methods can clearly reveal the overall winner of the World Cup competition history as well as the strong and weak countries. Furthermore, one can analyze and compare the performance of each country for each year along the context with their overall performance. This enables us to confirm the expected and discover the unexpected.

1 Introduction

Recent technological advances have led to the production of a lot of data, and consequently have led to many large and complex network models in many domains. Examples include:

– Social networks: These include telephone call graphs (used to trace terrorists), money movement networks (used to detect money laundering), and citation networks or collaboration networks. These networks can be very large.

M.L. Huang et al. (eds.), *Visual Information Communication*,
DOI 10.1007/978-1-4419-0312-9_2, © Springer Science+Business Media, LLC 2010

- Biological networks: Protein-protein interaction (PPI) networks, metabolic pathways, gene regulatory networks and phylogenetic networks are used by biologists to analyze and engineer biochemical materials. In general, they have only a few thousand nodes; however, the relationships are very complex.
- Software engineering: Large-scale software engineering deals with very large sets of software modules and relationships between them. Analysis of such networks is essential for design, performance tuning, and refactoring legacy code.
- Webgraphs, where the nodes are web pages and relationships are hyperlinks, are somewhat similar to social networks and software graphs. They are huge: the whole web consists of billions of nodes.

Visualization can be an effective analysis tool for such networks. Good visualization reveals the hidden structure of the networks and amplifies human understanding, thus leading to new insights, findings and predictions. However, constructing good visualizations of such networks can be very challenging.

Recently, many methods for visualization of large graphs have been suggested. For example, see the recent proceedings of Graph Drawing and Information Visualization conferences. Methods include fast multi-level force directed methods [7], geometric or combinatorial clustering methods [12, 14], and multidimensional methods [8]. However, current visualization methods tend to exhibit one or more of the following problems: *scalability*, *visual complexity*, *domain complexity* and *interaction*.

Note that some of the network structures exhibit more complex relationships, i.e, multiple relationships, dynamic relationships or temporal relationships. Methods are available for visualization of such temporal or dynamic networks including using an animation or a 2.5D visualization [1, 6, 11]. However, they only considered the dynamics of network topologies, i.e. addition or deletion of nodes and edges based on different time frames. On the other hand, recently a method for visualizing affiliation dynamics of the IMDB (Internet Movie Data Base) was introduced [4].

In this paper, we consider a more complex network model of both *dynamic topology* and *dynamic properties* (or attributes). More specifically, we consider a dynamic temporal network with two attributes: dynamic hierarchy and geographic clustering structure, and present three visualization methods for dynamic network with dynamic hierarchy and geographic clustering: *wheel* layout, *radial* layout, and *hierarchical* layout.

Our methods are evaluated with a social network, history of the FIFA World Cup Competition data set. More specifically, we derive a dynamic network with geographic clustering from the history of the FIFA World Cup Competition data, based on *whobeats-whom relationship*.

Combined with the *centrality* analysis from the social network analysis [3, 15] which defines dynamic hierarchy, and the use of the *union of graphs* which determines the overall layout topology, our visualization methods can clearly reveal the overall winner of the World Cup competition history as well as the strong and weak countries.

Furthermore, one can analyze and compare the performance of each country for each year along the context with their overall performance. This enables us to confirm the expected and discover the unexpected [13].

This paper is organized as follows. In Section 2, we explain our network model with example data set, the FIFA World Cup competition data. We describe our analysis method in Section 3. Our visualization techniques and results are presented in Section 4. Section 5 concludes.

2 The FIFA World Cup Competition History Data Set

Our research was originally motivated from the Graph Drawing Competition 2006 to visualize the evolution of the FIFA World Cup competition history. We first briefly explain the details of the data set in order to explain the network model that we derived from the given data set, which eventually motivated the design of our new techniques.

The FIFA (Federation Internationale de Football Association) World Cup is one of the most popular and long-lasting sports event in the world. As a record of the World Cup history, the results of each tournament are widely available and frequently used by the sports teams as well as the general public. For example, every four years, during the the tournament's final phase, many media outlets analyze such historical record to predict the performance of the teams.

The FIFA World Cup competition history data set has complex relationships between the teams from each country changing over time, thus leading to a set of directed graphs which consist of nodes representing each country and edges representing their matches. Recently, the data set became a popular challenging data set for both social network community (i.e. Sunbelt 2004 Viszard Session) and graph drawing community (i.e. Graph Drawing Competition 2006) for analysis and visualization purpose.

More specifically, the data set contains the results of all the matches played in the final rounds since the Cup's founding in 1930. The FIFA has organized the World Cup every four years, but due to the World War II, only 18 tournaments have been held so far.

There are in total 79 countries that have ever joined the Cup's final rounds. Further, they can be clustered based on their geographic locations and the Football Federations. There are six different federations: AFC (Asia), CAF (Africa), CONCACAF (North America), CONMEBOL (South America), OFC (Oceania) and UEFA (Europe). Therefore, from the data set, we can derive a series of 18 directed graphs with the following properties:

- Dynamic network: Each year, the graph has been dynamically changing. That is, some nodes are disappeared and some new nodes are added. In addition, the edge sets are dynamically changing based on their matches. There is some overlap of nodes between each year, as most of the strong countries joined the final games many times.
- Temporal network: Each network has a time stamp. Thus the ordering of each graph is fixed by the time series.
- Geographic clustering structure: Each network can be clustered according to the 6 continental confederations.

3 Centrality Analysis for Dynamic Hierarchy

In this section, we now describe how to define a dynamic hierarchy for the dynamic network of the FIFA World Cup data set.

The overall result of each match can inherently define a hierarchy between countries. Some countries won many matches, whereas the other countries lost many matches. Furthermore, some countries joined the final game many times, whereas the other countries joined only a few times. Obviously, the most interesting question to ask is to analyze the overall winner of the World Cup history, and to identify the top countries of strong performance in order to predict the next winner.

Based on the previous *centrality* analysis from the Sunbelt 2004 Viszard Session, we also used the centrality analysis from the social network analysis to define a hierarchical attribute for each node in the network. Centrality index is an important concept in network analysis for analyzing the importance of actors embedded in the social network [3, 15]. Recently, centrality analysis has been widely used by visualization researchers, see [5]. Note that in our case, the centrality analysis define a *dynamic hierarchy*, based on the performance of each country in each year.

In particular, we compute both the overall performance and the performance of each year, to confirm the expected events and detect the unexpected events. For this purpose, we designed a new approach based on the *union* of a dynamic graph as follows: For each year, we construct a directed graph G_i, $i =1,..., 18$, based on the results of matches in each year. Then, we construct the union of graphs $G = G_1 \cup G_2 \cup ... \cup G_{18}$ in order to analyze the global performance.

There are many centrality measures available based on the different definition of the importance in specific applications, such as degree, betweenness, stress, and the eigenvalue centralities. For details of each definition, see [3, 15]. We performed several centrality analysis on each G_i as well as the union graph G, as used in the Sunbelt 2004 Viszard Session. Based on the results, we finally chose the *degree* centrality to roughly approximate the overall winner.

Degree centrality $c_D(v)$ of a node v is the number of edges incident to v in undirected graphs. The use of degree centrality makes sense, as in general, strong teams participated and played many times than weak teams. For example, Brazil played in every world cup so far, and won against many other teams.

4 Visualization of Dynamic Networks with Dynamic Hierarchy

In this section, we describe our new layout methods for visual analysis of dynamic networks with dynamic hierarchy: wheel layout, radial layout and hierarchical layout.

4.1 Wheel Layout

In the *wheel* layout, we place each country in the outermost circle of the wheel, and then represent the performance (i.e. the centrality value) of each country for each year using the size of nodes along each wheel as an inner circle.

More specifically, we first divide a wheel into 6 wedges based on the federations clustering, and then place each country inside each wedge alphabetically in counter-clockwise order. Alternatively, one may use the overall centrality values instead.

The centrality values of each country are represented by the size of the nodes along each wheel. The centrality values for the same year form an inner concentric circle with the same node color. The inner circle near the center corresponds to year 1930, and the circle next to the outermost circle corresponds to year 2006. Figure 1 shows a wheel layout based on the degree centrality.

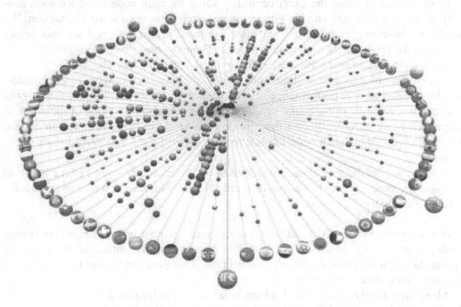

Fig. 1. Wheel layout with degree centrality analysis.

Note that in the wheel layout, the *overview* of the evolution of the performance of each country over the years can be easily seen on its corresponding line. For example, it is clear that Brazil, Germany and Italy are the strongest group in the history of FIFA World Cup, as they have many large circles along the wheel. Moreover, one can compare the performance between countries of a specific year, by inspecting the sizes along the concentric circle represented by the same color.

Furthermore, one can easily compare the performance between the continents and inside each continent. For example, in general the European countries are much stronger than the other continents. Among the Asian countries, South Korea performed relatively well.

However, one of the disadvantages in the Wheel layout is that it does not show the network topology structure of each graph. To support this property, we designed a radial layout and hierarchical layout, which clearly display the network structure of each year to find out more *details*.

4.2 Radial Layout

In order to simultaneously display the network topology and the performance, we used a radial drawing convention from social network analysis for displaying centrality [3, 15]. That is, we place the node with the highest centrality value in the union graph G at the center of the drawing, and then place the nodes with the next high centrality values using the concentric circles. However, we made the following important modifications.

First, instead of using the exact centrality value for each node to define each concentric circle, which may end up with too many circles, we used some abstraction. We divide all the countries into a winner plus 3 groups (i.e. strong, medium and weak), based on the range of their centrality values. Then we place the strong group in the innermost circle, and place the weak category in the outermost circle.

Second, in order to enable simultaneous *global* analysis (i.e. overall performance) and *local* analysis (i.e. performance of the specific year), we fix the location of each country in each circle of the radial layout, based on the centrality value of the union of graphs G. More specifically, we first divide each circle into federation regions, and then evenly distribute each node in each region, sorted by the centrality values of the nodes in G.

Finally, we use the size of each node based on the centrality values of the graph G_i of a specific year, in order to enable the local analysis. Next we describe more specific details of each step.

Circle assignment We divide all the countries into a winner and 3 groups (i.e. strong, medium and weak), based on the range of their centrality values in the union of graphs G. Then we place the strong group in the innermost circle, and place the weak category in the outermost circle.

More specifically, the circle L of each node v is determined by the *normalized* degree centrality value $C_D(v)$ of the union graph G as follows:

$$
L(v) = \begin{cases} 0 & if\ c_D(v) = 1 \\ 1 & if\ 0.45 \le c_D(v) < 1 \\ 2 & if\ 0.15 \le c_D(v) < 0.45 \\ 4 & if\ c_D(v) < 0.15 \end{cases}
$$

As a result, Brazil is the overall winner by the degree centrality, and there are 8 countries in the innermost circle: Italy, West Germany, England, France, Spain, Sweden from Europe, plus Argentina and Mexico. There are 21 countries in the middle circle, and 49 countries in the outermost circle.

Node placement and geographic clustering To enable simultaneous visual analysis for both overall performance and performance of a specific year, and to preserve the mental map [10] of the dynamic networks, we fix the location of each country in the radial layout of the union graph G and G_i, i =1,..., 18.

We first divide each circle into 6 federation regions to preserve a geographic clustering and to enable analysis between the continents. Then we evenly distribute each node in each region, sorted by the centrality values of the nodes in G.

To distribute the nodes in each circle evenly, the position of a node v is computed as follows:

$$x(v) = L(v)R(v)\cos(2\pi \frac{i(v)}{N(v)}) \tag{1}$$

$$y(v) = L(v)R(v)\sin(2\pi \frac{i(v)}{N(v)}) \tag{2}$$

where $L(v)$ represents the circle assignment, $R(v)$ represents the radius of the inner most circle, $N(v)$ represents the number of nodes in that circle, and $i(v)$ represents an ordering of the node in the circle.

We also color each cluster in order to support analysis and comparison of the performance of each federation using the area with a specific color. The color codes are: red -UEFA (Europe), pink -CONCACAF (North America), green -CONMEBOL (South America), yellow -AFC (Asia), black -CAF (Africa), blue -OFC (Australia and New Zealand).

Figure 2 shows the result of the circle assignment, node ordering and geographic clustering. Figure 3 shows the radial layout of the union of graph G.

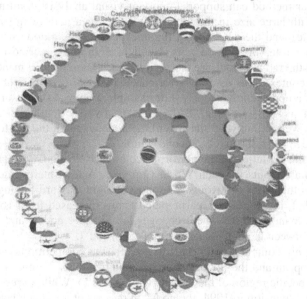

Fig. 2. Result of circle assignment, node ordering and geographic clustering.

Centrality mapping for local analysis and results To produce a radial layout for each graph $G_i, i = 1,..., 18$, we use the same layout as the union of graph G, with the size of each node represented by the centrality values of the nodes in G_i, in order to enable both the global and local analysis. In addition, as the direction of the edges, which represents "who beats whom" relationship, can be meaningful for detailed analysis, we represent each edge with directions.

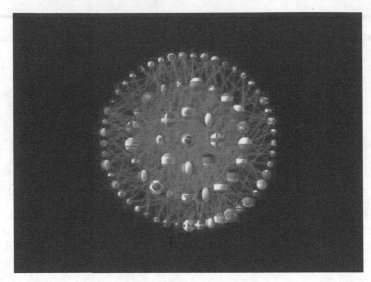

Fig. 3. The union of graphs.

Note that our method can support important visual analysis: confirm the expected (i.e., a node with large size in the innermost circle, or a node with small size in the outermost circle), and the detection of the unexpected (i.e., a node with large size in the outermost circle, or a node with small size in the innermost circle). More specifically, in the radial layout, we can analyze each team's performance of a specific year along the context of its overall performance, by looking at the embedded position and the size of a node simultaneously. For example, Figure 4 shows a radial layout of year 2002. It is obvious that Turkey (respectively, South Korea) performed extraordinarily well in that year: the size of the node is one of the top four, although it is placed in the third (respectively, second) circle.

To analyze the evolution of the performance of each World Cup year, we produced a series of radial layouts for each World Cup year. A few interesting events can be found out from the series of layouts. The most straight-forward finding is the change of rules. In 1982, the number of participated teams increased from 16 to 24, then in 1994, it was expanded to 32. These changes led to more nodes, and more complex relationships between them. Compare Figures 5, 6, and 7.

For geographic comparison, in the early years, the competitions were mainly between the European and the South American counties, thus the nodes were appeared only in some specific region of the layout (see Figures 5). While in recent years, especially after the expansion in 1994, the nodes in the layout are much better distributed, which may indicates a "fairer" game (see Figures 4).

For a specific country, we can see that, Brazil actually did not perform very well in the early years of World Cup history, although now it is undoubtedly the best performer overall. Also, note that from the given data set, one can find West Germany in the innermost circle, and (the united) Germany in the middle circle, and East Germany in the outermost circle.

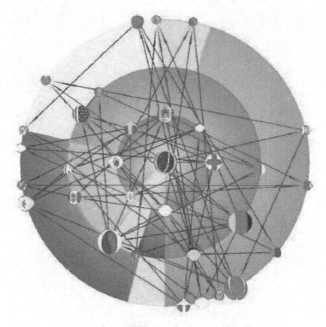

Fig. 4. Radial layout of year 2002.

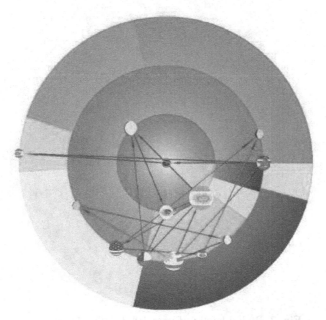

Fig. 5. Radial layout of year 1930 with 16 teams.

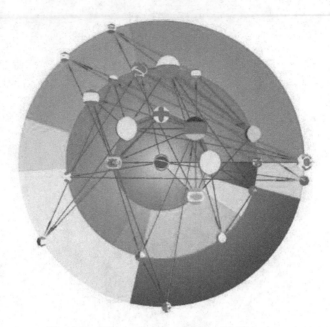

Fig. 6. Radial layout of year 1982 with 24 teams.

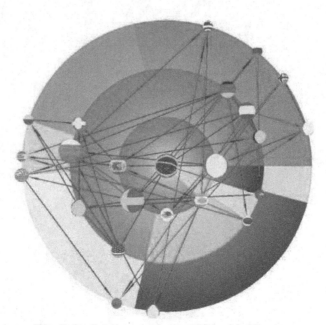

Fig. 7. Radial layout of year 1994 with 32 teams.

In summary, compared with the wheel layout, the radial layout can display the topology of the network, i.e. who-beats-whom relationships. It clearly shows the overall winner, Brazil in the center. Further, visual comparison between regional performance is clearly visible based on the use of coloring.

However, it shows many edge crossings, as the ordering of nodes inside each geographic clustering is not based on the crossing minimization method. This can be improved by using one of the crossing minimization method for radial graph layout, or using a curve representation instead of straight-line edge representation [9].

4.3 Hierarchical layout

As an alternative view of the radial layout for displaying centrality, we also designed a hierarchical layout for displaying centrality. The main idea of using the centrality analysis and the union of graphs are similar to the radial layout. However, there are two main differences:

- For each year, the teams are placed on layers (i.e. parallel lines) instead of concentric circles. The level indicates a team's overall performance: the higher the level, the better the performance.
- In each layer, the football federation clustering is preserved: each federation is shown as a coloured region. Within each region, countries are sorted by their centrality value in decreasing order from left to right.

More specifically, the layout of the union graph G is computed according to the centrality values, as in the radial layout (i.e. into 4 layers with Brazil on the top layer). Once the layering is done, the nodes within each layer are clustered first according to football federation, and then sorted by the centrality value within each cluster.

The resulting visualization of the union graph G is shown in Figure 8. Note that the dominance of the European teams (shown in red region) is very clear.

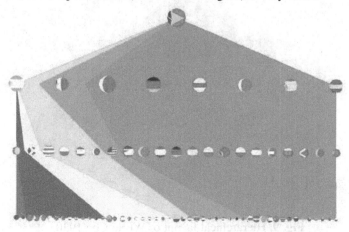

Fig. 8. Hierarchical layout of the union graph.

As with the radial layout, the union graph layout (i.e., the same layering and the same ordering inside each layer) is used for the layout of each individual World Cup graph to preserve the mental map [10] and to support simultaneous visual analysis (i.e. the global performance and the local performance).

We also used the size of node to represent the performance of the particular year. In this way, we can confirm the expected (i.e. we expect the countries in the upper layer perform better than the lower ones; similarly, we expect the countries in the left side perform better than the right ones in the same level), and detect the unexpected (i.e. the country in the lowest layer with large node size, or the country in the top upper layer with small size; similarly, the country in the right side with larger node size, or the country in the left side with smaller size in the same level).

As with the radial layout, to analyze the evolution of the performance of each World Cup year, we produced a series of hierarchical layouts for each World Cup year. From the layering method, we expect that teams on the upper layer (good overall performance) with large node size (good performance of that particular year). However, this is not always true, as observed in most of the World Cup games. For instance, the performance of Brazil in the top layer was not so good in 1930 (Figure 9), whereas Turkey from the lowest layer performed very well in 2002 (Figure 11).

From the series of hierarchical layout, it is also possible to see the change of World Cup team structure visually. Here "structure" refers to the number of teams in each layer, the ratio of teams from different football federation, and team performance. For example, the structure of the 1930 World Cup graph (Figure 9) is significantly different from that of the union World Cup graph (Figure 8); whereas recent World Cups, such as 1986 (Figure 10) and 2002 (Figure 11), have a similar structure to that of the union graph.

1930

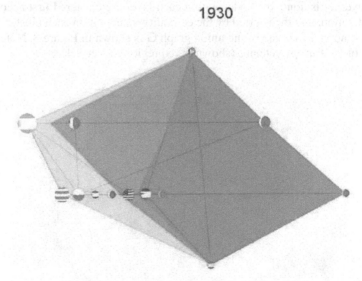

Fig. 9. Hierarchical layout of World Cup 1930

1986

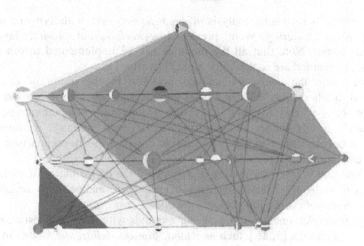

Fig. 10. Hierarchical layout of World Cup 1986.

2002

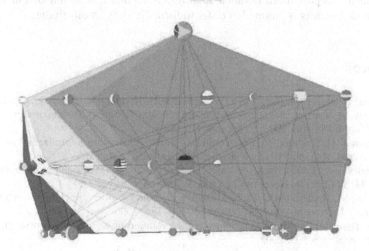

Fig. 11. Hierarchical layout of World Cup 2002.

In summary, compared with the radial layout, the hierarchical layout tends to create less crossings. It also preserves geographic clustering between the layers continuously, which makes the overall visual comparison between regional performance more visible.

However, the use of straight-line edge representation makes some of intra-layer edges not clearly visible. This can be improved by using a curve representation for such case, where any overlap between intra-layer edges occurs [2].

5 Conclusion

Three new methods for visual analysis of dynamic networks with dynamic hierarchy and geographic clustering were presented: *wheel* layout, *radial* layout and *hierarchical* layout. Note that all the methods can be implemented to run in linear time. Thus, our method are scalable for large networks.

Combined with the *centrality* analysis and use of the *union of graphs*, our visualization methods can clearly reveal the overall winner of the World Cup competition history, and identify the strong groups and weak countries. Further analysis such as evolution of performance of each country, comparison of performance between the continents and inside each continent, comparison between different years are also supported.

More importantly, one can analyze and compare the performance of each country for each year along the context of their overall performance. This enables us to *confirm the expected* events and *discover the unexpected* events [13].

For large networks, one can combine our methods with other well-established network analysis methods [3, 15] such as *island*, *blockmodelling*, or *k-core* in order to reduce the size of the network.

Our future work include combination with different analysis methods and more dynamic version of the union of graphs, and integration with interaction methods for each layout to support more detailed findings. A formal evaluation of our methods with different data sets is planned in order to formally support our findings.

References

1. A. Ahmed, T. Dwyer, M. F. X. Fu, J. W. K. Ho, S.-H. Hong, D. Koschuetzki, C. Murray, N. S. Nikolov, R. Taib, A. Tarassov, and K. Xu. Geomi: Geometry for maximum insight. In Proc. of Graph Drawing 2005, pages 468–479, 2005.
2. C. Bachmaier, H. Buchner, M. Forster, and S.-H. Hong. Crossing minimization in extended level drawings of graphs. Discrete Applied Mathematics, to appear.
3. U. Brandes and T. Erlebach, editors. Network Analysis: Methodological Foundations, volume 3418 of Lecture Notes in Computer Science. Springer, 2005.
4. U. Brandes, M. Hoefer, and C. Pich. Affiliation dynamics with an application to movie-actor biographies. In Proc. of EuroVis 2006, pages 179–186, 2006.
5. C. Chen. The centrality of pivotal points in the evolution of scientific networks. In Proc. of IUI 2005, pages 98–105, 2005.
6. X. Fu, S.-H. Hong, N. S. Nikolov, X. Shen, Y. Wu, and K. Xu. Visualization and analysis of email networks. In Proc. of APVIS 2007, pages 1–8, 2007.
7. P. Gajer, M. T. Goodrich, and S. G. Kobourov. A multi-dimensional approach to force-directed layouts of large graphs. In Proc. of Graph Drawing 2000, pages 211–221, 2000.
8. D. Harel and Y. Koren. Graph drawing by high-dimensional embedding. In Proc. of Graph Drawing 2002, pages 207–219, 2002.
9. S.-H. Hong and H. Nagamochi. Approximating crossing minimization in radial layouts. In Proc. of LATIN 2008, pages 461–472, 2008.
10. K. Misue, P. Eades, W. Lai, and K. Sugiyama. Layout adjustment and the mental map. J. Vis. Lang. Comput., 6(2):183–210, 1995.

11. J. Moody, D. McFarland, and S. Bender-deMoll. Dynamic network visualization. American Journal of Sociology, 110(4):1206–41, 2005.

12. A. J. Quigley and P. Eades. Fade: Graph drawing, clustering, and visual abstraction. In Proc. of Graph Drawing 2000, pages 197–210, 2000.

13. J. J. Thomas and K. A. Cook. Illuminating the Path: The Research and Development Agenda for Visual Analytics. National Visualization and Analytics Ctr, 2005.

14. C. Walshaw. A multilevel algorithm for force-directed graph drawing. In Proc. of Graph Drawing 2000, pages 171–182, 2000.

15. S. Wasserman and K. Faust. Social Network Analysis: Methods and Applicaitons. Cambridge University Press, 1995.

From Tree to Graph - Experiments with E-Spring Algorithm

Pushpa Kumar[1], Kang Zhang[1], and Mao Lin Huang[2]

[1] University of Texas at Dallas, 2601 N. Floyd Road, Richardson, TX 75063, USA
{pkumar, kzhang}@utdallas.edu
[2] University of Technology, PO Box 123, Broadway NSW 2007, Sydney, Australia
{maolin}@ it.uts.edu.au

Abstract. Graph drawing and visualization represent structural information as diagrams of abstract graphs and networks. *E-Spring* Algorithm, derived from the popular spring embedder model, was proposed to eliminate node overlaps in the drawings of clustered directed acyclic graphs Gc. In this paper, we apply the E-Spring algorithm to general graphs by minimizing edge-node intersections. Initially, a tree structure is extracted from the original graph using the breadth-first search (BFS) algorithm. The extracted tree is then visualized without node overlaps using the E-Spring algorithm, and the remaining non-tree edges are appended to this visualization. A post-processing step that implements edge routing is performed on the obtained visualization to eliminate residual edge-node intersections. This method has been validated by visualizing eBay buyer-seller relationships and Graph Catalog benchmarking data.

Keywords: node overlaps, edge-node intersections, edge routing, graph visualization

1 Introduction

Graph visualization is an area of extensive research in recent years. Applications of graph visualization include genealogy, cartography, sociology, software engineering, VLSI design, and visual analysis. Cluttered drawings of graphs generally produce undesirable visual presentation that could increase the cognitive overhead in understanding of the structural information. Various criteria for determining the graph quality have been proposed [2][16][35]. A graph drawing is sometimes measured by how well it meets the following aesthetic criteria [29][32][37]:

- Minimization of *edge crossings*.
- Minimization of *edge-node intersections:* Edges should not intersect with finite-size labeled nodes.
- *Symmetry*: Nodes should be sufficiently far apart from their nearest neighbor to be easily distinguished and to avoid occlusion.
- *Readability*: Labels must have legible sizes.

M.L. Huang et al. (eds.), *Visual Information Communication*,
DOI 10.1007/978-1-4419-0312-9_3, © Springer Science+Business Media, LLC 2010

- Minimization of *area*: Visual space is often at a premium and reducing the overall area of the bounding box of the graph is often desirable.
- Avoidance of *Overlap*: Labels should not overlap with other labels or other graphical features.

Various algorithms [2][14][15][16][23][29] have been proposed for removing node overlaps in graphs. Being most widely used, Spring algorithms [9] are a class of algorithms for drawing graphs in an aesthetically pleasing way by positioning the nodes of a graph in two or three dimensional space so that all the edges are of more or less equal length, and there are as few crossing edges as possible. They assign forces as if the edges were springs following Hooke's law, the forces are applied to the nodes, pulling them closer together or pushing them further apart. At equilibrium, node overlap is gradually reduced [14][29][36]. Spring algorithms are regarded as effective tools for visualizing undirected graphs.

E-Spring algorithm [20] derived from the popular spring embedder model [9] was proposed to eliminate node overlaps in clustered directed acyclic graphs (DAGs). A combination of spring and electrostatic forces act on the physical system to remove node overlaps at equilibrium. E-Spring algorithm uses animation for drawing clustered DAGs to preserve the user's mental map [11]. Enhancements to this algorithm include determination of a *stop condition* that utilizes graph geometry to determine an upper bound on graph expansion during animated drawing. DAG expansion automatically stops when this condition is met. This minimizes the overall area of the DAG visualization and leads to effective utilization of screen space. Further optimization of this algorithm includes performing *node interleaving* in the top and bottom DAG cluster regions to remove residual node overlaps particularly effective for graphs with long node labels [21]. *E-Spring* algorithm ensures removal of all node overlaps [22].

Graphs have been extensively used to represent various important concepts or objects. A graph is generally drawn or represented in the plane so that we can understand and study its structure and properties [33]. Directed acyclic graphs (DAGs) are an important *subset of graphs*, and have been used to visualize various eBusiness and other applications [17][28]. It is essential that E-Spring algorithm can not only visualize graph subsets but also graphs in general. The usefulness of a graph drawing depends on its *readability* [1]. In this paper, we apply the E-Spring algorithm to visualize graphs without node overlaps and edge-node intersections. The new method consists of the following four steps:

1. One or more trees are extracted from a given input graph using the graph traversal algorithm, *breadth-first search* (BFS) [3].
2. The extracted trees are visualized using the *E-Spring* algorithm, which removes all node overlaps.
3. Non-tree edges (that are not traversed by BFS algorithm) are then appended to the visualization so that the whole graph structure can be visualized.
4. An *edge routing* procedure is performed to remove any residual edge-node intersections.

The proposed method greatly improves the *readability* of node labels in the graph layouts. We evaluate our method by visualizing eBay social network data and Graph

Catalog benchmark data. Using our method, all node overlaps and edge-node intersections are removed in the obtained final layouts.

The rest of this paper is organized as follows. Section 2 describes related work. Section 3 presents details of the E-Spring algorithm. Section 4 describes our method for visualizing graphs which includes the clustered graph model, tree extraction, and removing edge-node intersections. Section 5 provides details of our implementation and experimental results. Finally, a conclusion is given in Section 6.

2 Related Work

We review related work on visualization of graphs without node overlap and edge-node intersections, tree search and retrieval algorithms, and edge routing in layouts that served as a motivation for this paper. The family of spring algorithms was developed for adjusting cluttered graphs without node overlaps, and includes force scan (FS) [23], force transfer (FT) [14], dynamic natural length spring (DNLS) and orthogonal dynamic natural length spring (ODNLS) [29]. The Force-scan method (FS) scans in both the horizontal and vertical directions of a graph to find overlapping nodes and uses a force along the line connecting the center of two overlapping nodes in an iterative fashion to remove node overlaps. In Force-transfer method (FT), forces are applied with left-to-right and top-to-bottom scans, and some nodes are moved either horizontally or vertically. Outputs using FS method have smaller area than those of FT. Dynamic natural length spring (DNLS) and orthogonal dynamic natural length spring (ODNLS) modify attractive and/or repulsive spring forces between nodes to achieve node overlap removal. Both DNLS and ODNLS have a better performance than FS and FT in terms of aesthetic criteria such as display symmetry and uniform edge. A fast algorithm (FADE) for two dimensional drawing, geometric clustering and multilevel viewing of large undirected graphs is presented in [36]. The decomposition tree provides a systematic way to determine the degree of closeness between nodes without explicitly calculating the distance between each node. For large clustered undirected graphs, three types of spring forces - internal spring, external spring and virtual spring that operate between the vertices of a graph are defined for the navigation and visualization of these graphs [10]. In addition to spring forces, there are gravitational repulsion forces between all nodes.

A general framework called "User Hints" treats the map labeling processes as an optimization task and supports human interaction along with automated methods [32]. *Simulated annealing* (SA) is a flexible optimization method and solves the problem of drawing nice-looking undirected straight-line graphs without node overlaps. The SA method uses rules that are derived from an analogy to the process in which liquids are cooled to a crystalline form, a process called annealing [5]. A three-dimensional system based on the simulated annealing algorithm extends straight-line two-dimensional drawings of general undirected graphs to three dimensions [4]. This system features an advanced 3D user interface that assists the user in choosing and modifying the cost function and the optimization components on-line. Various approaches for removing node overlapping based on constr*ained optimization* techniques are proposed in [31]. These include minimal linear scaling, formulating the node overlapping problem as a convex quadratic programming problem to be solved by any quadratic solver, local search methods based on adaptation of the EGENET solver, and form of Lagrangian multiplier method.

Graph theory algorithms such as Breadth-first search (BFS) and Depth-first search (DFS) efficiently *search* a given unweighted graph beginning with any source vertex [3]. They can used to determine whether a graph is connected and what components are connected. While BFS searches for discovered and undiscovered vertices across the breadth of the graph, DFS performs search along the graph depth. Two minimum-spanning tree (MST) determination algorithms for weighted graphs are Kruskal [18] and Prim [34]. Kruskal's algorithm is based directly on the generic minimum-spanning-tree algorithm to find a safe edge to the growing forest by finding and edge of the least weight. Prim's algorithm is a special case of the generic minimum-spanning-tree algorithm and has the property that the edges in a set always form a single tree. Dijkstra's algorithm [6] is a graph search algorithm that solves the single-source shortest path problem for a graph with non-negative edge path costs, producing a shortest path tree and is often used in routing. It can also be used for finding costs of shortest paths from a single vertex to a single destination vertex.

An approach to remove *edge-node intersections* for graphs with non-trivial node sizes using the force-scan (FS) algorithm has been proposed in [24]. This method integrates the force-scan algorithm and applies it successfully to prevent edge-node intersections and overlapping edges. A new method for the analysis of the inter-relation of clusters and levels, and their influence on edge crossings and cluster/edge crossings has been proposed [12]. It applies two-level crossing reduction algorithms for clustered level graphs and retains the optimality of a one-sided two-level crossing reduction algorithm. To solve the problem of edge-node intersections, routing algorithms that originate in robot motion planning [25][26][30] have been proposed. They are designed for finding a shortest path between two specified points while avoiding intersections. Applications such as Microsoft Visio [41] and Concept Draw [38] provide object-avoiding connector routing. The routes are updated only after object movement has been completed rather than as the action is happening. Another well-known library for edge routing in graph layout is the Spline-o-matic library developed for GraphViz [40]. This supports poly-line and Bezier curve edge routing. An algorithm that draws only the edges with fixed node positions and does not make any use of the layered structure is provided in [7]. It starts by drawing the edge as a direct line between the source node and the destination node and then re-routes the line away from the nodes that intersect with the line. Another method for integration of edge-routing techniques into a force-directed layout is based on constrained stress majorisation [8]. It takes an initial layout for the graph, including poly-line paths for the edges, and improves this layout by moving the nodes to reduce stress and moving edge bend points to straighten the edges and reduce their overall length. Separation constraints between nodes and edge bend points are used to ensure that node labels do not overlap edges.

3 E-Spring Algorithm

E-Spring algorithm [20] was proposed to eliminate node overlaps in the drawing D(Gc) of clustered directed acyclic graphs (Gc), especially for labeled nodes with finite length string labels. In this algorithm, nodes are modeled as unequally charged particles, with springs representing edges of the graph. The spring force is derived from the following force formula according to Hooke's law:

$$F_s(d) = C_1 \log(d/C_2) \tag{1}$$

where d is the spring length and C_1 and C_2 are constants. The new electrostatic force generated between any two charged particles representing two connected nodes is derived from Coulomb's law as follows:

$$F_c = k_c q_1 q_2 / r^2 \tag{2}$$

where q_1 is the charge on one body, q_2 is the charge on the other body, r is the distance between them, and k_c is the Coulomb's force constant. The combination of F_s and F_c is the resultant force between two connected nodes. Note that for each pair of non-connected nodes, the combined force is equal to F_c.

The magnitude of charges is obtained by calculating the weight associated with each source node. The force function calculated from the weights modeled on electrostatic charges eliminates node overlap. The weight of each source node is determined by the number of sink nodes in its immediate vicinity, number of hierarchy levels in the tree, and a force scaling factor. A classification mechanism identifies nodes as parents or children. A parent node along with all its direct child leaf nodes constitutes a *cluster* c_i. A new force function based on the weights is applied and the additional displacement contributes to node overlap removal. The forces are applied to each node and the positions are updated accordingly. The attractive forces on the springs and the repulsive forces between the positive charges act together to generate a drawing free of node overlaps. A final layout is obtained with a locally minimum energy on the nodes when the total force on each node in |V| is zero. Enhancements to this algorithm includes introduction of a '*stop condition*' to reduce the overall size of DAGs leading to more efficient utilization of screen space, and '*node-interleaving*' to remove any residual node overlaps [21]. *E-Spring* algorithm ensures that all node overlaps in a DAG are removed [22].

E-Spring Algorithm

---

input: a drawing D(G_D) of clustered G_c(V,E) with overlapping nodes
output : a new drawing D^{new}(G_c) with no node overlaps

---

   begin
      mark parent nodes p_k
      compute force factor f
         for each subtree i = 0 to k do
            compute weight W_i
            calculate new forces F_{newi}
      move nodes based on minimum distance threshold δ and compute final layout
      until stopping condition
end

---

4 Graph Visualization Methodology

To visualize a given graph using the E-Spring layout algorithm, we first extract the underlying tree structure from the graph. For this purpose, we utilize Breadth-First search (BFS) algorithm, because the derived tree is a 'fat' tree [27] that can used for generating tree clusters. A fat tree becomes fatter as one moves up the tree towards the root, so a parent node has more children in its vicinity to form clusters. Section 4.1 presents the clustered graph model. Section 4.2 describes the tree extraction method. An edge routing method that removes unnecessary edge-node intersections as the 4th step of our approach is described in Section 4.3.

4.1 Clustered Graph Model

Our clustered graph model is built on its own backbone tree T derived from the existing graph structure. This backbone tree T is a spanning tree which is extracted through the implementation of a Breadth-First-Search (BFS) algorithm.

Definition 1: Consider a graph $G(V, E)$ with a set of nodes $V = \{ v1, v2, ..., vn\}$, and the set of edges $E \subseteq V \times V$. A spanning tree $T(V_t, E_t, r)$ obtained through the *BFS* on G contains edges *in* E_t. A set of unreachable edges that are not included in T is contained in $E' = E - E_t$.

Definition 2: Consider a graph $G(V, E)$ with a set of nodes $V = \{v1, v2, ..., vn\}$, and the set of edges $E \subseteq V \times V$. The *BFS* algorithm expands node exploration uniformly across the breadth of the graph; a parent node v^p *in* V_t of the spanning tree T has a set of direct child leaf nodes $L_r \subset Vi$ in its immediate vicinity. A parent node together with all its direct child leaf nodes forms a *cluster* $c_i = \{v^p, L_i\}$, where v^p is a parent node of all children in L_i.

Definition 3: A clustered graph $G_C(C, V', E')$ consists of a set of clusters $C = \{c_1, c_2, ...c_k\}$ that are derived from the spanning tree T extracted from G as defined above, a set of non-tree nodes V' and a set of non-tree edges E'.

4.2 Tree Extraction

E-Spring algorithm [20][21][22] works well with graphs that follow a clustered tree structure, where a parent node has many child nodes in its vicinity to form clusters, and nodes have finite length string labels. For the purpose of using E-Spring algorithm for graph visualization, the method we choose for tree extraction has to produce fat trees [27]. A fat tree becomes fatter as one moves up the tree towards the root, so a parent node can have more direct child nodes. We therefore choose the graph search algorithm breadth-first search (BFS) that begins at the root node and explores all the neighboring nodes. Then for each of those nearest nodes, it explores their unexplored neighbor nodes and so on, until it finds the shortest path and generates a minimum spanning tree 'T' starting from the root node. Depth-first search (DFS) is another algorithm for graph traversal that starts at the root and explores as far as possible along each branch before backtracking. But this method does not produce fat trees.

Extraction of the tree is performed using the BFS method. Breadth-First search (BFS) is a graph traversal algorithm that can be used to find connected components in a graph. Given a graph $G = (V, E)$ and a distinguished source vertex 's', BFS explores the edges of G to "discover" every vertex that is reachable from 's' by computing the distance (smallest number of edges) from 's' to each reachable vertex [3]. The algorithm is given below:

BFS(G,s)

---

      unmark all vertices in G
      choose some starting vertex 's' as root node
      mark 's'
      Enqueue(Q,s)
      $T \leftarrow s$
      while Q non-empty
          choose some vertex 'v' from beginning of queue
          visit 'v'
          for each unmarked neighbor 'w'
              mark 'w'
              Enqueue(Q,w),
              $T \leftarrow vw$

BFS generates a spanning tree T with root r that contains all reachable vertices. The breadth first search tree T is the shortest path tree starting from its root r.

Using E-Spring layout algorithm, the extracted spanning tree T can be visualized with the elimination of node overlaps. The missing non-tree nodes in V' and edges in E' are then be appended to the visualization. Each edge is drawn as a straight line connecting the centers of the two nodes it links. The resultant visualization thus contains all nodes and edges from the initial graph G. To improvise the obtained layouts, we aim to remove residual edge-node intersections.

4.3 Removing Edge-Node Intersections

Typically, the drawing of a graph is accompanied by optimizing some cost function such as area, number of bends, number of edge crossings, uniformity in the placement of vertices, minimum angle etc. [33]. Computation of an aesthetic cost of a drawing involves node overlaps, and edge-node intersections [1]. We aim to minimize this cost by removing both node overlaps and edge-node intersections. The visualizations obtained after applying the E-Spring algorithm do not contain node overlaps, but suffer from intersections between edges and nodes, which greatly hinder *readability* of node labels. To remove these edge-node intersections, we apply edge routing on these layouts as a post-processing step. For edge routes in a graph layout, several relevant readability [24] criteria are:

- Minimizing the number of edge bends
- Minimizing the total length of edges
- Minimizing the number of edge crossings

Our clustered graph model is built on its own backbone tree T derived from the existing graph structure. This backbone tree T is a spanning tree which is extracted through the implementation of a Breadth-First-Search (BFS) algorithm.

'Orthogonal edge routing' was implemented for removing edge-node intersections in graphs with non-uniform nodes of finite length [24]. Since E-Spring algorithm works well with node labels of finite string label length, we aim to implement orthogonal edge routing for the obtained visualizations from Section 4.1. In this type of edge routing, a diagram's edges are routed using vertical and horizontal line segments only. An example of orthogonal edge routing is shown in Fig. 1a, b. Fig. 1a shows the actual edge-node intersection between edge $e(a,c)$ and node 'b' before re-routing. If an algorithm for orthogonal routing drawings is chosen, the output is shown in Fig. 1b with removal of the intersection.

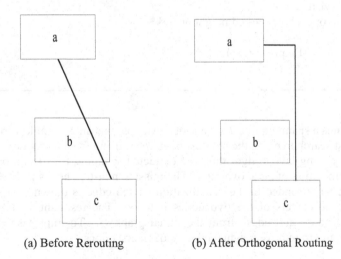

(a) Before Rerouting   (b) After Orthogonal Routing

Fig. 1. Orthogonal Edge Routing.

For performing the post-processing step, we utilized 'yFiles' Graph Layout Library available from yWorks [42]. Automatic edge routing is provided by 'OrthogonalEdgeRouter' which is a versatile and powerful layout algorithm. This tool also reduces the total number of edge crossings. We captured individual node, edge information such as node graphical position co-ordinates (X,Y) and edge connections from the obtained visualization data structure. Since 'yFiles' Library has a 'graphml' interface, we inserted the retrieved node, edge information for the visualization into a graphml file. This file was then loaded into the orthogonal edge routing application to remove edge-node intersections.

5 Implementation/Experimental Results

We have implemented the graph visualization method using *E-Spring* algorithm presented in Section 4 for eBay data and graph benchmark data. In this implementation, graph $G = (V, E)$ has the following parameters:

- Total number of nodes $1 \leq |N| \leq 100$
- Individual node label string length $3 \leq S \leq 10$

Input data for this implementation came from the following sources:

- eBay buyer/seller relationships obtained from eBay [19], where user-name string length 'S' is chosen from the following two cases: i) S = 3 ii) S = 10.

- Graph catalog benchmark data (AT & T graphs) obtained from the Graph drawing Web site [39] for the following three cases: i) |N| = 60, S = 10, r_n = 9 ii) |N| = 60, S = 10, r_n = 39 iii) |N| = 100, S = 10.

The Breadth-First search (BFS) algorithm presented in Section 4.2 was implemented using the Java programming language. The 4th step for edge routing presented in Section 4.3 was implemented using the 'yFiles' Graph Layout Library from yWorks [42]. The implementation results for the above cases are presented in this section.

5.1 eBay Data

We plotted the social network graph $G(V, E)$ extracted from eBay [19]. eBay customer data for various buyers and sellers was mined from its production environment using the Web services API. The buyer-seller interaction was captured by the *social network graph*. The graph has total number of nodes |N| = 30, number of edges |E| = 41. This graph is depicted in Fig. 2a. The java code of the BFS algorithm was implemented on this graph with chosen root node r_n = 5 (highlighted in yellow), and the corresponding tree 'T' extracted is depicted in Fig. 2b.

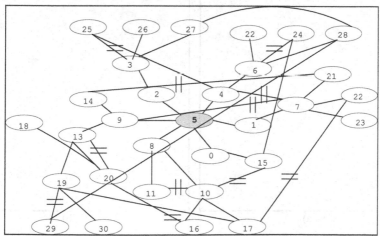

a)

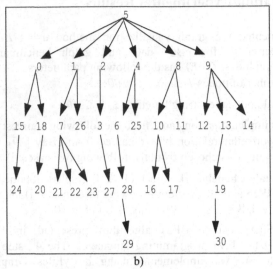

b)

Fig. 2. eBay Data Graph and extracted tree structure.

Fig. 3a, b depict screenshots of the tree visualization obtained using *E-Spring* algorithm, for *Case 1*: S = 3. Fig. 4a, b depict screenshots of the same for *Case 2*: S = 10. Fig. 3a, 4a represent extracted tree *T* while Fig. 3b, 4b represent screenshots after non-tree tree edges contained in *E'* were appended to the visualizations in Fig. 3a, 4a. Fig. 3c, 4c depict screenshots after 4th step using orthogonal edge routing method was applied to remove the edge-node intersections.

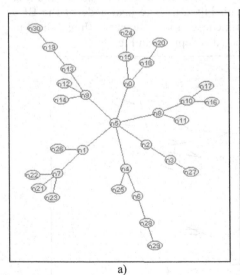

a)

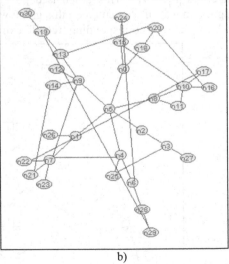

b)

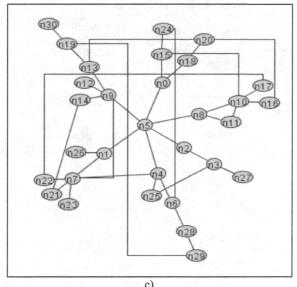

c)

Fig. 3. eBay data Case '1' |N| = 30, |E| = 41, S = 3.

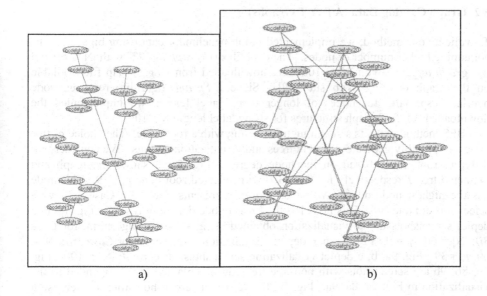

a)   b)

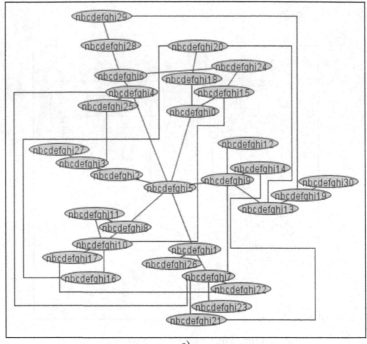

c)

Fig. 4. eBay data Case '2' |N| = 30, |E| = 41, S = 10.

5.2 Graph Catalog Data (AT & T Graphs)

To validate our method, we implemented graph benchmark data using bigger graphs containing higher number of nodes. The data files i) "*graph ug_97*" with |N| = 60 and ii) "*graph ug_379*" with |N| = 100 were downloaded from "*ug.gz*" zip file available on the graph drawing Web site [39]. Since *E-Spring* algorithm removes node overlaps especially for nodes of longer string label length, we implemented the downloaded AT & T graph structures for string label length S = 10.

BFS method extracts a spanning tree starting with a root node. The choice of this node can possibly generate different trees and visualization layouts. We consider two different root nodes based on the node degree. Fig. 5a, b shows the graph and extracted tree T respectively for Case 3 *i)* with selected root node r_n = 9. This node has the highest node degree N_D = 16. Fig. 6 represents tree T for Case 3 *ii)* with selected root node '39'. This node has the lowest node degree of N_D = 7. Fig. 7a, b, c depict screenshots of the visualization obtained using *E-Spring* algorithm, for *Case 3i)*: |N| = 60, r_n = 9. Fig. 8a, b, c depict visualization screenshots for *Case 3ii)*: |N| = 60, r_n =39. Fig. 9a, b, c depict visualization screenshots for *Case 4*: |N| = 100. Fig. 7b, 8b, 9b are screenshots with non-tree tree edges contained in E' appended to the visualization in Fig. 7a, 8a, 9a. Fig. 7c, 8c, 9c depict screenshots after 4th step using orthogonal edge routing was applied to remove edge-node intersections.

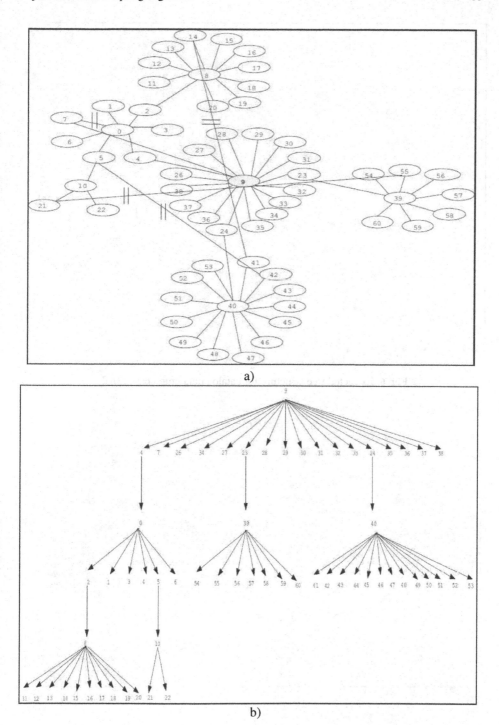

a)

b)

Fig. 5. Catalog data graph and extracted tree structure for Case '3 i)'.

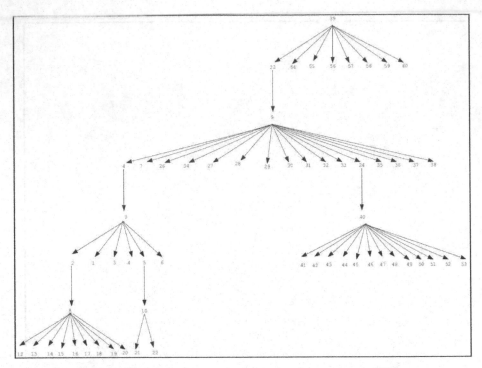

Fig. 6. Extracted tree structure for catalog data graph case '3ii)'

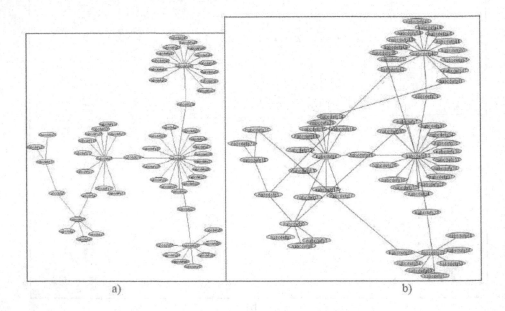

a)   b)

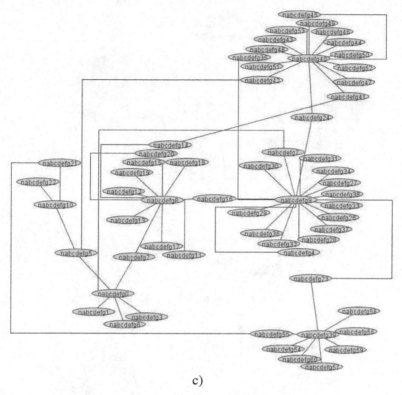

c)

Fig. 7. Catalog data graph Case '3 i)' $|N| = 60$, $|E| = 59$, $S = 10$, Root node $(r_n) = 9$.

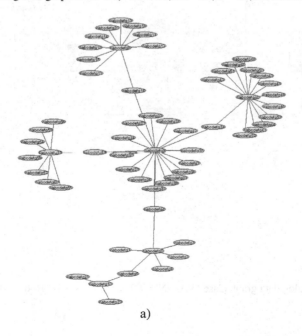

a)

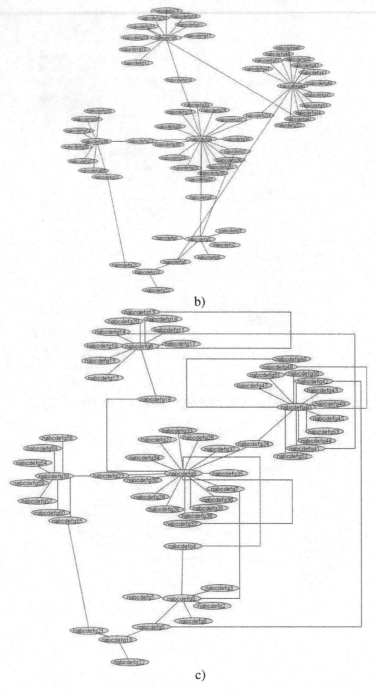

b)

c)

Fig. 8. Catalog data graph Case '3 ii)' |N| = 60, |E| = 59, S = 10, Root node (r_n) = 39.

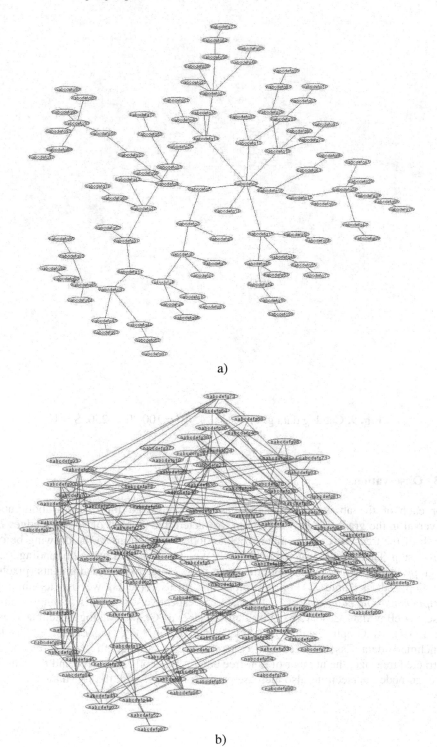

a)

b)

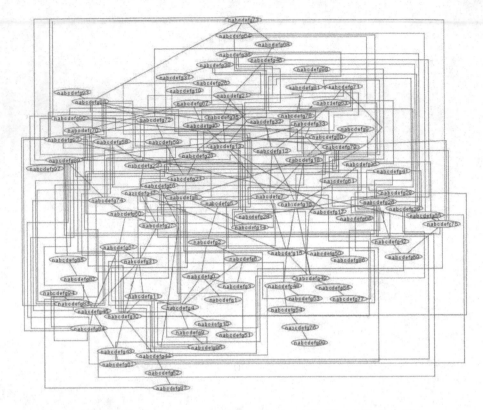

Fig. 9. Catalog data graph Case '4' |N| = 100, |E| = 250, S = 10.

5.3 Observations

For each of the above implemented cases, we retrieved information about node traversal in the graph for *BFS* algorithm, extracted tree T, a set of non-tree edges *E'*, depth of the tree 'Dr', and number of edge-node intersections in the drawing before the 4th step. This data is depicted in Table 1. We also measured overall bounding areas of graph visualizations before and after post-processing. Area measurements (pixels^2) are depicted in Table 2. For our plots and measurements, we use terminology "*Implementation Data source*" 1, 2, 3, 4, 5 respectively for the five implemented cases a) eBay data Case 1, b) eBay data Case 2, c) Graph Catalog benchmark data Case 3 i), d) Graph Catalog benchmark data Case 3 ii), and e) Graph Catalog benchmark data Case 4. We have observed that as the graph size increases, the extracted tree size, the number of non-tree edges, the depth of the tree and the number of edge-node intersections also increase proportionately for all the five data sources. This is due to the presence of larger number of nodes and edges in the input graphs. These measurements are depicted as plotted curves in Fig. 10.

We observed that the choice of the source root node (r_n) affects the tree depth, number of edge-node intersections, and the overall graph area. When source node with the highest node degree is chosen (r_n = 9) in Case *3 i)*, the extracted tree depth is lower (D_T = 5) so more children are present for every parent node in each cluster. The corresponding tree structure has higher tree depth (D_T = 7) when source node with lowest node degree is chosen (r_n = 39) in Case *3 ii)*. After missing edges are appended, the obtained visualizations indicate the presence of higher number of edge-node intersections (18) for Case *3 ii)* with lowest degree source root node (r_n = 39). The higher depth of the tree also causes the overall graph area to increase by 20% for Case *3 ii)* for Graph Catalog data with lowest degree source root node (r_n = 39). Hence, the selection of the *highest degree* node as the starting node for breadth-first search (BFS) algorithm produces better visualizations for our method.

After the 4th step of our approach, we observed that the obtained visualizations have greater area for nodes with longer string labels ($S = 10$) and larger graphs ($|N|$ = 60, $|N|$ = 100). This is because smaller label size nodes contain more in-between node gaps for performing orthogonal edge routing internally as compared to longer label size nodes. For nodes with longer string label lengths, the edge route sometimes has to be re-routed externally causing an increase in the graph area. Area measurement curves are plotted in Fig. 11. A trade-off exists between removal of edge-node intersections and graph area reduction with our method, especially for larger graphs with greater label sized nodes. From the obtained layout visualizations we observed that no node overlaps occurred in spanning trees drawn by *E-Spring* algorithm. The 4th step preserves the mental map, since the node positions were captured from the obtained visualization. We also observe that after the 4th step, all edge-node intersections in graph layouts have been removed.

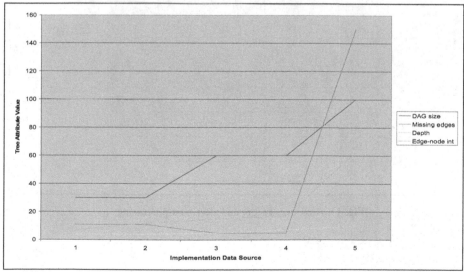

Fig. 10. Attribute values of extracted tree.

Table 1. Data Attributes of Extracted Tree Structure.

Data Source	Extracted tree size	Non-tree edges	Tree Depth	Edge-node intersections
1	30	11	4	7
2	30	11	4	12
3	60	5	5	15
4	60	5	7	18
5	100	150	10	62

Table 2. Graph Area Measurements

Data Source	Area before post-processing	Area after post-processing
1	101775	101775
2	155800	171000
3	534435	562275
4	671824	704740
5	870499	900467

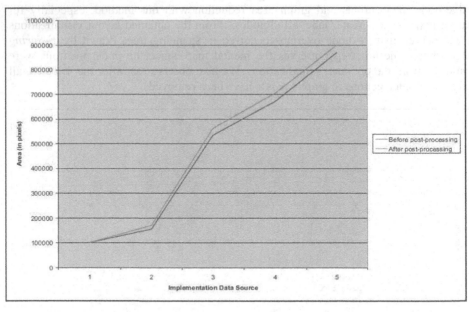

Fig. 11. Area sizes before and after post-processing.

6 Conclusion

E-Spring algorithm was proposed to draw clustered directed acyclic graphs (DAGs), and uses physical properties of electric charges and spring constants to remove overlaps between node labels. Since DAGs are only a *subset* of graphs, we apply E-Spring algorithm to include *general graphs*. The usefulness of a graph drawing depends on its *readability*, which is the capability of conveying the meaning of a diagram quickly and clearly. Readability issues are expressed by aesthetics such as minimization of crossings among edges and nodes, and removal of node overlaps. Our clustering structure of the graph is built on its own backbone tree derived from the existing graph structure. This backbone tree T is a spanning tree which is extracted through the implementation of breadth-first-search algorithm. The E-Spring algorithm guarantees that the visualized tree is free of node overlaps. We further improved graph readability by removing residual edge-node crossings using the edge routing method after the non-tree edges are inserted. The choice of the root node with the *highest node degree* for breadth-first search (BFS) algorithm results in better visualizations. Implementation was performed on eBay data and Graph catalog benchmark data with varying graph sizes, nodes with varying label string lengths, different source node selections and our experimental visualization results are promising. The resultant graph layouts are free of node overlaps and edge-node intersections. Future work includes enhancing E-Spring algorithm to accept input graphs for visualization, aesthetic comparisons for various graphs, and improving the quality of resultant drawings for large graphs.

References

1. Battista, G.D., Eades, P.: Algorithms for drawing graphs: an annotated bibliography. Computational Geometry. 4, 235--282 (1994)
2. Battista, G.D., Eades, P., Tamassia, R., Tollis, I.G.: Graph Drawing: Algorithms for the Visualization of Graphs. Prentice Hall, New Jersey, USA (1999)
3. Cormen, T.H., Leiserson, C.E., Rivest, R.L., Stein, C.: Introduction to Algorithms. MIT Press and McGraw-Hill, New York, USA (2001)
4. Cruz, I.F., Twarog, J.P.: 3D Graph Drawing with Simulated Annealing. In: Proceedings of the Symposium on Graph Drawing, pp. 162--165. Springer-Verlag, London, UK (1995)
5. Davidson, R., Harel, D.: Drawing Graphs Nicely Using Simulated Annealing, ACM Transactions on Graphics. 15, 301--331 (1996)
6. Dijksta, E.W.: A note on two problems in connexion with graphs. Numerische Mathematik. 1, 269--271 (1959)
7. Dolulil, J., Katreniakova, J.: Edge Routing with Fixed Node Positions. In: Proceedings of the 12th International Conference Information Visualisation, pp. 626--631. IEEE Computer Society Washington, DC, USA (2008)
8. Dwyer, T., Marriott, K., Wybrow, M.: Integrating edge routing into force-directed layout. In: Proceedings 14th Intl. Symp. Graph Drawing (GD '06), pp. 8--19. Springer-Verlag, Berlin, Heidelberg (2007)
9. Eades, P.: A heuristic for graph drawing. Congressus Numerantium. 42, 149--160 (1984)
10. Eades, P., Huang, M.L.: Navigating Clustered Graphs using Force-Directed Methods, Journal of Graph Algorithms and Applications. 4, 157--181 (2000)

11. Eades, P., Lai, W., Misue, K., Sugiyama, K.: Layout adjustment and the mental map. Journal of Visual Languages and Computing. 6, 83--210 (1995)

12. Forster, M.: Crossings in Clustered Level Graphs, Ph.D.Dissertation (2004)

13. Healy, P., Nikolov, N.S.: Graph Drawing. Springer-Verlag, Berlin, Heidelberg (2006)

14. Huang, X., Lai, W., Sajeev, A.S.M., Gao, J.: A new algorithm for removing node overlapping in graph visualization. Information Sciences. 177, 2821--2844 (2007)

15. Kakoulis, K.G., Tollis, I.G.: A unified approach to labeling graphical features. In: Proceedings 14th Annual ACM Symposium of Computational Geometry (SoCG'98), pp. 347--356. ACM New York, NY, USA (1998)

16. Kaufmann, M., Dorothea, W.: Drawing graphs, methods and models. Springer-Verlag, Berlin, Heidelberg (2001)

17. Korb, K.B., Nicholson, A.E.: Bayesian Artificial Intelligence. Chapman & Hall, London, UK (2004)

18. Kruskal, J.B.: On the Shortest Spanning Subtree of a Graph and the Traveling Salesman Problem. American Mathematical Society. 7, 48--50 (1956)

19. Kumar, P., Zhang, K.: Social Network Analysis of Online Marketplaces. In: Proceedings IEEE International Conference on e-Business Engineering, pp. 363--367. IEEE Computer Society Washington, DC, USA (2007)

20. Kumar, P., Zhang, K., Wang, Y.: Visualization of Clustered Directed Acyclic Graphs without Node Overlapping. In: Proceedings 12th International Conference on Information Visualization, pp. 38--43. IEEE Computer Society Washington, DC, USA (2008)

21. Kumar, P., Zhang K.: Visualization of Clustered Directed Acyclic Graphs with Node Interleaving. In: Proceedings of the 24th Annual ACM Symposium on Applied Computing (SAC '09), pp. 1800--1805. ACM New York, NY, USA (2009)

22. Kumar, P., Zhang, K.: Node Overlap Removal in Clustered Directed Acyclic Graphs. Journal of Visual Languages and Computing (JVLC). Article in press, doi:10.1016/j.jvlc.2009.04.007 (2009)

23. Lai, W.: Layout Adjustment and Boundary Detection for a Diagram. In: Proceedings of Computer Graphics International (CGI '01), pp. 351--354. IEEE Computer Society Washington, DC, USA (2001)

24. Lai, W., Eades, P.: Removing edge-node intersections in drawings of graphs. Information Processing Letters. 81, 105--110 (2002)

25. Larson, R.C., Li, V.O.K.: Finding minimum rectilinear distance paths in the paths in the presence of barriers. Networks. 11, 285--304 (1981)

26. Lee, D.T., Preparata, F.P.: Euclidean shortest paths in the presence of rectilinear barriers. Networks. 14, 393--410 (1984)

27. Leiserson, C.E.: Fat-Trees: Universal Networks for Hardware-Efficient Supercomputing. IEEE Transactions on Computers. 34, 892--901 (1985)

28. Leymann, F.: Web Services Flow Language (WSFL 1.0), IBM (2001)

29. Li, W., Eades, P., Nikolov, N.: Using spring algorithms to remove node overlapping. In: Proceedings of the 2005 Asia-Pacific symposium on Information visualization (APVIS '05), pp. 131--140. Australian Computer Society, Inc. Darlinghurst, Australia (2005)

30. Lozano-Perez, T., Wesley, M.A.: An algorithm for planning collision-free paths among polyhedral obstacles. Communications of ACM. 22, 22560--22570 (1979)

31. Marriott, K., Stuckey, P., Vam, T., He, W.: Removing Node Overlapping in Graph Layout Using Constrained Optimization. Constraints. 8, 143--171 (2003)

32. Nascimento, H.A.D., Eades, P.: User Hints for map labeling. Journal of Visual Languages and Computing. 19, 39--74 (2008)

33. Papakostas, A., Tollis, I.G.: Interactive Orthogonal Graph Drawing. IEEE Transactions on Computers. 47, 1297--1309 (1998)

34. Prim, R.C.: Shortest connection networks and some generalizations. Bell System Technical Journal. 36, 1389--1401 (1957)

35.Purchase, H.C., Cohen, R.F., James, M.: Validating Graph Drawing Aesthetics. In: Proceedings of the Symposium on Graph Drawing (GD '95), pp. 435--446. Springer-Verlag, London, UK (1995)
36.Quigley A., Eades, P.: Graph Drawing, Clustering, and Visual Abstraction. In: Proceedings of the 8th International Symposium on Graph Drawing (GD '00), pp. 197--210. Springer-Verlag, Berlin, Heidelberg (2000)
37.Taylor, M., Rodgers, P.: Applying Graphical Design Techniques to Graph Visualization. In: Proceedings of the Ninth International Conference on Information Visualization (IV '05), pp. 651--656. IEEE Computer Society Washington, DC, USA (2005)
38.ConceptDraw, http://www.conceptdraw.com/en/products/cd5/main.php
39.Home of Graphdrawing, http://www.graphdrawing.org
40.Graphviz - Graph Visualization Software, http://www.graphviz.org
41.Microsoft Office Online – Visio, http://office.microsoft.com/en-us/visio/default.aspx
42.yWorks, http://www.yworks.com/products/yfiles/doc/developers-guide/index.html

Visual Navigation with Schematic Maps

Steffen Bogen[1], Ulrik Brandes[2], and Hendrik Ziezold[2],

[1] Art History & Media Studies, University of Konstanz
[2] Computer & Information Science, University of Konstanz

Abstract. A prototypical example of the operational dimensions of visual information communication is the use of schematic maps for visual navigation. The implementation of maps on location-sensitive or handheld devices has changed the preliminaries of common mapping techniques. By an analysis of selected examples, both historic and current, we want to open up the space for innovative map design options. Our approach blends art history and computer science, and is based on a systematic, operational perspective. It may be unexpected, though, that it starts from the way that graphic design supports imaginative navigation on the map, rather than considering its utility for navigation in the physical space directly.

1 Introduction

Since navigation is a pervasive task, navigational information and instructions exist in audible, visual, tactile, or even multi-modal form. The most common tool to explore navigational opportunities systematically is the visual map. A map communicates comprehensive information about places and relations between them. It is a generic navigation aid if a-priori undetermined origins, destinations and paths connecting them can be singled out on demand. We are particularly interested in this process of instantiation, by which a user turns a map into an aid for a specific navigational task. With the goal to better understand the functioning of visual maps as an aid in navigation, we start from the proposition that the actual spatial navigation with maps is complemented by an imaginative navigation on them. This idea is not foreign to the vast literature on maps [1, 3, 7, 9, 17], but the argument has not been elaborated systematically, yet. Our assumptions imply that users actually explore, experience, and validate navigational information by duplication: on the map and in space. Not only is a map design more intuitive and convincing if derived from first principles, but it is also easier to evaluate, because such principles suggest hypotheses that can be tested in user studies.

M.L. Huang et al. (eds.), *Visual Information Communication*,
DOI 10.1007/978-1-4419-0312-9_4, © Springer Science+Business Media, LLC 2010

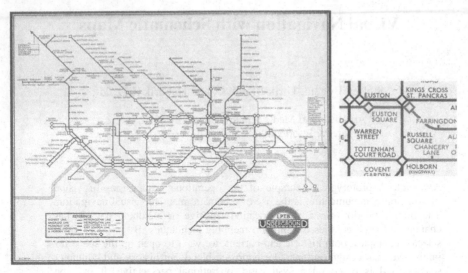

Fig. 1. The London Tube Map by Harry Beck, 1931 [8]

1.1 Dynamic Maps on Mobile Devices

Map layouts are often schematic in that physical reality is reduced to match a specific concept, which also emphasizes that "Design, however, is choice" [22, p. 191]. Since all maps are in essence conceptual [11] [18, p. 5], in an extreme view all map layouts are schematic. We ponder on this view because of the vast design space it implies. By reducing the content of the map its layout can be arranged so that the focused information is easier to read.

Static paper maps are restricted to a single layout. To remain useful for various use cases they are oftentimes generalized. The implementation of maps on computers has changed this preconditions of the medium. Now, the map animation opens up new possibilities of tuning level-of-detail and schematization interactively. A user can interact with the map and thereby can adapt the layout on demand to support a certain use case. That way the map can be temporarily specialized to fit a specific situation and orientational configuration.

On paper maps finding an index remains in the hands of the user. To find his current position and facing direction a paper map has to be folded out and turned. A location-sensitive mobile device can assist the search process by adapting the map dynamically. The device always keeps the map centered at the user's current position. Additionally the map might be rotated triggered by a change of the user's alignment. Also other layout parameters can be changed interactively. The user may want to change the level of detail or resolution, or select a different layout, etc. To apply these changes a digital map producer can take the time axis as an additional display dimension. Along this time axis several changes can be animated by: zooming, panning, information filtering, tuning level-of-detail or other transformations of the map layout.

Though mobile devices offer more possibilities for map visualization on the one hand, they cause some new demands in respect to their medium and use case scenario on the other. The main disadvantage of mobile devices is their small display size. To overcome this disadvantage is one task of current map visualization techniques [5].

1.2 An Operational Perspective

We focus on the process by which a user turns the map into an aid for a specific navigational task. Possible starting points, destinations, and routes have to be singled out. Schematic maps support these operations by reducing the world to an operational concept and by clearly visualizing its relations. Typical relations for operations are for example temporal or spatial distances or possible travel connections. Maps that depict the same places but visualize other relation types often also differ in scale, level-of-detail, or similar parameters.

To formulate these conceptual differences we break down the use of maps into different operational steps, or actions. We posit that, aside from aesthetics, design options mainly concern the following three activities.

to situate
The act of situating identifies spatial relations as operational opportunities for a person who holds respective abilities and might be interested in using them. For example, looking at the London tube map in Fig. 1 (even while sitting far away at Sydney's Harbour Bay), traveling with London transport is imagined.

to orient
For the act of orienting, we imagine someone to be at a concrete position and identify the relations between his position and other places on the map: what is in the surroundings? What distances or connections to other places are there? This person can also be imagined with a facing direction. On the London tube map, for example, someone could be positioned at King's Cross, and lines are identified that are connected and aligned towards a neighboring station or towards one end of a line.

to navigate
The act of navigating is changing an orientational configuration iteratively, i.e. operational opportunities and conditions to reach a destination are identified. In the process of planning several operations are selected and combined to one route. For example, for navigating from King's Cross to Tottenham Court Road it can be deduced from the tube map that one has to change at Holborn.

The modular concepts are developed for looking on a flat map space. Often the operations on the map can be linked to operations in real space. We call this operational index. Operations planned on the map are linked to operations and movements of our own body. Therefore we need to connect our perspective upon the flat map with our perspective to the real world [14]. In doing so, we become users of the map. The spatial knowledge gained can be transferred in both directions: operations can be planned ahead in map space and later be executed as movements in the real-world, and real-world movements can be followed by respective operations on the map. For navigation on the go it is always important to keep all operations synchronized.

Some of our historic examples are focused on only one operational aspect. Though their layouts are convincing in displaying certain information, they are too specific to actually be useful for the whole process of navigation on the go. For that reason modern static maps for navigation usually incorporate all operational aspects at once. However, as stated in Sect. 1.1, maps implemented on a mobile device can instantiate more than one layout, so that different operational aspects can be addressed temporarily. Thus, we claim that dynamic map design can still be informed by historic mappers' know-how. Applying our modular perspective to maps on mobile devices we aim to recover some strong ideas about schematic map layout.

2 Operating on Maps by Example

The following examples, both historic and current, are selected and analyzed as design options that support the introduced aspects of operating with maps: situating, orienting, and navigating. We choose schematic maps that emphasize single aspects. In Sect. 3 we reflect how the observed design options can be recombined and animated innovatively.

2.1 Situating

Situating with maps on location-sensitive mobile devices Fig. 2 shows a map (from Google Maps[1]) implemented on a location-sensitive mobile device. Situating with a location sensitive device is a shared process, partly achieved by the user who chooses a certain kind of map, and partly achieved by the device that detects the user's current position and environment. A mobile device using A-GPS (Assisted GPS) identifies the user's approximate current environment and orientation by its approximate position within the cellular network and by interpreting GPS signals. Map tiles representing the current environment are downloaded and displayed. If the GPS signal fails, localization can only rely on the approximate positioning within the cellular network. Then the user's current approximate surroundings are encircled by a disconnected blue crosshair on the map. Within the circle the user's potential whereabouts and operational opportunities are represented.

The resulting map concentrates on a certain kind of spatial relation, here geographic distances. The map is adjusted to display areas that are assumed to be of the user's interest. That way the user is assisted in situating. If the exact position can be determined by GPS signals, this position is visualized by a dark blue dot on the map. Thus, the user would even be assisted in orienting.

---

[1] maps.google.com

Fig. 2. Google Maps on a smartphone.

There are computer implemented maps that additionally enable the user to adjust the map himself to improve its usability for a certain situation. He can filter out specific details or mark specific points of interest. The user can even share such an annotated map with others.

Golden Seal of Louis IV In Europe, 700 years ago, only an emperor could realize and distribute a map that represented places according to his interests.

Fig. 3 shows a midget map on the golden seal of the bavarian king Louis IV. It was made in 1328 AD, the year the king was crowned in Rome as Roman emperor against the pope's opposition. The seal has a circular shape similar to the blue rimmed circle on the Google Map. The circular form of the seal invites to understand the represented area as a specific situation. Anyone who is familiar with the city of Rome will recognize buildings that define the city as town of the roman emperors: the Colosseum, the Capitol, the Pantheon, an emperor column and a triumphal arch. The buildings are represented by small images, shown in perspective. Their positions within the town are defined by the city wall and the Tiber river. A point of view is created, that overlooks the selected buildings.

The recto of the seal shows Louis IV on his throne. The combination reflects the political claim to reign in succession of the Roman emperors. We argue that the emperor is depicted on both sides of the seal: On its recto side in effigy, on its verso side as the person who peers implicitly at the city of Rome and gives it the meaning of the imperial city. In fact at the end of the ritual of coronation the emperor left the town and climbed the Monte Mario. From there he looked back on the town lying to his feet [23]. With this final view the emperor took possession of Rome visually and tried to recapitulate places of his coronation way. In reality it was hard to get this

Fig. 3. Golden Seal of Louis IV, Staatsarchiv Bamberg, Brandenburg-Bayreuth Urkunde 142.

view because the viewing point on the Monte Mario is too low and the symbolic places of interest are too distant. In contrast the midget map on the seal shows the situating of the emperor as a perfect visual scheme. It is even possible to imagine his ritual way through Rome: from St. Peter, where he was crowned, over a bridge, then up the stairs to the entrance of the senatorial palace. There he presented himself as the emperor to the people of Rome. From there he walked to the Porta Flaminia, represented at the bottom left of the seal, that leads to the Monte Mario outside the walls.

No matter who looks at the seal, the person who has to be situated on the map, is the emperor. The two sides of the seal – that is the map and the emperor who has to be situated on it – stand for a circular justification of power. Today companies like Google and others suggest that we all may become little emperors, who can create their own maps. By doing so, the users should be aware that the companies can collect their personality profiles too. Collecting profile information from personalized maps is somehow similar to our interpretation of the golden seal as the emperor's crowning situation.

2.2 Orienting

Map of the Surroundings of Nuremberg The map of the surroundings of Nuremberg (Fig. 4) is one of the oldest printed maps in Germany [21, 6, 19] (1492 AD). It is famous as one of the first true to scale regional maps that was extracted from travel experience, written itineraries, and some additional measurements. As a common feature of systematical map layouts, distances and directions can also be deduced that have not been set explicitly.

Nuremberg was the hometown of Erhard Etzlaub and Georg Glockendon who were maker and printer of the woodcut. Similar to the previous examples a circle is a prominent feature of the map. It surrounds potential points of interest around Nuremberg. The center of the circular map is marked by the city arms of Nuremberg. This central sign can be compared to the point "my place" on modern maps. Within the circle over a hundred names of towns are spelled out. Single letters encode additional information concerning the political status of a town, as "r" signifies a "Reichsstadt" (ger. imperial town), or "b" signifies a "Bischofsstadt" (ger. episcopal town). Rivers and their sources are represented by a straight line. Political borders are marked with a dotted line. The circle is enclosed by a rectangular frame. The cardinal directions are inscribed at the borders of the frame, "mittemtag" (ger. noon, south) is represented at the top of the map. Etzlaub may have derived this convention from the sundials he also produced.

The graphical entries are positioned on the map according to their true to scale distances. The scale bar and an explanation how to use it are printed at the bottom of the map. The radius of the circle scales to 16 german miles (ca. 120 km). By measuring the distance between dots on the map one can calculate the distance between the towns in real space. As the scale bar represents only 20 german miles, measurements through the whole diameter are not directly supported. But the bar is sufficient to translate distances between Nuremberg, as preselected center of orientation, and any other town. Thus, typical questions of orientation can be answered in relation to Nuremberg: how far is it from Nuremberg to town X? In which direction is town Y located?

It may be surprising, though, that neither streets are shown, nor bridges or other possibilities to pass the rivers. It is evident that the map was not intended to be used on the road for navigational tasks but rather to be studied in libraries or to be used for the documentation of places. As an indication, the represented copy, colored by hand, was preserved by Hartmann Schedel, who included the map in his own copy of his "Weltchronik". The originally intended user of the map was the political establishment of Nuremberg. Certainly they were proud to show a map that represented their town as the prominent center of orientation within its surroundings.

Halos The historic examples arranged their circular layout around a given center of orientation. As we stated above, maps implemented on mobile devices can be dynamized. This offers the possibilty to dynamically adjust maps to the user's current orientational configuration.

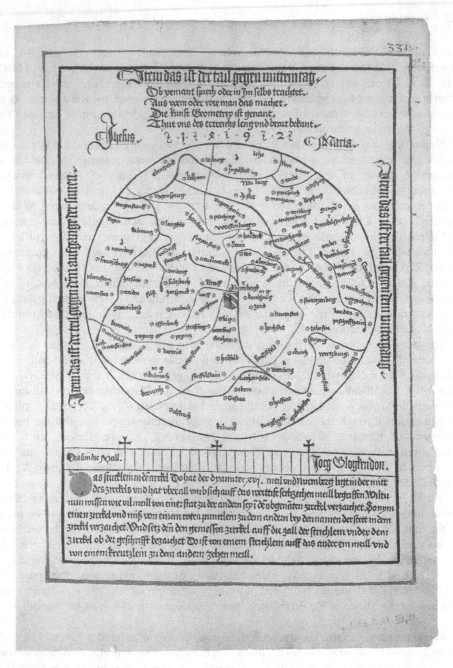

Fig. 4. Surroundings of Nuremberg (N¨urnberger Umgebungskarte), Erhard Etzlaub, 29.7×27.3 cm, 1492, copy of Munich, Bayerische Staatsbibliothek, Rar 287, fol. 331r.

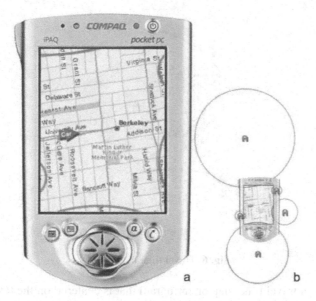

Fig. 5. Halos [2]

A typical orientational practice is to read out the direction and distance relations to certain points of interest. Favourably, these points of interests are displayed on the map. As the display of a mobile device is very small, some points of interest in the user's surroundings might not fit into the display. Unless the user pans or zooms to make them appear, he cannot read out any distances or directions towards off-screen destinations.

Halos, a focus and context technique developed by Baudisch and Rosenholtz [2], aim to overcome this disadvantage of maps on mobile devices (see Fig. 5). Here, an imaginary isoline circle is drawn around potential destinations (point of interest) that are located off-screen. These circles are dynamically resized until they extend to the border of the display. When changing location the map is updated to keep the current location in the center of the display. Accordingly, the radius of every circle is adjusted. Though only small segments of the circles are visible, the user is still able to anticipate the distances between his current location and his respective points of interest. The arc length of each circle segment is contingent on the distance to its respective point of interest. Halos emphasize distances and directions to the user's points of interest. Their orientational configuration and possible destinations are visualized and dynamically adjusted whenever the user position changes. But since points of interest located further away are more noticeably visualized than places located closer, this visualization technique might confuse the user. User studies should be accomplished to evaluate this method.

Travel Time Maps Another example for maps on which the relations are calibrated on one point of orientation are travel time maps. A travel time map visualizes temporal distances from one place to several possible travel destinations, for example if travelling by public transportation.

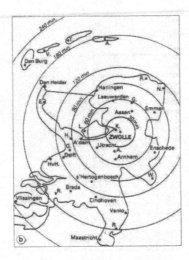

Fig. 6. Travel time map [10]

Fig. 6 shows a travel time map or cartogram that is centered on the town of Zwolle (Netherlands) and visualizes temporal distances to certain travel destinations within the Netherlands [10]. The map visualizes only one temporal distance between Zwolle and each of the travel destinations, i.e. the destination points are positioned on the map according to their shortest travel time distance starting at Zwolle. As an alternative layout the map layout could consist of a graph, in which Zwolle and all destinations would be visualized as nodes and travel time distances would be visualized as edges. Goedvolk chooses an area map to still display the whole Netherlands. He therefore distorts the coastlines and boundaries in respect to the time positions of the travel destinations. That way the map provides approximate temporal orientation to all places even if they are not marked on the map.

This results in a map that we would use if we were located in Zwolle and would want to orient ourselves in respect to our time-dependent travel opportunities. We might then align ourselves to one of the possible travel destinations. But for navigating on the go, we would want to take a different map at hand.

Circular Prospect of Nuremberg As another examples for retaining the principle of preselecting a center of orientation for all operations on the map Fig. 7 shows a circular prospect of Nuremberg. It is a large map, a woodcut with a square frame, commissioned at the end of the 16th century by the town of Nuremberg [21, p. 223]. It shows the surroundings of Nuremberg in an artificial circular prospect. There are earlier examples of such layouts from Vienna and elsewhere. At the center of the map the municipal area of Nuremberg is represented only as a trefoil of coats of arms within an idealized circle. The coats of arms are two city arms and the national emblem of the German Empire. Besides the town walls that surround the municipal area and that serve for orientation, no streets and buildings are shown. Cardinal points such as gates, towers, the entrance and exit of the river Pegnitz are represented and labeled. The map helps everyone who is familiar with the town to orientate himself in the surroundings.

Fig. 7. Circular prospect of Nuremberg (Rundprospekt N¨urnberg), Stefan Gans¨oder and Paulus Reinhart, 95,5×96,0, 1577-81, Staatsarchiv Nuremberg, Reichsstadt N¨urnberg, Karten und Pl¨ane Nr. 202

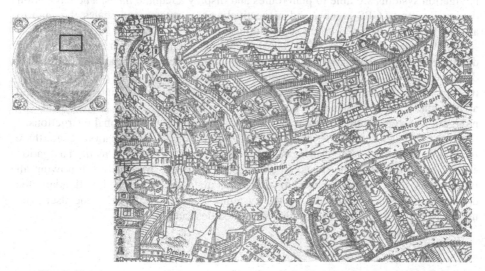

Fig. 8. Circular prospect of Nuremberg (Rundprospekt N¨urnberg), cutout enlarged.

The surroundings are represented by pictorial means: images of buildings, streets and hills, forests, rivers and fields (see Fig. 8). There are humans and animals inserted to give a vivid impression of possible uses of space. So, all these elements are stimuli to imaginative operations on the map. For a better orientation many places and streets are named. Cardinal directions are marked at the border of the horizon. At the edges personifications of the cardinal winds are placed, already known from the circular route maps.

The map explicates the concept of view-and-horizon or detail-in-context that also underlies all the other circular maps. Every image and letter is oriented towards the center, so everything seems to be viewed from the central town.

The artificial projection causes some distortions. Nevertheless, the map is useful not only for orientation but also for planning navigation. The user can grasp a lot of visual information for linking navigation on the map with navigation in real space. Crucial points for navigation as crossings, bridges or the skirts of a forest are depicted. But the ways trail away in the hills or the forests towards the horizon. So the perspective of the map is only useful for navigation within the immediate surroundings of the central town.

There are even current layouts that apply similar detail-in-context techniques. E.g., the variable-scale map layout of the authors Harrie, Sarjakoski and Lehto [12], that comprises different scales and levels of detail.

2.3 Navigating

Navigation Systems Without the use of a car navigation system the planning of the route and the interacting with the map had to be achieved by the user. Now common navigation systems are able to plan routes and display adequate maps. The navigation device interprets GPS signals and respectively pans, rotates and scales the map to always focus the driver's current surroundings.

Fig. 9 shows the display of a Falk navigation system on which the position and driving direction is indicated by a blue line and a small red triangle at the bottom. The displayed section of the map is in a bird's eye view that augments the driver's view through the windscreen. In addition, the further route is charted into the map, and arrows mark the points where navigational instructions have to be followed. That way navigation systems animate a map to display a sequence of navigational instructions.

Once the user has started the navigation system, he selects a destination. Then, there is actually no need for the user to be oriented in space all the time, as the navigation system tells him where he is and where to go next. If the driver is not following all instructions, the navigation system will recalculate the route and will adapt the displayed map accordingly. Thus, the system concurrently provides the user with navigational information towards his preselected destination.

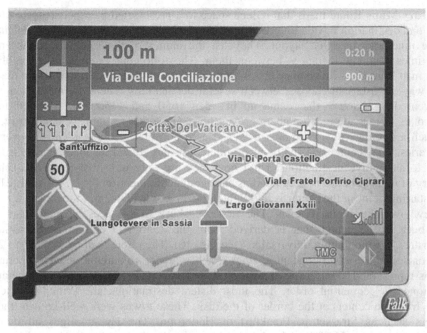

Fig. 9. Display of a contemporary navigation system (Falk).

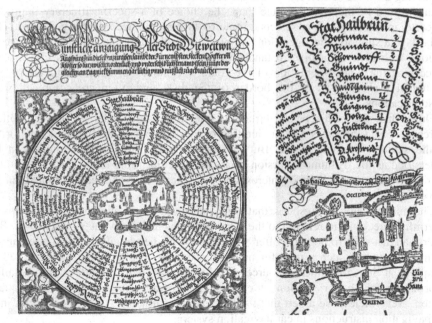

Fig. 10. Circular route map of Augsburg (Augsburger Meilenscheibe), Hans Rogel, 38.2×29.7 cm, 1565, copy of Augsburg, Maximilianmuseum, gr. 32.

Itinerary Maps Route maps that reduce space to a preselected path between starting point and destination have a long tradition. There are historical examples that display single itineraries in a list layout. They list the names of the route's stations and sometimes state the distances between them. The following example is a circular route map from the 17th century that integrates different itineraries into a single map. This way the user can choose between several destinations. There are more than 12 different disks known, that came up between 1650 and 1750 AD. Most of the exemplars were made in Nuremberg or Augsburg. One other example centers Erfurt.

Such a circular route map was designed as a concentric arrangement of several itineraries. They center one station as origin and display itineraries that emanate from there to alternative destinations. Until now they are only object of research to the history of roads, but are not regarded as cartographical invention [15], [16], and [21]. The starting point in the center is highlighted by an iconic element: in most cases it is a view over the focused town. The first Augsburg disk places a small map of Augsburg in the center that is derived from the 1550 AD edition of Sebastian M¨unsters "cosmographia universalis" (see Fig. 10). The circle is divided in 12 to 24 segments, and 10 to 30 concentric rings. Each segment contains a written itinerary that is represented along a ray emanating from the center. All itinerary stations are positioned in sequential order. The most distant destinations are written (furthest away from the center) at the border of the disk. These towns were well-known trade centers such as Strassburg, Frankfurt or Heilbronn. The layout aligns all items towards the center. Useful navigational information is displayed only along the rays emanating from the center, not on the concentric rings.

In the case of the circular route map, the choice of a specific itinerary implies a concrete operation: the user selects a route by turning the accordant ray upward. The radial layout supports this operation. Along the rays the user can read the sequence of stations with their respective distances in both directions. He also gets information concerning the main orientation of the route: the names of cardinal directions are written at the center or at the border of the disk, and often are combined with personifications.

Other than the Halos or the circles of the travel time map, the radius neither represents exact distances nor the duration of journey, but rather the sequential order of the station within its route. But in other respects the Halo technique can be understood as the dynamic inversion of a static circular route map. The Halo circles are drawn around the points of interest and their radius is dynamically adapted due to movement.

The midget map of Augsburg, that is placed in the center of our example, helps to determine directions in relation to the main buildings and main gates of the town. But other than that such route maps often withheld any further details for local orientation. So in order to use such a map for navigation on the go one would have needed to complement it with other resources of knowledge that provide more detailed information for the orientation at each station towards its respective subsequent station. Nevertheless we assert that the list feature of itineraries gets a new relevance for navigation instructions in car navigation system.

3 Applied Recombination of Operational Aspects

By analyzing current and historic map examples, we described the impact layout can have on operations with maps. We observed that the step of situating may be supported by pictorial elements, a certain point of view, and information filtering. Circular layouts are appropriate to guide orientation from a given starting point. Preplanned navigational routes are best represented as clearly arranged sequences of selected stations. We will now use these insights to introduce new approaches to map design. Their underlying operational concepts recombine the three observed operational aspects and design options innovatively.

3.1 Dynamic Detail-in-Context List for Navigation

A map on a common navigation system is concurrently updated triggered by a change of position and orientation (see Fig. 9). By looking at the display the driver can read out birds-eye view details about his local environment and can gain some additional route information.

But we claim that what is considered relevant information should differ dependently on the operational stage the user is currently in. On the one side, during navigation the user arrives at points where he needs to perform a navigational instruction. Then he needs to orient himself within his local environment, because the instruction has to be performed at the correct position and with the correct alignment in space. In that case the user needs a more detailed map about the local environment. On the other side, while only following one and the same street, being oriented within his local environment is not as important. The driver is rather interested in his sequential position within the route and his distance to the next navigational instruction. But a map would be of advantage that is showing orientational information about the local environment of the next navigational instruction. That way the driver could mentally prepare this step in advance.

On a navigation system, it is no problem to alternate layouts that either emphasize orientation within the route or orientation within a local environment. Inspired by historic itineraries (see Fig. 4) we propose to display a dynamic list layout that takes the differing requirements into account. A drawing of a circular Google Maps cutout[2] representing the surroundings of a navigational instruction is displayed in Fig. 11. In order to align all local cutouts in driving direction from bottom to top, just as most navigation systems do, we propose to connect the cutouts by Bezier curves. The hybrid connected list of map cutouts is then to be animated, so that the user's position is always centered on the display. According to the user's position either the schematic line passes the center, whenever following a street, or a local cutout surrounds the center, whenever the user needs to follow a navigational instruction. For orientation within the route a small true to scale map of the route should be provided in one corner of the display. On that the driver's position is concurrently marked.

---

[2] maps.google.com

Fig. 11. Draft for a dynamic detail-in-context list for navigation

3.2 Warping Zoom

Although a generalized map is capable of serving various situations, it might not always be the best choice for each separate situation. If a user only needs to consider a single situation, he could more easily gain relevant information from a specialized map, since its layout and content is adjusted to fit the specific situational needs best. Consequently, such a map is useful in a smaller diversity of situations. For a combined navigational task a change of situations (i.e. navigational spaces) is required. So, for performing such a combined navigational task one would usually take two specialized maps at hand. When the user arrives at a situation his specialized map at hand does not support, he replaces it with a respective other one. After the user has exchanged maps, he has to find his orientational configuration within the new layout again.

For example beholding the case, in which a user needs to accomplish walking on the streets together with using a public transportation network. The user has to come to navigational decisions concerning the street level and the transportation net. He would take a schematic map of the transportation net and a common city plan at hand. However, there are even some ideas to overcome the necessity of two separate maps for this task. One approach is a so-called Spider Map[3,4]. Here, a city plan cutout around a specific station is integrated in a schematic transportation map. But the original schematic transportation net layout has to be adjusted in a way that the cutout fits in. So these maps only provide street-level details for a single station. Maps still need to be swapped whenever the surroundings of another station are of interest.

Another approach is to combine the different map layouts into one dynamic interactive map. This way the information of both maps can be maintained. The generation of a compound map by warping techniques is discussed by Reilly and Inkpen [20] and Boettger, Brandes, Deussen and Ziezold [4]. Basically, Reilly et al. use raster-graphics based maps. Their map distortion demonstrates that two optimized layouts can be morphed into each other. They additionally couple their warping

---

[3] sfcityscape.com/maps/spider.html
[4] tfl.gov.uk/tfl/gettingaround/maps/buses

animation with fading the respective other map. This simple morphing application aids index finding.

Boettger et al. use vector data and keep the operational information that was relevant in the previous situation as context information for the other respective layout. Furthermore, they account for other situational requirements, as there is a need to change level-of-detail and enlargement scale. The layout of the compound map of Boettger et al. is smoothly adjusted to facilitate the reading of the currently relevant information and to preserve the user's orientational index and embedding. This technique is called warping zoom.

In practical terms, if the user wants to reach a nearby metro station by walking, he covers short distances and thus he only needs street-level information of his current surroundings. But when arriving at a metro station, he can suddenly cover longer distances within range of the whole metro network. This sudden switch of situations is considered by the warping zoom technique. Switching from walking to riding metro trains, the user zooms out and simultaneously warps the map layout to a schematic overview map of the metro network. Switching from riding metro trains to walking he zooms in and simultaneously warps back to the geographical layout of street level information (see Fig. 12 or the authors' demo video[5]). If the situation of the user can be determined by the device, the warping zoom could also be controlled automatically. For example, location sensitive devices can derive the user's current location and travel speed from GPS signals. As these parameters can serve as an indication of the user's current situation, the map can be zoomed and warped to the respective layout.

Boettger et al. suggest a second technique for the integration of two differing layouts into one map. Inspired by the circular prospect of Nuremberg (see Fig. 7 and 8) and by modern fisheye techniques [13] they implement a fisheye lens. This lens dynamically unwarps a circular area within the warped compound map layout (see Fig. 13). While under the lens street level information is easier to read, outside the lens the map is adapted to give an overview of metro network connections. Thus, if the user is in pedestrian situation, he is provided with street level details in metro network context. If he is in the situation of a metro network user, he can read out the network details in street level context.

Summary

Starting from the proposition that map navigation is understood better when also considering the imaginative act of navigating on the map, we discussed several design options that support the basic operational dimensions of situating, orienting, and navigating in various ways.

We analyzed both current and historic maps to inform map designs that address specific and complex operations. We then formulated an innovative perspective on how to reactivate ideas of historical maps. Our examples demonstrated how historical map features can provide design options for keyframe layouts in map animation, and we thereby aim to motivate further map design variations.

---

[5] http://www.inf.uni-konstanz.de/algo/research/mapwarping/demo.avi

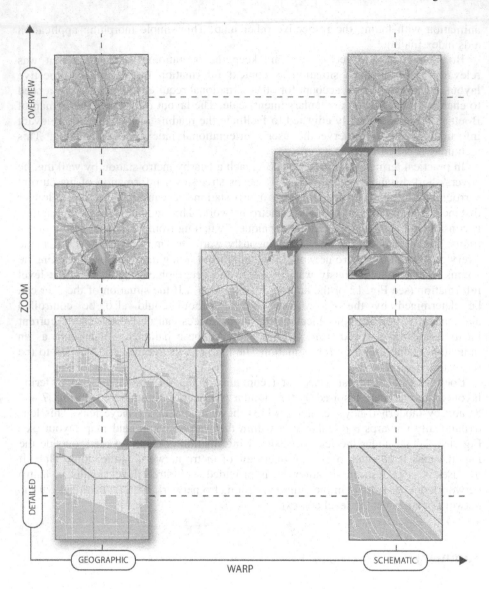

Fig. 12. Warping Zoom [4]

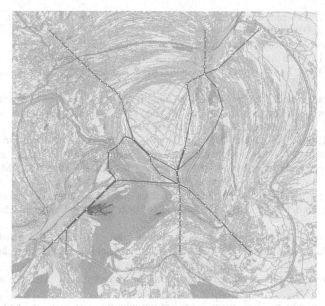

Fig. 13. Fisheye lens [4]

Acknowledgments This work was supported by Volkswagen Foundation under grant II/81425 (project "Visual Navigation"). We would like to thank Christian Ehinger, Gesa Henselmans, Albert K"ummel-Schnur, Ilka Ludwig, Felix Th"urlemann, and Julia Zons for helpful comments and suggestions.

References

1. James R. Akerman. Cartographies of travel and navigation. Univ. of Chicago Press, Chicago u.a., 2006.
2. Patrick Baudisch and Ruth Rosenholtz. Halo: A technique for visualizing off-screen locations. Proc.CHI 03, pages 481–488, 2003.
3. Gabriele Brandstetter. Figur und Inversion. Kartographie als Dispositiv von Bewegung, pages 223–245. de figura. Fink, Paderborn, 2002.
4. Joachim B"ottger, Ulrik Brandes, Oliver Deussen, and Hendrik Ziezold. Map warping for the annotation of metro maps. IEEE Computer Graphics and Applications, 28(5):56–65, 2008.
5. Stefano Burigat and Luca Chittaro. Geographical data visualization on mobile devices for user's navigation and decision support activities. Spatial Data on the Web–Modelling and Management, page 261–284, 2007.
6. Tony Campbell. The earliest printed maps 1472-1500. British Library, London, 1987.
7. Michel de Certeau. L'invention du quotidien. Arts de faire. Union Generale d'Editions, Paris, 1980.
8. Ken Garland. Mr Beck's Underground Map. Capital Transport Publishing, 38 Long Elmes, Harrow Eeald, Middlesex, 1994.
9. Alfred Gell. How to read a map: Remarks on the practical logic of navigation. Man. The Journal of the Royal Anthropological Institute, 20:271–286, 1985.

10.A. Goedvolk. De nieuwe relatieve afstand voor het openbaar vervoer. De nieuwe geografenkrant, 1988(10):6–7, 1988.
11.J. Brian Harley. Deconstructing the map. Cartographica, 26.2:1–20, 1989.
12.Lars Harrie, L. Tiina Sarjakoski, and Lassi Lehto. A variable-scale map for small-display cartography. Proc. Symposium on GeoSpatial Theory, Processing, and Applications, pages 8–12, 2002.
13.T. Alan Keahey and Edward L. Robertson. Techniques for non-linear magnification transformations. In Proceedings of the IEEE Symposium on Information Visualization, pages 38–45, San Francisco, CA, USA, October 1996.
14.Alexander Klippel, Kai-Florian Richter, Thomas Barkowsky, and Christian Freska. The cognitive reality of schematic maps. In Liqiu Meng, Alexander Zipf, and Tumasch Reichenbacher, editors, Map-based Mobile Services -Theories, Methods and Implementations, pages 57–74, Berlin, 2005. Springer.
15.Herbert Kr¨uger. Oberdeutsche Meilenscheiben des 16. und 17. Jahrhunderts als strassengeschichtliche Quellen, I. Teil. Jahrbuch f¨ur fr¨ankische Landesforschung, 23:171–195, 1963.
16.Herbert Kr¨uger. Oberdeutsche Meilenscheiben des 16. und 17. Jahrhunderts als strassengeschichtliche Quellen, II. Teil. Jahrbuch f¨ur fr¨ankische Landesforschung, 24:167–206, 1964.
17.Sybille Kr¨amer. Medium, Bote, Ubertragung kleine Metaphysik der Medialit¨at. Suhrkamp, Frankfurt/M, 2008.
18.Alan M. MacEachren. How maps work. representation, visualization, and design. The Guilford Press, New York u.a., 2004.
19.Peter H. Meurer. Cartography in the German Lands, 1450 -1650, volume 3.2 of Cartography in the European Renaissance, pages 1172–1245. Chicago; London, 2007.
20.Derek F. Reilly and Kori M. Inkpen. White rooms and morphing don't mix: setting and the evaluation of visualization techniques. Proceedings of the SIGCHI conference on Human factors in computing systems, pages 111–120, 2007.
21.Franz Schiermeier. Stadtatlas N¨urnberg Karten und Modelle der Stadt N¨urnberg von 1492 bis heute. Schiermeier, M¨unchen, 2006.
22.Edward R. Tufte. Visual explanations images and quantities, evidence and narrative. Graphics Press, Cheshire, Conn., 1997.
23.Marco Vencani. Rom als multiple Figur. Zur Geschichte einer umkaempften Stadtwahrnehmung (12. -14. Jh.). In Gottfried Boehm, Gabriele Brandstetter, and Achatz von M¨uller, editors, Figur und Figuration. Studien zu Wahrnehmung und Wissen, pages 357–370, Paderborn, 2007.

DOI-Wave: A Focus+Context Interaction Technique for Networks Based on Attention-Reactive Interface

Lei Ren[1,1], Lin Zhang[1], Dongxing Teng[2], Guozhong Dai[2], Qian Li[3]

[1] School of Automation Science and Electrical Engineering, Beihang University, Beijing 100191, China
[2] Institute of Software, The Chinese Academy of Sciences, Beijing 100190, China
[3] School of Information Technology, Shangdong Institute of Commerce and Technology, Jinan, 250103, China
leo.renlei@gmail.com, johnlin9999@163.com, tengdongxing@ios.cn, dgz@iel.iscas.ac.cn, liqian.daisy@gmail.com

Abstract. This paper presents DOI-Wave, a Focus+Context technique for interactive exploration of networks, whose layout depends dynamically on the user's degree-of-interest (DOI). DOI-Wave uses the hierarchical clustered graph paradigm, in which, the view of a graph is dynamically determined by the selection of a single node as the focus node. The layout algorithm could change the view of graph animatedly, as the selected focus node is changed, according to each node's DOI value computed by a DOI function. The Focus+Context paradigm in DOI-Wave, from user's perspective, makes it easy to understand the relationships between the focus node and the other nodes. And the hierarchical cluster paradigm, which adapts to display space dynamically, leads to simultaneously clear and compact visualization. We have applied DOI-Wave to visualizing and exploring social networks. Evaluation results show DOI-Wave is effective.

Keywords: information visualization, user interface, graph visualization, interaction techniques, Focus+Context, attention-reactive user interface.

1   Introduction

Graph visualization, which has been studied extensively by researchers over the past years [1, 2], is an important topic in the information visualization community that can

---

[1] Lei Ren and Lin Zhang are with the School of Automation Science and Electrical Engineering, Beihang University. E-mail: leo.renlei@gmail.com, johnlin9999@163.com.

Dongxing Teng and Guozhong Dai are with the Human-Computer Interaction Lab and the Institute of Software, The Chinese Academy of Sciences. E-mail: tengdongxing@ios.cn, dgz@iel.iscas.ac.cn.

Qian Li is with the School of Information, Shangdong Institute of Commerce and Technology. Email: liqian.daisy@gmail.com

M.L. Huang et al. (eds.), *Visual Information Communication*,
DOI 10.1007/978-1-4419-0312-9_5, © Springer Science+Business Media, LLC 2010

be used in many application areas such as social network theory, communication network topology, and biology.

Hot issues in graph visualization include graph drawing algorithms for the aesthetic layout of large scale graph structures and interaction techniques for good understanding of complex network relationships. Perhaps the graph drawing algorithms [1] and software package in Graphviz [3] are well known, but most of these techniques are focused on providing static drawings of relatively large graph. Users need highly-interactive visualizations to gain insight, for example, it's quite necessary for social network analysts to explore an interested node's degree of connectivity and network distance from other nodes [4].

One group of the interaction techniques has used the clustered graph navigation paradigm to explore graphs (such as [5, 6, 7], which is limited in practice because it assumes the structure of the input graph is like a hierarchy. A second group transforms a graph into a tree (e.g. spanning tree) by using a fast algorithm and navigates this tree rather than the graph [8, 9], which often hides links among nodes and can't respond well to the change of graph structure according to use's attention. A third, very sparse group has used Focus+Context paradigm [10], such as graph fisheye technique with geometric distortion [11] and Radial Graph technique without geometric distortion [4]. Focus+Context techniques, using user's attention to dynamically allocate display resources through calculations of user's degree-of-interest (DOI) [16], meet user's intuition in visual information exploration that users need a way to pay attention to particular details they are focused on and also need some surrounding context [10]. However, current Focus+Context techniques with distortion for graph are difficult for users to comprehend the hierarchical relationships in complex graph since the nodes may be very close together, and the Focus+Context techniques without distortion, for example, Radial Graph that lays out nodes in the concentric rings, can't make the best of the rectangle display space and make users feel hard to explore nodes in every directions all 360 degrees.

To address these concerns, we propose DOI-Wave, a Focus+Context technique for interactive exploration of network whose layout depends dynamically on the user's estimated degree-of-interest (DOI). DOI-Wave, based on attention-reactive user interface [16], uses the hierarchical clustered graph paradigm in which the view of a graph is dynamically determined by the selection of a single node as the focus node user pay most attention to. The layout algorithm would change the view of graph animatedly, as the selected focus node is changed, according to each node's DOI value computed by a network DOI function. The Focus+Context paradigm in DOI-Wave, from user's perspective, makes it easier to understand the relationships between the focus node and the other nodes, and the hierarchical cluster paradigm, which adapts to display space, leads to simultaneously clearer and more compact visualization than graph fisheye and Radial Graph. We applied DOI-Wave to visualizing and exploring social networks. Evaluation results show DOI-Wave is effective.

2   Related Work

Graph visualization has been a hot research area in information visualization community over last few decades [2, 12]. There are a variety of graph drawing algorithms, e.g. [1, 2, 12], to calculate the positions of the nodes and the edges to display on the screen. However, most classic graph drawing algorithms are focused on producing static and nice layout of graph layout, which do not provide interactive solutions to support user's exploration.

In recent years the research on graph visualization has begun moving towards more interaction techniques, including the clustered graph navigation paradigm [5, 6, 7, 13, 14], tree navigation [8, 9], and Focus+Context paradigm [4, 11]. The cluster graph navigation paradigm, e.g. force-directed clustered graph [6] and ASK-GraphView [7], which allows the users to navigate a large graph by interactively expanding or collapsing aggregate nodes or edges, can be divided into two categories: nodes cluster [5, 6, 7, 13] and edge cluster [14]. The cluster navigation paradigm can be effective for revealing patterns and clusters in large graphs, but it would not work well if users want to explore the relationships between nodes that belong to the different clusters far away from one another. Tree navigation techniques, e.g. H3Viewer [15], hyperbolic hierarchical graph [8] and TreePlus [9], extracting trees from graphs to visualize the hierarchy, can be easy to understand for users and nicely support abstraction and generalization [9]. Although hierarchy is easier to read, current tree navigation techniques for graphs can't provide more support for the strategy of attention-reactive user interface than Focus+Context techniques do. Focus+Context techniques for graph consist of two categories. One is inspired by the geometric distortion of the Fisheye Lens metaphor, e.g. graph fisheye technique [11]. The other is without distortion, dynamically transforming the layout of graphs according to the selection of focus node. Radial Graph [4] is a method for animating the transition to a new layout as a new focus node is selected, which lays out focus node at the center of a circle and other nodes on a serial of concentric rings according to network distance from the focus node.

DOI-Wave combines three major ideas from existing interaction techniques mentioned above. In contrast with current clustered navigation and tree navigation techniques, DOI-Wave provides Focus+Context technique to support attention-reactive user interface. Besides, it can dynamically yield hierarchical clustered graph depended on the selection of the focus node, which leads to a more clear and compact layout for user's efficient understanding of the meaning of relationships than current Focus+Context techniques.

3   DOI-Wave

3.1   Preliminary Definition

We give the definitions of networks which will be used in the DOI-Wave algorithm.

*Definition 1: A **Node** is a 7-tuple (NodeID, DOI, CenterPoint, NodeWidth, NodeHeight, Level, NodeList, Text, Flag), where NodeID is the ID of the node, DOI is the value of degree of interest, CenterPoint is the center point of the bounding box of the node, NodeWidth and NodeHeight are the width and height of the bounding box, Level is the layer level in the clustered hierarchy the node belongs to, NodeList is the set of the nodes' IDs which are linked to the node, Text is the label, and Flag is a boolean flag with the initial value false.*

*Definition 2: An **Edge** is a 4-tuple (EdgeID, StartNode, EndNode, Text), Where EdgeID is the ID of the edge, StartNode and EndNode are the NodeIDs of two endpoint nodes of the edge, and Text is the label.*

*Definition 3: A **Network** is a 2-tuple (NodeSet, EdgeSet), where NodeSet is the set of nodes, and EdgeSet is the set of edges.*

3.2   DOI Model

Let N be a *Network* consisting of n nodes. Let Nd_f be the focus node user has selected. Let Nd_i be any node in N, $Nd_f \neq Nd_i$. Let Tr be a spanning tree of N with Nd_f as the root node. Let Nd_p be the parent node of Nd_i in Tr. DOI function is defined as follows.

$$DOI(Nd_i) = DOI(Nd_p) - C . \tag{1}$$

In DOI function, C is a constant. DOI Computing Algorithm is described as follows.

Step 1: Initiate DOI value of the focus node, $DOI(Nd_f) = n*C$. Make the *Flag* of Nd_p be true, $Nd_p.Flag$ = true.

Step 2: Traverse N with breadth first order and get the nodes' set *NodeList* of Nd_f.

Step 3: For any $Nd_j \in NodeList$, if the *Flag* of Nd_j is false, $DOI(Nd_j) = DOI(Nd_f) - C$. Then make the *Flag* of Nd_j be true, $Nd_j.Flag$ = true.

Step 4: For any $Nd_j \in NodeList$, make Nd_j be the new Nd_f. Then go to step 2.

3.3   DOI-Wave Layout Algorithm

Fig. 1 shows the layout method when a node is selected as the focus of attention. Let the left-top point of the rectangle display area be the origin of a two-dimensional coordinate system, the horizontal axis be X axis, and vertical axis be Y axis. Let w be the width of the rectangle in X axis, and h, the height in Y axis. For Nd_f and N, the DOI-Wave layout algorithm is described as follows.

Step 1: For each node $Nd_i \in NodeSet$, compute $DOI(Nd_i)$ by the DOI Computing Algorithm.

Step 2: For each node $Nd_i \neq Nd_f$, sort all the nodes in descending order according to $DOI(Nd_i)$. Then put them into sets SL_0, SL_{01}, SL_2, $\cdots$, SL_m where for $Nd_j \in SL_i$, $DOI(Nd_i) = (n-i-1)*a$.

Step 3: Put Nd_f at the point ($a + NodeWidth(Nd_f)$, $h/2$).

Step 4: For the nodes in each set SL_k ($k = 0$ to m), lay out them evenly in the arc L_k. The equation of L_k is $(x - s - k*d)^2 + (y - h/2)^2 = R^2$, where $t \leqslant y \leqslant h-2t$. If $k = 0$, draw each edge between Nd_f and Nd_i where $Nd_i \in L_k$. If $k \neq 0$, draw each edge between Nd_i and Nd_j, where $Nd_i \in L_{k-1}$ and $Nd_j \in L_k$.

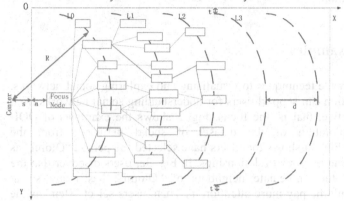

Fig. 1. The DOI-Wave Layout.

Since the display region is often like a rectangle, the focus node is moved to the middle on one side, and the other nodes are dynamically re-arranged on a serial of arcs. Each node lies on the arc according to its DOI value. Immediate neighbors of the focus, on the nearest arc, have the maximum DOI values, and their neighbors with the minor DOI values lie on the second nearest arc, and so on. The layout can be adaptive dynamically to the display space, that means, the radius R (see Fig. 1) of the arc varies with the height of the rectangle, and the distance d (see Fig. 1) between two adjacent arcs, varies with the width, as illustrated in Fig. 2.

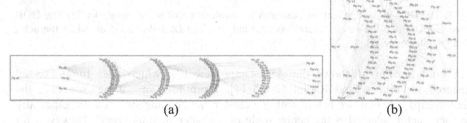

(a)   (b)

Fig. 2. The adaptive layout to the display space.

This layout differs from Radial Graph [4] in that users can understand the focus node's degree of connectivity and network distance from other nodes in a single direction, rather than explore nodes in every directions all 360 degrees, which can reduce cognition burdens. Besides, the adaptive visualization mechanism can achieve more effective display space utilization since the layout takes advantage of the rectangular space rather than the circular space used by Radial Graph. Indeed, although the layout of DOI-Wave is similar to TreePlus except that a radial layout rather than a vertical layout is used, it differs from TreePlus in that DOI-Wave pays more attention on the relationships between the focus node and the others. Besides, the adaptive visualization mechanism can avoid more interaction operations such as panning and zooming. As a result, DOI-Wave might obtain higher interaction efficiency than TreePlus especially in understanding the links and network distance according to user's attention.

4   Application Examples

We have applied DOI-Wave techniques to visualizing and exploring social networks. This interactive exploration can support users for understanding social networks from a single actor's perspective, that is, the focus. Fig. 3 shows the examples of DOI-Wave layout for exploration of the dataset of social networks from the RadialGraphView [17]. Fig. 3a shows that users have selected the person "Otomi" as the focus actor to examine his social relationships. In Fig. 3a, users discover that the person "Ben", one of the immediate neighbors of "Otomi", has many social relationships which should be pay more attention to. Then, users select "Ben" as the new focus actor for further exploration, as illustrated in Fig. 3b.

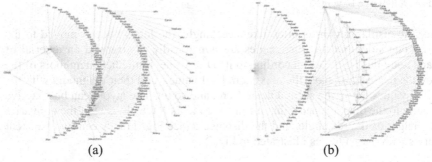

(a)   (b)

Fig. 3. The DOI-Wave application examples for exploration of social networks. (a) The DOI-Wave layout when the actor "Otomi" is selected. (b) The DOI-Wave layout when the actor "Ben" is selected in (a).

In contrast, Fig. 4 shows the ASK-Graphview [7], which uses force-directed clustered techniques, and Radial Graph [4]. From Fig. 4a we can see that, the relationships between two actors within a cluster can be understood easily, especially the focus actor selected is the center node of a cluster such as "Ben". However, for those who don't apparently belong to any clusters, such as "Otomi" in Fig. 4a, it's difficult to comprehend the relationships and network distance from other actors. From Fig. 4b we can see that, users always need to explore actors in every direction all around the rings, especially when examining the relationship between two actors who are far away from each other in network distance, such as "Otomi" who is at the center and "Sam" who is at the outer ring, as illustrated in Fig. 4b.

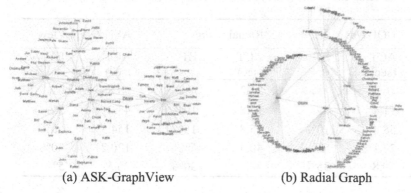

| (a) ASK-GraphView | (b) Radial Graph |

Fig. 4. The ASK-GraphView and Radial Graph for exploration of social networks.

5   Evaluation

To evaluate the usability of DOI-Wave, we compared DOI-Wave with ASK-GraphView and Radial Graph for certain tasks. We chose Radial Graph because DOI-Wave could be seemed as a special case of the general Radial Graph technique, and they both used the Focus+Context paradigm based on attention-reactive user interface. Since ASK-GraphView is one of the typical techniques using the clustered graph navigation paradigm, we also chose it for contrast.

We recruited 10 participants (5 males and 5 females) for this evaluation. They were mainly computer science students in our lab who were familiar with computers and understood graph definitions, but they had never used graph visualization tools such as ASK-GraphView and Radial Graph for exploration. To increase motivation, they received 3 dollars for their participation. Participants were first received a brief training on the three tools for about 30 minutes. Then, each participant was asked to use the three tools to carry out five tasks as follows. The first task was to follow a path of length 4, with the purpose of testing the basic navigation of reading and browsing. The second task was that, in the direct neighbors of a given actor, finding the one who has the maximum degree of connectivity. This task was targeted for observing the understanding of a node's degree of connectivity. The third task was to find the ones that were distance 1, 2, 3 away from the given actor. This task concerned one of most common tasks, identifying the links from a focus node. The forth task was to find the shortest path between a given pair actors, which focused on another common task, counting the network distance from one to another. The fifth task was to find the one who has the most direct relationships with others. This task concerned the structural clustered issues. The given actors were marked with red circles in the tasks above. The tasks were recorded for later analysis. Then there was a short interview lasting about 10 minutes, in which participates were asked about their experiences and the difficulties they had encountered.

Table 1. Average completion times (ACT) and error rates (ET) for tasks 1 through 5.

	DOI-Wave		Radial Graph		ASK-GraphView	
	ACT (sec)	ET	ACT (sec)	ET	ACT (sec)	ET
Task 1	16.6	0%	25.2	0%	38.8	0%
Task 2	11.4	8%	12.8	10%	43.2	5%
Task 3	58.4	10%	65.8	15%	154.5	60%
Task 4	27.1	5%	40.4	6%	120.2	30%
Task 5	59.8	35%	48.2	30%	26.5	5%

The results showed all participants completed the five tasks. The average completion times and error rates for the tasks are shown in Table 1. In the first task, the data showed DOI-Wave did better than the other two in the basic tasks such as browsing and reading. The participants thought the tree layout benefited the browsing process. There was no significant effect of completion times and error rates between DOI-Wave and Radial Graph in the second task, which meant they both favored the understanding of a node's degree of connectivity. At the same time, ASK-GraphView got the lowest error rates in this task because the compact cluster was more distinct in this layout than the other two. DOI-Wave worked best, with the lowest completion times and error rates, in the third task about the links finding and the forth task about the network distance counting. These two tasks were among the most important tasks in network visualization and navigation. As the participants said in the interview, they felt good because the Focus+Context paradigm in the layout could be reactive to their attention. Besides, they said it was easier to understand the focus node's links and network distance from other nodes in DOI-Wave than Radial Graph because they only navigated in a single direction rather than in every direction all 360 degrees. In the last task, ASK-GraphView performed best because it made the compact and clustered nodes clearer than the other two. We also found the error rates were high both in DOI-Wave and Radial Graph in this task, because participants were inclined to estimate the size of a cluster by the angle of the sector of the arc. To improve this problem, the adaptive visualization mechanism was used by the participants to perform the fifth task again, and then DOI-Wave got a lower error rate than Radial Graph, because the dense nodes and links became loose as the height and width were enlarging and the layout got clear.

As a result of the evaluation, DOI-Wave achieved overall higher efficiency than ASK-GraphView and Radial Graph, especially for understanding of the focus node's links and network distance from other nodes.

6   Conclusions and Future Work

This paper presented DOI-Wave, a Focus+Context interaction technique for networks, whose layout depends dynamically on the user's estimated degree-of-interest. DOI-

Wave uses the hierarchical clustered graph paradigm in which the view of a graph is dynamically determined by the selection of a single node as the focus node user pay most attention to. The layout algorithm could change the view of graph animatedly, as the selected focus node is changed, according to each node's DOI value computed by a DOI function. The Focus+Context paradigm in DOI-Wave, from user's perspective, makes it easier to understand the relationships between the focus node and the other nodes, and the hierarchical cluster paradigm and adaptive visualization mechanism lead to simultaneously clear and compact visualization. We have applied DOI-Wave to visualizing and exploring social networks and evaluation results validated its effectiveness.

As known to all, no graph layout is a definite solution for all network patterns. It will work for specific network patterns and it will not be applicable to other network patterns. DOI-Wave works well especially when the structure of the input graph is like a hierarchy, just as Radial Graph and ASK-GraphView do. Then, what is the definition of the good graphs that fit the DOI-Wave methodology will be our future work. Future work also includes user study to compare DOI-Wave with TreePlus, because the layout of DOI-Wave seems very similar to Treeplus except that the layouts of the nodes are radial rather than vertical. However, DOI-Wave differs from TreePlus in that: 1) DOI-Wave pays more attention on the understanding of the relationships between the focus node and the other nodes, and 2) DOI-Wave can adapt the layout dynamically to the display area. As for the scalability problems, since the dataset in the application examples and user study is relatively small and with low density, the improvement of the layout algorithm for very large graph is also in our plans.

Acknowledgments. This research is supported by the National High-Tech Research and Development Plan of China under Grant NO.2007AA04Z153, the National Grand Fundamental Research 973 Program of China under Grant No. 2007CB310900, 2006CB303105, and the National Natural Science Foundation of China under Grant No. U0735004, 60703078.

References

1. Battista G.D., Eades P., Tamassia R., Tollis I.G.: Graph Drawing Algorithms for the Visualization of Graphs. Prentice Hall, New Jersey (1999)
2. Herman I., Mellancon G., Marshall M.S.: Graph Visualization and Navigation in Information Visualization: a Survey. IEEE Transactions on Visualization and Computer Graphics. 6, 24--43 (2000)
3. Graphviz, http://www.research.att.com/tools/graphviz
4. Yee K.P., Fisher D., Dhamija R., Hearst M.S.: Animated exploration of dynamic graphs with radial layout. In: Proceedings of IEEE Symposium on Information(InfoVis'01), pp. 43--50. IEEE Computer Science Press, Los Alamitos (2001)
5. Eades P., Feng Q.W.: Multilevel Visualization of Clustered Graphs. In: Proceedings of the 4th International Symposium on Graph Drawing, pp. 101--112. Springer, Heidelberg (1996)
6. Eades P., Huang M.L.: Navigating Clustered Graphs using Force-Directed Methods. Journal of Graph Algorithms and Applications, 4, 157--181 (2000)

7. Abello J., Van H.F., Krishnan N.: ASK-GraphView: a large scale graph visualization system. IEEE Transactions on Visualization and Computer Graphics. 12, 669--676 (2006)

8. Hao M.C., Hsu M., Dayal U., Krug A.: Web-Based Visualization of Large Hierarchical Graphs Using Invisible Links in a Hyperbolic Space. In: Proceedings of Fifth Working Conference Visual Database Systems, pp. 83--94 (2000)

9. Lee B., Parr C.S., Plaisant C., Berderson B.B.: TreePlus: Interactive exploration of networks with enhanced tree layouts. IEEE Transactions on Visualization and Computer Graphics. 12, 1414--1426 (2006)

10. Furnas G.W.: A fisheye follow-up: further reflections on focus+context. In: Proceedings of the SIGCHI conference on Human Factors in computing systems, pp. 999--1008. ACM Press, New York (2006)

11. Sarkar M., Brown M.: Graphical fisheye views. Communications of the ACM. 37, 73--84 (1994)

12. Battista G.D., Eades P., Tamassia R., Tollis I.G.: Algorithms for Drawing Graphs: an Annotated Bibliography. Computational Geometry:Theory and Applications. 4, 235--282 (1994)

13. Jia Y., Hoberock J., Garland M., Hart J.: On the Visualization of Social and other Scale-Free Networks. IEEE Transactions on Visualization and Computer Graphics. 14, 1285--1292 (2008)

14. Cui W., Zhou H., Qu H., Wong P.C., Li X.: Geometry-based edge clustering for graph visualization. IEEE Transactions on Visualization and Computer Graphics, 14, 1277--1284 (2008)

15. Munzner T.: Drawing Large Graphs with H3Viewer and SiteManager. In: Proceedings of Graph Drawing. LNCS, vol. 1547, pp. 384--393. Springer, Heidelberg (1998)

16. Card S.K., Nation D.: Degree-of-Interest Trees: A Component of an Attention-Reactive User Interface. In: Proceedings of Advanced Visual Interfaces. (2002)

17. Radialgraphview, http://prefuse.org/gallery/radialgraphview

Multi-dimensional Data Visualization using Concentric Coordinates

Jiawan Zhang [1], Yuan Wen [1], Quang Vinh Nguyen [2] Liangfu Lu [3,1,*],

Maolin Huang [4], Jiadong Yang [1], Jizhou Sun [1]

1. School of Computer Science and Technology, Tianjin University , Tianjin ， P.R.China; 2. School of Computing & Mathematics, University of Western Sydney, Australia; 3. Mathematics Department, Tianjin University, Tianjin, P.R.China,300072; 4.Faculty of information Technology,University of Technology,Sydney,Australia
*Corresponding Author E-mail: liangfulv@gmail.com

Abstract. This paper proposes a new method called Concentric Coordinate for visualizing multidimensional datasets. To reduce the overlapping and edge crossings among curves, axes are arranged as concentric circles rather than parallel lines that are commonly used in the traditional approach. Edges which represent data items are drawn as segments of curves rather than poly-lines drawn in the classical parallel coordinate approach. Some heuristics are applied in our new method in order to improve the readability of views. The paper demonstrates the advantages of new method. In comparison with the parallel coordinate method, our concentric circle approach can reduce more than 15 % of the edge overlaps and crossings by visualizing the same dataset. In our new approach, we further enhance the readability of views by increasing the crossing angle. Finally, a visual interactive network scans detection system called CCScanViewer is developed based on our new visualization method to represent traffic activities in network flows, and the experiments show that the new approach is effective in detecting unusual patterns of network scans, port scans, the hidden scans, DDoS attacks etc.

Keywords: Concentric Coordinates, Multi-dimensional Data Visualization, Crossing Reduction, Security Visualization

1   Introduction

As we all know, visualizing multidimensional data is a challenging problem. Among the existing multidimensional visualization techniques, parallel coordinates [1] is one of the most popular methods, in which multiple dimensions are allocated one-to-one to an equal number of parallel axes and each data set is mapped as a poly-line intersecting the parallel axes at points which represent values of the individual data dimensions, see Fig 1(a). Unfortunately, as the volume of data increases, a large number of line crossings and overlaps would produce unreadable images that suffer from excessive visual clutter. Several improvements have been proposed to reduce the quantity of displayed elements. These methods either focus on the interactive

M.L. Huang et al. (eds.), *Visual Information Communication*,
DOI 10.1007/978-1-4419-0312-9_6, © Springer Science+Business Media, LLC 2010

techniques [12] or rely on the data preprocessing techniques such as clustering [13] and aggregation [16].

In this paper we solve the above problems by using a new visual coordinate: in which the axis are organized as concentric circles rather than parallel lines. The polylines are transformed into segments of curves to represent each dimensional space, see Fig 1(b). Our experiment shows that the new approach can reduce more than 15% of the line crossings in comparison with the traditional parallel coordinate scheme. At the same time, the new method can increase the crossing angles partially which can increase the readability of views. A visual interactive network scans detection system called CCScanViewer has been developed based on the new visualization to represent network traffic activities that were extracted from a large volume of network flows and their patterns. Experiments showed that the new approach is effective in the application of monitoring and detection of network intrusion. Using CCScanViewer we can easily detect the unusual patterns from network scans, port scans, the hidden scans, and DDoS attacks etc.

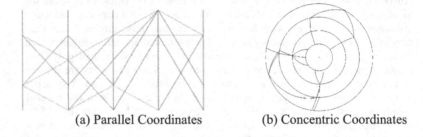

(a) Parallel Coordinates   (b) Concentric Coordinates

Fig. 1. Comparison of parallel coordinates and concentric coordinates.

The rest of the paper is organized as follows. In section 2 we give an overview of existing techniques for reducing the overlapping and crossings in parallel coordinates technique. Section 3 provides the general layout of concentric coordinates, and the new method is proposed theoretically to reduce the overlapping and crossings. Comparison between parallel coordinates and concentric coordinates is discussed in section 4. Case studies are presented in section 5. Finally, we give the conclusions and future work in section 6.

2   Related Work

Many techniques have been proposed to overcome the drawback of parallel coordinate visualization, such as the use of associated interaction method to focus on the interested data [22, 11]. Peng et al. suggested that reordering dimensions can reduce clutter and reveal relationships among the data in parallel coordinates [23]. Authors in [12, 17] introduce a structure-based brush to perform selection and navigation in hierarchically structured datasets. Ellis and Dix [20, 15] proposed a technique that reduces the display density through the use of sampling lens to produce focus+context view of particular regions. Adjusting the scope of visualization manually may get a better representation while the interaction is time-consuming and boring sometimes. For example, if the user wants to use "zoom-in" to focus on a particular subset of the poly-lines, N range values is that required to specify once for each dimension.

Therefore, it's more effective to reduce display elements automatically corresponding to the data characteristics. Johansson et al. use the K-means algorithm to cluster the data [18] and construct clusters of the original information [13]. In addition to clustering, Novotny and Hauser [16] divide the original data space into a set of bins to reveal outliers and trends. Artero et al. [21] reduces visual clusters by presenting frequency or density information in parallel coordinates visualizations. Kosara et al. [14] also combine frequency representation to display the category data instead of continuous variables. Our approach is different from all of the above techniques since it primarily concerns with the original data sets and rearranges the layout to reduce clutter and reveal the pattern among data.

There have been some efforts for improving the readability of views by changing classical layout to radial or concentric circles in graph visualization. Bachmaier extends Sugiyama's framework in radial drawings to visualizing hierarchical information [9]. Keim et al. build hierarchic radial layouts visualizing and analyze network activity of computer hosts on a network [24]; Vliegen et al. transform the classical treemap into a concentric drawing to visualize business data [25] and Brandes et al. map social network structure to geometric centrality [10]. Giacomo et al. analyze the advantages and disadvantages in radial drawings of graphs theoretically [19]. But all these approaches cannot visualize multidimensional datasets effectively. The work presented here focuses on the visualizations for multi-dimensional datasets. This makes the new method effective in some complicated network traffic detections such as scans, DDoS attacks etc.

3 n-Dimensional Graph Model and Layout

The layout of curves is described in this section. Before describing the layout, the relationship between dataset and its abstract graph model is defined. According to the transformation, the corresponding graph model can be extracted from the multi-dimensional dataset. In order to shorten the length of curves to avoid unnecessary windings, the layout of curves, which represents the data items, is optimized. With the decrease of length, the possibility of edge crossing is reduced, and this will also be discussed in this section.

3.1   Transformation between Dataset and Graph

We are dealing with an n-dimension discrete data set

$$D^n = \{d_i\} \ . \tag{1}$$

where

$$D^n \subset R^n \ .$$

(2)

$$d_i = (d_{i,1}, d_{i,2}, \ldots d_{i,n}) \ .$$

(3)

A n-dimensional graph $G = (V, E)$ that represents D^n can be defined as follows: The vertex set consists of n subsets, namely

$$V = V_1 \cup V_2 \cup \ldots \cup V_n \ .$$

(4)

There is an existing map between each dimension value in every data item and each vertex:

$$f_v : d_{i,j} \rightarrow v_{i,j} \in V_i$$

(5)

The edges set is partitioned into n-1 subsets

$$E = E_{1,2} \cup E_{2,3} \cup \ldots \cup E_{n-1,n}$$

(6)

where

$$E_{i,i+1} = \left\{ e_{u,v} \middle| u \in V_i, v \in V_{i+1} \right\}$$

(7)

For each item $d_i = (d_{i,1}, d_{i,2}, \ldots d_{i,n})$ in D^n, we can define a one-to-one map

$$f_e : d_i \rightarrow X = \left\{ (e_{v_1,v_2}, e_{v_2,v_3}, \ldots, e_{v_{n-1},v_n}) \middle| v_j = f_v(d_{i,j}) \right\}$$

(8)

Then we use

$$\gamma_{i,i+1} = \frac{|E_{i,i+1}|}{|V_i| \cdot |V_{i+1}|}$$

(9)

to describe how edges connected between two neighboring vertex subsets, which also reflects the data density between two dimensions.

After the original data set is transformed into an abstract graph, representation of the abstract graph is just the task of geometrical layout of the graph for display. Classical parallel coordinates arrange every vertex on a parallel axe. However, we locate a vertex $v_{i,j} \in V_i$ on the circle ρ_i with radius r_i, which represents the ith dimension. The location of the vertex depends on $\rho = r_i$ and the relative angle θ in polar coordinates, i.e. $v(\theta, \rho)$ $(0 \leq \theta < 2\pi)$. Under the mapping f_v and f_e, one data object corresponds to a series of spirals intersecting with the dimension circles, just as the poly-line crosses the axes set in classical parallel coordinates method.

3.2 Positioning of Circular Axes

Similar to the classical parallel coordinates, the position of axes in graph layout is quite essential for users to percept the date items and their values. Especially the order of these axes plays a significant role in the design of visualization. Therefore, it is very important to optimize the arrangement of dimension axes. Since it has been proved in [5] that it is a *NP* hard problem to find an optimal order of dimension axes in considering the similarity between dimensions, it is reasonable to import some additional factors to optimize the arrangement of dimension axes.

Because the length of dimension axes that appear in concentric circles differs with each other, the dimension with higher density should be put outside to reduce the overlap relatively. It can get a better view when the area between neighbor circles is identical with the data density.

3.3 The drawing of Curves

In the classical parallel coordinate visualization, the end vertices are placed on parallel coordinates in advance, and then the straight line is drawn between the end vertices. However, in our approach, there are some other factors needed to be considered in the drawing of curves, such as the winding direction, the curve shape and etc.

3.3.1 Winding Direction

Obviously, for the same connection between a pair of vertices, two different winding directions, clockwise or counter-clockwise, will produce different lengths and shapes of a given curve. Without loss of generality, we make rules that all the curves start from the inner circle and point outward. In such cases, clockwise means that the angle increases along the curves, and counter-clockwise inversely, see Fig 2. Clearly, in comparison with the curve shown in Fig 2(b), the curve shown in Fig 2(a) produces a shorter path and is more concise which should be adopted for the drawing.

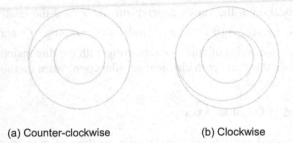

(a) Counter-clockwise   (b) Clockwise

Fig. 2. Winding Direction.

As discussed above, the winding direction is defined as below, which should make the angle span of the curve , $|\theta_a - \theta_b|$, less than $\pi/2$. In other words, the winding direction, $\delta : E \to \{-1,1\}$, shortens the length of the spiral as much as possible.

$$\delta(e) = \begin{cases} 1, & \text{if } \mathrm{sgn}(\Delta\theta) \cdot (|\Delta\theta| - \pi) \geq 0 \\ -1, & \text{if } \mathrm{sgn}(\Delta\theta) \cdot (|\Delta\theta| - \pi) < 0 \end{cases}. \tag{10}$$

where $\mathrm{sgn} : R \to \{1,-1\}$, $\Delta\theta = \theta_a - \theta_b$, $\rho_a < \rho_b$. It denotes clockwise when $\delta = 1$ and counter-clockwise when $\delta = -1$.

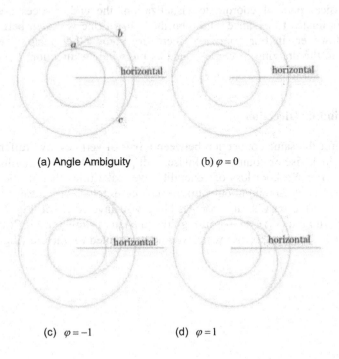

(a) Angle Ambiguity   (b) $\varphi = 0$

(c) $\varphi = -1$ (d) $\varphi = 1$

Fig. 3. Angle Ambiguity.

The periodicity of polar coordinates produces ambiguity when the curve crosses the horizontal line $\rho = 0$, see Fig 3(a). Both curves wind clockwise, but $\theta_a < \theta_b$ and $\theta_a > \theta_c$. Therefore, another variable called span, $\varphi : E \to \{-1,0,1\}$, is introduced to tag that character.

$$\varphi(e) = \begin{cases} 1, & if \quad \delta(e) = 1 \quad and \quad (\theta_a - \theta_b) > 0 \\ -1, & if \quad \delta(e) = -1 \quad and \quad (\theta_a - \theta_b) < 0 \\ 0, & otherwise \end{cases} \quad (11)$$

3.3.2   Curve drawing

Bezier curve is the common way to connect two points in the plane smoothly, and we use it to draw curves. In the polar coordinates, the curve is

$$\begin{cases} \theta(t) = \theta_a + (1-t)\theta_b \\ \rho(t) = \rho_a + (1-t)\rho_b \end{cases} , (0 < t < 1) \quad . \quad (12)$$

where $\rho_a < \rho_b$. The point $p(\theta, \rho)$ on the curve generated by (12) should satisfy the constraint $\theta_a < \theta_p < \theta_b$ and $\rho_a < \rho_p < \rho_b$. Considering the angle ambiguity, we modify (12) incorporated with (11):

$$\begin{cases} \theta(t) = \theta_a + (1-t)(\theta_b + 2\pi \cdot \varphi(e)) \\ \rho(t) = \rho_a + (1-t)\rho_b \end{cases} , (0 < t < 1) \quad . \quad (13)$$

3.3.3   Reduction of Edge Crossings

In section 3, we have extracted a graph model $G = (V, E)$ from the dataset $D'' = \{d_i\}$. In the graph G, the distribution of vertices, which represents the numerical values of dataset, affects the readability of the view heavily. For continuous data, the vertex can just fall on the circle increasingly or decreasingly. However, when disposing discrete data sets with weak monotonicity or the categorical data [14], the layout can be made more readable if breaking the monotonicity.

The edge crossing condition which is slightly different from the parallel coordinate approach will be discussed first in this section. The new definition sets up the bridge to apply heuristics in horizontal edge crossing reduction to our concentric fashion. On the other hand, we have found that the concentric circle approach can reduce up to

33% of edge crossings for the complete bipartite graph $K_{n,n}$ when n is large enough. The detail of the proof is shown below:

Theorem. Visualizing $K_{n,n}$ in two layers, concentric circle fashion can reduce up to 33% of the total edge crossings in comparison with the parallel coordinate layout when n is large enough.

Proof. In the parallel coordinate layout, for edge $e_{u,v}$, each edge $e_{i,j}$ with the end vertices $i \prec u$ and $j \succ v$ crosses $e_{u,v}$. The edge $e_{i,j}$ with $i \succ u$ and $j \prec v$ also crosses $e_{u,v}$, See Fig.4, that means that the total number of edge crossings for each edge $e_{u,v}$ is:

$$pEdgeCr(e_{u,v}) = \sum_{i=1}^{u} i \sum_{j=v+1}^{n} j + \sum_{j=1}^{v} j \sum_{j=u+1}^{n} i \tag{1}$$

Therefore, the total number of edge crossings in graph $K_{n,n}$ with parallel coordinate approach is:

$$pCr(K_{n,n}) = \frac{1}{2}\sum_{u=1}^{n}\sum_{v=1}^{n} pEdgeCr(e_{u,v}) = \frac{1}{4}n^4 - \frac{1}{2}n^3 + \frac{1}{4}n^2 \tag{2}$$

In section 3.3 we have defined rules to avoid angle span of curves those larger than $\pi/2$. If we unwind the circle along the *original line*, edges $e_{u,v}$ with $u - v > n/2$ will intersect *original line*, as showed in Fig. 5. Without losing generality, we assume that vertices are placed on axes or circles uniformly. Assuming that $u \prec v$ and $v - u = s$, the edge crossings for edge $e_{u,v}$ include four parts is described below:

If $i \prec u$ and $j \succ v$, then there will be $n/2 - (u - i)$ edges from vertex i crossing with $e_{u,v}$, see Fig.6 (a). The total number of edge crossings on this condition is:

$$\sum_{v-\frac{n}{2}<i<u} [n/2 - (u - i)] \tag{3}$$

If $i \succ u$, $j \prec v$ and $i \prec j$, there will be $n/2$ edges from vertex i crossing with $e_{u,v}$. The total number of edge crossings on this condition is $s \cdot n/2$, see Fig.6 (b).

If $i \succ u$, $j \prec v$, $i \succ j$ and $i \prec v$,there will be $v - i$ edges from vertex i crossing with $e_{u,v}$, see Fig.6(c). The total number of edge crossings on this condition is:

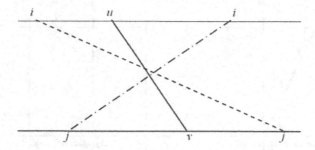

Fig. 4. Edge crossings in parallel layout.

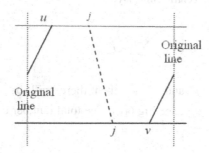

Fig. 5. Unwind the concentric circular layout.

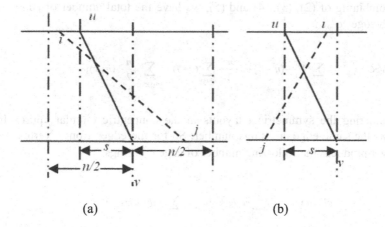

(a)   (b)

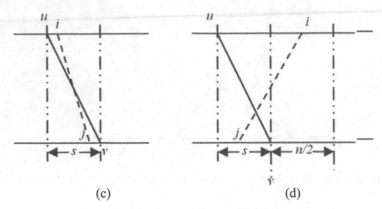

$$(c) \qquad\qquad\qquad (d)$$

Fig. 6. Edge crossings in concentric circle layout.

$$\sum_{u<i<v} v-i \tag{4}$$

If $i \succ u$, $j \prec v$, $i \succ j$ and $i \succ v$, then there will be $n/2-(i-v)$ edges from vertex i crossing with $e_{u,v}$, see Fig 6(d). The total number of edge crossings on this condition is:

$$\sum_{v<i<v+\frac{n}{2}} [n/2-(i-v)] \tag{5}$$

In combining of (2), (3), (4) and (5), we have the total number of edge crossings for each edge $e_{u,v}$ is

$$cEdgeCr(e_{u,v}) = \sum_{v-\frac{n}{2}<i<u} [\frac{n}{2}-(u-i)] + s \cdot \frac{n}{2} + \sum_{u<i<v} (v-i) + \sum_{v<i<v+\frac{n}{2}} [\frac{n}{2}-(i-v)] \tag{6}$$

Considering the symmetrical layouts in the concentric circular approach, every edge has the same edge crossings number. So for the edges from a vertex u in the first layer produces the following number of edge crossings:

$$cVertexCr(u) = \sum_{s=0}^{\frac{n}{2}} cEdgeCr(e_{u,v}) + \sum_{s=1}^{\frac{n}{2}} cEdgeCr(e_{u,v}) \tag{7}$$

Thus the total number of edge crossing in graph $K_{n,n}$ under the concentric circle scheme is

$$cCr(K_{n,n}) = \frac{1}{2}n \cdot cVertexCr(u) = \frac{1}{6}n^4 + \frac{3}{8}n^3 + \frac{1}{12}n^2 \qquad (8)$$

In combining of (2) and (8), we got the formula (9). It is obviously that when n becomes large enough, the concentric circle scheme can reduce up to 33% of the edge crossings in a complete bipartite graph $K_{n,n}$.

$$\lim_{n \to \infty} \frac{cCr(K_{n,n})}{pCr(K_{n,n})} = \lim_{n \to \infty} \frac{\frac{1}{6}n^4 + \frac{3}{8}n^3 + \frac{1}{12}n^2}{\frac{1}{4}n^4 - \frac{1}{2}n^3 + \frac{1}{4}n^2} = \frac{2}{3} \qquad (9)$$

Definition of Edge Crossing. In parallel coordinates, an edge crossing occurs between two poly-lines depends purely on the positions of their end vertices. In concentric coordinates, however, the edge crossings could be affected by some other factors, such as the direction of curve winding and the crossings with horizontal line as discussed in section 3.3.

If $\varphi(e_1) \neq 0$ or $\varphi(e_2) \neq 0$, it implies that there is a gap of 2π or -2π between the reality and the literal meanings of end vertices angles, see Fig 7. Relative to the other three vertexes, the angle of b_2 should be in $(2\pi, 4\pi)$, so $\theta(b_2)' = \theta(b_2) + 2\pi$. It can be decided whether two curves cross only by angles of their end vertices after such transformation.

$$Cross(e_1, e_2) = sgn\left(\theta(a_1)' - \theta(a_2)'\right) \wedge sgn\left(\theta(b_1)' - \theta(b_2)'\right) \qquad (10)$$

where $sgn : R \to \{1, -1\}$. It denotes there exists a crossing when $Cross(e_1, e_2) = 1$.

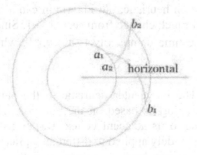

Fig. 7. Crossing Definition.

View Adjustment. After position the dimension axes and the drawing of curves, the improvement of readability of views becomes the task of optimizing the distribution of vertexes with the target of reduction of edge crossings. Instead of working globally, we attempted to minimize the edge crossings layer-by-layer. We initialize the vertexes ordering in the inner most circle first according to the monotonicity, and then gradually sweep to outer circles.

It has been proved that finding of the vertexes ordering which minimize the edge crossings between two layers of the graph in parallel coordinate is NP-hard even if the ordering of vertices in one layer of the graph is fixed [2], and Bachmaier points out that the same problem in radial layouts is also NP-hard [9]. As a consequence, it has been advised to find some heuristics to reach an efficient solution. Many methods have been developed to resolve the problem in the parallel layout [2]. Since the edge crossing definition has been expressed, we can derive from the heuristics in the parallel layout to solve the same problem in our concentric circle layout apparently.

Greedy Switch Heuristic. In parallel layout, the greedy switch heuristic [2] works in a similar way as bubble-sort [cite]. Suppose that u and v are two consecutive vertices on the same layer, u is prior to v $(u \prec v)$. Then, swapping their positions changes the total number of crossings by $C_{vu} - C_{uv}$, where C_{uv} denotes the number of the crossings between edges from u and edges from v. The algorithm scans all consecutive pairs and swaps them if this reduces the number of crossings. This process is repeated until no further swap is required.

Section 3.1 shows that the use of greedy heuristic swap can reduce crossings in the concentric layout if two curves crosses are dependent on their vertices' angles. Obviously, the algorithm has the same running time as the horizontal version, $O(|\rho|^2)$.

Sifting Heuristic. Sifting was originally introduced as a heuristic for vertex minimization of ordered binary decision diagrams [3], and it was later adapted for the (parallel) crossing minimization problem [4]. The algorithm determines optimal position of each vertex that positions of the other vertices are fixed.

As same as greedy switch heuristic, our algorithm can also be implemented in the concentric layout without much change from section 3.1. Since every vertex has to be set on every position, the time complexity is as $O(|\rho|^2)$, which remains the same as parallel layout.

Barycenter Heuristic. The barycenter heuristic in the parallel crossing reduction, which is also called averaging, is based on the intuition. There are fewer crossings when each vertex is close to its adjacent vertex. Because the method is simple and produces good result, it is widely applied to different applications.

In concentric layout, we can locate a vertex u on the outer circle whose angle equals to the average one of its adjacency on the inner circle.

$$\theta(u) = \frac{\sum\limits_{e_{(u,v)} \in E_{(\rho_1,\rho_2)}} \theta(v)}{\deg(u)} + \Delta \tag{15}$$

Where $\deg(u) = \left|\left\{(u,v)\,\middle|\,(u,v) \in E_{(\rho_1,\rho_2)}\right\}\right|$ and Δ is just a very small random number to prevent overlapping when two nodes have the same average values. The layout ensures that vertices with same or similar adjacent vertices will be placed near each other. The pattern can uncover some relationship in the initial data set, see Fig 8.

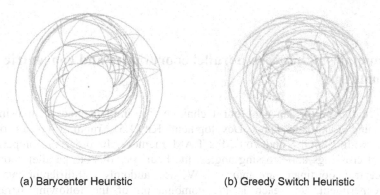

(a) Barycenter Heuristic   (b) Greedy Switch Heuristic

Fig. 8. Comparison of the barycenter and greedy switch heuristic.

Median Heuristic. Similar to the barycenter heuristic, median heuristic places vertices close to their adjacent vertices. However, median heuristic replaces the median with the average. Median heuristic generally distributes vertices in a denser way compared to barycenter heuristic because it is more likely to have the same median than average for two data groups, see Fig. 9.

The running time for computing the average or the median is proportional to the degree of u. Therefore the barycenter heuristic and median heuristic can be calculated in linear time.

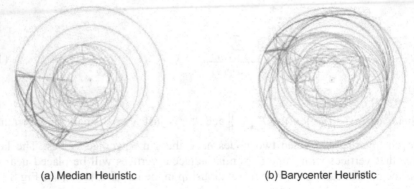

(a) Median Heuristic   (b) Barycenter Heuristic

Fig. 9. An example of the distributions in a) Median Heuristic and b) Barycenter Heuristic.

4   Comparison between parallel coordinates and concentric circle coordinates

To analyze the performance of our technique, we implemented them using Java Programming Language (Java Development Kit 1.5), running on an ordinary computer with 1.84Ghz and 768 Mbs RAM memory. In order to comparing the number of crossings and crossing angles, the heuristics of both parallel coordinates and concentric coordinates are analyzed. We use randomly 160 different data groups in our experiment, and each is the combination of the following parameters: $\gamma_{i,i+1} = \{0.2, 0.4, 0.6, 0.8\}$ and $|E_{i,i+1}| = \{10, 20, 30, 40\}$,   where i=1, 2, 3, 4.

4.1   Crossing Number

Under the same condition, the concentric layout can reduce the number of crossings obviously in comparison with the parallel layout. When the dimension or the density of data is low, the number of crossing can be reduced by 25 percent. The increase of the dimension or density also makes efficiency decline as well. It remains more than 15 percent, see Fig 11. Based on the discussion in section 3.3, concentric layout shortens the length of some edges, thus it avoids crossings better, see Fig 10. The experiment also shows that complete bipartite graph $K_{n,n}$, concentric layout can reduce crossings number 33% when n is large enough.

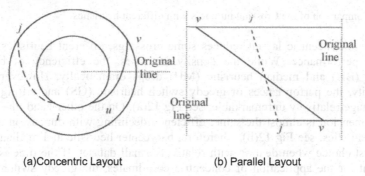

(a)Concentric Layout   (b) Parallel Layout

Fig. 10. An example shows that the concentric layout helps to shorten edges and reduce edge crossings.

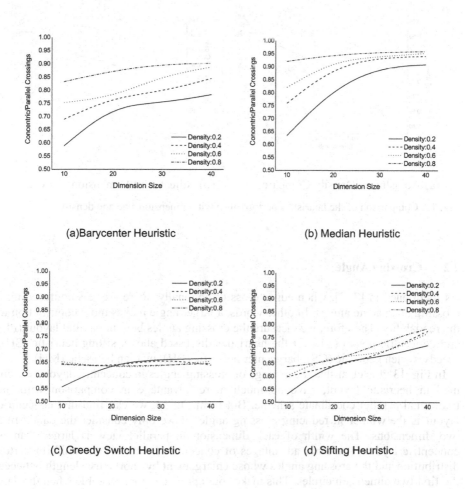

(a)Barycenter Heuristic   (b) Median Heuristic

(c) Greedy Switch Heuristic   (d) Sifting Heuristic

Fig. 11. Comparison of the Crossing numbers with different heuristics.

Although concentric layout reduces some crossings, different heuristics can give different performance. While the density increases, the efficiency of barycenter heuristic (BH) and median heuristic (MH) drops dramatically. However, at high complexity, the performances of greedy switch heuristic (GS) and sifting heuristic (SH) change relatively unremarkable; see Fig 12(a). On the other hand, the influence of the dimension is almost the same: efficiency declining with dimension increasing for all heuristics, see Fig 12(b). Therefore, barycenter heuristic and median heuristic is the first choice when dealing with relatively small dataset. If the time is not very important for the application of concentric coordinates, the greedy switch heuristic and sifting heuristic can provide more readable layout.

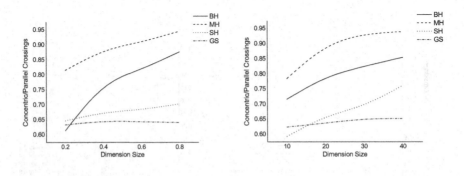

(a) Adjustment/Density Compare   (b) Adjustment/Dimension Compare

Fig. 12. Comparison of the heuristics performance with dimension size and density.

4.2 Crossing Angle

As mentioned in [7, 8], when edges cross orthogonally, there are less confused than crossing at an acute angles. In other words, a larger angle makes more contribution to the readability. Therefore, we measure the crossing angles both in parallel layout (PL) and concentric layout (CL) for the heuristics discussed above: sifting heuristic (SH), greedy switch heuristic (GS), barycenter heuristic (BH), median heuristic (MH).

In Fig. 13, it is clear that the average of crossing angles in concentric layout, except median heuristic layout, have no much more advantage in comparison with the traditional parallel coordinate scheme. But from Fig 14, we can find that concentric layout is the winner in reducing crossing angles if we only consider the data's first two dimensions. The width of each dimension in parallel view is larger than in concentric layout. The main advantages of concentric layout are the uniform vertex distribution and the crossing angles whose enlargement by short curve length between the first two dimension circles. This makes our approach more readable when the data contributes are closer to the center of the circles. Therefore, the above facts add a useful guideline in dimension arrangement: the important and complicated contribution of the data should be put in the center of the circles. This can help user realize and analyze the data effectively.

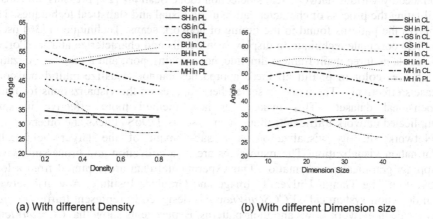

(a) With different Density   (b) With different Dimension size

Fig. 13. Crossing Angles in all dimensions.

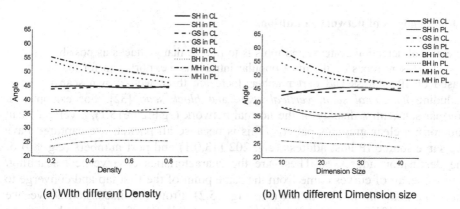

(a) WIth different Density   (b) With different Dimension size

Fig. 14. Crossing Angles between 1st and 2nd Dimensions.

5   Case studies

Scanning a network is a very common step in network intrusion. In order to gain information about a potential network intrusion, it is beneficial to analyze these network scans. The process of scanning a network is usually used to determine what is on the network. Now a day, networks and systems are becoming increasingly more and more complex. However, there is no absolute way to secure a network or system completely or indefinitely. The current techniques or tools of securing a network or system still heavily rely on human detection.

Researches of network scans have been popular for the last decade. Many research works in visualization have been introduced to work with large numbers of alerts produced by various network scans detection tools. ScanVis [29] presents a means of facilitating the process of characterization using visual and statistical techniques. This analyzes the patterns found in the timing of network scans. Technique in [30] uses a parallel-coordinate technique to display scan details and characterize attacks. PortVis [31] contains three main frames: timeline, hour (main), port, and a main visualization which uses color map. But all these approaches cannot visualize multidimensional datasets effectively. The work presented here focuses on the visualizations for multi-dimensional datasets. This makes our new method more effective in some complicated network traffic detections such as scans, DDoS attacks and others.

Network security visualization is a sub-domain of the larger field called information visualization. The main steps are data collection and processing, visual mapping, graphical representation. Our experimental data are captured from a local network at The Tianjin University Image and Graphics Institute. A visual network scan detection system called *CCScanViewer* is designed to represent traffic activities that reside in network flows and their patterns. Experiments show that *CCScanViewer* can easily detect the ports scans in the local area networks, and it is more readable than the parallel coordinates technique.

5.1   Analysis of network conditions

The aim of detection systems and tools is to find as many attacks as possible. At this first step, users focus on the most popular intrusions, i.e. port scan for the detection. Based on IP address and port number, there are three well-known scan methods, including *horizontal scan*, *vertical scan*, and *block scan* [32]. For example, in comparison with a display of the normal network (eg.Figure15.1), a vertical scan can form a clear graphics pattern. This is because all packets we captured have the same source IP host address (e.g. 202.113.0.1) and port numbers (e.g. 80) of the destination addresses. These are the characteristics of a vertical scanning. Therefore, all of curves come from the same point of the first lap and converge to the same point in the fourth lap (see Fig. 15.2). From the discussion above, we can see that sifting heuristic can make numerical points uniformly distribution. As a consequence, the curves cover evenly the two circles which represent the source IP of the host and the destination IP address. Figure15.3 displays the logic characteristics of scanning.

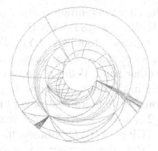

Fig. 15.1. The normal network state in CCScanViewer

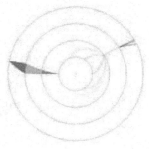

Fig. 15.2. Pattern of vertical scans in CCScanViewer

Fig. 15.3. Pattern of the logic characteristics of scanning in CCScanViewer

5.2   Detection of different scanning types

The aim of scanning a host or cluster is to obtain the status of a network. There are different ways to achieve it. For example, the abnormal flag of TCP packet in the TCP-IP protocol can cause the abnormal network. In order to establish a normal connection of two hosts, the majority of the flags in three-way handshakes should be

ACK (Acknowledgement) to ensure communications of two-side synchronization. This is shown in Figure 16.1. When a RST-SYN (Reset-Synchronize) attack occurs, the flags of SYN and RST increase obviously. SYN data segments are sent to the destination hosts in the process of scans. If the responses are the RST, it shows that the ports are closed. On the other hand, if the responses contain the SYN and ACK, this means the target ports are in the state of monitoring, and the connection has not yet been established. Therefore, this pattern is stronger hidden compared to the three-way handshakes. Figure 16.2 shows the RST-SYN scan. Figure 16.3 displays the statistics of TCP flags in the TCP packets. Obviously, the flags of FIN have a marked increasing in Figure 16.3. But the number in normal state should be rare. Consequently, we can easily see that there occurs a hidden FIN scan. This experiments show that the new approach can also find the patterns easily and effectively.

Fig. 16.1. Pattern of TCP flags of normal network traffic in CCScanViewer

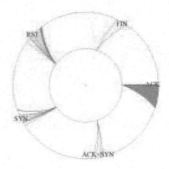

Fig. 16.2. Pattern of RST-SYN scans in CCScanViewer

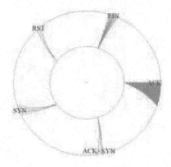

Fig. 16.3. Pattern of FIN scans in CCScanViewer

5.3   Comparison between parallel coordinates and concentric coordinates in DDoS attacks

In this section, we describe examples using CCScanViewer and parallel coordinates for displaying and analyzing DDoS attack. The characteristic of the DDoS attack is that within a short time, the attacked hosts can receive a lot of connected information and packets from a large number of strange IP addresses. Such as Smurf attack, whose console is communicated with large number of IP addresses in a short time and most IP addresses don't appear previously.

DDoS attack is detected very easily by the CCScanViewer. Comparing the Figure 17.1 and the Figure 17.2, we can find that concentric layout can obviously reduce the number of crossings and save space for the network traffic. According to section 3, concentric layout can be more useful and readable for large scale data packets. Therefore, in the case of an attack that has many of strange IP addresses connecting some host in short time, this system can detect effectively, and it can provide accurate pattern.

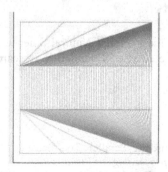

Fig. 17.1. Pattern of DDoS attacks in parallel coordinates.

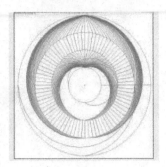

Fig. 17.2. Pattern of DDoS attacks in CCScanViewer

6   Conclusion and future work

This paper has proposed a new method, called Concentric Coordinates, to visualize multi-dimensional datasets. Our technique reduces the number of overlapping and crossings significantly. Some heuristics are applied in order to improve the readability of the views. Comparing to parallel layout, our concentric technique can reduce the number of crossings by more than 15 percent in some situations. The increase of crossing angles in our approach also makes the visualization more readable. A visual interactive network scans detection system called CCScanViewer has been implemented to represent traffic activities. The experiments show that the new approach is effective in finding the patterns of network scans, port scans, the hidden scans, DDoS attacks and others. We are planning to introduce more interaction techniques, such as linking and brushing techniques, it will potentially increase the usability of CCScanViewer.

7   Acknowledgments

This work is supported by the National Natural Science Foundation of China under Grant No.60673196 and the Applied Foundation Research Project of Tianjin under Grant No.07F2030.

References

1. A. Inselberg and B. Dimsdale. Parallel Coordinates: A Tool for Visualizing Multi-Dimensional Geometry. In *proceedings of Visualization '90,* pages 361–370, 1990.
2. M. Kaufmann and D. Wagner. Drawing Graphs, Springer, 2001.
3. R. Rudell. Dynamic Variable Ordering for Ordered Binary Decision Diagrams. In Proceedings of the 1993 IEEE/ACM International Conference on Computer-aided Design (ICCAD '93), pages 42–47.

4. C. Matuszewski, R. Schönfeld, and P. Molitor. Using Sifting for k-Layer Straightline Crossing Minimization. In Proceedings of 7th Graph Drawing Conference (GD '99), pages 217–224.

5. Daniel A. Keim. Designing Pixel-Oriented Visualization Techniques: Theory and Applications. IEEE Transaction on Visualization and Computer Graphics, 6(1):59–78, 2000.

6. E.R. Tufte. The Visual Display of Quantitative Information. Graphics Press, 1983.

7. Colin Ware, Helen Purchase, Linda Colpoys and Matthew McGill. Cognitive Measurements of Graph Aesthetics. Information Visualization, 1(2): 103–110, 2002.

8. Huang, W. and Eades, P. How people read graphs. In   Proceedings Asia Pacific Symposium on Information Visualization (APVIS 2005), 47–53.

9. Christian Bachmaier. A Radial Adaptation of the Sugiyama Framework for Visualizing Hierarchical Information. IEEE Transaction on Visualization and Computer Graphic, 13(3):583–594, 2007.

10. U. Brandes, P. Kenis, and D. Wagner. Communicating Centrality in Policy Network Drawings. IEEE Transaction on Visualization and Computer Graphics, 9(2):241–253, 2003.

11. Harri Siirtolam and Kari-Jouko Raiha. Interacting with parallel coordinates. Interacting with Computers, 18(6):1278–1309, 2006.

12. Y.-H. Fua, M. O. Ward, and E. A. Rundensteiner. Hierarchical parallel coordinates for exploration of large datasets. In Proc of IEEE Visualization, pages 43–50, 1999.

13. Jimmy Johansson, Patric Ljung,   Mikael Jern and Matthew Cooper. Revealing Structure within Clustered Parallel Coordinates Displays. In Proceedings of the 2005 IEEE Symposium on Information Visualization (INFOVIS'05), pages 125–132.

14. Robert Kosara, Fabian Bendix, and Helwig Hauser. Parallel Sets: Interactive Exploration and Visual Analysis of Categorical Data. IEEE Transaction on Visualization and Computer Graphics, 12(4):558–568, 2006.

15. Geoffrey Ellis and Alan Dix. Enabling Automatic Clutter Reduction in Parallel Coordinates Plots. IEEE Transaction on Visualization and Computer Graphics, 12(5):717–723, 2006.

16. Matej Novotny and Helwig Hauser. Outlier-preserving Focus+Context Visualization in Parallel Coordinates. IEEE Transaction on Visualization and Computer Graphics, 12(5):893-900, 2006.

17. Ying-Huey Fua, Matthew O. Ward and Elke A. Rundensteiner. Navigating Hierarchies with Structure-Based Brushes. In Proceedings of the 1999 IEEE Symposium on Information Visualization (INFOVIS'99), pages 58–64.

18. Jimmy Johansson, Matthew Cooper and Mikael Jern. 3-Dimensional Display for Clustered Multi-Relational Parallel Coordinates. In Proceedings of the Ninth International Conference on Information Visualisation (IV'05), pages 188–193.

19. Emilio Di Giacomo, Walter Didimo, Giuseppe Liotta. Radial Drawings of Graphs: Geometric Constraints and Trade-off. In Proceedings of 7th Graph Drawing Conference (GD'06), pages 355–366.

20. G.P. Ellis and A. Dix. Density control through random sampling : an architectural perspective. In Proceedings of International Conference on Information Visualization (IV'02), pages 82-90.

21. Almir Oivertte Artero, Maria Cristina Ferreira de Oliveria and Haim Levkowitz. Uncovering Clusters in Crowded Parallel Coordinates Visualizations. In Proceedings of the 2004 IEEE Symposium on Information Visualization (INFOVIS'04), pages 81–88.

22. Daniel A. Keim. Information Visualization and Visual Data Mining. IEEE Transaction on Visualization and Computer Graphics, 8(1):1–8, 2002.

23. Wei Peng, Matthew O. Ward, and Elke A. Rundensteiner. Clutter Reduction in Multi-Dimensional Data Visualization Using Dimension Reordering. In Proceedings of the IEEE Symposium on Information Visualization 2004 (INFOVIS'04), pages 89–96.

24. Keim, D.A.; Mansmann, F.; Schneidewind, J.; Schreck, T., Monitoring Network Traffic with Radial Traffic Analyzer Visual Analytics And Technology. In proceedings IEEE

Symposium on Visual Analytics Science and Technology 2006 (VAST 2006),   pages:123–128

25. Roel Vliegen, Jarke J.van Wijk and Erik-Jan van der Linden. Visualizing Business Data with Generalized Treemaps, IEEE Transaction on. Visualization and Computer Graphics, 12(5):789-796, 2006.
26. Wegenkittl R, Löffelmann H, Gröller E. Visualizing the behaviour of higher dimensional dynamical systems. IEEE Visualization 1997 (Phoenix, USA, 1997), ACM Press: New York; 119125
27. Tominski C, Abello J, Schumann H. Axes-based visualizations with radial layouts. ACM Symposium on Applied Computing 2004   (Nicosia, Cyprus, 2004), ACM Press: New York; 12421247.
28. Forsell C, Johansson J. Task-based evaluation of multi-relational 3D and standard 2D parallel coordinates. IS&T/SPIE's International Symposium on Electronic Imaging, Conference on Visualization and Data Analysis 2007 (San Jose, USA, 2007), SPIE: Bellingham and IS&T:Springfield; 64950C-112.
29. C.Muelder, , Ma, K.L., Bartoletti, T.: A visualization methodology for characterization of network scans. Visualization for Computer Security, IEEE Workshops, pp. 4–4 (2005)
30. G.Conti,Abdullah, K.: "Passive visual fingerprinting of network attack tools". VizSEC/DMSEC '04: Proceedings of the 2004 ACM Workshop on Visualization and Data Mining for Computer Security, 2004,pp. 45–54
31. J.McPherson, ,Ma, K.L., Krystosk, P., Bartoletti, T., Christensen,M.: Portvis: "A tool for port-based detection of security events". In: ACM VizSEC 2004 Workshop, 2004,pp.73–81
32. Pin Ren, Yan Gao and Zhichun Li, "IDGraphs: Intrusion Detection and Analysis Using Histographs", Visualization for Computer Security, 2005, pp.39-46

Construct Connotation Dictionary of Visual Symbols

Ping Xiao, Ernesto Arroyo, Josep Blat

Dept. Tecnologies de la Infornació i les Comunicacions, Universitat Pompeu Fabra, Roc Boronat. 138,
08018 Barcelona, Spain
{ping.xiao, josep.blat, ernesto.arroyo}@upf.edu

Abstract. We present the first version of an electronic dictionary (http://vis.upf.edu/CDVS/dic2.aspx) where designers can find pictures to represent abstract concepts. It aims at the expressiveness and variety of visual expressions for abstract concepts. This dictionary is driven by an automatic knowledge extraction method, which elicits pairs of abstract concept and picture from corpus. The extracted visual symbols look promising. A preliminary experiment was accomplished to test the quality and quantity of these visual symbols. We offer analysis of the experiment results and proposals to improve the knowledge extraction method.

Keywords: visual symbol, abstract concept, connotation, design, knowledge extraction, corpus, clustering, data mining, survey, user experiment, work efficiency

1 Introduction

The connotation of pictorial elements plays an active role in communication. The intentional use of connotations in design could be as ancient as leaving a lip print on a love letter, or as recent as juxtaposing a land rover with a hippo in an advertising image. In the love letter case, lip print means 'kiss' which is associated with 'love. In the advertisement for land rover, hippo is used as a symbol of 'being physically tough'. In terms of semiotics, pictorial elements are visual symbols. What picture actually depicts is called denotation. Besides, picture may associate with other concepts, as in the aforementioned two instances, which are called connotation.

'Love' and 'tough' are abstract concepts or quality. To express something abstract with something that can be seen, i.e. the visual, is a common task for designers, including graphic designers, product designers, architects, etc. It might be practiced by every layman to use lip print to say love. However, using hippo as a symbol of 'being physically tough' may not come into many people's mind at the first moment. Design, as a creative act, always asks for freshness. Very often, different visual symbols are pursued to express the same meaning in difference occasions. As a consequence, it is necessary for designers to have a huge repository of visual symbols in their mind. However, this requirement to designers faces two challenges. First, the capacity of this repository depends on the knowledge and experience of the

M.L. Huang et al. (eds.), *Visual Information Communication*,
DOI 10.1007/978-1-4419-0312-9_7, © Springer Science+Business Media, LLC 2010

individual. Second, it is not sure designers can quickly seek out enough candidate visual symbols on the spot.

Seeing the above two challenges, we think it would be helpful to construct an electronic dictionary which provides pictures expressing abstract concepts. We call it Connotation Dictionary of Visual Symbols (CDVS). The first version of CDVS is online at http://vis.upf.edu/CDVS/dic2.aspx. With this dictionary, designers will be provided a list of visual symbols to choose after inputting a concept, instead of spending time digging into the bottom of their brains or browsing through piles of photo books to look for a novel expression. An example of visual symbols offered by CDVS is shown in Fig. 1. For the concept 'peace', CDVS gives 18 visual symbols, which are presented in the descending order of association strength (from left to right and from top to bottom). Under each picture, there are two words which indicate the content of picture. Because of the limitation of figure size, these words are not illegible. We list them in Table 1 for better viewing.

Besides, we created an automatic real-time knowledge extraction process to supply entries to this dictionary. An automatic process can handle, in a very short time, a vast amount of information, to which the knowledge and experience owned by any individual cannot compare. Also, it allows the dictionary content to be dynamic. Being dynamic means different visual symbols can be provided according to specific cultures and time, which is impossible for most individuals.

CDVS is aimed to help designers at the early stage of design. It shows the variety of visual symbols, i.e. how abstract concepts can be represented by different objects or scenes. CDVS does not offer the exact picture to use. To choose a visual symbol means to decide the subject of pictures. Designers may proceed to search in image resources available to them for a specific picture of this subject, taking into account factors like colour, perspective, composition, etc.

In the rest part of this paper, we first outline the strategy to capture visual symbols of connotation. Secondly, we review the relevant literature. Thirdly, we explain the details of the automatic knowledge elicitation process to harvest pairs of connotations and pictures. Fourthly, we present the experiment which tests the quality and quantity of visual symbols found by our method. We also provide analysis of the experiment result and proposals for future work.

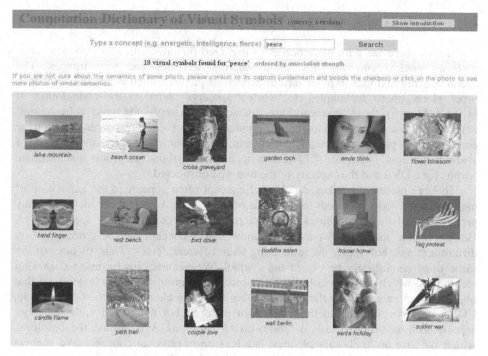

Fig. 1. Visual symbols of 'peace' provided by CDVS.

Table 1. The names of objects or scenes in the pictures which stand for 'peace'.

peace	Picture Content
	lake mountain
	beach ocean
	cross graveyard
	garden rock
	smile think
	flower blossom
	hand finger
	rest bench
	bird dove
	buddha asian
	house home
	flag protest
	candle flame
	path trial
	couple love
	wall berlin
	santa holiday
	soldier wall

2   Strategy of Capturing Visual Symbols of Abstract Concepts

Nowadays, there are a lot of resources of digitized pictures with accompanying text, such as stock photo websites, photo sharing websites and web images. The accompanying text may explain various aspects of pictures, such as content, concepts, time, place, photo technique, etc, while "concepts" refer to the connotation of pictures. Many of these "concepts" are abstract. For example, the word 'refreshment' is frequently found in the annotation of photos of kiwi. Picture resources, which have connotation as part of picture annotation, can be corpora to extract visual symbols of abstract concepts. In Section 4.1, we introduce what we think is a proper and adequate corpus for CDVS and the capacity of the one we constructed.

In large picture resources, an abstract concept often appears in the annotation of many pictures, from hundreds to hundreds of thousands. Among these pictures, many pictures are of the same things. Every picture is different, at a very specific level. However, note that CDVS pursues to show that a concept can be represented by different things, but not by the same thing with different details. Thus, pictures of the same thing should only be one visual symbol. We achieve this by using clustering techniques, which divide a collection of objects into groups (called *clusters*), so that objects are more similar to the objects within the same cluster than the ones outside. CDVS only concerns about the subjects of pictures, but not mixed with any other aspect, such as visual details or photo-taking locations. We assume the ontology, which we base on to classify pictures, is a lexicon of physical concepts. We achieve this by tag filtering. A lot of clustering algorithms have been proposed in the past. To select a proper one has to be based on both their overall performance and the different features of generated clusters. In Section 4.2.2, we explain our choice. For the purpose to show the variety of visual symbols, we designed a "window strategy" to determine the optimal number of clusters.

3   Literature Review and Contribution

The use of image search engines such as Google Image Search [1] is well appreciated by designers except the lack of precision [2]. Also, Google Image Search, as a general image search engine, may not satisfy designers' specific need. For example, as shown in Fig.2, among the top 18 images retrieved by Google for the word 'peace', 9 images are of peace sign. At the top of this page, Google also lists 4 related searches: 'peace sign', 'peace symbol', 'peace fingers' and 'peace hand'. 'Peace sign' and 'peace symbol' are different names for the same thing, which already spears on the first retrieved image page. This is also the case for 'peace fingers' and 'peace hand'. So, the 4 suggested related search terms do not bring in new visual symbols to designers.

Another popular source of inspiration is online stock photo databases, such as Getty Images [3], where photos are accurately annotated by photographers or editors. The retrieval precision is higher. But, the retrieved photos, normally thousands, are presented linearly. It often happens that the majority of photos on the first page are of the same thing. As demonstrated in Fig.3, among the top 24 photos provided by Getty Images for the word 'peace', 14 photos are of peace finger. On the left of the webpage, Getty offers search refinement. The retrieved photos can be further classified by people groups, location, concept, subject and style (composition, viewpoint and image technique). The classification by concept and subject are relevant to CDVS. In the classification by concept, the top 5 categories are 'tranquil scene', 'relaxation' 'serene people', 'tranquillity' and 'idyllic'. There are 3 category names among 5 are abstract concepts, i.e. 'relaxation', 'tranquillity' and 'idyllic'. From abstract to abstract is not the objective of CDVS. In the classification by subject, the top 4 categories offered are 'photography', 'outdoors', 'day' and 'nature'. All these are too general terms to tell what is actually in the photos.

Flickr [4], a popular online photo sharing site, offers clustering services to retrieved photos. Photos are divided into different semantic groups based on their tags. The number of clusters is up to 4 (as shown in Fig. 4), which is quite small considering the huge amount of photos retrieved by each concept. So, the partition is done at a very general level of semantics, i.e. each cluster has many sub-clusters. Inside each cluster, photos of different sub-clusters are mixed together and presented linearly, as Getty Images dose. Though each cluster also comes with a textual summary, comprised of a few most representative tags, each tag is not a unique pointer to a sub-cluster, i.e. several tags may refer to the same sub-cluster. So, there is no way to view photos of a sub-cluster. As a result, the clustering of photos offered by Flickr is rough, considering using it as a Connotation Dictionary of Visual Symbols.

Comparing Fig. 1 to Fig. 2, 3 and 4, we can see CDVS offers more accurate and diverse results, and requires lest search effort. CDVS is dedicated to the leap from abstract concepts to visual representations. We achieve these objectives by constructing a proper corpus, special tag filtering and a "window strategy" to determine the optimal number of clusters. The technical details are described in Section 4.

Fig. 2. First page of images retrieved by Google Image Search for 'peace' (as of June 15, 2009).

Fig. 3. First page of images retrieved by Getty Images for 'peace' (as of June 18, 2009).

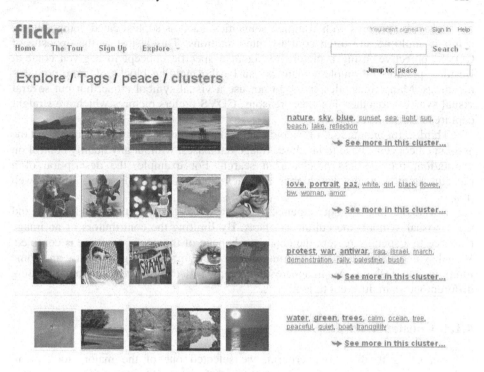

Fig. 4. Clustering of retrieved photos by Flickr for 'peace' (as of June 15, 2009).

4   Construct Connotation Dictionary of Visual Symbols

4.1   Corpus

4.1.1 Requirements of Corpus for CDVS

At present, there are plenty of resources of images with accompanying text. A proper corpus for eliciting visual symbols has to satisfy mainly 3 requirements, including

- broad topics and huge capacity,
- simple picture semantics,
- accurate annotation.

First of all, the image resource itself has to be a good approximation of the commonsense knowledge in a society. It means the image resource has to cover broad general topics, but not a specific field, such as only marine life pictures. It also means the capacity of the database has to be huge. Furthermore, huge capacity may imply a large number of contributors. Then, the leverage of all their opinion is closer to the real.

Secondly, pictures with complex semantics, such as sophisticated compositions, result in multiple and often contrast interpretations. This is just at the opposite of CDVS' objective, using a picture to signal a specific concept in a given context. Besides, pictures of simple semantics can be the building blocks of more complex meanings. Many times, designers do not use a visual symbol alone, but put several visual symbols together. For these reasons, CDVS prefers pictures which are straight captures of an object or scene.

Thirdly, for annotation, the depiction of image content has to be accurate and the associated concepts have to be close. Image databases, without any quality control on annotation, provide less precision in search. For example, the description of a museum item normally has higher accuracy than the text snippets around a web image.

Beside the above 3 requirements, there is also the consideration about culture and time. Visual symbols are culture artefacts. By limiting the contributors of an image resource to a specific region, the conceptual space of the image resource is confined. Visual symbols also evolve along time, with some symbols going out of use and some jumping into fashion. An image resource may reflect this evolution by providing different views in different time frames.

4.1.2 Construct Corpus

According to the above criteria, we selected one of the major stock photo websites, www.istockphoto.com, as our source of corpus. At present, iStockphoto has more than 5 million files and more than 4 million contributors all around the world (as of June 2009). Its capacity is increasing daily. iStockphoto has design professionals as one of its main clients. It only admits photos of simple composition and high quality. It achieved a good coverage of daily objects and scenes [5] by balancing the quantities of different subjects. iStockphoto uses a *Controlled Vocabulary* (CV) to regulate photographers' annotation (also called *tagging*). Photographer can only use standard words (tags) of certain language, such as English. CV is a lexicon of terms. What are included in CV depends on the whole content in iStockphoto and the need to facilitate search.

iStockphoto does not offer APIs to access its data in real time. It made an index of thumbnails public for a short time. We were able to download 187,081 big thumbnails (380 x 285 pixels) with the watermark of iStockphoto. At present, we do not place any constraints of culture and time, which can be easily implemented by collaborating with industry partners in the future. The number of tags owned by each photo ranges from a few to more than 100. We filtered photos which do not have any tag or have exact the same tags. It results in 140,953 photos with unique annotation. All the annotations are stored in a MySql database. Among all the annotations, there are 72,576 unique words. The most frequent word appears in 20081 annotations. There are 2,290 words which appear in more than 200 annotations, 1,045 words which appear in more than 500 annotations. This capacity is smaller than ideal. We expected to collect at least 1,000 photos for each familiar word.

4.2   Extract Visual Symbols from Corpus

For an arbitrary abstract concept, we first expand the query by adding synonyms of this concept. Then, we retrieve from corpus all the photos which have the concept or its synonyms in their annotation. Afterwards, we find photo groups of the same objects or scenes. For each group, we calculate the most representative photo, which is output as a visual symbol for the input abstract concept. The whole process runs online, whose steps are illustrated in Fig. 5.

What we use in clustering is the annotation of photos, because we want to classify photos by their semantics but not visual features. Photos of the same thing may look very different, and photos of different things may look very similar. [6] shows that it is better to only use textual information or visual features in clustering, but not mix them. [7] suggests that two kinds of clustering can be generated separately. Each photo belongs to certain cluster in each clustering, which is the connection point of the two clustering results. Users can navigate forth and back between these two clusterings through this connection point at any time they want.

Annotations are like short documents. Every retrieved photo collection corresponds to a collection of short documents. Therefore, our clustering problem is indeed a document clustering problem.

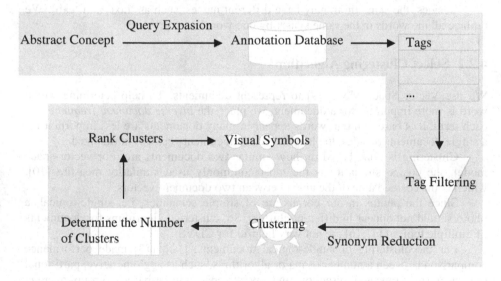

Fig. 5. Steps of extracting visual symbols.

4.2.1   Tag Filtering

The purpose of tag filtering is to delete tags which are irrelevant to clustering or even interfere this task.

Abstract exists as the opposite of physical. CDVS is dedicated to show abstract concepts can be represented by a variety of objects or scenes. It is a bridge from abstract concepts to physical concepts. For this reason, we intend to classify the retrieved photos only by their main subjects. Thus, the photo annotation, which will be input into clustering process, would better only contain tags describe what is actually in photos. For this purpose, tags of abstract concepts, photo techniques, popular photo classification terms and insignificant meaning should be filtered.

We use WordNet [8] to distil physical concepts. WordNet contains words of four major part of speech classes, including adjective, adverb, noun and verb. We take all adjective and adverb senses as abstract, and all verb senses as physical. WordNet puts noun senses into 25 source files, which are further grouped into 11 categories. We take the noun sense of the *abstraction* and *psychological features* categories as abstract. These two categories include noun senses of *attribute*, *quantity*, *relation*, *time*, *cognition*, *feeling* and *motivation*. A sense may map to more than one word. We only keep the nouns whose most frequently used sense is abstract, to avoid the danger of including any physical words.

We obtained tags of photo-taking techniques and popular photo classification terms from Getty Images [3]. Tags of photo techniques describe composition, viewpoint and image technique of photos. Popular photo classification terms are mainly terms of gender, ethnicity and age of people.

We also used a normal stop-word list contains words which are insignificant (i.e., articles, prepositions) or very common (i.e., how, least).

Besides, the same thing may have different names, such as 'taxi' and 'cab'. We replace all the words in the same synset by one word.

4.2.2 Select Clustering Algorithm

We use Vector Space Model [9] to represent documents. To help determine which word is more important for a document, we place the *inverse document frequency* on each term. It is based on that words appear in many documents are less important for a single document. Besides, the length of each document vector is normalized.

Clustering is done based on how similar two documents are. For vector-space model, the cosine similarity is the most commonly used similarity measure [10], which is the cosine value of the angel between two document vectors.

Since the photos in our corpus are of simple semantics, i.e. single-topical, a photo should not appear in different clusters. So, clustering algorithms for documents of multiple topics [11], [6] are not very helpful for CDVS.

For the clustering of single-topical documents, [12], [13] made performance comparison between a number of major algorithms, such as agglomerative, partitional (e.g. k-means, repeated bisection and spectral-partitioning-based), group average (UPGMA), single-link and complete link. Beside the quantitative evaluation, they also describe the features of clusters generated by different algorithms. They demonstrated that agglomerative algorithms group together documents that form small and reasonably cohesive clusters, a task in which partitional algorithms may fail as they may split such documents across cluster boundaries early during the partitional clustering process. As we stated before, the purpose of using clustering for CDVS is to group together photos of the same objects or scenes. Agglomerative clustering is a bottom-up process. It initially considers every document as a cluster. It repeatedly merges the most similar two clusters until there is only one cluster left. During the merge, photos which are close to each other get together, while photos which are far from any other photos stay alone. We can see agglomerative algorithm fits CDVS better than partitional algorithms. For agglomerative algorithms, the choice of cluster selection schemes generates solutions with varied accuracy. [13] evaluated the performance of all the aforementioned 9 cluster selection schemes (UPGMA, single-link, complete link, I_1, I_2, E_1, E_2, H_1 and H_2). It found that agglomerative algorithm with UPGMA provides the best clustering solutions.

4.2.3 Determine the Number of Cluster

For agglomerative algorithm, the number of cluster k has to be known a prior. But in our case, k is unknown. The merge process of agglomerative clustering can be represented by dendrogram, which is a hierarchical tree. Each node in the tree represents a merge step, and the height of node is the UPGMA vale between the two merged clusters. Inconsistency analysis can be applied to dendrogram to find the optimal number of clusters k. Inconsistency analysis compares the height of each node with the heights of the nodes below it. A node whose height differs noticeably from the height of the nodes below indicates that the clusters joined at this step are farther apart from each other than their components were. The node with the biggest inconsistency coefficient is the optimal k. However, this is just one level of the hierarchical clustering tree. The k might be quite small, e.g. 1000 photos are grouped into a few clusters. Within each cluster, photos converge at a quite general concept. Sometimes, the k could be very big, e.g. 1000 photos are divided into 200 groups. Within each group, photos not only converge at a specific concept, but also converge at more details, such as taken by the same photographer who uses very similar annotations for all these photos. In this case, photos of the same thing are distributed in different clusters. We want to find a number of clusters, a level of viewing the whole collection, which is not too general nor too divided. Our solution is to define lower and upper boundaries for possible ks. The lower bound is defined as $n/100$, where n is the number of documents. The upper bound is defined as $n/10$. Before applying this window, we only take the ks ($\leq n/2$) and sort all of them in the descending order of their inconsistency coefficients. The k with highest inconsistency coefficient is examined first. This examination stops at the first k which is within the window.

4.2.4 Rank Visual Symbols

Within a retrieved photo collection, the repetition of photos of the same objects or scenes from different contributors may correlate positively with the qualification of the photos to be visual symbols of the corresponding concept. We rank the obtained clusters by the number of photos they have. The bigger size, the higher rank. We also set a lower bound on the cluster size. Clusters, whose size is less than the lower bound, are seen as idiosyncratic and are ignored. Furthermore, the lower bound should be in proportion with the size of the whole retrieved photo collection. It is like voting. What works is not the absolute number, but the percentage. At present, we found 1% works fine for our data, which could be further investigated.

4.2.5 Most Representative Photo and Label of Cluster

We use the Cluto [14] implementation of the agglomerative algorithm and UPGMA. Cluto also provides statistics of the generated clusters besides clustering solution, such as internal and external z-scores for each document. Internal z-score is the similarity between the document to other documents of the same cluster. External z-score is the similarity between the document to the documents in other clusters. The most representative photo of a cluster has large values of the internal z-score and small values of the external z-score.

Besides, Cluto provides the most descriptive features of each cluster. We use the top 2 tag as the label of cluster.

5   Evaluation

We accomplished a preliminary test of the quality and quantity of visual symbols output by our knowledge extraction method. Quality refers to if the provided picture can stand for the intended concept. Quantity means if a sufficient number of visual symbols are offered for designers to choose from, when they are looking for something fresh and proper.

5.1   Experimental Apparatus

The experiment apparatus is a one page online survey at http://vis.upf.edu/CDVS/test.aspx. The interface is shown in Fig. 6. At the top of page, it is the experiment instruction. Below it, users can enter freely the concept to search for its visual symbols. After clicking the "Search" button, a list of visual symbols will be returned. Under each picture, there are a label and a checkbox. The label refers to the object or scene depicted in the picture. Users are invited to judge if each picture can stand for the input concept. If the answer is 'Yes', the corresponding checkbox should be checked. After the pictures, there are two questions asking about users' overall opinion about the provided visual symbols. The two questions are

- "are there any visual symbols new to you",
- "are there plenty of different visual symbols to choose".

They should be answered by saying "Yes" or "No". At the end of the page, users should click the "Submit" button, and all their response will be stored in a database.

5.2 Participants

Because of the limit of time, we were not able to organize strict onsite experiment with designers. Instead, invitations of participation were sent out to forums of advertising professions and graphic designers, and mailing lists of linguists and computer scientists. We expected some people might get interested and contributed some of their time. Google Analytics [15] was used to obtain the statistics of visits to our online survey.

5.3 Experiment Result and Analysis

From 12 to 19 May 2009, 171 unique visitors from 33 countries made 198 visits to our online survey. Average time on site is 3'30" per visit. In our database, 142 assessments are recorded. There are invalid assessments. For instance, an assessment says there are "fresh" and "plenty" visual symbols. But, at the same time, it says there is no "qualified" visual symbol. We suspect this is because the visitor was not willing to tick the checkbox under each picture one by one. All the invalid assessments amount to 41. Among the rest 101 valid assessments, 38.6% think there are "fresh" visual symbols. 52.48% think there are "plenty" of symbols to choose. For the assessment of "qualified" visual symbols, we first calculate the percentage of "qualified" visual symbols within each assessment. Then, we average it over the total 101 assessments. The result is 37.13%.

First of all, the above experiment result should be seen as the bottom-line performance of CDVS, because our current corpus is still inadequate and the experiment participants might not be serious.

Secondly, the percentage of "qualified" visual symbols is lower than our expectation. The photo annotation from iStockphoto should be able to ensure a basic level of association strength. In our own inspection of the generated visual symbols, we also thought the percentage of "qualified" visual symbols should be much higher. There may be two reasons for this discrepancy. One is that some experiment participants may not understand "symbolism" in the same way as designers do. The other reason is that the expressiveness of symbols also depends on the context. So, it is not very proper to judge "symbolism"when symbols stand alone. A more ideal experiment scenario is to involve designers in a specific design task.

Thirdly, we calculated the linear correlation coefficients between "fresh" and the number of visual symbols, and "plenty" and the number of visual symbols. The correlation between "fresh" and the number of visual symbols is 0.0204, which is not significant at all. The correlation between "plenty" and the number of visual symbols is 0.2934. So, the number of visual symbols does not affect much people's judgment on "fresh" and "plenty". We speculate they have more to do with the individual concepts. For example, people may give higher ratings for visual symbols of uncommon words, such as 'plump', than for familiar words. Another case is we found it is difficult to find pictures expressive enough, in all CDVS and 3 image resources mentioned in Literature Review, for certain specific concepts, such as 'ugly' and 'stupid'. Besides, for some concepts, such as 'uncertainty' and 'silence', naturally there are not many varied subjects in the retrieved photos, no matter how big the corpus is. We would like to know further about for which concepts our knowledge extraction method works well and for which it does not, as well as what characteristics divide these concepts. We also think that some psycholinguistic features of words, such as concreteness, imaginability, meaningfulness and familiarity [16], may shed some light on this problem. However, with current data, it is not possible to classify concepts, because the number of assessments is not enough. Among the 101 assessments, only 14 concepts have more than 1 assessment to see the judgements from different participants on the same visual symbols.

6 Future Work

In the future, we would like to expand the capacity of our corpus, with the objective of collecting at least 1000 photos for each familiar concept. We would also like to carry out another user experiment to test the usefulness of CDVS in specific design tasks and gather more data for differentiating concepts. We believe this differentiation will help improve the current knowledge extraction.

7 Conclusion

We created an online service, Connotation Dictionary of Visual Symbols (http://vis.upf.edu/CDVS/dic2.aspx), for visual communication designers to instantly find a variety of pictures for representing a given abstract concept. It is aimed at improving their productivity. This dictionary is backboned by an automatic knowledge extraction process, which elicits pairs of abstract concept and picture from corpus. The clustering process runs in real time and features tailored tag filtering and a "window strategy" to determine the optimal number of clusters. The extracted visual symbols look promising. An online survey was used to test their quality and quantity. Analysis of experiment result and proposal of improvement are also provided.

Acknowledgements. This work is supported by the FI-IQUC grant from Agència de Gesti'o d'Ajuts Universitaris I de Recerca, Catalunya, Spain. I also would like to thank the discussion and support from Rodrigo Roman and Fabien Girardin.

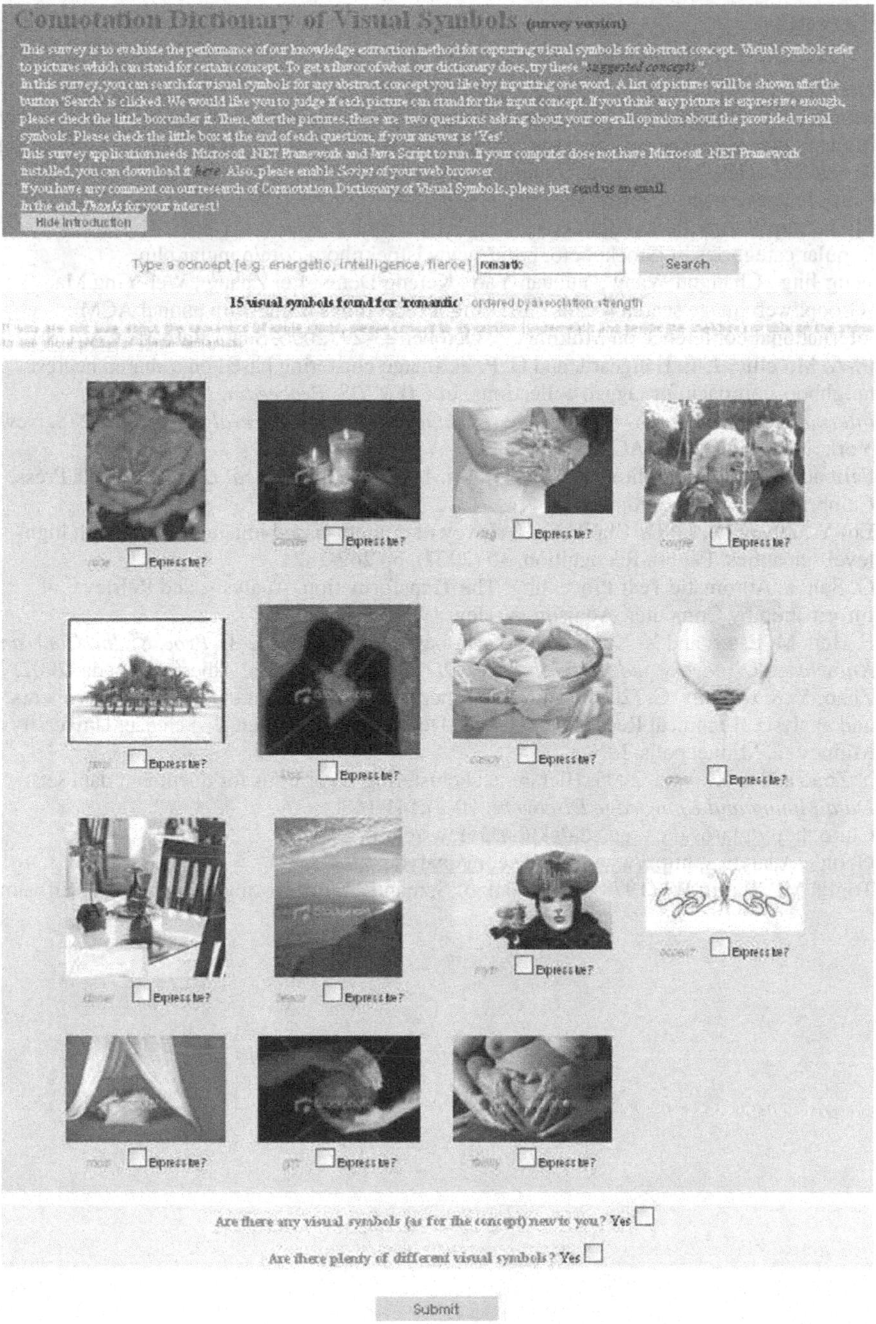

Fig. 6. Interface of web survey.

References

1. Google Image Search, http://images.google.com/.
2. Mougenot C., Bouchard C., Aoussat A., Fostering innovation in early design stage: a study of inspirational process in car design companies, Wonderground 2006 in proc. of the Design Research Society International conference, Portugal 2006.
3. Getty Images, www.gettyimages.com.
4. Flickr, http://www.flickr.com/.
5. Popular categories in iStockphoto, http://www.istockphoto.com/popular.php.
6. Feng Jing , Changhu Wang , Yuhuan Yao , Kefeng Deng , Lei Zhang , Wei-Ying Ma, IGroup: web image search results clustering, Proceedings of the 14th annual ACM international conference on Multimedia, October 23-27, 2006, Santa Barbara, CA, USA.
7. P.-A. Mo"ellic, J.-E. Haugeard, and G. Pitel. Image clustering based on a shared nearest neighbors approach for tagged collections. In *CIVR '08: Proceedings of the 2008 international conference onContent-based image and video retrieval*, pages 269–278, New York, NY, USA, 2008. ACM.
8. Fellbaum, Christiane, editor. 1998. *WordNet:An Electronic Lexical Database*. MIT Press, Cambridge, Massachusetts.
9. Liu Y., Zhang D., Lu G., Ma W.Y., A survey of content-based image retrieval with high-level semantics, Pattern Recognition, 40 (2007), pp 262-282.
10. G. Salton. Automatic Text Processing: The Transformation, Analysis, and Retrieval of Information by Computer. Addison-Wesley, 1989.
11. F. Beil, M. Ester, and X. Xu. Frequent term-based text clustering. In *Proc. 8th Int. Conf. on Knowledge Discovery and Data Mining (KDD)'2002*, Edmonton, Alberta, Canada, 2002.
12. Zhao, Y. & Karypis, G. (2001). Criterion functions for document clustering: Experiments and analysis. Technical Report TR #01--40, Department of Computer Science, University of Minnesota, Minneapolis, MN.
13. Y Zhao and G Karypis. 2005. Hierarchical clustering algorithms for document data sets. *Data Mining and Knowledge Discovery*, 10(2):141.168.
14. Cluto, http://glaros.dtc.umn.edu/gkhome/views/cluto.
15. Google Analytics, http://www.google.com/analytics/.
16. Toglia MP, Battig WF(1978): Handbook of Semantic Word Norms. Hillsdale, NJ: Erlbaum.

Constructing Confluent Context-sensitive Graph Grammars from Non-confluent Productions for Parsing Efficiency

Yang Zou[1,2], Jian Lü[1], Xiaoqin Zeng[2], Xiaoxing Ma[1] and Qiliang Yang[1,3]

[1] State Key Laboratory for Novel Software Technology, Nanjing University, Nanjing 210093, China
[2] Research Institute of Pattern Recognition and Intelligent System, Computer and Information Engineering College, Hohai University, Nanjing 210098, China
[3] Institute of Engineering Corps, PLA University of Sci. & Tech., Nanjing 210007, China
yzou08@gmail.com

Abstract. The efficient parsing algorithms are usually confined to confluent graph grammars in context-sensitive formalisms, whereas the confluence condition is not frequently met by graph grammars in practical applications. This paper, based on the Reserved Graph Grammar (RGG) formalism, proposes an extended formalism XRGG which allows imposing constraints characterizing application situations on graph productions. The constraints can make the redexes of the XRGG productions' right graphs mutually exclusive so as to ensure the confluence of the corresponding graph grammar. Then an algorithm is developed to construct a confluent XRGG graph grammar from an RGG grammar with non-confluent productions for tackling identical graph languages. This method can be easily generalized to other context-sensitive graph grammar formalisms, thus making the efficient parsing algorithm of the RGG that depends on confluent graph grammars more widely applicable.

Keywords: Context-sensitive graph grammar; confluence; parsing algorithm; constraint; extended productions

1 Introduction

Similar to formal grammars that are employed as syntax definition formalisms for textual languages, graph grammars are also natural mechanisms for the specification of graphical visual languages. And the parsing algorithms equipped with them can then be utilized to check the syntactic correctness and to interpret the semantics. As most of the context-free graph grammars have difficulty in tersely and intuitively describing visual languages, context-sensitive ones have attracted much attention in recent years.

Rekers and Schürr [1] developed a context-sensitive graph grammar, the Layered Graph Grammar formalism (LGG), to formally define graphical visual languages. The LGG formalism (abbreviated to "the LGG" hereafter) explicitly indicates in both sides of productions context elements to address the embedding problem, making the

M.L. Huang et al. (eds.), *Visual Information Communication*,
DOI 10.1007/978-1-4419-0312-9_8, © Springer Science+Business Media, LLC 2010

formalism rather too complicated but quite intuitive. Nevertheless, the lexicographical order enforcement on LGG productions for guaranteeing the decidability of the membership problem is intractable, and thus its parsing algorithm is intricate and extremely hard.

Another context-sensitive formalism Reserved Graph Grammar (RGG), proposed by Zhang et al [2], is an improvement over the LGG in terms of the form of productions and parsing algorithm. Besides the layer decomposition mechanism inherited from the LGG to handle the membership problem, the RGG invents a particular two-level node structure plus a marking technique to identify context elements, and introduces a general embedding rule to resolve the embedding problem. Compared to the LGG, this formalism is more succinct but not that intuitive. Moreover, a quite efficient Selection-Free Parsing Algorithm (SFPA) was developed for the RGG in [2] that has polynomial time complexity when applied to a set of confluent (called selection-free in [2]) graph productions, together with a pertinent conclusion which states that an RGG graph grammar is confluent if its production set is confluent.

The SFPA is one of the main contributions of the RGG. Equipped with the SFPA, the RGG has thus far been applied to a wide range of research fields, including XML document design and transformation [3], Multimedia layout adaptation [4], graphical user interface design [5], model management [6], and design pattern evolution [7], among others. In addition, the SFPA can also be exploited in several other context-sensitive graph grammar formalisms [8-9].

However, the assumption underlying the SFPA that the set of productions under consideration must be confluent seems not frequently satisfied by graph grammars in practical applications, since even an ordinary category of graphs, such as process flow diagrams, may be intuitively specified by a non-confluent set of graph productions. An example in this regard is illustrated in the next section. It is this observation that motivates the work in the paper.

In order to make the efficient SFPA applicable to context-sensitive graph grammars without restriction of confluent set of productions, the paper proposes a method to transform a set of non-confluent productions to confluent ones. The contribution of the paper is twofold. One is the proposal of an extended RGG formalism, called XRGG, which allows more detailed context information to be enclosed in productions as constraints, together with a few conclusions characterizing confluent XRGG graph grammars. The other is the development of an algorithm based on the conclusions for generating a confluent XRGG graph grammar from a set of originally non-confluent RGG productions with their languages being equivalent. The novelty of the method is the introduction of proper constraints that could lead to confluent graph grammars by making the redexes of productions' right graphs mutually exclusive. It is of great significance that the method can not only largely enlarge the application scope of the RGG, but also be effortlessly generalized to other context-sensitive graph grammar formalisms, thus making the efficient SFPA more widely applicable.

The rest of the paper is organized as follows. Section 2 reviews the RGG formalism in more detail, and exemplifies a non-confluent set of productions. Section 3 firstly defines the XRGG and draws a few conclusions on confluent graph grammars, and then develops an algorithm for generating a set of confluent XRGG productions from a non-confluent RGG one. A case study of the algorithm is subsequently elaborated in Section 4. Section 5 argues the effectiveness of the method and compares it to related work. Finally, Section 6 concludes the paper.

2   The RGG Formalism

Generally, a graph grammar consists of an initial graph and a collection of graph productions, and thus defines a set of graphs which can be generated from the initial graph by iteratively applying those productions in an arbitrary way. A graph production, also called rewriting rules, comprising two graphs, left graph and right graph respectively, can be applied to another graph called host graph. A redex is a subgraph in the host graph that is isomorphic to the left or right graph of a production. When a redex of the left graph of a production occurs in a host graph, one can substitute the right graph for this redex, which is called L-application of the production; symmetrically, R-application is the reverse replacement. The L-application defines the language of a graph grammar, and the R-application is adopted to parse a graph.

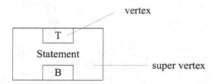

Fig. 1. Node structure of the RGG formalism.

The RGG is a context-sensitive graph grammar formalism [2]. It introduces a node-edge format to represent graphs in which a node is organized in a two-level structure, as illustrated in Figure 1, where the large surrounding rectangle is the first level, called super vertex, and other embedded small rectangles the second level, called vertices. Either super vertex or other vertices of a node can be the connecting point of an edge without any semantic difference.

In addition to the two-level structure of a node, a marking technique is also required to describe graph productions in the RGG which partitions all the vertices within a node into two categories, marked and unmarked ones with each marked vertex being assigned a unique number. Marked vertices, each of which appears simultaneously on both sides of a production, are used to preserve the context elements pertaining to it. In an R- (or L-) application of a production, those edges connected to such vertices in the redex of a host graph that have marked isomorphic correspondents in the right (or left) graph are reserved, which avoids the appearance of dangling edges in the replacement process provided that another rule is also enforced.

This embedding rule states that if a vetex in the right (or left) graph of a production is unmarked and has an isomorphic vertex in the redex of a host graph, then all the edges connected to the vertex should be completely inside the redex. Apparently, the embedding rule as well as the marking technique based on the special node structure properly handles the unmarked and marked vertices in the process of production application, which solves the embedding problem for the RGG.

As an example, an RGG specifying process flow diagrams is depicted in Figure 2.

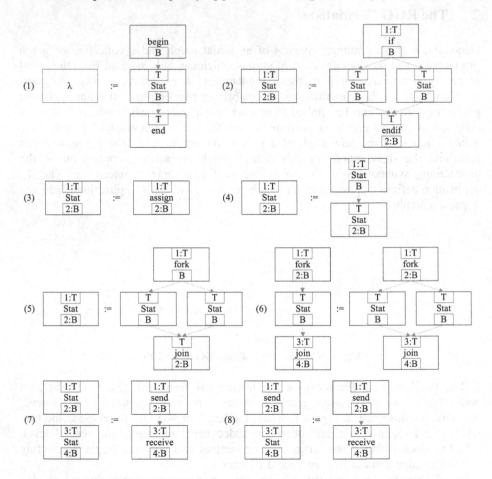

Fig. 2. An RGG for specifying process flow diagrams.

The RGG is equipped with a parsing algorithm SFPA, which can be applied to a graph grammar whose production set is confluent. A set of productions is confluent whenever any two productions in it are confluent. Two productions p_1, p_2 being confluent means that if a host graph contains the redexes of these two right graphs simultaneously, then it can be parsed in two different orders p_1, p_2 and p_2, p_1 with the resulting graphs being the same. It is proved for the RGG in [2] that a graph grammar is confluent if its production set is so. Informally, a confluent graph grammar guarantees that different sequences of production applications to a host graph result in the same graph.

However, as a counterexample of the condition, the set of productions shown in Figure 2 is non-confluent, so is the graph grammar. Notice that productions 5 and 6 which have exactly the same right graphs are non-confluent, since when a redex of the right graphs appearing in a host graph, the two resulting graphs from conducting the R-application of productions 5 and 6 respectively to the host graph are evidently different. An example in this regard is demonstrated in Figure 3, where the graph in the middle is a host graph, and the subgraph of it surrounded by dashed rectangle is a redex of the right graphs of both productions 5 and 6, which is then replaced respectively by the two left graphs in R-applications, resulting in two distinct graphs (in dashed rectangles) on each side. The one on the right side can be further deduced to the initial graph by implementing an R-application of production 1, while the other on the left cannot.

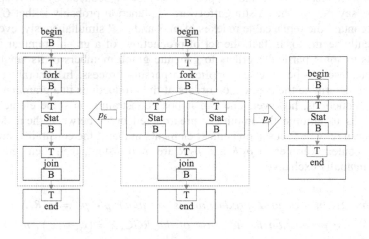

Fig. 3. An example violating the confluence condition.

3   Extended RGG

This section defines an extended RGG formalism, called XRGG, which inherits from the RGG the basic concepts and notations. Some of them are listed below for the sake of clarity and simplicity.

$p := (L, R)$: a production with a pair of graphs, left graph L and right graph R. $p.L$ and $p.R$ are used to denote the left graph and right graph of p, respectively.

$Rd(H, G)$: a set of redexes of graph G, which are subgraphs of graph H.

$G_1 \approx G_2$: graphs G_1 and G_2 are isomorphic.

Merger: a graph G is a merger of G_1 and G_2 if both of them are subgraphs of G and each node or edge in G is either from G_1 or from G_2.

$Merge(G_1, G_2)$: the set of mergers of graphs G_1 and G_2.

$H \to^L H'$: L-application or derivation of a production $p := (L, R)$ to a host graph H, yields H'.

$H \to^R H'$: R-application or reduction of a production $p := (L, R)$ to a host graph H, yields H'.

3.1 Definitions of the XRGG Formalism

Some circumstantial analysis on a set of non-confluent productions is necessary beforehand. To explain why two productions p_1 and p_2 are non-confluent, it is sufficient to analyze the relevant mergers leading to this failure, and two right graphs $p_1.R$ and $p_2.R$ in particular. Consider a merger G of two graphs A and B isomorphic to $p_1.R$ and $p_2.R$ respectively, and suppose G cannot be reduced by an R-application sequence, say p_1, p_2. Then a straightforward explanation probably is that G does not actually contain the replaceable redexes of $p_1.R$ and $p_2.R$ simultaneously, even though it apparently seems to. In fact, the set of productions of a graph grammar implicitly conforms to some particular orders to generate graph members of its language, and thus is supposed to be reversely applied in parsing process. In general, it is rather difficult to determine the application orders of the productions in a grammar. As for a pair of productions, however, one can impose constraints on some elements in the right graphs to enforce the implicitly prearranged order between them. Moreover, attention can only be focused on context elements in that if the constraints imposed on common context vertices of $p_1.R$ and $p_2.R$ are inconsistent, then their redexes in G must be mutually exclusive.

Definition 1 *An extended production is a quadruple $p^E := (L, R, X, C)$, where $p := (L, R)$ is a production in the sense of the RGG, $X = \{x_1, \cdots, x_n\}$, $n \geq 0$, a set of feature variables, and C a Boolean expression on X.*

Each x_i $(1 \leq i \leq n)$ in X represents a particular feature, such as degree, of a marked vertex within a node in R, and each component of the Boolean expression C is a constraint imposed on x_i, such as an equation. Then, C can be employed to characterize much more detailed contextual features for applying an R-application of the production. Notice that p is a special case of p^E when $X = \varnothing$ and C is T (true).

Given a production p, one can create many extended productions p^E with respect to p in terms of different feature variables X or Boolean expressions C. In the sequel, we simply use p^E to nominate an extended production with respect to p.

Definition 2 *A subgraph S of a graph H is a redex of the right graph of an extended production $p^E := (L, R, X, C)$, denoted by $S \in Rd(H, R, C)$, if*

- *S is a redex of R in the sense of the RGG,*
- *the Boolean expression C is T in H.*

Generally, $Rd(H,G,C)$ denotes the set of such subgaphs of H that not only are the redexes of G in the sense of the RGG but also satisfy the Boolean expression C. So, $Rd(H,G)$ that is identical to $Rd(H,G,T)$ where C is assigned to T can be viewed as a trivial case of it. For consistency, $Rd(H,G,C)$ is abbreviated to $Rd(H,G)$ as what it actually denotes is unambiguous from the context.

Definition 3 $gg := (A, P^E)$ is an extended RGG called XRGG, if (A,P) is an RGG, and $P^E = \{ p^E \mid p^E$ is an extended production with respect to p, and $p \in P \}$.

Definition 4 Let $gg := (A, P^E)$ be an XRGG of an $RGG(A,P)$, then its language $L(gg)$ is the same as that of the (A,P).

Definition 5 Let G be a merger of two graphs A and B, p_1^E and p_2^E two extended productions, and A and B isomorphic to $p_1.R$ and $p_2.R$, respectively. G is reducible with respect to p_1^E and p_2^E if $A \in Rd(G, p_1^E.R) \wedge B \in Rd(G, p_2^E.R)$

$$\Rightarrow \exists G_A, G_{AB}, G_B, G_{BA} (G \mapsto^A G_A \mapsto^B G_{AB} \wedge G \mapsto^B G_B \mapsto G_{BA} \wedge G_{AB} \approx G_{BA}).$$

Definition 6 Let P^E be a set of extended productions. P^E is confluent if for any p_1^E, $p_2^E \in P^E$, A and B are graphs isomorphic to $p_1.R$ and $p_2.R$ respectively, and for each $G \in Merge(A,B)$, G is reducible with respect to p_1^E and p_2^E.

Note that the definition of a confluent set P of RGG productions is also included in the above two definitions, since P is merely a special case of P^E.

Theorem 1 Let $gg := (A, P^E)$ be an XRGG. If P^E is confluent, then gg is confluent.

Proof. It is straightforward from Definitions 1, 2 and 3 and the theorem proved in [2] which states that an RGG is confluent whenever its production set is confluent.

Lemma 1 Let p_1 and p_2 be two productions, p_1^E and p_2^E extended productions with respect to them, and A and B graphs isomorphic to $p_1.R$ and $p_2.R$, respectively. For any $G \in Merge(A,B)$ such that $A \in Rd(G, p_1.R) \wedge B \in Rd(G, p_2.R)$, if G is reducible with respect to p_1 and p_2, then G is also reducible with respect to p_1^E and p_2^E.

Proof. Suppose that G is reducible with respect to p_1 and p_2, then, by Definition 5,

$$\exists G_A, G_{AB}, G_B, G_{BA} (G \mapsto^A G_A \mapsto^B G_{AB} \wedge G \mapsto^B G_B \mapsto G_{BA} \wedge G_{AB} \approx G_{BA}).$$

Since $A \in Rd(G, p_2.R) \wedge B \in Rd(G, p_2.R)$, if the Boolean expressions of p_1^E and p_2^E are simultaneously satisfied by G, then $A \in Rd(G, p_1^E.R) \wedge B \in Rd(G, p_2^E.R)$ according to Definition 2. Therefore, the conclusion holds by Definition 5. If the two Boolean expressions are not simultaneously satisfied by G, $A \notin Rd(G, p_1^E.R) \vee B \notin Rd(G, p_2^E.R)$, by Definition 2. Thus, G is also reducible with respect to p_1^E and p_2^E from Definition 5.

Theorem 2 *Suppose P^E be a set of extended productions with respect to a set P of productions. If P is confluent then P^E is confluent.*

Proof. It is evident from Lemma1 and Definition 6.

The converse does not necessarily hold. This theorem, underlying the algorithm for transforming a non-confluent set of productions to a confluent one, unveils that it suffices to extend only those pairs of productions that are non-confluent.

3.2   Algorithm for Constructing Confluent Productions

The algorithm comprises two steps. Firstly, we shall make sure that the set of productions being considered is actually non-confluent, which is determined by checking if each pair of productions in the set is confluent. Whether a pair of productions is confluent will not be known until all the possible mergers of the right graphs of them are attempted. When a set of productions is judged to be non-confluent, those pairs of productions being non-confluent should be enumerated and stored for further treatment in the subsequent process.

The second step is the transforming process for non-confluent productions, which requires the participation of graph grammar designers. They are requested to create for each one of a pair of productions a couple of variables characterizing the context vertices as well as a constraint on them to make the redexes of two right graphs in all possible mergers mutually exclusive. Each of the non-confluent productions is processed in this manner as many times as it appears in those pairs. Then, an extended production with respect to a non-confluent production is such formed that the variable set X is the union of all the variables created for that production and the Boolean expression C the conjunction of all the constraints imposed on it.

Algorithm *Confluence*
    Input: A set of productions $P = \{p_1, \cdots, p_n\}$
    Output: P if P is confluent; an extended set of productions P^E, otherwise
    {
        $ncpset := \varnothing$;   // to store the pairs of non-confluent productions
        for (any $p_i, p_j \in P$, $i \neq j$)
            for (any merger G of Merge($p_i.R$, $p_j.R$))
                if $\neg$ (G is reducible) **then** $ncpset := ncpset \cup \{\{p_i, p_j\}\}$;
        if ($ncpset = \varnothing$) **return** P;

      else $\{ncset := \bigcup ncpset;$ // to store all the non-confluent productions
          $expset := ncset;$
          // to store extended productions with X initially empty and C true
          for (any pair of productions $p_i, p_j \in ncpset$)$\{$
               create variables V and constraint Ct for both p_i and p_j in $expset$;
               // such that $p_i.Ct$ and $p_j.Ct$ are mutually exclusive in all the mergers
               if $(p_i.V = \varnothing \wedge p_j.V = \varnothing)$ **return failure**;
               $p_i.X := p_i.X \cup p_i.V;$ $p_i.C := p_i.C \wedge p_i.Ct;$
               $p_j.X := p_j.X \cup p_j.V;$ $p_j.C := p_j.C \wedge p_j.Ct;$
          $\}$
          $P^E := (P \setminus ncset) \cup expset;$
          return P^E;
$\}$

Apparently, the first step of the algorithm that decides whether the set of productions is confluent accounts for most of the time complexity, which is exponential in the maximal number of nodes in the right graphs of the productions in P. Practically, however, either the number of productions in a graph grammar or that of nodes in a production's right graph is regularly small. So, the exponential time complexity is actually not a crucial problem for the application of the algorithm.

In the second step, the algorithm may fail to output a set of confluent extended productions if the designers have difficulty in distinguishing the situations of applying a production from that of another. However, this doubt will be dismissed through discussions in the following two sections.

4   A Case Study

In order to demonstrate how the above algorithm operates, especially how to generate the feature variables and constraints when acting as a graph grammar designer, we reexamine the set P of productions depicted in Figure 2.

Undoubtedly, the two pairs of productions, $\{p_5, p_6\}$ and $\{p_7, p_8\}$, result in the non-confluence of P. According to the algorithm, the pair p_7, p_8 is detected to be non-confluent in that all the three mergers of two graphs isomorphic to $p_7.R$ and $p_8.R$ are not reducible by Definition 5, as pictured in Figure 4, where the subgraph enclosed in dashed rectangle of each merger is the overlap of the two graphs.

The thought of the grammar designer when designing productions p_7 and p_8 can be reasonably conjectured as follows: firstly utilize two "Stat"s to generate a pair of "send" and "receive", then iteratively use a "send" and a "Stat" to produce more "receive"s. Note also from Figure 4 that the difference between the redexes in the three mergers is the degrees of vertices "B" or "T". From these observations, we can create explicit feature variables for $p_7.R$ and $p_8.R$ as follows: $p_7.X = \{x_1, x_2\}$(here X is chosen other than V in that p_7 appears just once in the non-confluent pairs) and $p_8.X = \{x_3, x_4\}$, where $x_i (i = 1, 3)$ is the number of edges leaving the vertex "B" of node "send" for "receive" nodes, and $x_j (j=2, 4)$ the number of edges leaving "send" nodes for the vertex "T" of node "receive" in the right graphs of them. Under the assumptions, the constraints for the two productions are intuitively built, as described in Figure 5.

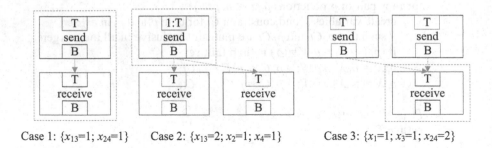

Case 1: $\{x_{13}=1; x_{24}=1\}$ Case 2: $\{x_{13}=2; x_2=1; x_4=1\}$ Case 3: $\{x_1=1; x_3=1; x_{24}=2\}$

Fig. 4. All the three mergers of two graphs isomorphic to $p_7.R$ and $p_8.R$.

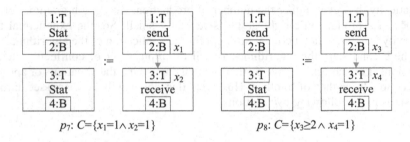

p_7: $C=\{x_1=1 \wedge x_2=1\}$ p_8: $C=\{x_3 \geq 2 \wedge x_4=1\}$

Fig. 5. Extended productions p_7^E and p_8^E.

We still need to check whether these originally not reducible mergers are reducible or not with respect to the extended productions. It is trivial to conclude according to Definition 5 that all the three mergers are actually reducible to $\{p_7^E, p_8^E\}$ as shown in Figure 4, where x_{13} means x_1 and x_3, so does x_{24}, for the corresponding two nodes of the two graphs isomorphic to $p_7.R$ and $p_8.R$ are overlapped in the mergers.

As to the other pair of productions $\{p_5, p_6\}$, an extended set that is confluent can be analogously achieved, as illustrated in Figures 6 and 7, where $p_5.X=\{x_1, x_2\}$, $p_6.X=\{x_3, x_4\}$, and x_i ($i=1, 3$) is the outdegree of vertex "B" in the node "fork" and x_j ($j=2, 4$) the indegree of vertex "T" in the node "join" in the right graphs of them. The constraints $x_1=x_2$ and $x_3=x_4$ exclude the possibility of the third merger to contain redexes of p_5^E or p_6^E, for the graphs including the merger as a subgraph are not members of the graph language defined by the graph grammar in Figure 2.

Beneficially, Theorem 2 ensures that the originally reducible mergers with respect to a pair of productions will never be irreducible after it has been extended. For instance, the pair $\{p_4, p_5\}$ is confluent, so does $\{p_4, p_5^E\}$. Therefore, the P^E with four productions of P extended and others unaltered is confluent.

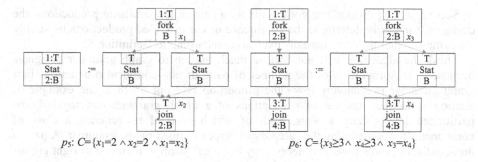

p_5: $C=\{x_1=2 \wedge x_2=2 \wedge x_1=x_2\}$ p_6: $C=\{x_3\geq3 \wedge x_4\geq3 \wedge x_3=x_4\}$

Fig. 6. Extended productions p_5^E and p_6^E.

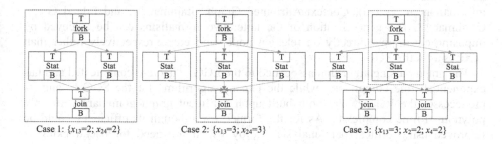

Case 1: $\{x_{13}=2; x_{24}=2\}$ Case 2: $\{x_{13}=3; x_{24}=3\}$ Case 3: $\{x_{13}=3; x_2=2; x_4=2\}$

Fig. 7. Three of the mergers of two graphs isomorphic to $p_5.R$ and $p_6.R$.

5   Discussion and Related Work

To better illustrate the effectiveness of the algorithm *Confluence*, further remarks are given in four aspects. First, the feasibility of the algorithm, especially the participation of graph grammar designers, is argued on account of two factors. One is that how context elements will be arranged in productions of a graph grammar is primarily dependent upon its designer's domain knowledge. Then, it is expected that the designer can sufficiently foresee for each production the possible situations in which it will be applied to derive graphs, and these situations can be helpful for the designer to set the constraint on the production. The other is that all the mergers leading to the non-confluence of a pair of productions can be provided for the designer by the algorithm itself. This will largely assists the designer with the creation of constraints on grammar productions. Therefore, it is reasonable and feasible for grammar designers to design for each production the constraint imposed on its context elements characterizing the situations in which it will be applied.

Second, having created two constraints for a pair of non-confluent productions, the designers can easily determine the confluence of the extended productions by simply checking whether they are mutually exclusive, according to Definition 5.

Third, the algorithm will not impose much burden to graph grammar designers because of the proportion of the number of pairs of non-confluent productions in a graph grammar is relatively low. The proportion is 2 out of 28 in the example of Section 4. In fact, the set of productions of a graph grammar can regularly be partitioned into several subsets, each of which is used to generate a class of components for constituting the category of graphs defined by the grammar. A pair of non-confluent productions that necessarily has a subgraph in common in right graphs is frequently from the same subset. Therefore, the number of pairs of non-confluent productions is small in ordinary graph grammars.

Fourth, this method can be effortlessly generalized to other context-sensitive graph grammar formalisms with context information implicitly indicated, such as Spatial Graph Grammar [5] (SGG, an extended formalism of the RGG with spatial information integrated), Context-Attributed Graph Grammar [8], and Edged Graph Grammar [9]. The generalization of the latter two formalisms can be achieved by imposing constraints directly on relevant nodes and edges respectively rather than vertices as in the RGG.

The graph parsing algorithm associated to the LGG [1] is quite complicated and has exponential time complexity, while the parsing algorithms for the SGG [5] and its predecessor the RGG [2] are both built upon confluent graph grammars with only polynomial time complexity. As for the former, even though its efficiency could be improved using critical pair analysis [11], by which the need for backtracking is reduced via identification of critical pairs, its complexity is not reduced. As for the latter, the confluence condition undoubtedly limits their application scope, since designers may create non-confluent graph grammars in an intuitive way. To overcome the limitation, a more general algorithm has been proposed for the RGG that has no such requirement that the graph grammar is confluent [10], yet the time complexity of it is exponential in the number of nodes of the host graph to be parsed. Comparatively, the algorithm *Confluence* which does not demand much additional effort from graph grammar designers can considerably enlarge the application scope of the efficient SFPA.

6   Conclusion

This paper presents an extended graph grammar formalism of XRGG from that of the RGG, which encloses more detailed context information as constraints in productions that can lead to confluent graph grammars when the redexes of their right graphs under the constraints are mutually exclusive. In the paper, some conclusions characterizing confluent XRGG graph grammars are drawn, and based on them an algorithm is proposed for constructing a confluent XRGG graph grammar from a set of non-confluent RGG productions with their languages being equivalent. This method can not only largely enlarge the application scope of the RGG formalism, but also be easily generalized to other context-sensitive graph grammar formalisms, thus making the efficient SFPA of the RGG that is confined to confluent graph grammars more widely applicable. It is worthy of noticing that the detailed context information included in XRGG productions can be employed to improve the efficiency of parsing algorithms. How to further and properly make use of context information remains to be a significant issue for our future consideration.

Acknowledgments. This work is supported by the National Grand Fundamental Research Program of China (973) under grant 2009CB320702, and the National Natural Science Foundation of China under grants 60571948, 60673186, 60736015 and 60721002.

References

1. Rekers J., Schürr A.: Defining and Parsing Visual Languages with Layered Graph Grammars. Journal of Visual Languages and Computing 8(1), 27--55 (1997)
2. Zhang D.Q., Zhang K., Cao J.: A Context-Sensitive Graph Grammar Formalism for the Specification of Visual Languages. The Computer Journal 44(3), 187--200 (2001)
3. Zhang K., Zhang D.Q., Deng Y.: A Visual Approach to XML Document Design and Transformation. In: 18th IEEE International Symposium on Human-Centric Computing Languages and Environments, pp. 312--319. IEEE Press, Washington, DC (2001)
4. Zhang K., Kong J., Qiu M.K., G.L. Song: Multimedia Layout Adaptation through Grammatical Specifications. ACM/Springer Multimedia Systems 10(3), 245--260 (2005)
5. Kong J., Zhang K., Zeng X.: Spatial Graph Grammars for Graphical User Interfaces. ACM Transactions on Computer-Human Interaction 13(2), 268--307 (2006)
6. Song G.L., Zhang K., Kong J.: Model Management through Graph Transformations. In: 21st IEEE International Symposium on Visual Languages and Human-Centric Computing, pp. 75--82. IEEE Press, Washington, DC (2004)
7. Zhao C.Y., Kong J., Dong J., Zhang K.: Pattern Based Design Evolution Using Graph Transformation. Journal of Visual Languages and Computing 18(4), 378--398 (2007)
8. Zou Y., Zeng X.Q., Han X.Q., Zhang K.: Context-Attributed Graph Grammar Framework for Specifying Visual Languages. Journal of Southeast University (English Edition) 24(4), 455-461 (2008)
9. Zeng X.Q., Han X.Q., Zou Y.: An Edge-Based Context-Sensitive Graph Grammar Formalism. Journal of Software 19(8), 1893--1901 (2008) (in Chinese)
10. Zeng X.Q., Zhang K., Kong J., Song G.L.: RGG+: An Enhancement to the Reserved Graph Grammar Formalism. In: 22nd IEEE International Symposium on Visual Languages and Human-Centric Computing, pp. 272--274. IEEE Press, Washington, DC (2005)
11. Bottoni P., Taentzer G., Schürr A.: Efficient Parsing of Visual Languages based on Critical Pair Analysis and Contextual Layered Graph Transformation. In: 17th IEEE International Symposium on Visual Languages, pp.5--60. IEEE Press, Washington, DC (2000)

Experimental Color in Computer Icons

Yan-Peng Lim[1] and Peter Charles Woods[2]

[1] Faculty of Creative Multimedia, Multimedia University
63100 Cyberjaya, Selangor, Malaysia
[2] Knowledge Management in the Faculty of Creative Multimedia, Multimedia University,
63100 Cyberjaya, Selangor Malaysia

forestlim@yahoo.com

Abstract. Color selection is important as color could adversely affect the entire design if not appropriately applied in icon design. Color is also visually important to make a design more attractive, legible and viewer-friendly. The function of icons in computer display is for direction and navigation. Color and icon are both of equal importance in Graphical User Interface environments. The combination of color and icon makes for a powerful tool that allows information to be pleasantly presented on screen in a manner that is both clear and easy to comprehend. This study divided into Part 1, 2 and 3 comprises three research questions.The objective of this study is to encourage the 73 participants to explore the RGB color model by applying the color for a pair of previous and next icons. The findings from this study show that students still need to be given a systematic list of color combinations for foreground and background color choices.

Keywords: Color, Icon, RGB Color.

1 Introduction

The PC is no longer a luxury item afforded by affluent residents of the first world, but a basic tool akin to the slate boards and notebooks of yesteryear. Current graphic user interfaces have made the on-screen world as comfortable, intuitive and non-threatening a realm to millions of diverse users as the physical environments in which they live and thrive [1]. A key basis of this comfort is the now popular use of iconography and color. The use of colors and icons has parallel roles in providing users with an understandable graphical interface that makes up the main concern of this paper.

In the computer environment, graphic icons act like "road signs" – they guide users towards their destination and lead them quickly towards the content they seek [2],[3]. Icons are used increasingly in interfaces because they are compact, universally understandable pictographic representations of a computer's functionality and processes [4], [5], [6]. Color it is useful to discriminating object and distinguishes the surface received by the eye [7].

M.L. Huang et al. (eds.), *Visual Information Communication*,
DOI 10.1007/978-1-4419-0312-9_9, © Springer Science+Business Media, LLC 2010

In the field of communication, it has been demonstrated that if used correctly, color can be a powerful tool [8]. In the hands of a skilled designer, it allows information to be pleasantly presented on posters, brochures, textbooks, newspapers and computer screens in a manner that is both clear and easy to comprehend. [9], a human factors researcher, believes that if used properly, "color can be a powerful tool to improve the usefulness of an information display." Huang, Shieh and Chi stated that "color should be used in icon design".

The user's ability to recognise the icon does not depend on his or her understanding of a particular language or code of symbols. "The human mind has powerful image memory and processing capabilities" [10] and because of this, people find images "natural" [11]. Icons make up and facilitate an intuitive grasp of the organization and location of information. Baecker et al. reinforced this point, saying that images "... possess more universality than text. Iconic interfaces can, therefore,... reduce the learning curve" in both time and effort, and facilitate user performance while "reducing errors".

Payne mentioned that "Icons have become an inseparable part of Graphical User Interfaces" [11]. In graphical user interfaces, color often helps create distinct groupings of icons [12]. It also allows information to be visually divided in a way that directs a user's attention to meaningful and relevant segments [13], [14]. Color scientists, artists, and designers describe color phenomena in different terms. One useful set of terms is hue, value and chroma [8], [15]. In essence, the word 'hue' refers to the colour in its purest form such as red, yellow, green and blue. The word "value" defines its lightness or darkness based on the amount of black and white mixed into the color. Chroma with saturated color is high in intensity while unsaturated colors look dull.

The purpose of this experimental study is to examine the knowledge of color of this group of participants. Although the participants have been working with Adobe Photoshop for two semesters (28 weeks), the researcher discovered from their class assignments that they hardly use the RGB color model to mix colors. Color plays an important role in design classes. If colour is not appropriately applied, it affects legibility and visualization. It also encourages participants to explore the variety of colors based on the RGB colour model.

Participants from the first two classes who displayed their designs on computer screen were found to use very similar colors. For example, if green was applied, the other colors usually comprised other shades of green. Participants lacked confidence to mix colors in the RGB color model for their designs. The researcher found out from them that this was "because the RGB colour model contains 16 million colors which made it difficult to mix appropriate colors. In addition, they did not have the opportunity to explore all of the colors in previous classes. The main reason for this study is to encourage participants to gain experience and work with the colors provided in Adobe Photoshop.

The preliminary study was divided into three parts. These three sections in the preliminary study included part one (PSP1), part two (PSP2) and part three (PSP3). For part one and part three, the participants carried out self-exploration for colour study. Part two involved choosing their favourite icon to be combined with colors in the RGB model. The results from the preliminary study would be carried forward to the second study, which is based on pre-selected icons and the systematic choosing of colors based on the 16 million colors from Adobe Photoshop.

Although previous researchers have mentioned the importance of icon and color, there is very little literature relating to this field, in particular the combination of color and icon in design using the RGB colour model.

2 Methods

The procedures for conducting Preliminary Study Part 1, 2 and 3 (PSP1, 2, 3) are described in detail in this paper. The three parts of the preliminary study comprise analysis, results and discussion. The following are the research questions:

PSP1: Do all the participants know how to mix colors in the RGB color model?

PSP2: What are participants' favourite 'previous' and 'next' icons?

PSP3: Do participants' confidence in color combination increase with practice?

2.1 Preliminary Study Part One (PSP1): Color Experiment for Icon Design

The first study was to find out how much participants knew about color combinations for screen display based on the RGB color model using pairs of 'previous' and 'next' icons. The researcher also wanted to find out whether they had preference for specific colors for foreground and background. This assignment is fundamental in helping the researcher understand the participants' level of knowledge in using the RGB color model to produce digital colors for icons. It is also important as a gauge to decide the worthiness of continuing along this line of research.

This group of 73 participants learned about color in their Alpha year but their knowledge was confined only to paper and ink as they did not have the opportunity to explore RGB colors on screen displays. In designing or applying colors for screens, a designer must include the numerical color coding to be used. For example, 0,0,255 is a blue color but 0,28,208 and 0, 107, 246 are also blue. Therefore, it is necessary to include the numerical color coding, instead of merely mentioning the name of the color, in order to be more accurate. The researcher found out that the participants did not even bother to apply numerical coding in their color indications. The researcher decided to use a familiar object such as an icon to allow participants to explore and mix colors using the RGB color model. For this assignment, participants have to take into consideration the background color with the icon as foreground color.

2.2 Experimental Procedures for Preliminary Study Part One

A total of 73 participants (second year students from the Digital Media Department, FCM, MMU) were asked to choose 30 combinations of a foreground and background color (based on pairs of 'previous' and 'next' icons). Throughout the experiment, the participants were allowed to explore and mix colors for their color combination choice based on the RGB color model. Participants were also encouraged to use the

RGB color model as a tool to make their individual and independent color selection without having any guidelines to follow. This group of participants was more accustomed to doing assignments based on instructions from the lecturer. Participants were given one week to complete this assignment in class (3 hours) and but were allowed to continue to work at home. Submission of work was to be done on the following week.

2.3 The Results

Based on observations in class for the first two weeks of the design assignment, it was found that the participants were lacking in the area of color exploration. The data was collected from participants who wrote down their experiences throughout their experimental study of color. By grouping similar responses together, the results obtained from the 73 participants are as shown in Table 1.

The second column in Table 1 indicates the number of participants with similar responses. From the results, participants were excited about this assignment as it was their first time doing color combination on computer screen while having the freedom to choose their personal color preferences. However, based on the results, it can be seen that they were unable to make color selections as the RGB model contains 16 million colors and participants did not have the confidence to choose colors. They were also confused between CMYK and RGB colors and lacked knowledge about RGB color combinations. It would seem that participants would have preferred a more structured assignment or one that required them to provide information such as details of icons and on color study rather than choose colors entirely independently.

The results of the study on participants' knowledge of the RGB color model are summarized and presented in Table 1. The main purpose for this study is to provide participants with the opportunity to explore colors for icon design. The results from the assignments were not intended to show the capability of participants working with appropriate colors.

Table 1. Participants' responses on the assignment in study one

Participants' (N=73) responses	No of Participants
Do not understand how or have the knowledge to choose RGB colors.	5
Loved this exercise because there were no guidelines or structures and I could learn from mistakes.	3
I learned and understood colors better through this exercise.	6
I do not know about RGB colors or I may have forgotten.	4
I always have problems choosing the right colors.	9
I do not know about RGB colors or how to apply the right color.	6
I would like to learn more about iconography and colors because it is important for my future career.	4
This assignment helped me to better design my work.	3

Color is important to design a good interactive program.	2
It enhanced my understanding about icon and color design.	2
It was a guide for me to have a clearer view of icons and color design.	2
I would have preferred to have been given some brief theories or concepts about iconography and color design before the assignment.	2
I am not sure at all about iconography and color study.	5
I do not think I have enough knowledge. If we are clear about colors, we can create a better design with a good sense of color combination.	7
I would like to learn more about icons and colors.	5
I am still unclear about and weak in icon and color design. It is important to have guidelines and a structure for iconography and color.	3
Icons and colors are useful for our future careers.	5
	Total = 73

2.4 Discussion

From the findings, it was impossible for the participants to explore all the 16 million colors in the RGB model. Participants selected color combinations in a rather disorganised manner. They also lacked confidence and needed help to choose better combinations to enhance their icon design. This was probably because they did not have enough experience in color studies. Their lack of experience affected the results of their icon appearance on screen displays. Color selection is important as color could adversely affect the entire design if not appropriately applied in icon design. Color is also visually important to make a design more attractive, legible and viewer-friendly.

2.5 Summary

Based on the feedback shown in Table 1, it can be concluded that exploring all 16 million colors in one assignment is problematic. The participants did not know how or where to start based on the RGB color model provided in Adobe Photoshop. They did not even describe about color combination in terms of hue, value and chrome for colors and icons. For the next study, it would be more beneficial for participants to focus on RGB color combinations rather than select icons again. For the second study, participants will be asked to select pairs of 'previous' and 'next' icon designs. In the third study, participants will be asked to apply colors for foreground and background color combinations based on the selected color background and icon. The background colors will be limited to red, green and blue only. These three colors are the basic primary colors that can be mixed to create the color selection.

3   Preliminary Study Part 2 (PSP2): Favourite Pair of Icons

Based on the first study, the researcher found that the participants were not familiar with icons and the RGB color model. Thus, the researcher decided to conduct a second study to allow the participants to select a pair of their favourite 'previous' and 'next' icons. A third study would then be conducted for them to focus on color selection. The overall favourite pair of icons would be used in the third study.

The participants found it difficult to select the icon design due to the wide selection presented. Without any guidelines, it took them a longer time to make their decision. This reflects their lack of experience in independent study and decision-making as they have all this while been used to being given instructions to complete assignments. However, they were excited about the study in spite of their lack of experience in independent exploration.

The same 73 participants from the first study were asked to take part in this second study. Based on the first study, the researcher discovered that the participants had a difficult time choosing both icons and color at the same time. They could not decide which colors were suitable for which icons. In addition, they also lacked knowledge in the RGB color model.

3.1   Experimental Procedures

The participants were given three lessons by the researcher on icon design based on Horton's book, 'The Icon Book' in the three weeks prior to the study. As such, the participants had basic knowledge of icon design before taking part in the second study. A total of 38 pairs of 'previous' and 'next' icon designs in black and white (refer to Table 2) were displayed on a 17-inch screen for participants to view and select. Each pair of icon design had a number below it and participants were only allowed to choose one pair of icons.

The participants were divided into 4 groups. After the procedures had been explained, the participants made their choices, writing them on a piece of paper and then putting the paper into a box. Each group took an average of 23 minutes to complete their selection.

Table 2. 38 pairs of 'previous' and 'next' icon design

I← →I	← →	↵ ↳	↰ ↱	↵ ↳	⇗ ⇖	⇇ ⇉	← →
1	2	3	4	5	6	7	8
← →	◄ ►	⇦⇨	⇦⇨	⇦⇨	⇦⇨	⇦⇨	← →
9	10	11	12	13	14	15	16
← →	← →	◄ →	← →	← →	← →	◄ ►	◄ ►
17	18	19	20	21	22	23	24
← ⇒	◄ ►	⇨◄	↵ ↳	↰ ↱	← →	← →	⇐⇒
25	26	27	28	29	30	31	32
⊂ ⊃	← →	↑ ↓	↖ ↗	◄ ►	‹ ›		
33	34	35	36	37	38		

3.2 The Results

Based on the results, 52 out of 73 participants preferred icon design number 37 (refer to Table 2). The other 21 participants selected a mixture of icon designs. Icon design number 37 shows icons which are triangular and black. They are simple shapes that viewers can easily identify and are very legible, giving them the best appearance on screen.

3.3 Discussion and Summary

Based on observation, this pair of icons usually appears in the World Wide Web and on electronic players. It is possible that participants selected these icons due to their familiarity with them. The knowledge that they gained from lectures helped them to decide simple icon designs for the 'previous' and 'next' icons and on appropriate icons for further study. This pair of icons will be used as objects for foreground color in the third study.

4 Preliminary Study Part Three (PSP3): Color Experiment

Based on the findings from the first study, it was evident that the participants lacked knowledge in the RGB color model. In the first study, the researcher found that choosing icon design and color at the same time proved to be too difficult and confusing for the participants. Hence, the second study focused only on icon design. In this third study, the focus was only on color preference. The researcher hoped that the participants would be able to learn and explore more about the variety of colors through the RGB color model in order to enhance their knowledge as it is very relevant to the study of design.

This study on color exploration was the participants' second experience as it was part of the exploration in the first study. They were asked to use Adobe Photoshop© for their color selection as it is a program they have been using since their Alpha year.

4.1 Experimental Procedures for Preliminary Study Part Three

The participants were given three lessons on basic color study and introduced to the RGB model color combinations prior to the second study. The same 73 participants from the first and second study were asked to take part in this third study. They were asked to choose 30 combinations of a foreground color based on the selected 'previous' and 'next' icons from the second study. In the first study, participants were free to apply any color. They also had to choose the background color from a choice of red, green and blue only. However, they had the freedom to choose any color for the foreground. Their choice of color combinations had to be written in numerical code. Participants were given one week to complete this assignment and were also required to write down their experience of color study. The researcher wanted to find out whether this assignment increased their confidence in applying color in icon through exploration.

4.2   The Results

The findings of the third study showed that there was a lack of consistency in color combination for foreground and background colors. Although this was their second attempt at color combination, the participants did not try out the range of color combinations available. They did not apply much of the range of RGB colors from the top, middle and bottom of the model. The researcher noted that if they chose a bright color, then the rest of the choices would also be bright colors. The same was for choices of dark colors. Furthermore, some of the foreground colors could not stand out against the background color because they used adjacent colors. The results from the participants show an increase in confidence in color combination using the RGB color model. The responses from the participants are summarized and presented in Table 2.

Table 3. Participants' responses on color combination in the third study

Comments (N=73)	No of Participants
We are clear about colors but there are still too many colors in the RGB color model.	11
This study can help me to have a better sense of color combinations to create better designs.	7
I learned something new about RGB color combinations.	3
It is important to go through this study as it gives me a reference for color combinations.	12
If I do not apply color properly, it will affect the icon design.	9
I am interested in icon design and would like to learn more.	3

It is not enough if I leave university without knowledge of color combinations.	3
Experimenting with 2 to 3 colors is adequate for RGB color study.	3
I need a lot of guidelines to help me create good and suitable icons for multimedia applications. Knowledge in color design will help me develop a good sense of color.	6
I would like to learn more about color theories.	3
We lack exposure to color and icon study in our course.	2
We are still very weak in designing color and icons.	5
I still do not quite understand how to choose a good color combination.	6
	Total = 73

4.3 Discussion

The participants' color choice is still weak in spite of learning about Hue, Value and Chroma color combinations in their design class and trying out mixing colored ink on paper. They did not apply the knowledge and skill which they learned from their ink color study to this digital color combination experiment. The researcher had also given them three lessons on digital color combination before the study. The findings from the third study show that students still need to be given a systematic list of color combinations for foreground and background color choices.

4.4 Conclusion and Future Study

The results from the color and icon experiment based on study 1 to 3 show that the participants are gradually improving. They had a better sense of color combination based on exploration. This skill is practical and helps to develop their knowledge of combing colors in icon use.

For the next study, the researcher will cover a range of colors where participants randomly select colors from a scale of 0 to 255 from the RGB color model to experiment with. This is intended to help them have a more in-depth study of color selection. The background colors will be limited to the basic primary colors red, green and blue, which can be mixed to create 16 million colors.

References

1. Huang, Shieh and Chi.: Factor affecting the design of computer icons. International Journal of Industrial Ergonomics. Volume 29, Issue 4, p. 211-218. Elsevier Science (2002).

2. Horton, W.: The icon book: visual symbols for computer system and documentation, John and Sons (1994).
3. Sassoon, R. and A.: Signs, symbols and Icons: Pre-history to the computer age. Intellect Book (1997).
4. Catarci, T., Massari, A. and Santucci, G.: Iconic and diagrammatic interface: an integrated approach. IEEE (1991).
5. Bartram, L. Ware, C. and Calvert, T.: Moving icons: detection and distraction. Human-Computer Interaction-INTRACT'01, 1OS Press (2001).
6 Szabo, A.J.: Graphical user interface for database system, US Patent Issued on. October 12, 1999. Retrieved March. 26, 2007 from: http://www.patentstorm.us/patents/5966126-description.html.
7 Conway, B.R.: Color vision, cones, and color-coding in the cortex. The neuroscientist, Jun 2009, vol 15: pp.274-291 (2009).
8 Marcus, A.: Principles of effective visual communication for graphical user interface design. Human-Computer interaction: toward the year 2000. Morgan Kaufmann Publishers Inc. San Francisco, CA, USA (1995).
9 Murch, G.: Color graphics - blessing or ballyhoo. Human-Computer Interaction: Toward the Year 2000. Excerpt in: Baecker, Ronald M. et al. (etd.). Morgan Kaufmann, (1995), p 442-443.San Francisco, CA (1995).
10 Baecker, R., Small I, and Mander R.: Bringing icons to life. Conference on Human Factors in Computing Systems. Proceedings of the SIGCHI conference on Human factors in computing systems: Reaching through technology. (1-6). ACM Press, New York, NY, USA (1991).
11 Payne R.O and Starren, J.: Presentation discovery: Building a better icon. Conference on Human Factors in Computing Systems. CHI 2006, April 22-27, 2006, Montreal, Quebec, Canada.ACM Press, New York, NY, USA (2006).
12 Meier, B.J.: ACE:A color expert system for user interface design. Symposium on User Interface Software and Technology. Proceedings of the 1st annual ACM SIGGRAPH symposium on User Interface Software. ACM Press New York, NY, USA (1988).
13 Lamberski, R.: The instructional effect of color in immediate and delayed retention. Journal of Instructional Psychology, pp.122-131 (1982).
14 Tufte, E.: Envisioning information. Graphics Press, Cheshire, Connecticut, USA (1990).
15 Pett, D. and Wilson, T.: Color research and its application to the design of instructional materials. ETR&D. Vol. 44, No. 3, 1996. pp.19 (1999).

Hidden Cluster Detection for Infectious Disease Control and Quarantine Management

Yain-Whar Si, Kan-Ion Leong, Robert P. Biuk-Aghai, and Simon Fong

Faculty of Science and Technology, University of Macau
{fstasp,ma46511,robertb,ccfong}@umac.mo

Abstract. Infectious diseases that are caused by pathogenic microorganisms can spread fast and far, from one person to another, directly or indirectly. Prompt quarantining of the infected from the rest, coupled with contact tracing, has been an effective measure to encounter outbreaks. However, urban life and international travel make containment difficult. Furthermore, the length of incubation periods of some contagious diseases like SARS enable infected passengers to elude health screenings before first symptoms appear and thus to carry the disease further. Detecting and visualizing contact–tracing networks, and immediately identifying the routes of infection, are thus important. We apply information visualization and hidden cluster detection for finding cliques of potentially infected people during incubation. Preemptive control and early quarantine are hence possible by our method. Our prototype Infectious Disease Detection and Quarantine Management System (IDDQMS), which can identify and trace clusters of infection by mining patients' history, is introduced in this paper.

Keywords: Infectious Disease, Cluster Detection, Contact Tracing, SARS, Health Care Information System.

1 Introduction

Infectious disease prevention and control is one of the most important research areas in the 21st century. The SARS (Severe Acute Respiratory Syndrome) outbreak in 2003 and recent world–wide avian flu infections have contributed to the urgent need to search for efficient methods for prevention and control of highly infectious diseases. During the SARS outbreak of 2003, there were 8096 probable cases and 774 deaths reported in 29 countries including China, Taiwan, Hong Kong, Canada, Singapore, and Vietnam [1]. According to a WHO (World Health Organization) report [2], three influenza pandemics were recorded in history: "Spanish influenza" in 1918, "Asian influenza" in 1957, and "Hong Kong influenza" in 1968. The 1918 Spanish influenza pandemic killed an estimated 40 to 50 million people worldwide.

When a patient is diagnosed with a highly infectious disease or is suspected of being infected, it is crucial to locate the source of infection (also known as ground zero or super spreader) and to identify future probable cases within a short time. Such measures aim to limit the secondary spread during the outbreak. Although numerous

M.L. Huang et al. (eds.), *Visual Information Communication*,
DOI 10.1007/978-1-4419-0312-9_10, © Springer Science+Business Media, LLC 2010

researches have been undertaken to find effective vaccines and cure, relatively less attention was devoted to devising software programs which are capable of assisting medical planners with rapid decision making in tracing the source of an outbreak based on information obtained from patients. In addition, currently available health–care information systems from hospitals are not designed to deal with the complex and delicate task of managing quarantine for potentially large numbers of suspected cases.

Given this background, this research aims to develop a decision support system which can be used to locate the source of an outbreak by mining clusters and communities from the patients' past activities (testimonies) using techniques from infectious disease control, information visualization, and database management systems. Our developed system also allows categorizing individuals who are likely to be infected into different risk groups whereby members from the high risk group are subjected to immediate isolation whereas members from the low risk group are monitored periodically. The system also includes visualization capabilities for medical experts to analyze the outbreak as the clusters of infection depicted as inter–connected graphs, and graphs for different risk groups. The system is also designed to provide medical planners with quarantine management capabilities such as administering the data of (1) persons currently being quarantined, (2) persons being monitored for symptoms but not in quarantine, and (3) persons who were recently identified for possible infection but have yet to be contacted.

This paper is structured as follows. We briefly review related work in section 2. An introduction of IDDQMS is given in section 3. The extraction of detailed epidemiological history and data analysis is described in section 4. The identification of index case and tracing the source of outbreak is described in section 5. Identifying clusters of infections is detailed in section 6. The need for a quarantine management system is discussed in section 7. We summarize our ideas in section 8.

2 Related Work

Recent work on infectious disease informatics projects also deploys information visualization methods. In the West Nile Virus and Botulism Portal project [3], spatial temporal data sets are overlaid onto geographic maps including land information and demographic data. The Portal System also allows web–enabled access to data related to West Nile Virus and Botulism [3].

SAHANA [4] is an open source disaster management system which is designed to assist in tracking of missing victims and managing of relief supplies. SAHANA is a web–enabled system powered by a set of modules including volunteer coordination, camp management, and supply chain management. The main difference between our work and SAHANA is that our system focuses on discovering hidden clusters of infection using data mining methods whereas the main objective of SAHANA is to provide web–enabled coordination functions to different organizations during a disaster.

Similar methods have been applied in the context of crime data mining. Chen et al. [5, 6] have proposed an automated Social Network Analysis approach to analyze structural properties of criminal networks and to investigate patterns of interaction. Chen et al. use the concept space approach to create networks automatically and deploy the complete–link algorithm for partitioning networks. In [5], MDS algorithm [7] is used to visualize criminal networks.

3 Overview

IDDQMS (see Figure 1) consists of four modules; information extraction, data analysis, hidden cluster detection, and quarantine management. The current system was developed in the Java programming language, JUNG [8], and MySQL database management system [9]. JUNG is a JAVA based open–source software library for the modeling, analysis, and visualization of data.

Once an outbreak is reported, one of the crucial steps is to collect information from the patients and transform them into an appropriate format for data mining tasks. During the course of an isolated outbreak, the load of extracted epidemiological and virological information is generally low. However, the amount of data and its growth may become unmanageable in the event of a major outbreak. In the following section, we describe the information extraction tasks and propose an event–based framework for recording patients' activities.

4 Information Extraction

Recording detailed epidemiological history of relevant travel or contact history was identified as one of the key factors in identifying potential SARS cases [10]. When a patient is diagnosed with a highly infectious disease such as SARS, emergency medical planners may need to decide whom they should quarantine after analyzing the patient's history spanning the entire incubation period (e.g. approximately 10 days for the case of SARS). The information extraction phase can be carried out by a medical practitioner to record patient's name, identification number (or Passport number), address, family members, colleagues or classmates, friends, workplace address, and activities happened during the last 10 days. The extracted information is then structured into a set of events which include four primary attributes: (1) duration, (2) persons contacted during that period, (3) location visited (e.g. enclosed spaces such as offices, air planes, etc.), and (4) food taken. A snapshot of information extraction menus designed for the SARS infectious disease for entering visiting activities is depicted in Figure 2. A separate menu is also designed to view all the visiting activities of the persons in the infectious disease as depicted in Figure 3. As a note, the data in Figures 2 and 3 are simulated data which are used for demonstration only. In a similar way, information on persons contacted and food intake are recorded in the other information extraction menus in our system. Since the proposed system is intended for emergency medical planners, we assume that the confidentiality of the extracted information is guaranteed in a way similar to other health care information systems.

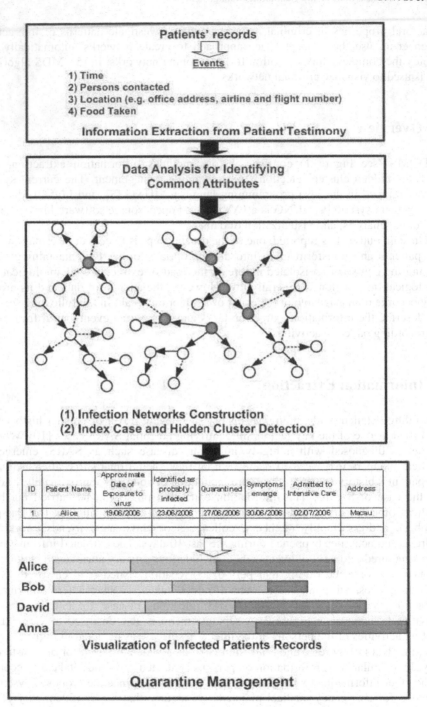

Fig. 1. Overview of the IDDQMS system.

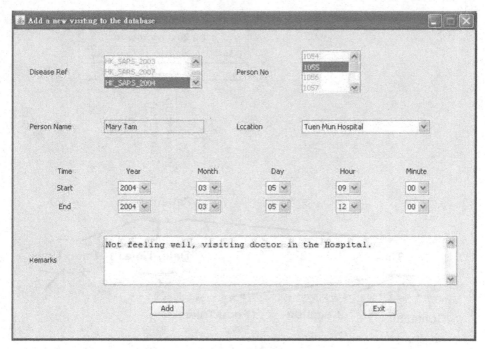

Fig. 2. Entering patient's visiting activities.

Visit No	Disease Ref	Person No	Name	Start Time	End Time	Location
155	HK_SARS_2004	1055	Mary Tam	2004-03-02 09:00:00	2004-03-02 14:00:00	Tai Po Hospital
156	HK_SARS_2004	1056	Nancy Lok	2004-03-02 12:00:00	2004-03-03 10:00:00	Tai Po Hospital
157	HK_SARS_2004	1057	Derek Kwan	2004-03-03 09:00:00	2004-03-03 12:00:00	Tai Po Hospital
158	HK_SARS_2004	1055	Mary Tam	2004-03-03 10:00:00	2004-03-04 09:00:00	Queen Mary Hospital
159	HK_SARS_2004	1054	Peter Chan	2004-03-04 08:00:00	2004-03-04 14:00:00	Queen Mary Hospital
160	HK_SARS_2004	1058	Lina Wong	2004-03-03 08:00:00	2004-03-03 17:00:00	Tai Po Hospital
161	HK_SARS_2004	1059	Tommy Lee	2004-03-04 08:00:00	2004-03-04 12:00:00	Tai Po Hospital
162	HK_SARS_2004	1060	Rita Wong	2004-03-02 08:00:00	2004-03-03 08:00:00	Tuen Mun Hospital
163	HK_SARS_2004	1061	Thomas Chu	2004-03-02 12:00:00	2004-03-03 12:00:00	Tuen Mun Hospital
164	HK_SARS_2004	1060	Rita Wong	2004-03-04 12:00:00	2004-03-04 18:00:00	Tai Po Hospital
165	HK_SARS_2004	1054	Peter Chan	2004-03-05 08:00:00	2004-03-05 12:00:00	Tuen Mun Hospital
166	HK_SARS_2004	1056	Nancy Lok	2004-03-04 12:00:00	2004-03-05 08:00:00	Queen Mary Hospital
167	HK_SARS_2004	1055	Mary Tam	2004-03-05 09:00:00	2004-03-05 12:00:00	Tuen Mun Hospital

Fig. 3. Viewing all the visiting activities of the persons of the infectious disease; the entry in Figure 2 corresponds to the last record in current figure.

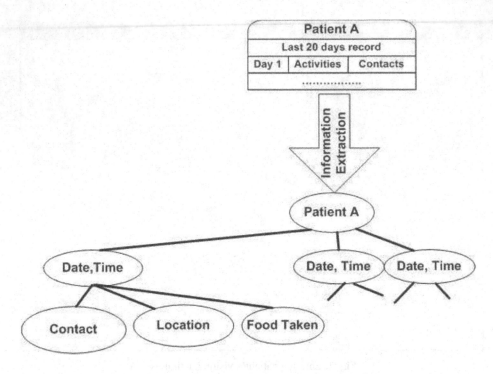

Fig. 4. Extracted episodes from patient's records.

Based on the extracted information, past activities of the patients are constructed as networks of events carrying respective time–stamps (see Figure 4). These networks are then used for visualization of the patients' past activities as well as for mining clusters of infection and identifying index cases.

Based on the extracted information, emergency medical planners may decide on the status of individuals:

– who need to be quarantined immediately as they pose the highest risk (e.g. family member and colleagues who have had direct contact with the patient),
– who should be put under surveillance as they may have been in the same enclosed space, and
– who should be put under notice as they may live in nearby apartments or may have had contact with the patient's family members (secondary infection).

5   Data Analysis for Identifying Common Attributes

The task of tracing an outbreak can be performed efficiently and promptly in combating any infectious disease by comparing elements extracted from the patients' episodes. A similar approach has been used by investigators to detect deceptive information in criminal records [11]. An example of identifying similar elements from extracted patients' record is depicted in Figure 5. Patient 1 and patient 2 from Figure 5 are suspected of having the disease and they both have traveled on the same train (number 15) on 2 April 2006. In that case, one of them may have been carrying the disease at that time or they may have contracted the disease from a third person. Medical experts may then further examine whether patient 1 or patient 2 have contracted the disease from other sources (e.g. contaminated food) or if there was indeed a third person who may have infected them and traveled on the same train. If contraction from contaminated food is less likely, then it is crucial to identify the third person before he/she can spread the disease to the healthy population.

Tracing the source of infection from patients' episodes is a complex and tedious task as the information provided by the patients may contain errors and inconsistencies. For instance, the addresses extracted from two patients may not be identical and hence such overlapping depicted in Figure 5 may not be obvious. In that case, methods from identifying partial matching of strings or locating patterns in strings is employed to find any overlapping and users of the system will be prompted when similarity among elements are identified in the event data. A screen shot captured from the data analysis module of IDDQMS is depicted in Figure 6. In this module, patients' activities are visualized as segmented horizontal bars arranged along a time axis, and overlapping activities are grouped using separate colors. The scale of the horizontal bars is adjusted based on the longest duration from the recorded past activities of the patients being monitored. For the sake of simplicity, locations which appear in more than one patient's past activities are extracted and grouped for visual identification. The data analysis module in Figure 6 provides effective visualization capabilities to medical experts in identifying overlapping locations, and thus points of potential contamination among patients.

However, in the event of a large scale outbreak, pattern matching of extracted information from event data alone may not be sufficient for identifying hidden clusters of infection. For instance, the family members of patient 1 from Figure 5 may have contracted the virus and in turn, they may have passed the disease to other persons before being quarantined. In that case, comparing elements from extracted information alone may not be sufficient to identify probable clusters of infection.

6 Identifying clusters of infection

In [12], we proposed the principles and the algorithms for cluster detection in IDDQMS. The practice of cluster detection is generally referred to as contact tracing in the medical context. The proposed approach utilizes the visiting records are collected and input into the system. For finding clusters of cases and the infection tree of an infectious disease during its outbreak, three main algorithms were presented in [12]: an algorithm for detecting clusters of cases, an algorithm for detecting the infection tree of a cluster, and an algorithm for constructing the infection tree of an outbreak. In worst case scenarios, the space and time complexity of these algorithms is $O(n^2)$.

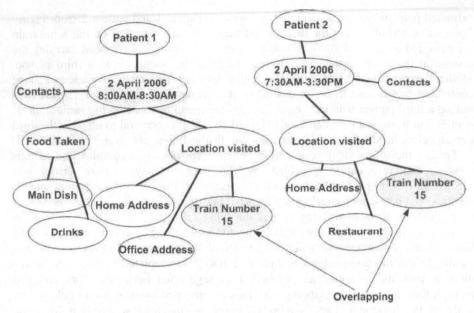

Fig. 5. Example of overlapping in patients' activities.

Based on the theoretical framework proposed in [12], in this paper we tested IDDQMS with a case study of the year 2003 Hong Kong SARS outbreak. In this case study, the real–life information, such as incubation period, onset date, confirmed date, etc, of the patients from the related medical institutions, were collected from [13–16]. To the best of our knowledge, this set of information is adequate to outline the 2003 Hong Kong SARS outbreak in its initial stage. We have used the collected information to fit in the algorithms and have deduced the infection trees (or cluster trees) of the clusters of the outbreak in its initial stage as shown in Figure 7. By following the transmission routes of the patients, we connect the separate individual infection trees, to construct a whole infection tree in Figure 8.

Here we give a brief account of the outbreak as a summary from [13–16]. In Figure 7, *n1* who is a professor from Guangzhou, China is the index case (or index patient) of the outbreak. He came to Hong Kong to celebrate the wedding of his nephew. After a family dinner, he checked into the Metropole Hotel. During the night, the professor felt feverish. The next day, the professor felt so ill that he was admitted to the nearest hospital, Kwong Wah Hospital (KWH). In the hospital, he infected a nurse, *n4*.

In Figure 7, epidemiological investigation confirmed that *n2* was the index case of St Pauls Hospital (SPH) in which *n2* infected three nurses while *n3* was the index case of Prince of Wales Hospital (PWH) in which *n3* infected three doctors and three nurses. In PWH, it then caused a SARS outbreak among the healthcare workers (HCWs). Since then, SARS cases were prevalent in the community as the diseases continued to propagate progressively on their down lines. Further epidemiological investigation showed that the infection of both *n2* and *n3* took place in the Metropole Hotel while the professor was staying there, so the clusters were linked together as shown in Figure 8.

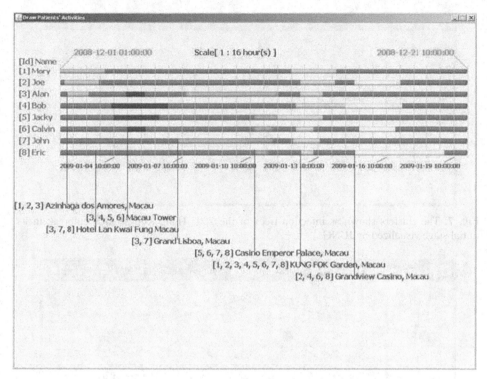

Fig. 6. Tracing/Locating source of infection.

7 Quarantine Management

During the year 2003 SARS epidemic in Beijing, more than a thousand confirmed cases and hundreds of suspected cases were identified. In the event of a major outbreak, the total number of patients who should be quarantined, monitored, or tracked may vastly increase as the disease may spread to densely populated urban areas. Therefore, managing and analyzing infection networks from all these cases and extraction of event data can easily overwhelm an existing information system. In this research, we develop an integrated system which not only includes data mining functionalities as described in the previous section but also contains tailor–made programs for managing patient records and their quarantine status. By using our integrated system, medical workers may decide appropriate quarantine actions such as admitting to intensive care units, isolating in purpose–built medical wards, and monitoring probable cases. These decision making procedures are depicted in Figure 8.

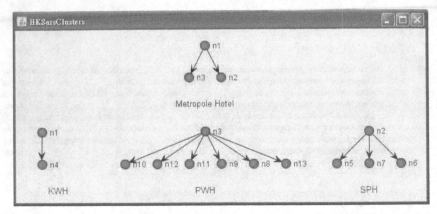

Fig. 7. The clusters shown as infection trees of the 2003 Hong Kong SARS outbreak in its initial stage visualized by JUNG..

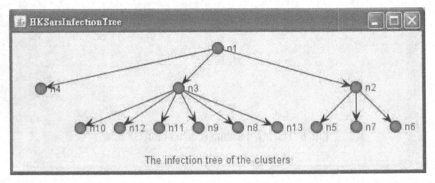

Fig. 8. The whole infection tree constructed from the infection trees in Fig 6 visualized by JUNG.

When a person is reported to have made contact with an infectious disease (through one of the possible mediums such as another person carrying the disease, a common location or contact with an object), he/she will need to be classified as either a confirmed case or a suspected case by observing his/her symptoms and recent medical records. Any suspected case has to be further classified either for quarantine or for monitoring procedure. This situation is depicted in the top part of Figure 8. The quarantine management decision making process described in Figure 8 is applied to every patient who is suspected of being exposed to the disease.

In addition, IDDQMS also provides visualization of incubation period, quarantine, and treatment status for a selected number of patients using scaled vectors. Such capabilities are useful when a number of patients within a cluster need to be compared based on their respective durations. Five time points are used in Figure 9, time of infection (confirmed), quarantined, monitored, onset of symptom, and end date of treatment.

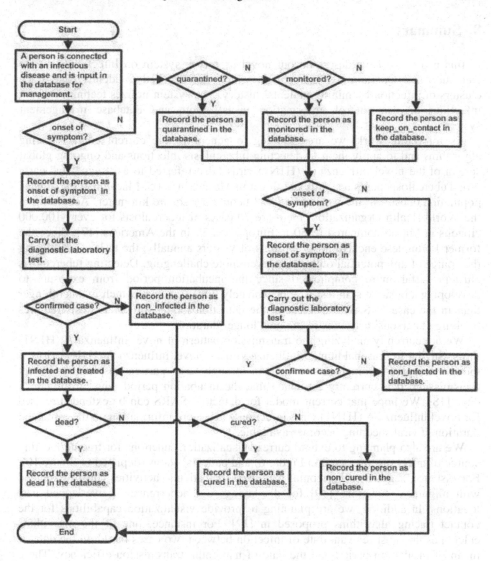

Fig. 9. Deciding patients' status for quarantine

8 Summary

In this paper, we have described our novel prototype system on Infectious Disease Detection and Quarantine Management, which can be used to identify and trace clusters of infection by mining patients' history. The system utilizes techniques from infectious disease control, information visualization, and database management systems.

As for future work, we are planning to generalize the current contact tracing algorithms and to apply them to detecting tuberculosis infections and ongoing global spread of the novel influenza A (H1N1) virus (also referred to as "swine flu" early on). Tuberculosis poses a significant threat to Macau. In 2005, Macau had the highest population density in the world at 18,428 people per square kilometer. According to the World Health Organization, there are 70 cases of tuberculosis for every 100,000 citizens in Macau compared to 50 in Europe and 39 in the Americas [17]. Since the former Portuguese enclave hosts millions of visitors annually, the task of identifying the source of any potential outbreak is even more challenging. Detecting tuberculosis clusters is far more complicated since the incubation period from exposure to developing a positive skin test is approximately 2 to 12 weeks, which is much longer than in the case of SARS. Therefore, the detection model for tuberculosis requires tracking of persons' activities for a much longer duration.

We are currently analyzing the transmission pattern of novel influenza A (H1N1) virus. Similar to seasonal human influenza viruses, novel influenza A (H1N1) virus is thought to spread from person to person through large–particle respiratory droplet transmission. It is currently estimated that the incubation period range from 1 to 7 days [18]. We hope that current model for detecting SARS can be extended/revised for novel influenza A (H1N1) virus infection when more information on the estimated duration of viral shedding becomes available.

We are also planning to extend current visualization functions for tracing/locating source of infections (depicted in Figure 6) and patients' status (depicted in Figure 10). For instance, segmented horizontal bars used for patients' activities can be extended with alignment functions [19] for displaying first occurrence of overlapped past locations. In addition, we are planning to provide visualization capabilities for the contact tracing algorithms proposed in [12]. For instance, one of the algorithms calculates the most relevant date of infection between two cases based on the date of mean of incubation period and the date of maximum transmission efficiency. These dates as well as the meeting dates of patients' can be presented chronologically on one or more horizontal time–lines.

We are also currently testing information extraction software LingPipe [20] to extend our information extraction phase by employing the Named Entity Recognition (NER) algorithm [21] to locate and classify atomic elements. For instance, NER can be used to arrange these elements into predefined categories such as the names of persons, organizations, locations, times, quantities, and numbers.

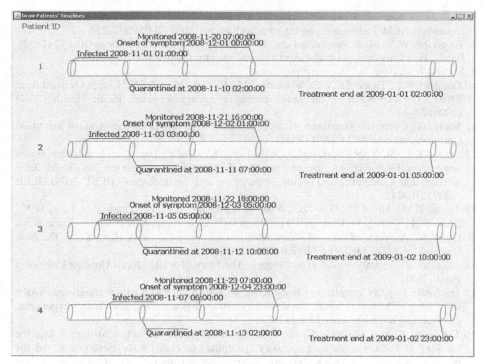

Fig. 10. Visualization of patients' status

Acknowledgments. This work is funded by the University of Macau Research Grant "Hidden Cluster Detection and Visual Data Mining Framework for Infectious Disease Control and Quarantine Management". The authors thank Dr. Lam Chong, Coordinator for Control of Communicable Disease and Surveillance of Diseases, CDC, Government of Special Administrative Region Health Bureau, Macau, for his insightful comments on the project.

References

1. World Health Organization: Summary of probable SARS cases with onset of illness from 1 November 2002 to 31 July 2003. http://www.who.int/csr/sars/country/ table2004_04_21/en/
2. World Health Organization: Ten things you need to know about pandemic influenza. http://www.who.int/csr/disease/influenza/pandemic10things/en/
3. Zeng, D., Chen, H., Tseng, C., Larson, C.A., Eidson, M., Gotham, I., Lynch, C., Ascher, M.: Towards a national infectious disease information infrastructure: a case study in West Nile virus and botulism. In: 2004 Annual National Conference on Digital Government Research, Seattle, WA, IEEE (2004) 1–10
4. SAHANA, Free and open source disaster management system. http://www. sahana.lk/
5. Xu, J.J., Chen, H.: Criminal network analysis and visualization. Communications of ACM 48(6) (2005) 100–107

6. Xu, J.J., Chen, H.: CrimeNet explorer: a framework for criminal network knowledge discovery. ACM Transactions on Information Systems 23(2) (2005) 201–226
7. Torgerson, W.S.: Multidimensional scaling: I. Theory and method. Psychometrika 17 (1952)
8. JUNG, Java Universal Network/Graph Framework. http://jung.sourceforge. net/
9. MySQL homepage. http://www.mysql.com/
10. Goddard, N.L., Delpecha, V.C., Watsona, J.M., Reganb, M., , A., N.: Lessons learned from SARS: The experience of the health protection agency, England. Public Health 120(1) (2006) 27–32
11. Wang, G., Chen, H., Atabakhsh, H.: Automatically detecting deceptive criminal identities. Communication of ACM 47(3) (2004) 70–76
12. Leong, K.I., Si, Y.W., Biuk-Aghai, R.P., Fong, S.: Contact tracing in health-care digital ecosystems for infectious disease control and quarantine management. In: Third IEEE International Conference on Digital Ecosystems and Technologies (DEST 2009), IEEE (2009) 210–215
13. Tsang, K.W., Ho, P.L., Ooi, G.C., Yee, W.K., Wang, T., Chan-Yeung, M., Lam, W.K., Seto, W.H., Yam, L.Y., Cheung, T.M., Wong, P.C., Lam, B., Ip, M.S., Chan, J., Yuen, K.Y., Lai, K.N.: A cluster of cases of severe acute respiratory syndrome in Hong Kong. The New England Journal of Medicine 348(20) (2003) 1977–85
14. Abraham, T.: Twenty–First Century Plague -The Story of SARS. Johns Hopkins University Press (2005)
15. The SARS Expert Committee of Hong Kong: Report of the SARS expert committee -SARS in hong kong: from experience to action. http://www.sars-expertcom. gov.hk/english/reports/reports.html (2003)
16. The Hong Kong Legislative Council: Report of the select committee to inquire into the handling of the severe acute respiratory syndrome outbreak by the government and the hospital authority. http://www.legco.gov.hk/yr03-04/english/sc/sc_ sars/reports/sars_rpt.htm (July 2004)
17. Huxtable, N.: Population density hinders fight against TB. Macau Daily Times (28 June 2008)
18. Centers for Disease Control and Prevention: Interim guidance for clinicians on identifying and caring for patients with Swine–origin Influenza A (H1N1) virus infection. http://www.cdc.gov/h1n1flu/identifyingpatients.htm
19. Wang, T.D., Plaisant, C., Quinn, A.J., Stanchak, R., Murphy, S., Shneiderman, B.: Aligning temporal data by sentinel events: discovering patterns in electronic health records. In: The twenty-sixth annual SIGCHI conference on Human factors in computing systems, CHI '08, New York, NY, USA, ACM (2008) 457–466
20. LingPipe. http://www.alias-i.com/lingpipe/
21. Cohen, W.W., Arawagi, S.: Exploiting dictionaries in named entity extraction: combining semi-Markov extraction processes and data integration methods. In: Tenth ACM SIGKDD International Conference on Knowledge Discovery and Data Mining, KDD '04, New York, NY, ACM (2004) 89–98

Multi-scale Vortex Extraction of Ocean Flow

Cui Xie[1], Lihua Xing[1], Cunna Liu[1], Xiaocong Li[1]

Computer Science Department, Ocean University of China,
[1] 238,Songling Road, Qingdao, Shandong Province,China, 266100
xiecuidlmu@163.com

Abstract. A simple and intuitionistic method of vortices extraction is put forward in this paper. It includes two parts work: the vortex core detection and the vortex hull extraction. The former is based on Sperner's Lemma to label the velocity vector direction of triangle vertices and identifies the fully-labeling triangle cells that are most likely to contain critical points. Combining with triangle subdivision scheme and recording the number and the position of the intersection of a surround streamline with the four axes under the coordinate system originated from the examined vortex core to determine the existence of the swirling flow pattern of vortices. Thus from visual and logical perspective, the actual vortex core regions are verified and the specific swirling range of vortex can be obtained by recording the outmost ring of the intersection points on the swirling streamlines surrounding the examined core. This approach can not only suppress false positives but also make the vortex extraction process easily and efficiently. Furthermore, an interactive vortex-scale factor is used for selective extracting and visualizing the vortex in ocean flow. This method is very flexible for user to perform multi-scale vortex feature analysis. The visualization results of the real ocean investigation data can prove the effectiveness of our method by comparing our results to the method of Jiang's. In addition, it also shows the potential of the interactive visual analysis by the abstraction properties of feature extraction process in physical oceanography and in engineering practice.

Keywords: Vortex detection, feature extraction, ocean flow visualization

1 Introduction

In the recent years, information visualization has become powerful enough to be truly instrumental in many fields, which use of computer-supported, interactive, visual representation of abstract data to amplify cognition [1]. Since vortex is one of the most important features in ocean flow field, which usually can not be rapidly and easily detected from massive ocean flow data. Immediately, directly mining vortices in large scale and complex ocean flow field is a real challenge. This paper focuses on vortex detection and visualization for ocean flow because vortices represent the vortical flow with lots of energy transportation, strongly affecting flow evolution over time. A fundamental issue for vortex extraction is the lack of a unique clear formal

---

M.L. Huang et al. (eds.), *Visual Information Communication*,
DOI 10.1007/978-1-4419-0312-9_11, © Springer Science+Business Media, LLC 2010

mathematical or physical definition of a vortex for it's extremely complex [2] [3]. A typical definition of a vortex is [4] as follows:

A vortex exists when instantaneous streamlines mapped onto a plane normal to the vortex core exhibit a roughly circular or spiral pattern, when viewed from a reference frame moving with the center of the vortex core.

This definition points out that, the identification of a vortex region requires the direction of its core in advance. It is hard to find an effective algorithm supporting this definition. Portela[5] developed a collection of mathematically rigorous definitions for a vortex, using mathematical theory of differential geometry. In fact, vortices have two integral aspects: the central core region and the swirling streamlines surrounding it. Both aspects are indispensable.

The basic idea of this paper is to enrich the vortex core regions detecting method of Jiang's[6], which is a point-based, and local vortex criterion. It is based on an idea derived from a lemma in combinatorial topology: Sperner's lemma[7][8], which labels the velocity vector direction of grid cell vertices to find the candidate vortex core region. But this method will inevitably produce the false positives and it can not distinguish the false positives from the true swirling features due to the local techniques. Although Jiang etc[9] presented a geometric approach to verify an actual vortex core, which is based on the 2 swirling criterion to measure certain differential geometry properties of the surrounding streamlines to determine whether or not these streamlines are swirling around the core region. This process is time-expensive for lots computing on angles and vectors.

In this paper, we present a simple approach to verify actual vortex core in 2D ocean flow field by detect the existence of swirling streamlines surrounding these candidate core regions based on the statistical analysis method. Given a candidate vortex core, we count the number of the intersection of a surround streamline with the coordinate axes originated from the examined vortex core, if the number on four direction of coordinate axes is all more than one, then from a visual and logical perspective, the candidate vortex core is an actual vortex core, since the existence of swirling flow patterns that surround the candidate vortex cores are identified. Meanwhile, the outmost ring of the swirling streamlines surrounding the examined core can be determined by this counting method conveniently, which directly depicts the main range of the vortex hull. So we can easily extract vortices from the complex flow fields. Moreover, this vortex extraction method is simple and efficient, which facilitates the following quick interaction with the flow by users to show the multi-scale vortex visualization.

2. Previous Work

There are many different definitions of vortices and like wise many different vortex detection algorithms, with respective advantages and disadvantages [10]. In this section, we briefly review several vortex detection algorithms in the literature. Though these reviews are not meant to be exhaustive, they provide a fairly good overview of the state of the art in vortex detection. The existing vortex identification methods can be roughly divided into the following types:

1)The method based on solving velocity gradient or derivative

Jeong and Hussain [11] proposed a region-based, local vortex criterion is the λ2 method, which is based on the evaluation of the Jacobian of the vector field by matrix decomposition and eigenvalue computation. The major limitation of λ2, however, lies in its incapacity to isolate individual structures. The parallel-vectors approach [12] is proposed to find the vortex core line where vorticity is parallel to velocity. They use the parallel-vectors operator to trace ridge and valley lines of local criteria like λ2 from local extremum points [13] and to track core lines over time [14]. Recently, Weinkauf et al. [15] have extended this class of algorithms by proposing the coplanar vectors operator, which is applied to the extraction of cores of swirling particle motion in transient flows. However, the higher-order derivatives of the λ2 scalar field that are required by this class of method, which increase the cost of computation and the possibility of detection error to some extent, such as the false core lines. Moreover, since this class of method requires derivative computation it is very sensitive to noise.

2)Geometric methods

Portela [5] using differential geometry to search the vortex comprised of a central core region surrounded by swirling streamlines, which detects vortices by verifying whether or not the winding angle of streamlines around a grid point is a scalar multiple of 2π. Sadarjoen et al. [16, 17] proposed a simplification to the 2D winding-angle method, by using the summation of signed angles along a streamline instead. The main disadvantage with these methods is that they lack a viable 3D counterpart to their 2D approach – winding angles are only meaningful in 2D and also has some false results.

Topology-based methods is also can be used for facilitate the detection of vortex core based on the computing the singularities of the flow fields [18]. Howerver, it also need for the computing of the Jacobian of the vector field by matrix decomposition and eigenvalue computation [19,20]. The approach is so far restricted to regular grid data and the computations involved provide topological information only, and also return false positives in some cases. Other typical algorithms use helicity or magnitude of vorticity for vortex core extraction, including [21,22,23,24]. Other comprehensive related work can be referenced by the paper [25,26].

3 Theoretical Background

Definition 1: Critical Point

All velocity components of point P0 are zero, and there is a neighborhood surrounding P0 in which the velocity vectors of any point except P0 are not zero, then P0 is a critical point.

Theorem 1: Brouwer's fixed point theorem

Every continuous mapping $f: \sigma \rightarrow \sigma$ where σ is a p-simplex has a fixed point[27].

Theorem 2: Sperner's lemma

Sperner's lemma states that every sperner coloring of a triangulation of an n-dimensional simplex contains a cell colored with a complete set of colors. The two-dimensional case is the one referred to most frequently. It is stated as follows:

Given a triangle ABC, we can assign to each vertex of the triangle a unique label A, B or C, which means a fully labeled triangle. Then triangulate it into subtriangles T and assign to each vertex of the subtriangles a label from {A;B;C }. NOTE: any vertex along the edge of a fully labeled triangle can only choose from the labels at the two vertices of that edge. There are no restrictions for vertices introduced inside a fully labeled triangle. If the initial vertices of the triangle ABC are fully labeled, then there exist an odd number of fully labeled subtriangles inside the triangle ABC. Figure 1 shows the idea of Sperner labeling. The original fully labeled triangle ABC is arbitrarily subdivided, resulting in three fully labeled subtriangles that are colored gray. The Sperner's lemma guarantees us that any subdivison of the triangle would result in a fully labeled subtriangle.

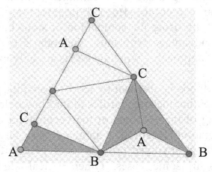

Fig. 1. Sperner labeling and simplicial subdivision of the original fully labeled triangle ABC result in three fully labeled subtriangles, colored gray.

4 Our Algorithm

4.1 Applying Sperner's Lemma into Vector Field

Henle [27] pointed out the duality between fully-labelled sub-triangles and fully-labelled vector field. Furthermore, the author argues that this duality leads to the correspondence between fully-labeled sub-triangles and the fixed points, such as critical points of a vector field. Since Sperner's lemma is a theory in combinatorial topology associated with the Brouwer's fixed point theorem. With proofs of invariance of domain and from the perspective of critical point theory, Sperner's lemma guarantees the existence of at least one critical point under the condition of a fully labeled vector field domain. Furthermore, by subdivision of the original fully labeled triangle more, the fixed points (critical points of a vector field) can be obtained. Hence, the technique provides a way to approximate fixed points.

The goal of this paper is to design a simple and intuitionistic method of vortex extraction, which detects the actual vortex core and the range of vortex. Therefore, we pull Sperner's lemma into our algorithm to increase efficiency in vortex core detection, since Sperner's lemma guarantees the existence of at least one critical point under the condition of a fully-labeled vector field which can be regarded as the candidate of vortex core areas.

4.2   Direction Labeling of Vector Field

Figure 2 illustrates the design principle of labeling each triangle of vector field. The task is to identify the direction ranges of the vector of each vertex in which it point just as labeling a triangulation. In this case, we have three equally spaced direction ranges, as illustrated in figure 2(a), each with a corresponding label chosen from {1;2;3}. A fully labeled triangular cell, in this case, corresponds to a property that each vector at the vertex of a cell point in a unique direction range. This would mean that all three vectors can point in different directions labeled 1, 2 and 3 respectively (figure 2b), forming the fully labeled "triangular" cell accordingly.

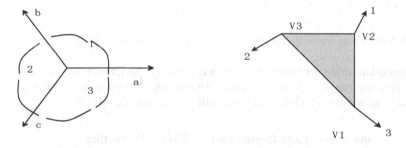

Fig. 2. (a) The three equally spaced direction ranges. (b) Direction labeling of the triangular cell of vector field.

4.3   Vortex Extraction

4.3.1   2D Vortex Core Regions Detection

Unlike the algorithm of Jiang's [6], which examines the velocity vectors of each grid point's immediate neighbors to see if they satisfy the direction-spanning property. If so, then that grid point is extracted as part of a vortex core region. Here, our algorithm is to examine the vector direction of each triangle cell vertex (figure 3), if it satisfies direction distribution principle of fully-labeled cell then this triangle cell is marked as a candidate of vortex core areas (the grey triangles), which need not compute the velocity vectors of the neighborhood points like Jiang's [6]. Thus result in the performance enhancement.

It is fast for the stepwise refinement to discern where the core lies. The detection procedure traverse the labeled flow field, find out the candidate of vortex core triangles and successively approximate the position of the vortex core by subdivision the fully-labeled triangles (as is shown in figure 4) recursively until three vectors of the subtriangle is similar to each another, which means there exist a vector that would be near to all three vectors. The only vector that can point in all three directions at once is the zero vector(i.e., a critical point). Note that when the value of velocity vectors on grid vertex is 0, it is treated specially as a critical point in that case.

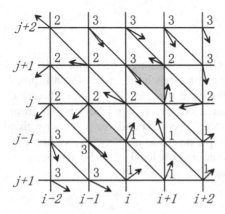   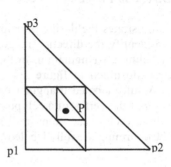

Fig. 3. Vortex core region detection   **Fig. 4.**   Triangle subdivision

Another important thing for vortex extraction is to verify the actual vortex core and identify the swirling range of vortices, which isolates one's feature from other's or other flow patterns nearby. The following part will discuss it in detail.

4.3.2   Verifying the Vortex Core Region and 2D Vortex Extraction

Given a candidate vortex core (as shown in figure 5), where p is the approximation of the position of vortex core and the origin of the coordinate axis x and y, streamline S surrounding the candidate vortex core is generated by integration based on fourth-order Runge-kutta method, eight dots marked as points of intersection of streamline with each axis in four directions. We record the number and the position of these intersections by comparing the magnitude of x, y component of the point p and other points on streamline near axes in four directions. If the number of intersection on four direction of coordinate axis is all more than one, then the existence of swirling flow patterns that surround the candidate vortex cores is identified. So the examined vortex core is an actual vortex core.

Meanwhile, the intersection scheme provides a convenient way to find the swirling range of a vortex. In this paper, the seed points are planted evenly around the critical point p to generate several streamlines. We find out the outmost ring of all the swirling streamlines surrounding one examined core by find the outmost four intersections of the streamline with each axis in four directions, which directly depicts the main range of the vortex hull. So we can easily extract vortices from the complex flow fields with positive vortex core and clearly determined range of vortex.

Moreover, this vortex extraction method is simple and efficient, which facilitates the following quick interaction with the flow by the user to show the multi-scale vortex visualization.

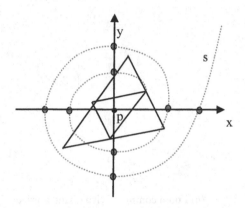

Fig. 5. Verifying the Vortex Core Region and 2D Vortex Extraction

5 Multi-Scale Description of Vortex

Due to the complexity of ocean flow field, visualization of the vortices appears to be a powerful approach to disclose the inherent laws of the flow and understand of vortices and their creation. In order to accurately analyse and visualize vortex feature of complex flow field, we provide a simple tool to perform multi-scale vortices extraction and visualization of flow field. Through the design of scale option factor K, the user can interactively pick the interested vortex in certain scale and achieve vortex feature visualization of different scales which he or she wants to analyze. K is the smallest radius of vortex required to demonstrate. However, on the screen the actual size showed is K/n, n is a scale factor, which is relevant to the distribution of flow data, and it can adjust the size of vortex on the screen. Figure 6 shows the Screenshot of the vortex core extraction of flow field with different scale factor setting of K.

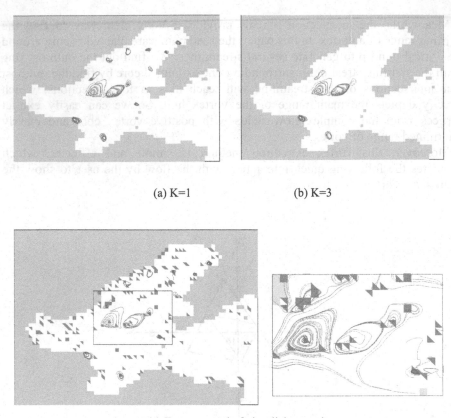

(a) K=1   (b) K=3

(c) Zoom control of visualizing vortices

Fig. 6. The Screenshot of the vortex feature extraction of flow field with different setting of K, where in picture (a) k=1; (b) k=3; (c) shows the zoom control of visualizing vortices.

Contrasting figure 6(a) with figure 6(b), when the scale factor K increases, it can effectively extract the vortex of large-scale flow field (radius of vortex greater than or equal to K), filter out of smaller-scale (radius less than K), and enhance the vortex feature. Selected part of flow field in the left part of figure 6(c) was shown in the right like zooming in. It can show the vortex feature of flow field more effectively and clearly, facilitating the feature observation and study. In figure 6, the background light yellow color denotes the land around the Bohai Sea.

6   Experimental Results and Discussion

We test the approach of vortex extraction proposed in this article with observation data of the Bohai sea (68 × 49) , developed upon a PC with processor Pentium 1.70GHz, CPU 512M and Visual C++ 6.0, the experiment results is shown in figure 7-10. Although topology analysis method shows the whole appearance of the flow (as is shown in Figure 7), the scale of the vortex and their position and range are difficult to obtain clearly. While our method is effective for vortex extraction quickly, combined with multi-scale method, we can get an immediate and direct viewing of the typical feature of whole flow field (figure 8). In figure 8, the red triangle is the candidate vortex core areas. The blue swirling streamlines indicate the swirling pattern around the cores.

Fig. 7. The flow field visualization using topological analysis method

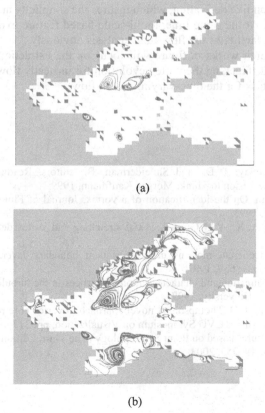

(a)

(b)

Fig. 8. (a) The vortex extraction using our method, (b) is the vortex extraction using Jiang's method[9].

Contrasting figure 7 with figure 8, we can see that the vortex core region obtained by using our method and topology analysis is consistent, which confirms the validity of our method. However our method can shows the vortices more exact and specific, since there are many misguided impressions of existence of vortices in the field. Comparing figure 8 (a) with (b), our method can not only extract the vortex core but also suppress the false positive and determine the swirling range of vortices exactly with a less computing cost, since we just perform value comparison not perform time-consuming computing of so many angles.

7   Conclusions and Future Works

In this paper, a simple and intuitionistic method of vortices extraction is put forward, which focus on two integral aspects: the extraction of actual vortex cores and their swirling range. The method is based on Sperner lemma in combinatorial topology to determine the candidate vortex core region by identifying the fully-direction-labeling velocity vector of triangle cell vertices. Then by a simple counting scheme, the actual vortex core and the swirling range of each vortex can be determined. With comparison to most existing vortex detection technology, this method does not need complex computation like derivation, which insures the simplicity and accuracy of the detecting of vortex. At the same time, multi-scale-based feature extraction is applied in this paper, which facilitates the flow field analysis obviously.

The related research works in future will focus on the extraction of vortex in the 3D flow vector field. Tracking the vortex evolution for unsteady flow fields is another important research task for the time-varying ocean flow.

References

1.Card, S. K., Mackinlay, J. D., and Shneiderman, B., editors. Readings in Information Visualization:Using Vision to Think. Morgan Kaufmann, 1999.
2. J. Jeong, F. Hussain. On the identification of a vortex. Journal of Fluid Mechanics. Vol1, No.285, pp: 69~94, 1995.
3. WU J.-Z., XIONG A.-K., YANG Y.-T.: Axial stretching and vortex definition. Physics of Fluids 17 , 2005.
4. S. K. Robinson. Coherent motions in the turbulent boundary layer. Ann. Rev. Fluid Mechanics, 23, pp: 601~639, 1991.
5. L. M. Portela. Identification and characterization of vortices in the turbulent boundary layer. PhD thesis, Stanford University, 1997.
6. M. Jiang, R. Machiraju, D. Thompson. A novel approach to vortex core region detection. In: Joint Eurographics-IEEE TCVG Symposium on Visualization, pp: 217~225, 2002.
7. Jincheng Xiong,Lectures based on Point Set Topology (The Third Edition), Bejing Education Publishing House. 249~255, 2003.

8. Sobolev, V. I., "Brouwer theorem", in Hazewinkel, Michiel, Encyclopaedia of Mathematics, Kluwer Academic Publishers, 2001.

9. M. Jiang, R. Machiraju, and D. S. Thompson, Geometric Verification of Swirling Features in Flow Fields. In IEEE Visualization '02, pages 307–314, 2002.

10. POST F. H., VROLIJK B., HAUSER H., LARAMEE R. S., DOLEISCH H.: The state of the art in flow visualization: Feature extraction and tracking. Computer Graphics Forum 22, 4 (2003), 775–792.

11. JEONG J., HUSSAIN F.: On the identification of a vortex. Journal of Fluid Mechanics 285 (1995), 69–94. 6 (1990), 721–724.

12. PEIKERT R., ROTH M.: The "parallel vectors" operator –a vector field visualization primitive. In Proc. IEEE Visualization '99 (1999), pp. 263–270.

13. SAHNER J., WEINKAUF T., HEGE H.-C.: Galilean invariant extraction and iconic representation of vortex core lines. In Proc. EG / IEEE VGTC Symposium on Visualization (Eurovis)(2005), pp. 151–160.

14. STEGMAIER S., RIST U., ERTL T.: Opening the can of worms: An exploration tool for vortical flows. In Proc. IEEE Visualization '05 (2005), pp. 463–470.

15. THEISEL H., SAHNER J., WEINKAUF T., HEGE H.-C., SEIDEL H.-P.: Extraction of parallel vector surfaces in 3D time-dependent fields and application to vortex core line tracking.In Proc. IEEE Visualization '05 (2005), pp. 631–638.

16. WEINKAUF T., SAHNER J., THEISEL H., HEGE H.-C.: Cores of swirling particle motion in unsteady flows. IEEE Transactions on Visualization and Computer Graphics (Proc. Visualization 2007) 13, 6 (2007), 1759–1766.

17. I. A. Sadarjoen. Extraction and Visualization of Geometries in Fluid Flow Fields. PhD thesis, Delft University of Technology, 1999.

18. I. A. Sadarjoen, F. H. Post, B. Ma, D. C. Banks, and H.-G. Pagendarm. Selective Visualization of Vortices in Hydrodynamic Flows. In Proc. Visualization '98, pages 419–422,558, 1998.

19. F. H. Post., W. C. DeLeeuw, I. Ari Sadarjoen, et al. Global, geometric, and feature-based techniques for vector field visualization. Future Generation Computer Systems, pp: 87~98, 1999.

20. SCHEUERMANN G., HAGEN H., KRÜGER H., MENZEL M., ROCKWOOD A.: Visualization of higher order singularities in vector fields. In VIS '97: Proceedings of the 8th conference on Visualization '97 (1997), IEEE Computer Society Press, pp. 67–74.

21. BAUER D., PEIKERT R.: Vortex tracking in scale-space. In Proc. EG / IEEE TCVG Symposium on Visualization '02 (2002), pp. 233–240.

22. SINGER B. A., BANKS D. C.: A predictor-corrector scheme for vortex identification. Tech. Rep. ICASE 94-11, NASA CR-194882, 1994.

23. SAHNER J., WEINKAUF T., HEGE H.-C.: Galilean invariant extraction and iconic representation of vortex core lines. In Proc. EG / IEEE VGTC Symposium on Visualization (Eurovis) (2005), pp. 151–160.

24. SUJUDI D., HAIMES R.: Identification of swirling flow in 3D vector fields. Tech. Rep. AIAA 95-1715, Dept. of Aeronautics and Astronautics, MIT, Cambridge, MA, 1995.

25. JIANG M., MACHIRAJU R., THOMPSON D.: Detection and visualization of vortices. In The Visualization Handbook, Hansen C. D., Johnson C. R., (Eds.). Elsevier, Amsterdam, 2005, pp. 295–309.

26. HASSOUNA M. S., FARAG A. A.: On the extraction of curve skeletons using gradient vector flow. Proc. ICCV 2007 (2007), 1–8.

27. M. Henle. A Combinatorial Introduction to Topology. Dover, 1979.

A Novel Visualization Method for Detecting DDoS Network Attacks

Jiawan Zhang[1], Guoqiang Yang[1], Liangfu Lu[2,*], MaoLin Huang[3], Ming Che[1]

1. School of Computer Science and Technology, Tianjin University, Tianjin ，P.R.China;
2. Mathematics Department, Tianjin University, Tianjin, P.R.China, 300072;
3. Faculty of information Technology, University of Technology, Sydney, Australia
*Corresponding Author E-mail: liangfulv@gmail.com

Abstract. With the rapid growth of networks in size and complexity, netwok administrators today are facing more and more challenges for protecting their networked computers and other devices from all kinds of attacks. Unlike the traditional methods of analyzing textual log data, a visual interactive system called DDoSViewer is proposed in this paper for detecting DDoS kind of network attacks. DDoSViewer is specifically designed for detecting DDoS attacks through the analysis of visual patterns. Wc will discuss the data sources, visual structures and interactive functions that are used in the proposed visualization system. We will also discuss the advantages and disadvantages of the existing visual solutions for DDoS detection. The extraction and analysis of network data, the calculation and display of graphic elements' attributes and the pre-characteristics of DDoS attacks are all included in the new visualization technique. The experiments showed that the new system can detect DDoS attacks effectively.

Keywords: network security; DDoS attacks; information visualization; port scan

1   Introduction

Networks and data communication systems are becoming more and more complex [1]. However, there is no absolute solution to secure a networked system perfectly. Most existing network security techniques and tools still rely heavily on human detection of intrusions. These techniques require users to analyze and detect the anomalies and intrusions manually. To enhance the human perception and understanding of all kinds of network intrusion and attacks, network visualization has become a hot research field in recent years that attempts to speed up the intrusion detection process through the visual analytics. Unlike the traditional methods of analyzing textual log data, visualization can increase the efficiency and effectiveness of network intrusion detection significantly. It can not only help analysts to deal with the large-volume of analytical network data effectively, but also help network administrators to detect anomalies through the pattern recognition in visual graphs. It can even be used for discovering new types of attacks and forecasting the trend of unexpected events.

M.L. Huang et al. (eds.), *Visual Information Communication*,
DOI 10.1007/978-1-4419-0312-9_12, © Springer Science+Business Media, LLC 2010

Some visualization techniques and tools have been proposed recently for detecting hostile attacks [2,3,4]. However, these techniques are more focusing on how to produce novel visual structures for general real-time monitoring of large volume of network traffic data, and they are not specifically designed for detecting DDoS (Distributed Denial of Service) attacks. Up to now there are no specific tools available for DDoS attack detection.

This paper proposes a novel visualization system called DDoSViewer that uses a new visual representation to display the main features and characteristics of DDoS attack. The proposed technique utilizes a variety of visual elements to map a collection of datagram to the graph for emphasizing DDoS patterns. The focus+context viewing and interaction techniques used in our system will also be discussed. The experiments have shown that the new system is able to detect port scans and many other kinds of DDoS attacks quickly and effectively.

The rest of the paper is organized as follows. Section 2 presents some of the related work. We describe our approach in section 3, including the details of data collection and processing, nodes coordinates calculation and their visualization. Case studies are shown in section 4. Finally, we give the conclusions and future work in section 5.

2   Related work

The study of DDoS attack detection has been popular for the last decade. Some works have been done in finding ways to detect DDoS attacks in large-volume alerts produced detection tools which employed visualization methods. Pearlman [5] proposed a new visualization in 2007 for network security by approaching the problem from a service-oriented perspective. This research provides a real time system for network administrators to monitor service activities, enabling for the early stage detection of attacks, including Denial of Service (DoS) attacks. Chris Lee etc [6] proposed a VisualFirewall in 2005 that seeks to aid in the configuration of firewalls and monitoring of networks by providing four simultaneous views that display varying levels of detail and time-scales as well as correctly visualizing firewall reactions to individual packets. Christos etc [7] introduced 3D interactive auto-stereoscopic (AS) displays for visual representations of attacks.

Although the above visualization techniques can assist network analysts in analyzing abnormal (or unusual) patterns of network data in the early stage of network intrusion detection, they can only produce alarms and in most cases the accuracy rate of alarming for real attacks is very low. Therefore, the actual identifications and classifications of a variety of attacks are still rely on human brain. Furthermore, so far there is no specific tools developed for detecting DDoS attacks, and the above approaches are only focusing on the visualization of suspicious network activities and they do not help in the analysis of network event characteristics.

In this work, we focused on both the analysis of DDoS features and the investigation of novel visual representations. This enables the new system work effectively in some complex situations for DDoS attack detections, such as Smurf attacks detection, port scans detection etc.

3   Our new approach: DDoSViewer

Network Visualization (NV) is a part of the information visualization. The main steps involved in NV are 1) data collection and pre-process, 2) visual mapping, and 3) graphics generation. we will discuss these three steps with the details in the design stage.

3.1   Data collection and pre-process

The current network security requires information visualization to be able to display sufficient network information with a meaningful visual format, and efficiency in visual processing. The multiple dimensional visualization of raw network data is one of such meaningful visual format that attracted many researches working on it for several years. In multi-dimensional visualization, the dimension reduction technique is essential to be considered first, and then the format of the data including source IP, destination IP, destination port, packet size and time-stamp can be obtained accordingly.

To analyze the raw data, a hash-table is used for data storage, and the keywords are expressed by the strings, which includes three parts: *source IP, port numbers* and *time-stamps* which are chosen by user to set the time interval $\mathcal{K}$. Any difference between the three parts in the new element will be inserted into the hash-table, and will be rendered as a new node, which expresses the relationship between the two hosts. The value corresponding to each keyword denotes the total amount of data transmitted between two linked nodes. After having selected a time interval $\mathcal{K}$ in the interface (default value as the beginning of the programming), $\mathcal{K}$ will be introduced into the statistical module. Statistical module uses the window that built by the scale of $\mathcal{K}$ processing the data from the beginning of the raw data to the end. The data which included in the scale of $\mathcal{K}$ will be processed and the others will not.

3.2   Drawing of Nodes

The key to the visualization is drawing of the nodes for showing the present network status. Thus, the calculation of the geometrical positioning of nodes is essential. In our work the principle of the nodes positioning is based on the geometrical distance and the communication frequency between the new node and the center node which have the same trend. That is, if a console node communicates with the central console node more frequently, it will be moved away from the central one more further. There are two core issues for better visualization:

1). Positioning a new node: Based on the communicated frequency, the liner distance between a Console Node n_c and the Central Console Node n_{cc} is calculated by the following model. First, we define some constants and valuables:

F_{max} is the maximum communicated frequency, F_{min} is the minimum communicated frequency, and R_{max} is the maximum radius of the available

screen space. R_{unit} is a unit radius that is defined in formula (2), where
d represents the greatest difference of the frequency defined in formula (1).

Suppose that F_n is the frequency value of a new console node n_c calculated from statisticas. R_n is the radius of n_c, defined by formula (3). After we get the radius, we can calculate the geometrical position of n_c, $D(n_c)=(x, y)$ using formula (4).

In Fig. 1, the point O is the Center Console Node n_{cc}, and n_c is a new console node. The absolute value of the abscissa of the point X is in the range of $[-R_x, R_x]$. Using the formula (4) we can obtain the values, and then we can calculate y using (5).

$$d = F_{max} - F_{min} .\tag{1}$$

$$R_{unit} = \frac{R_{max}}{d} .\tag{2}$$

$$R_x = F_x \times R_{unit} .\tag{3}$$

$$x = Random(\ ) \times R_x .\tag{4}$$

$$R_x = \sqrt{(x-x_0)^2 + (y-y_0)^2} \rightarrow y = \pm\sqrt{R_x^2 - (x-x_0)^2} + y_0 .\tag{5}$$

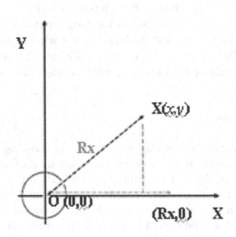

Fig. 1. Node positioning

2) Node overlapping problem If some nodes are overlapped in the visualization, then the main graphic attributes of nodes may not be completely displayed. For example, the attributes of the line between console nodes and the colors of the console nodes may be hidden when node overlap occurs. In our visualization, we addressed

this problem with an effective and simple method. When a new node is to be generated, the visualization will search all the existing positions of displayed nodes. If there is a node overlap found, the system will then re-generate a new X coordinate, and calculate Y coordinate using the formula (5) for the new node. However, this problem cannot be completely solved. Although the scope of the X, Y coordinates is sequential and unlimited, we still can not obtain a clear view with no node overlaps if the number of nodes to be displayed in the same radius becomes large. Considering the arc length with the same radius is always limited, and the size of the node can't be modified. The technique of "magnifier" can be used to solve this problem by adjusting R_{unit} defined in the formula (2) manually. It can be enlarged in the local view through adjusting the parameters to achieve amplification.

3.3   Graphic Design of Nodes

After the positioning of nodes, the information of the geometrical location of nodes (date items) will be stored in the program, and then the nodes will be drawn graphically through the graphic design module, which is depends on the domain characteristics of nodes. The graphic design model can be described below:

The networking connection between a node n_c and n_{cc} can be described by several domain specific attributes and the value of these attributes can be measured in a certain time interval $\mathcal{K}$. In our graphic design, we attempted to map the domain specific attribute (the networking attributes) into the graphical attributes (the coloring scheme). For example, we may use the "red" color to represent the high value of a certain networking attribute. In our graphic model, a console node n_c is consisting of a range of concentric circles, and the number of ports involved in the networking connection is represented by the color contrast grade.

Each node is displayed as a range of concentric circles (see Fig 2) which have equal width between each pair of circles, C_i and C_{i+1}. Each circle displays one color in a N-level color scheme (see Fig 2). The color of the consecutive circle is mapped the consecutive color ribbon. At the same time the width P express the distance between the consecutive colors. The width P is determined by the number of the ports connected between nodes n_c and n_{cc}. If the connection is based on many ports, the span between colors would be very larger and the nodes' color contrast grade would be stronger. Oppositely, the span could be smaller and its color trends to be a single color. All of these are shown in Fig. 2[13]

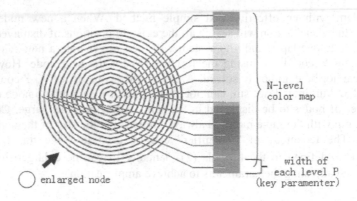

Fig. 2 The color scheme in node design

For detecting different abnormities and identifying different types of attacks, we need to utilize different value of the parameters. Therefore the adjustment of the parameter is critical to the system. The characteristics of DDoS attack are best to be presented by multidimensional and large scale visualizations. However the limit of the display space is a problem. Therefore, the interactive zooming technique is crucial for users to have both the global view of the nodes interaction and the detail view of a node that can help in identifying the type of attacks. In this model, the user can adjust the value of parameters in the system to catch the optimized view for detecting abnormal actions. For example, the user can manually adjust the length of radius that liking a "magnifying glass" can help user to observe the local characteristic of the graphic, and the time intervals K in the real-time raw data to catch the most identical features of DDoS attacks.

4   Case studies

In this section we describe several examples of using DDoSViewer for visual analysis and detection of DDoS attacks. One remarkable characteristic of DDoS attacks can be described as that in a short time the attacked host receives a lot of date packets sending from a large number of strange IP addresses. For example, the characteristic of Smurf attack is that in a short time one host may communicate with large number of IP addresses simultaneously and most of the source IP addresses have never appeared in the current host before. The experimental data we used are caught from LNA in the Image and Graphics Institute, Tianjin University.

By using DDoSViewer, DDoS attacks can be detected very easily. In Fig. 3, there are three isolated nodes around the center host. The interactive technique allows the exploration of detailed attributes of nodes easily. By having a close look of detailed data shown in Fig 3, we can easily find that these network connections are mainly related to port 23 and 80. Thus, the analysts may assume that these nodes may perform data transmission services, such as ftp transmissions (in port 23) or web transmissions (in port 80), and there is nothing abnormal. In comparison with other nodes, the line color between the third node and the center host is deeper (the red color), and from Fig. 3, we can see that there are more data communications with port 43969 of one host. If we want to have a close look of this host, we can get its IP address 59.247.12.45.So it can be assumed that the user is using a file transfer service. We can also see that there are many nodes surrounding the center node in Fig. 3. After interactively exploring the detail of nodes, we discovered that all of the surrounding nodes have different IP addresses. All log data items are collected in the same time interval: $\mathcal{K}$=2. By looking over detailed information of these surrounding nodes, we also found that all the nodes are connecting with the port 7 of the center host at the same time: 2008-4-2 18:05:02. The sizes of the transmitted data between the surrounding nodes and the center host are very small. It could be just an Echo message, such as a returned message after the host receives a PING packet. Therefore, we can then identify this visual pattern shown in Fig 3 as a typical "Smurf" attack, which is quiet different from the other patterns we generated through DDoSViewer. In fact, our system can detect Smurf attacks that are not restricted to the Echo package. Rather the system could extend its pattern recognition capacity to identify other abnormalities (or attacks) based on the identical features of the visualization generated by DDoSViewer.

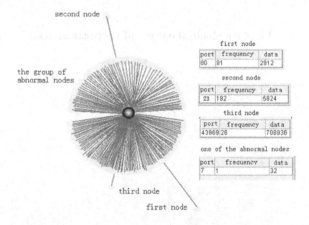

Fig. 3 An identical pattern of Smurf attack: many nodes surrounding the host node with small data packages and stranger IP addresses.

Port-Scan is another preliminary type of DDoS attacks and we can also extract its main domain specific features and generate identical visual patterns for analysts to quickly detect it. In Fig. 4, we can see that there are two obvious abnormal nodes, the first node and the second node. In comparison with other nodes in visualization (for example nodes in group A), these nodes are far away from the center node. The main features of abnormal nodes are that they have more color levels than others and they also have a larger amount of networking traffic (data transmissions) with the center node. In Fig. 5, we can easily find that in each port of the abnormal nodes only transfer a very small data package, but the scanned ports received a large-volume of data, and the colors of the abnormal nodes are very complicated. We believe that the identical visual pattern generated as shown in Fig 4 is clear enough for network analysts to easily and quickly identifying the port-scan attackers.

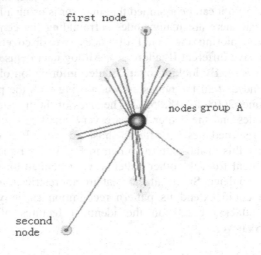

Fig. 4 An identical pattern of port-scan attack.

traffic of the first node			traffic of the second node			one of the node group A		
port	frequency	data	port	frequency	data	port	frequency	data
3611	1	32	12511	1	32	80	1	3941
43615	1	32	44949	1	32			
23767	1	32	25172	1	32			
31231	1	32	24083	1	32			
13098	1	32	38784	1	32			
3431	1	32	32196	1	32			
4241	1	32	257	1	32			
41600	1	32	31956	1	32			
62162	1	32	60017	1	32			
61449	1	32	51542	1	32			
1108	1	32	44648	1	32			
37170	1	32	15389	1	32			
17183	1	32	469	1	32			
10717	1	32	43454	1	32			
36134	1	32	25438	1	32			
36679	1	32	6280	1	32			
24714	1	32	23892	1	32			
26489	1	32	39437	1	32			
49049	1	32	37255	1	32			
37614	1	32	21851	1	32			
17777	1	32	13131	1	32			
22928	1	32	18796	1	32			
62017	1	32	29221	1	32			
2524	1	32	57906	1	32			
10727	1	32	3704	1	32			
20186	1	32	64333	1	32			

Fig. 5 the detail information of nodes displayed in Fig 4.

5 Conclusion and future work

This paper proposed a new visualization method called DDoSViewer that focuses on creating of identical visual patterns for analysts to effectively and efficiently detect DDoS attacks, such as the Smurf attacks and port-scan attacks. The new system is working mainly based on the statistics model of the time-stamp, rather than the traditional packets analysis model. Interaction techniques with multiple-views are used to display both the overall view of the linkage attributes and the detailed view of node attributes, which are represented by geometrical attributes and rich graphic properties, such as colors and the locality of nodes.. The experiments have shown that the pattern of the attacks can be distinctively generated in DDoSViewer and these identical patterns could significantly assist the analysts in detecting DDoS attacks. In the future, we plan to draw the graphics in 3D visual spaces, and set up more visualization functions to improve the representations of nodes that could increase the accuracy of network attack detections.

Acknowledgments. This work has been supported by National Natural Science Foundation of China under Grant No.60673196; the Natural Science Foundation of Tianjin, P.R. of China, under Grant No. 07F2030.

References

1. X. Yin, W. Yurcik,: et al. "VisFlowConnect: NetFlow Visualizations of Link Relationships for Security Situational Awareness." Proceedings of the 2004 ACM Workshop on Visualization and Data Mining for Computer Security. Washington, DC, USA, ACM Press.
2. Robert F. Erbacher.: "Visual traffic monitoring and evaluation". In Proceedings of the Conference on Internet Performance and Control of Network Systems II, 2001, pp 153–160.
3. L. Girardin and D. Brodbeck.: "A visual approach for monitoring logs". In Proceedings of the 12th Usenix System Administration conference, 1998, pp 299–308.
4. Chris Muelder, Kwan-Liu Ma and Tony Bartoletti,: A Visualization Methodology for Characterization of Network Scans, Visualization for Computer Security, 2005, pp.29-38
5. J. Pearlman, P.R.: Visualizing Network Security Events Using Compound Glyphs from a Service-Oriented Perspective. In Visualization for Computer Security. VizSEC 2007: Proceedings of the Workshop on Visualization for Computer Security, 2007, pp. 131~146.
6. Chris P. Lee, J.T., Nicholas Gibbs,Raheem Beyah,John A. Copeland.: Visual Firewall: Real-time Network Security Monitor. in IEEE Workshop on Visualization for Computer Security 2005 (VizSEC 05), 2005:129~136.
7. Christos Papadopoulos, C.K., Alexander Sawchuk, Xinming He. CyberSeer: 3D Audio-Visual Immersion for Network Security and Management. in the 2004 ACM Workshop on Visualization and Data Mining for Computer Security. 2004. Washington, DC, USA: ACM Press,pp:90~98.
8. A. Hussain, J.H.a.C.P.: A Framework for Classifying Denial of Service Attacks. in Sigcomm 2003. Karlsruhe, Germany. 2003:99~110.

9. Muelder, C., Ma, K.L., Bartoletti, T.: A visualization methodology for characterization of network scans. Visualization for Computer Security, IEEE Workshops, 2005, pp. 4 - 4.

10. Conti, G., Abdullah, K.: "Passive visual fingerprinting of network attack tools". VizSEC/DMSEC ' 04: Proceedings of the 2004 ACM Workshop on Visualization and Data Mining for Computer Security, 2004,pp. 45 - 54

11. Jonathan McPherson, Kwan-Liu Ma, Paul Krystosk, Tony Bartoletti, Marvin Christensen.: Portvis: "A tool for port-based detection of security events". In: ACM VizSEC 2004 Workshop, 2004, pp. 73 - 81

12. Pin Ren, Yan Gao and Zhichun Li,: "IDGraphs: Intrusion Detection and Analysis Using Histographs", Visualization for Computer Security, 2005, pp.39-46

13. Stuart K. Card, Jock D. Mackinlay and Ben Shneiderman,: "Readings in information visualization: using vision to think", Morgan Kaufmann Publishers, 1999

14. Rawiroj Robert Kasemsri,: "A Survey, Taxonomy, and Analysis of Network Security Visualization Techniques": [Master Paper], USA, Georgia State University, 2005

15. Richard A. Becker, Stephen G. Eick, and Allan R.Wilks. :"Visualizing network data". IEEE Transactions on Visualization and ComputerGraphics,1995 1(1):pp.16–28.

16. Prefuse, http://www.prefuse.org/

17. Mukosaka, S.;,Koike, H.:"Integrated visualization system for monitoring security in large-scale local area network Visualization",APVIS '.2007 6th International Asia-Pacific Symposium, 2007,pp.41– 44

18. Musa, Shahrulniza, Parish,etc.: "Visualizing Communication Network Security Attacks", Information Visualization,IV '07. 11th Internati onal Conference, 2007, pp. 726-733

19. Pavel Minarik1 , Tomas Dymacek.: "NetFlow Data Visualization Based on Graphs", In Visualization for Computer Security ,VizSEC 2008: Proceedings of the Workshop on Visualization for Computer Security, 2008, pp. 144-151

A Pool of Topics: Interactive Relational Topic Visualization for Information Discovery

Inessa Seifert and Michael Kruppa

German Research Center for Artificial Intelligence (DFKI GmbH),
Alt-Moabit 91c, Berlin, 10559, Germany
inessa.seifert@dfki.de, michael.kruppa@dfki.de
http://www.dfki.de

Abstract. In this paper, we present a novel relational visualization that supports people at information discovery tasks in digital libraries. This visualization displays search query results structured into topics and highlights the intersections between them. The proposed visual representation introduces interactive drag-and-drop operations for manipulation of the generated topics. These operations mirror the human online searching strategies that involve boolean AND, OR, and NOT operators. In doing so, the information seeker can refine (or relax) a search query in an interactive way during a focusing or a defocusing phase. The intersections of topics are made explicitly visible to enable the information seeker to avoid frustrating "no hits" situations.

Keywords: information visualization, boolean operators, information discovery, online search strategies.

1 Introduction

Modern digital libraries provide a seamless access to a vast amount of scientific literature. The amount of information available on the Internet has tremendously increased over the past years. Retrieving an article of a known title (or an author) is sufficiently fast and easy today. However, finding appropriate literature on a topic the information seeker is not familiar with is a time consuming task. During information seeking and discovery tasks, the lack of domain specific knowledge leads to underdetermined and unclear search goals that are reflected in the definition of vague search queries. Such search queries contribute to a huge number of resulting hits. Examining a great amount of scientific literature is a time consuming endeavor. Therefore, such vaguely defined queries are usually followed by a more focused formulation of different search terms combined with boolean AND, OR, and NOT operators. Yet, too many, or too specific search terms often deliver no results[1]. In such situations, people try to broaden their search goals by returning to less specified queries. The information seeking process encompasses series of focusing phases that

---

[1] up to 30-50% of queries containing boolean operators together with precisely defined search terms deliver no results [1,2]

M.L. Huang et al. (eds.), *Visual Information Communication*,
DOI 10.1007/978-1-4419-0312-9_13, © Springer Science+Business Media, LLC 2010

are followed by defocusing phases, in which people examine the retrieved hits, learn more about the topic, and continuously change their attitude toward the search goals.

In this paper, we present a novel relational visualization approach that displays query results structured into topics and highlights the intersections between them. The proposed visual representation introduces interactive drag-and-drop operations for manipulation of the generated topics. These operations mirror the logical AND, OR, and NOT operators that enable the information seeker to refine (or relax) the search queries during a search session. The intersections of topics are made explicitly visible to enable the information seeker to avoid frustrating "no hits" situations.

2 Information Seeking

Information seeking is a complex and cognitively demanding task that has a close relation to learning and problem solving [3].

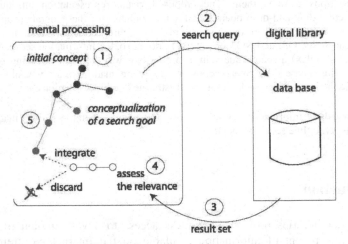

Fig. 1. Information seeking process

The information seeker starts with an initial concept of the search goal (Fig. 1, step 1) that is derived from the prior knowledge about the problem domain and defines an initial search query (Fig. 1, step 2). Based on the new knowledge acquired from the analysis of the query results (Fig. 1, step 3), people think of new concepts, revise their search goals, and formulate new queries. The search goals as well as criteria for assessing the relevance of articles from the query results (Fig. 1, steps 4 and 5) evolve during the information seeking process and cannot be specified in advance [4]. Having no specific well-defined goal and also no specific criteria for determining the solution quality, information seeking is regarded as an ill-structured problem [5]. The information seeking process terminates as soon as a user finds appropriate articles or decides to interrupt the search.

Looking at the information seeking process from the problem solving point of view, we have to identify the dimensions of the problem domain, possible actions that people can perform during the search to reach a new problem solving state, as well as search strategies that help people to reduce the amount of information they have to process.

2.1 Dimensions

A scientific article is characterized by the meta-data that makes it unique: *title*, *author(s)*, *editor(s)*, *year*, publishing *source* (e.g., the name of the journal, or conference proceedings, volume, issuer), abstract, and its *text*. Some digital libraries (e.g., ACM[2], CiteSeer[3]) provide further information such as *keywords*, *categories*, and links to the *referenced articles*.

In the following, we will discuss possible search paths resulting from the information choices accessible to the information seeker.

Each article is distinguished by a title, a short description (i.e., abstract), and its text. These attributes can contain specific words that trigger the formulation of refined search queries. Author names are usually augmented with contact information, such as e-mail and author's affiliation, i.e., name and address of an institution. Familiarity with the work of a specific author as well as the reputation of a scientific institution are important factors that can guide the information seeker to the publications of a particular author, groups of scientists, or research institutions [6,7]. A year is derived from the publishing date of an article in a scientific journal or a conference proceeding that represents a source. Examining articles that belong to a particular conference proceeding or a journal is another path that can be taken by the information seeker to continue the search. Referenced articles can provide even more hints about where further information about specific topics can be found.

The variety of the illustrated possibilities to follow different search paths leads to a vast growth of the search space. To reduce the amount of information to be processed and to facilitate the search, publications contained in a digital library are structured into different categories and augmented with key words.

Categories are traditionally maintained by librarians who are responsible for the creation and preparation of literature catalogs. Modern data mining and clustering methods automatically structure query results into different clusters and accordingly label them with frequently occurring terms, i.e., *topics* [8].

Key words are usually assigned either by authors of the corresponding articles or by librarians[4].

2.2 Online searching strategies

To deal with a huge amount of data that has to be processed during information seeking tasks, people developed sophisticated online searching strategies. Marchionini [9] defines a strategy as "the approach an information seeker takes to a problem. Strategies are sets of ordered tactics that are consciously selected, applied

---

[2] http://portal.acm.org/
[3] http://citeseerx.ist.psu.edu/
[4] for example, the primary and secondary index of the ACM digital library

and monitored to solve an information problem.[...] Tactics are discrete intellectual choices or prompts manifested as behavioral actions during an information-seeking session." He distinguishes four general strategies commonly employed during information seeking and information seeking tasks that represent these behavioral actions.

A first online searching strategy is called the "building blocks" approach [10]. During problem definition, the information seeker identifies the main facets and concept groups associated with the problem. Concepts are specific terms that frame the content of a search topic. For example, a user is interested in methods for improving the interaction with digital libraries. He/she can specify search terms that resemble this concept such as "usability for digital libraries," "user interaction," or "queries in digital libraries." (see Fig. 2)

Facets reflect meta-data, for example, a year of publication, research institutions, or specific properties of a document, for example, its format [11]. Concepts are employed for query formulations that include search terms combined with logical operators. Facets are used to filter the retrieved query results. In other words, concepts help to dice and facets help to slice the data space into observable portions. If a combination of topics delivers no results, the user can use synonyms or replace one of them with another topic.

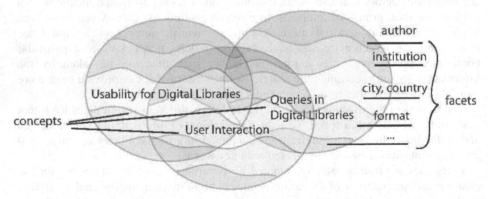

Fig. 2. "Building blocks" strategy: slicing and dicing the data space into facets and concepts.

A second strategy that is widely used is the "successive fractions" approach [12]. This approach works well if a user has a vague or broad conceptualization of the search goals. Like the first strategy, it is based on the commonly known "divide and conquer" problem solving principle. Using this strategy, the information seeker successively refines a large subset of data retrieved from a information system by introducing search terms that become more and more specific in each problem solving step. For example, the user can start with a general term "digital library", and make it more specific by constructing a search query "digital library AND user interaction".

The "building blocks" strategy as well as "successive fractions" facilitate the search process by breaking it into a sequence of systematic and discrete steps.

A third general strategy is the "pearl growing" approach [12]. The user starts with a specific document or document set that is relevant (a pearl) and uses the characteristics of that document to successively retrieve further relevant documents.

The information seeker uses assigned key words, title or text words, names, citations, a year of publication, or other features to construct queries in order to find similar documents.

A fourth general strategy was described by Hawkins & Wagers [13] as "interactive scanning". This strategy requires a more intensive interaction with the content of the documents from a user. The information seeker starts with a selection of documents relevant to the problem area sorted out from the initial result set. He/she scans these documents in order to identify key features (e.g., authors, terminology, methods) that trigger the formulation of successive queries.

Another less popular but still effective strategy proposed by Vigil [14] is called "closed-loop relevance clustering." This strategy uses the NOT operator to successively remove redundant documents from sets formed as a result of query modifications and combinations.

In this contribution, we will present an approach for visualization and manipulation of information that implements a combination of the "building blocks," "successive refinement" and provides support for the "close-loop relevance clustering" strategy.

2.3 Visual Representations

In this section, we will outline suitable visualization approaches for representing the hierarchical structure of digital libraries that were pursued so far. A more detailed overview about different visualization techniques can be found in [15]. We will discuss how these approaches communicate the structure of the data space and which interactive operations are provided to the user to perform an information seeking task.

The basic structural elements of relational visualizations (also termed graphs) encompass nodes and edges between them.

Spatially inspired concept spaces display different concepts that involve central terms retrieved from a data base using, for example, an automated thesaurus generation algorithm [16]. Spatial distance between the concepts conveys similarity relations between them.

Topic maps provided by HighWire digital library consist of tree-based structures that include hierarchically structured topics[5]. Edges are used to visualize the hierarchical relations between topics and subtopics. The interactive operations allow for expanding nodes in order to change the level of granularity.

3D visualizations present the content of a digital library as cone trees [17,18]. Cones stand for different topics and subtopics that contain documents represented as leaves of a tree. The user can interactively rotate the cones to examine the titles of the documents.

The outlined representations support browsing operations such that the user can interactively select, expand, or collapse different nodes in order to examine the data space at different levels of granularity. These operations, however, do not allow for applying the logical AND, OR, and NOT operators that are essential for the online searching strategies addressed in section 2.2.

---

[5] http://highwire.stanford.edu/help/hbt/

3   Interactive Relational Topic Visualization

Cutting et al. [8] proposed an efficient online clustering technique for structuring query results into topics. This approach enabled the information seeker to use the extracted topics for the formulation of successive queries that included logical AND, OR, and NOT operators. Yet, inappropriate combinations can often deliver no results. Our vision is to support the selection of logical operators by making the critical combinations of topics that can deliver no results visually accessible before a user states a new query.

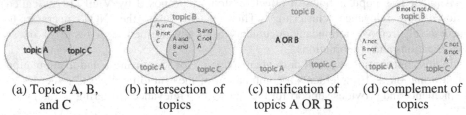

(a) Topics A, B,   (b) intersection of   (c) unification of   (d) complement of
    and C   topics   topics A OR B   topics

Fig. 3. Some variations of possible relations between topics A, B, and C.

Usually, such relations are visualized using Venn diagrams [19] that depict topics as overlapping circles (see Fig. 3). The results of the logical AND operator belong to the intersection of the circles (Fig. 3(b)), the OR operator unifies the topics (Fig. 3(c)), and the NOT operator includes only the part of a topic that does not overlap with the second topic (Fig. 3(d)). It seems that Venn diagrams are very well suited as a graphical representation to support people at construction of search queries. Yet, determining all possible variations in advance is a computationally demanding task (n! combinations). The same applies for the perceptual inspection of Venn diagrams. Intersections of two or three topics are visually tractable. Examining various intersections of a considerable amount of topics is difficult. To keep the response times of our system short, we refrain from determining all possible variations. To provide a better visual access to the relations between different topics, we focus on critical relations that can lead to "no hits" situations. If an intersection of two topics is empty, the NOT operation will be useless and the AND operation will deliver an empty result set. To prevent this, we retrieve in addition to topics pairwise intersections between them. The main idea behind this approach is to give the user an immediate impression of the relationships between generated topics.

3.1   A pool of topics

Figure 4 shows the user interface of the **D**igital **L**ibrary **A**ssistant (DILIA). The screen is separated into two parts. The left side illustrates an example pool of topics generated from the search query *digital library*. In the top left corner of the screen is a query panel. Here, a user can formulate a search query, for example *digital library*. On the right side of the screen, the user can examine the resulting hits.

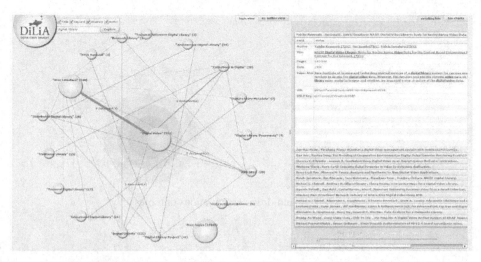

Fig. 4. Topics generated from the example search query *digital library*.

In the first step, DILIA processes the search query and generates a set of topics visualized as round blobs. The size of a blob stands for the number of documents that belong to a topic. The blobs are labeled with retrieved topic names together with the number of the corresponding documents. In the second step, it determines how many documents are shared between each pair of topics (with $O(n^2)$ run-time complexity, where n is the number of topics). Finally, the number of shared documents is visualized as an edge between topics. The edge thickness depends on the number of documents shared between the topics. By rolling over a topic, DILIA highlights the corresponding edges together with the number of shared documents.

3.2 Interactive drag-and-drop manipulation of topics

The user can drag and drop the blobs representing topics. This operation invokes an event that shows possible logical AND, OR, and NOT operations on a combination of topics that leads to further results. In doing so, DILIA enables the user to apply the "building blocks" strategy. If the intersection between the topics is empty, the system proposes only OR operation. In figure 5(a) the logical AND operation between topics "Digital Objects" AND "Digital Information" is automatically generated from the example search query digital library. Figure 5(b) shows another alternative combination of the involved topics, i.e., "Digital Objects" OR "Digital Information." Figure 6(a) shows the result of the AND combination of the topics "Digital Objects" AND "Digital Information." Figure 6(b) shows the corresponding OR combination of the topics. The edges of the AND combination become thin depicting the precision of the constructed sub-query. The edges of the OR combination are more prominent, since they include more documents as compared to the original pool of topics. In the same way, the user can employ NOT operators to remove documents contained in the dragged topic from the target topic. The NOT operation gives the user the opportunity to apply the "close-loop relevance clustering" strategy.

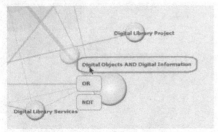
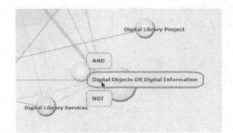

(a) "Digital Objects" AND "Digital Information"

(b) "Digital Objects" OR "Digital Information"

Fig. 5. Drag-and-drop manipulations of topics

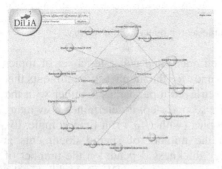
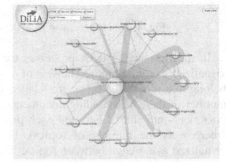

(a) "Digital Objects" AND "Digital Information"

(b) "Digital Objects" OR "Digital Information"

Fig. 6. Example query results performed using drag and drop operations

After a user defines a new logical combination by dropping a topic on a target topic, DILIA determines the intersections between the remaining topics and the new logical combination of the two topics. To avoid an increasing number of topics in each drag-and-drop interaction, we decided to remove the modified topics from the screen. This combination of topics is than displayed in the center of the pool of topics.

A single click on a topic puts the selected topic in the center of the pool and filters the lists of articles on the right side of the screen according to the selected topic. This allows for a better inspection of intersections among the revolving topics and corresponding articles that belong to the topic in the center.

A double click on a topic invokes an event that extends the current search query included in the query panel with the clicked topic label. As a response, the system processes the new search query and generates new topics and corresponding topic intersections. This procedure corresponds to the "successive fractions" approach described in section 2.2.

4 Realization

For our prototype implementation, we make use of a web-based client server architecture. On the client side, we have developed a Rich Internet Application (RIA) realized in Adobe Flex[6]. This application follows the model-view-controller (MVC) concept. We have build the flex prototype based on the Cairngorm[7] MVC implementation which allowed us to ensure a consequent MVC realization. The client utilizes server side PHP[8] classes to query the digital library database which is realized as a Lucene[9] index. In order to call Lucene methods from PHP we utilize the PHP Javabridge[10]. Finally, the communication between Flex (which is compiled into a Flash Movie) and the server side PHP classes is realized using Weborb[11]. Weborb handles the serialization/deserialization of data and the interfacing of methods between PHP and Flex. To determine the topic labels, we use the Carrot clustering engine[12].

The server side environment is based on the Apache HTTP Server[13] and Apache Tomcat[14]. The information flow between server and client is visualized in figure 7.

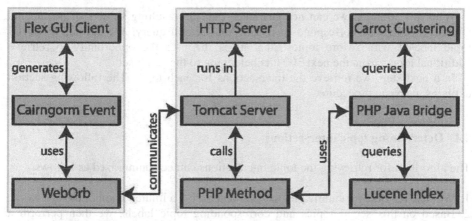

Fig. 7. Communication flow between client (left box) and server (right box)

The computational effort for deriving content clusters is quite high due to the complexity and mere size of the underlying data structures (more than one million data sets). Since the envisioned prototype should be able to do these calculations in real time, we decided to take a different approach. Similar to [8], instead of clustering the complete query result set, we used a clustering algorithm only on a subset of the

---

[6] http://www.adobe.com/products/flex/
[7] http://opensource.adobe.com/wiki/display/cairngorm/
[8] http://www.php.net
[9] http://lucene.apache.org/
[10] http://php-java-bridge.sourceforge.net
[11] http://www.themidnightcoders.com/products/weborb-for-php/
[12] http://project.carrot2.org/
[13] http://httpd.apache.org/
[14] http://tomcat.apache.org/

result list. By clustering only the first 300 hits, we can efficiently retrieve topics with corresponding labels.

Since the Lucene Index can efficiently process query requests that can return more than 200.000 hits, we interpreted the extracted topics as sub-queries. To arrive at a subset of documents that correspond to each extracted topic, we simply form a new Lucene query combining the original query with each subquery (using the logical operator AND). The following example illustrates the idea:

```
Initial Query: digital library

Extracted topics: "visual interfaces", "usability"...

1. topic sub-query: (digital library) AND "visual
interfaces"

2. topic sub-query: (digital library) AND "usability"
```

With this strategy, we can not guarantee that the resulting subsets of documents contain all hits that correspond to the original search query. We defined a special topic labeled with "More topics" that gives the user the opportunity to retrieve additional topics from the next 300 hits belonging to the result set.

In a next step, we retrieve the intersections for each topic. The following section explains the basic procedure.

4.1 Determining topic intersections

The algorithm for retrieving the topic intersections can be summarized as follows.

1. We take the query submitted by the user and derive a limited number of topics.
2. Based on this set of topics and corresponding topic labels, we then perform a number of Lucene sub-queries.
3. Each sub-query is a combination of the original query and one of the determined topic labels. In this way, we can find out the number of documents included in each topic.
4. Based on these results, we then construct a $n \times n$ matrix (where n is the number of topics derived from the current query). The matrix contains the number of documents that belong to the intersections between the topics (except for the special label "More topics") (see Fig. 8).
5. In order to fill the cells of the matrix, we again perform concatenated Lucene queries for each combination of topics and the original query.

After this final operation, we get a matrix representing the topics derived from the initial query, the number of documents contained in each of these topics, and the number of documents contained in each pairwise intersection of the topics.

Retrieved topic labels	"Digital Information" (267)	"Evaluation of Digital..." (15)	"Digital Library Project" (49)	"Digital Objects" (145)	"Digital Library Services" (42)	"User Interaction" (81)	"Digital Resources" (98)	"Queries in Digital..." (5)	"Digital Library Search" (17)	"Usability for Digital..." (13)	"Digital Music Libraries" (15)	"Digital Documents" (201)	"Research Libraries" (24)	"Library Interface" (21)	"Image Retrieval" (173)
"Digital Information"	267	-	-	7	1	2	5	-	-	-	-	5	2	-	-
"Evaluation of Digital..."	-	15	-	-	-	-	-	-	-	-	-	-	-	-	-
"Digital Library Project"	-	-	49	-	-	-	1	-	-	-	-	-	-	-	-
"Digital Objects"	-	-	-	145	1	1	1	-	-		-	1	1	-	-
...	...	...	...	...	...	...	...	...	...	...	...	...	...	...	...
"Image Retrieval"	-	-	-	-	-	-	-	-	-	-	-	-	-	-	173

Fig. 8. Topic intersections matrix resulting from query: "digital library"

5 Outlook and future work

In this contribution, we proposed an interactive Flex-based visualization capable of displaying topics extracted from query results and intersections between them. This visualization provides the user with interactive drag-and-drop operations that allow for employing boolean AND, OR, and NOT operators for combining the generated topics in order to obtain further results. Such combinations of topics enable the user to employ commonly used online searching strategies such as the "building blocks," "successive fractions," and "closed-loop relevance clustering" approach. In order to support the "pearl growing" approach, we need to modify the currently used clustering procedure. Therefore, we consider the support for the "pearl growing" approach by DILIA (Digital Library Assistant) as matter of future work. Our next steps in developing DILIA encompass usability studies with human users in order to evaluate the proposed interaction with topics and their visualization.

In the current implementation, the user can manipulate only those topics that are proposed by the information system. To support the "interactive scanning" approach and allow for more flexibility, we plan to extend the topic view with a possibility to specify additional user-defined topics. The system can determine intersections between the retrieved and the user-defined topics and highlight them, for example, with a distinct color.

The Rich Internet Application (RIA) technology employed for the prototype implementation of DILIA demonstrates new perspectives for the interaction design and user interface development to support the information discovery tasks. In doing so, the proposed relational topic visualization makes the structures concealed in a digital library visually accessible to information seekers and enables the exploration of unfamiliar problem domains in an efficient and aesthetically pleasing way.

Acknowledgments

The research project DILIA (Digital Library Assistant) is co-funded by the European Regional Development Fund (EFRE) under grant number 10140159. We gratefully acknowledge this support.

References

1. Borgman, C.L.: Why are online catalogs hard to use? lessons learned from information-retrieval studies. Journal of the American Society for Information Science 37(6) (1986) 387–400
2. Bates, M.: Subject access in online catalogs: A design model. Journal of the American Society for Information Science 37(6) (1986) 357–376
3. Vakkari, P.: Task complexity, problem structure and information actions -integrating studies on information seeking and retrieval. Information Processing and Management 35(6) (1999) 819–837
4. Bates, M.: The design of browsing and berrypicking techniques for the online search interface. Online Review 13(5) (1989) 407–424
5. Simon, H.A.: The structure of ill-structured problems. Artificial Intelligence 4 (1973) 181–201
6. Barry, C.L.: User-defined relevance criteria: An exploratory study. Journal of the American Society for Information Science 45(3) (1994) 149–159
7. Anderson, T.D.: Studying human judgments of relevance: interactions in context. In Ruthven, I., ed.: Proceedings of the 1st international conference on Information interaction in context, ACM (2006) 6–14
8. Cutting, D.R., Karger, D.R., Pedersen, J.O., Tukey, J.W.: Scatter/gather: a cluster-based approach to browsing large document collections. In: SIGIR '92: Proceedings of the 15th annual international ACM SIGIR conference on Research and development in information retrieval, New York, NY, USA, ACM Press (1992) 318–329
9. Marchionini, G.: Information seeking in electronic environments. Cambridge University Press, New York, NY, USA (1995)
10. Harter, S.: Online information retrieval: Concepts, principles, and techniques. Academic Press, Orlando, FL (1986)
11. Hearst, M.A.: Uis for faceted navigation: Recent advances and remaining open problems. In: in the Workshop on Computer Interaction and Information Retrieval, HCIR 2008. (2008)
12. Meadow, C., Cochrane, P.: Basics of online searching. John Wiley and Sons, New York (1981)
13. Hawkins, D.T., Wagers, R.: Online bibliographic search strategy development. (1989) 88–95

14.Vigil, P.J.: The psychology of online searching. Journal of the American Society for Information Science 34(4) (1983) 281–287

15.McKiernan, G.: New age navigation: Innovative information interfaces for electronic journals. The Serials Librarian 45(2) (2003) 87–123

16.Zhang, J., Mostafa, J., Tripathy, H.: Information retrieval by semantic analysis and visualization of the concept space of d-lib magazine. D-Lib Magazine 8(10) (October 2002)

17.Robertson, G.G., Mackinlay, J.D., Card, S.K.: Cone trees: animated 3d visualizations of hierarchical information. In: CHI '91: Proceedings of the SIGCHI conference on Human factors in computing systems, New York, NY, USA, ACM (1991) 189–194

18.Mizukoshi, D., Hori, Y., Gotho, T.: Extension models of cone tree visualizations to large scale knowledge base with semantic relations. In: The 14th International Conference in Central Europe on Computer Graphics, Visualization and Computer Vision'2006. (2006)

19.Venn, J.: On the diagrammatic and mechanical representation of propositions and reasonings. Philosophical Magazine and Journal of Science 9(50) (1880)

DaisyViz: A Model-based User Interfaces Toolkit for Development of Interactive Information Visualization

Lei Ren[1,1], Feng Tian[2], Lin Zhang[1], and Guozhong Dai[2]

[1] School of Automation Science and Electrical Engineering, Beihang University, Beijing 100191, China
[2] Institute of Software, The Chinese Academy of Sciences, Beijing 100190, China
leo.renlei@gmail.com, post.wimp@gmail.com, johnlin9999@163.com, dgz@iel.iscas.ac.cn

Abstract. Although the increasing hordes of information visualization technologies are recognized both in industry and research community, there are seldom toolkits for non-expert users or end-users to rapidly design and develop domain-specific information visualization applications. Such toolkits should provide support for the unified data structures suited to tree, network, temporal and multi-dimensional data, well-known visualization techniques and interaction techniques, and generic visualization tasks. We built DaisyViz, a model-based user interfaces toolkit, which enables end-users to rapidly develop domain-specific information visualization applications without traditional programming. DaisyViz is based on an interface model called UIMI consisting of three declarative models – data model, visualization model, and control model. In the development process, users visually construct UIMI which could be used to generate profiles. Those profiles can be parsed by DaisyViz to automatically generate a prototype system. We firstly give the formal definition of UIMI, and then discuss the architecture of DaisyViz. To evaluate DasyViz we built an application in a manufacturing enterprise and performed a user study. The results show DaisyViz is usable and effective.

Keywords: User interface, information visualization, toolkit, multiple coordinated views, model-based interface development.

1 Introduction

The past 20 years have witnessed an abundance of information visualization (*infovis*) novel work on visual representation and interaction techniques. There are so many layout algorithms, mainly for tree, network, multi-dimensional and temporal data of the seven data types [1], to make complex data easy to understand in a data-rich world.

---

[1] Lei Ren and Lin Zhang are with the School of Automation Science and Electrical Engineering, Beihang University. E-mail: leo.renlei@gmail.com, johnlin9999@163.com.
    Feng Tian and Guozhong Dai are with the Human-Computer Interaction Lab and the Institute of Software, The Chinese Academy of Sciences. E-mail: post.wimp@gmail.com, dgz@iel.iscas.ac.cn.

M.L. Huang et al. (eds.), *Visual Information Communication*,
DOI 10.1007/978-1-4419-0312-9_14, © Springer Science+Business Media, LLC 2010

And interaction techniques, at the same time, including dynamic query [2], overview+detail [3], focus+context [4], panning+zooming [3] and multiple coordinated views [5], provide powerful support for user's tasks in Visual Information-Seeking Mantra [6]. Although *infovis* is recognized as an effective media for gaining insight in many application domains such as business intelligence, sociology and biology, wide-spread development for interactive information visualization is difficult which requires domain-specific customization and programming accessible only to specialist [7]. Indeed, non-expert users or end-users need a toolkit which could offer high-level support for the unified data structures suited to tree, network, multi-dimensional and temporal data, special visualization techniques and interaction techniques, and well-known generic *infovis* tasks. However, current toolkits attempting to rapidly prototype domain applications, such as PAD++ [8], Jazz [9], Piccolo [10], Snap-Together [11], GeoVista [12], Improvise [41], PRISMA [13], Polaris [14], XML toolkit [15], Fekete's *infovis* toolkit [16], prefuse [7], Many Eyes [17], and ComVis [18], can't cover all relevant aspects mentioned above.

Model-based systems for user interface development use a declarative interface model, a high-level abstract model of domain requirements, to drive the interface development process. This paradigm offers a number of key benefits: user-centered development cycle, centralized user interface specification, comprehensive design tools for interactive and automated development, and re-use of user interface designs [19]. It's much easier for end-users to craft an interface model than to implement complex algorithms from scratch. Therefore, leveraging model-based development approaches to build domain *infovis* applications may be valuable for end-users. From an end-user's perspective, when creating a domain *infovis* application, he should be able to visualize and explore many facets of a single conceptual information entity to gain insight of complex information collections [5]. There are several questions for them to answer: What facets of the target information should be visualized? What data source of each facet and what relationships among all the facets? What layout algorithm to visualize each facet? What interactive techniques for each facet to support *infovis* tasks? Here, we often use a window or view to represent a facet. For example, to analyze the reason of the bottleneck in a product line, end-users need three facets: a view about the product line graph for revealing the bottleneck node, a view about the production tasks tree for analyzing the tasks related to the bottleneck node, and a view about the multi-dimensional information related to the task execution for uncovering the deep reasons why some tasks are delayed. In the model-based development, the task of end-users is to transform the answers of above questions to a declarative model. Thus, the *infovis* applications can be generated automatically by mapping the model to the implementation.

To address these issues, we built DaisyViz, a model-based user interfaces toolkit for development of interactive *infovis* system with multiple coordinated views. The key features of DaisyViz include:

- Unified data models suited to the seven data types and multiple coordinated views.
- A variety of specific layout algorithms, which are extensible, mainly for tree, graph, multi-dimensional and temporal data.

- Interaction techniques including dynamic query, overview+detail, panning+zooming, focus+context, and multiple coordinated views to support extended *infovis* tasks such as overview, pan, zoom, filter by data attributes (i.e., dynamic query), filter by legends, keyword search, detail tooltip (i.e., detail-on-demand), coordination (e.g., brushing-and-linking and drill-down).
- Model-based interfaces development for end-users.

The goal of DaisyViz is to simplify the design and implement of *infovis* applications in a given domain. DaisyViz is based on an interface model called UIMI consisting of three declarative models – data model, visualization model, and control model. End-users construct interface models and then generate profiles which can be parsed by DaisyViz to automatically generate an interactive *infovis* application. To evaluate DasyViz we built an application in a manufacturing enterprise and performed a user study. The results show that DaisyViz is usable and effective. The paper is organized as follows. Section 2 is a survey about related work. Section 3 presents the formal definition of UIMI. Section 4 describes the architecture of DaisyViz, including the model-based approach, the core components and libraries. Section 5 evaluates DasiyViz through an application example and a user study. Section 6 concludes the paper and outlines future work.

2   Related Work

Over last few decades, there has been a great deal of work on *infovis*, which has produced novel visual representations to visualize information, new interaction techniques for manipulation of the visual representations to reveal underlying information, and new tools for supporting the creation of *infovis* applications. The examples of popular visual representation designs include tree visualizations (e.g., TreeMaps [20], Cone Trees [21], Hyperbolic trees [22], SpaceTrees [23], DOITrees [24], InterRing [25], and CirclePacking [26]), graph visualization (e.g., Clustered Graph [27], Force-Directed Graph [28], and Radial Graph [29]), multi-dimensional visualizations (e.g., Scatterplots [30] and Parallel coordinates [31]) and temporal visualizations (e.g., Theme River [32], Circle View [33], and TimeWhell [34]). Advances also came in the research on interaction techniques, including dynamic query [2], overview+detail [3], focus+context [4], panning+zooming [3] and multiple coordinated views [5], which support users for navigation and exploration of visual information.

Some *infovis* tools have been developed especially for the visualization of a given data type, such as *infovis* tools for static graph visualization (e.g., Graphviz [35] and GVF [36]), *infovis* tools for interactive graph visualization with zoomable user interfaces (e.g., PAD++ [8], Jazz [9] and Piccolo [10]) and *infovis* tools for multi-dimensional visualization (e.g., Polaris [14]). However, these tools can't cover the seven data types [6], especially the popular data types of tree, graph, multi-dimensional and temporal data. In contrast, DaisyViz can provide generic data models suited to the seven data types and multiple coordinated views.

The technique of multiple coordinated views, using two or more coordinated visualizations, is a proven technology for interactive visual analysis. When faced with complex information datasets, users should visualize and explore many facets of the information conceptual entity to gain insight of each facet and, most importantly, to understand the hidden relationships among the facets. There have been some *infovis* tools to support multiple coordinated views, such as Snap-Together [11], GeoVista [12], Improvise [41], PRISMA [13], and ComVis [18]. These tools, however, focusing only on implementing the coordination mechanisms, provide less support for the combination of a wide range of visualization and interaction techniques, such as the visualizations for tree, graph, multi-dimensional and temporal data, and the interaction techniques for overview, zoom, filter, and details-on-demand. DaisyViz, in contrast, in addition to implementing multiple coordinated mechanisms, can carry out multiple well-known tasks which extended Shneiderman's taxonomy [6] in each visualization view.

Among the *infovis* toolkits, the most similar to DaisyViz are XML toolkit [15], Fekete's *infovis* toolkit [16], prefuse [7], and Many Eyes [17]. They all aim at simplifying design and implementation of *infovis* domain applications, by providing generic data models to cover a variety of data types and visualization components that encapsulate algorithms into widgets. XML toolkit, based on the standard Java data structures (e.g., Treemodel), is a package of *infovis* algorithms, rather than a toolkit for end-users. Although Fekete's *infovis* toolkit provides a library of existing visualization widgets to support well-known layout algorithms and interaction techniques such as focus+context and dynamic query, it lacks flexibility and reusable components for constructing novel *infovis* applications [7]. Prefuse, as a software framework to build domain-specific interactive *infovis* applications, gives support to both structured (i.e., tree and graph) and unstructured (i.e., multi-dimensional) data, and enable users to craft applications by stringing together finer-grained program blocks called "action". Prefuse provides a degree of flexibility supporting many popular visualization and interaction techniques such as dynamic query, overview+detail, focus+context, and panning+zooming. However, since it hasn't given a design tool with GUI for end-users, users still have to craft a lot of codes according to its predefined standards when customizing complex domain-specific applications, for example, enterprise *infovis* applications with multiple coordinated views. The goal of Many Eyes is to support collaboration for visualization at internet scale. Many Eyes pays more attention to end-users for creation of the visualizations on internet, and its mechanisms for data models, visualization and interaction techniques are relatively simple so that it can't meet the demands of interactive *infovis* applications for complex domain. In contrast to current solutions mentioned above, DaisyViz can provide a model-based design toolkit for end-users to simply create domain-specific interactive *infovis* applications that support unified data models, a wide range of well-known visualizations and interaction techniques for exploration of multiple coordinated views.

3   UIMI: A User Interface Model for Infovis

DaisyViz exploits the idea of model-based interface development [19], which uses a declarative model of user interfaces to drive the development process. A user interface model should abstract the features and represent all the relevant aspects of a user interface in some type of formal languages. The user interface model, as the core of development process, will be parsed according to knowledge bases in order to generate the applications. From the perspective of the end-users, what they should do is to construct the interface model. For the users of interactive *infovis* applications, they need answer several questions as follows. What facets of the target information should be visualized? What data source of each facet and what relations among all the facets? What layout algorithm to visualize each facet? What interactive techniques for each facet (i.e., view) to support *infovis* tasks? These answers can be abstracted to a User Interface Model for *Infovis* (UIMI) including three declarative models of data, visualization, and control.

3.1 Definition of Data Model of UIMI

The data model of UIMI is to describe the data structures of multiple relevant facets of the target information. The target information, from different points of view, can be divided into several facets, and every facet organize data into relations (i.e., tables) where each row in a table corresponds to a basic data item and each column represents an attribute of that data item [37]. Hence, multi-dimensional and temporal data can be represented by a multi-dimensional relational table. And for tree and graph data, two tables can be used to organize nodes and edges. Therefore, the relational data schemas provide unified data model for tree, graph, multi-dimensional, and temporal data. Furthermore, the relationships among the facets can be described by foreign keys so as to support the coordination mechanisms of multiple views. The formal definitions are as follows.

*Definition 1 A **DataItem** DN = <DIID, Attribute$_1$, Attribute$_2$, ···, Attribute$_n$>. DIID is the ID of a data item. Attribute$_i$ = <AttrName$_i$, MetaData$_i$> is a property of DI, where AttrName$_i$ is the property name of Attribute$_i$, and MetaData$_i$ is the metadata type of nominal, ordinal, and quantitative [1]. Here intervals are treating as quantitative.*

*Definition 2 A **DataItemRelation** DIR = <SourceDIID, TargetDIID, Direction> where SourceDIID and TargetDIID are the IDs of two data items of a link. Direction ∈ {direct,undirect}.*

*Definition 3 An **InfoFacet** IF = <IFID, DISet, DIRSet, DataSource> is a facet of the target information. IFID is the ID of the facet of the target information. DISet is a set of DIs. DIRSet is a set of DIRs. DataSource is a pointer to different data sources, from formatted text files to XML and relational databases. For formatted text files and XML, DataSource would be the path. For relational databases, DataSource would be connection strings including server, database, user, password, SQL, etc.*

*Definition 4 An **InfoFacetRelation** IFR = <SourceIFID, TargetIFID, KeyAttri, Direction> is a relationship between two facets. SourceIFID and TargetIFID are IDs of two relevant facets. Let SourceAttriSet be the set of attributes of data items in facet SourceIFID, and TargetAttriSet be the set of attributes of data items in facet TargetIFID. KeyAttri ∈ SourceAttriSet ∩ TargetAttriSet. Direction ∈ {direct, undirect}.*

*Definition 5 **Data** = <IFSet, IFRSet>. IFSet is a set of facets of the target information, and IFRSet is a set of relationships among the facets.*

3.2   Definition of Visualization Model of UIMI

The visualization model of UIMI, describing the visual representations of data in the user interface, can be divided into two categories: coordinated views and visual structure in each view. The coordinated views are a set of view containers, and the relationships among views are to support the coordination mechanisms. The visual structure, including layout algorithm, spatial substrate, and graphical mark mappings [1]. Spatial substrate should give the definition of a set of axises and the mapping attributes of data items for the axises. The graphical mark mappings should specify the encoded attributes of data items for retinal variables of graphical marks [1], such as shape, color, size, orientation, and texture. From the perspective of the end-users, they would answer how many views in the interface and what visualization in each view through the definition of this part. The formal definitions are as follows.

Definition 6** An **Axis = < *AxisID, AxisType, DIMappingAttri, ValueRange* >. *AxisID is the ID of the axis. AxisType* ∈{*NoAxis,NominalAxis,OrdinalAxis,QuantityAxis*} *is type of the axis. DIMappingAttri is the encoded attribute of data items. ValueRange is the predefined range of the axis.*

***Definition 7** A **SpatialSubstrate** is a set of axis.*

***Definition 8** A **GraphicalMarkMapping** GMM* = < *LabelMappingAttri, ShapeMappingAttri, ColorMappingAttri, SizeMappingAttri, OrientationMappingAttri* > *where LabelMappingAttri, ShapeMappingAttri, ColorMappingAttri, SizeMappingAttri, and OrientationMappingAttri are the encoded attributes of data items for retinal variables of graphical marks including label, shape, color, size, and orientation.*

***Definition 9** A **VisualStructure** VS* = < *VSID, LayoutAlgorithm, SpatialSubstrate, GMM* > *where VSID is the ID of VS, and LayoutAlgorithm is the name of layout algorithm. LayoutAlgorithm* ∈ {*TreeMaps, DOITrees, RadialGraph, ScatterPlot, ParallelCoordinates, ···*}. *And the set of LayoutAlgorithm can be extended when a new layout algorithm is added.*

***Definition 10** A **ViewContainer** VC* = <*VCID, IFID, VSID* > *where VCID is the ID of a view container, IFID is the ID of facet which will be visualized in this view container, and VSID is the ID of the visual structure in this view container.*

***Definition 11** A **ViewContainerRelation** VCR* = <*VCRID, SourceVCID, TargetVCID, KeyAttri* > *where SourceVCID and TargetVCID are the IDs of two coordinated views with the common attribute KeyAttri of data items.*

Definition 12** **Visualization = < *VCSet, VCRSet* > *where VCSet is a set of view containers, and VCRSet is a set of VCRs.*

3.3   Definition of Control Model of UIMI

The control model of UIMI is to describe the *infovis* tasks and the interaction techniques used in each view container. According to the new requirements of current toolkits [7-18] and based on Shneiderman's taxonomy of tasks (i.e., overview, zoom, filter, and details-on-demand), we give a more detailed taxonomy for *infovis* tasks, including overview of multiple views, overview of visualization in a view, pan, zoom, filter by data attributes (i.e., dynamic query), filter by legends, keyword search, detail tooltip (i.e., detail-on-demand), coordination (e.g., brushing-and-linking and drill-down). For the tasks of coordination, brushing-and-linking means selecting an item in one view highlights the corresponding items in another view, and drill-down means selecting an item in one view loads related items into another view [11].

Users should define what tasks they need to meet the requirements of applications. Then users need to specify the concrete control model for every task they have chosen. The interaction controls can be divided into two categories: direct manipulation and indirect manipulation. Direct manipulation is mainly used for overview of multiple views, overview of visualization in a view, pan, zoom, detail tooltip, and coordination. For the direct manipulation, users should specify that, according to a set of predefined events, which interaction events to achieve the tasks. For example, double click on the blank area in a view to overview the visualization, or drag and drop a graphical node from one view to another view to realize coordination. Indirect manipulation, using some controls such as sliders, text boxes, and legends, is targeted for dynamic query, keyword search, and filter by legends. Users should configure the mapping attributes of data items used by dynamic query sliders, keyword search boxes, and legends.

Definition 13 *A* **DirectManipulationEventSet** *DMES = <OnItemLeftClick, OnItemLeftDoubleClick, OnItemRightClick, OnItemRightDoubleClick, OnItemHover, OnItemLeftDragDrop,   OnItemRightDragDrop,   OnViewLeftClick, OnViewLeftDoubleClick,   OnViewRightClick,   OnViewRightDoubleClick, OnViewHover, OnViewLeftDragDrop, OnViewRightDragDrop, ······>. Here, some usual interaction events are predefined for user to choose to realize the direct manipulation.*

Definition 14 *A* **DirectManipulationTaskControl** *DMTC = <DMTask, DME>. DMTask ∈ { OverviewMultipleViews,   OverviewVisualization,   Pan,   Zoom, DetailTooltip, Brushing-and-LinkingCoordination, DrillDownCoordination } is one of the tasks using direct manipulation. DME ∈ DMES is the interaction event for DMTask.*

Definition 15 *A* **DynamicQueryControl** *DQC = <DQCID, VCID, DIAttri, ValueRange >. DQCID is the ID of a dynamic query slider. VCID is the view container where the slider works. DIAttri is the attribute of data items which will be used to do dynamic query. ValueRange is a predefined range of the slider.*

Definition 16 *A* **KeywordSearchControl** *KSC = <KSCID, VCID, DIAttri >. DQCID is the ID of a text box for keyword search. VCID is the view container where the textbox works. DIAttri is the attribute of data items which will be used to search items in the view.*

Definition 17 *A* **FilterbyLegendsControl** *FLC = <FLCID, VCID, RetinalVariables >. FLCID is the ID of legends control. VCID is the view container where the legends control works. RetinalVariables is the retinal variables of graphical marks which will be used to filter items in the view.*

Definition 18 *Control = < DirectManipulationTaskControlSet, IndirectManipulationTaskControlSet >. DirectManipulationTaskControlSet is a set of controls using direct manipulation to support related tasks. IndirectManipulationTaskControlSet = < DQCSet, KSCSet, FLCSet > is a set of controls using indirect manipulation to support related tasks.*

4   Architecture of DaisyViz

4.1   Overview

Fig. 1 illustrates the architecture of DaisyViz. DaisyViz is composed of four main parts: DaisyViz tools, DaisyViz core components, DaisyViz libraries, and Java APIs.

Java APIs, including JDBC, SAX, Graphical Editor Framework and so on, provide underlying support for all other parts. DaisyViz libraries, as the foundation of DaisyViz core components, cover the libraries used for data structures of information, data access, visual representation structures, visual mapping, graphical element rendering, and interaction events controlling. DaisyViz core components give support to the main development process. In this part, UIMI profile builder is responsible for UIMI modeling according to the requirements of domain applications, and then constructs the profiles of UIMI. Mapping parser, based on the mapping knowledge base, translates the declarative language in the UIMI profiles into runtime parameters for the system runtime framework. Runtime controller, as the master of runtime system, controls the runtime mechanisms such as data access, visual representation mapping, render, and response to interaction events. DaisyViz provides tools for end-users to design and run the domain-specific applications. DaisyViz Modeler can be used by users to build UIMI model and construct profiles. DaisyViz Runner, as a runtime tool, can generate the application system through parsing UIMI profiles and, thus, support user's visual analysis.

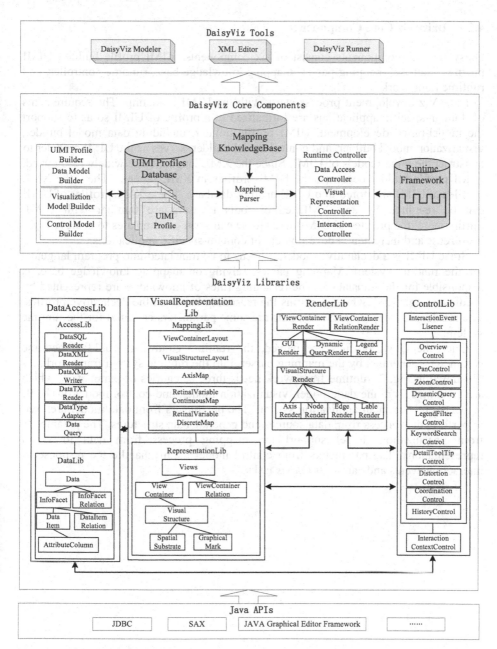

Fig. 1. Architecture of DaisyViz. It includes four main parts: DaisyViz tools, DaisyViz core components, DaisyViz libraries, and Java APIs.

4.2   DaisyViz Core Components

DaisyViz core components consist of six components: UIMI profile builder, UIMI profiles database, mapping parser, mapping knowledge base, runtime controller, and runtime framework.

DaisyViz development process starts with the UIMI modeling. The requirements of domain-specific applications are formalized to a profile of UIMI so as to support the model-based development. UIMI profile builder, including data model builder, visualization model builder, and control model builder, serves as the UIMI modeler to construct the three models of UIMI. Since the XML language has widely recognized, UIMI profile builder construct the UIMI profiles in XML schema. Then, the XML profiles of UIMI are stored into UIMI profiles database. These XML profiles of UIMI can be re-edited by any XML editor tools if users are familiar with UIMI. Furthermore, the profiles of UIMI in database can serve as templates to achieve high-level reuse and incremental development of domain-specific applications.

Since UIMI is a declarative model, it needs to be translated into program language for the runtime system. Mapping parser, relying on mapping knowledge base, is responsible for the translation. The reasoning rules of knowledge are represented by Predicate Logic [38], which performs the reasoning based on the declarative profiles. The results the mapping parser outputs are some parameters essential for the runtime system.

Once the UIMI profiles are parsed, the runtime controller would embed the parameters, generated by the mapping parser, into the runtime system framework. As illustrated in Fig. 2, runtime framework needs three categories of parameters, which are generated from the data model, visualization model, and control model of UIMI, respectively, to run an application system. The parameters from data model are used to perform data access from data sources and generate data structures. The parameters from visualization model support the mapping process from data to visual representations. The parameters from control model mainly handle the response to interaction events and carry out *infovis* tasks.

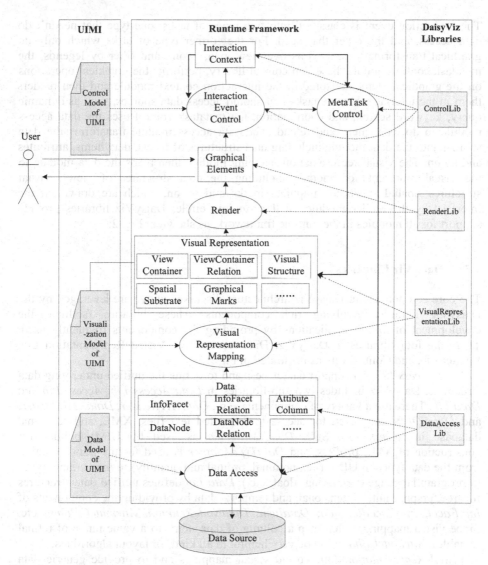

Fig. 2. Runtime framework of DaisyViz. Squares represent data structures whereas ellipses represent functions.

In runtime framework, there are five types of function modules, that is, data access module, visual representation mapping module, render module, interaction event control module, and metatask control module, and four types of data structure modules, that is, data module, visual representation module, graphical elements module, and interaction context module.

The runtime process starts with an interaction event triggered by user's interaction with the graphical elements in the interface. Then, based on the interaction context module, where current interaction state is recorded such as selected items and search results, the interaction event is recognized by the interaction event control module.

The interaction event is classified into two types of tasks: one type that needn't do data access, and the other that need. For the former type of tasks which only do graphical transformations, such as overview, pan, zoom, and filter by legends, the metatask control module, based on control library, performs the graphical operations on the graphical elements stored in the interaction context module and then renders them in the interface. For the tasks that should access data sources, such as dynamic query, keyword search, and coordination, the metatask control uses the data access module to do data query and reload. The data access module transforms the data sources into the data module including data structures of facets, data items, attributes and so on. The visual representation mapping module then maps the data module to the visual representation module including the data structures of views, visual structures, spatial substrate, graphical marks and so on, which are drawn on the interface by the render module. In this runtime circle, DaisyViz libraries provide support for all modules in the runtime framework, as shown in Fig. 2.

4.3   DaisyViz Libraries

The core components in DaisyViz architecture discussed above are leveraged by the DaisyViz libraries involving rich components. These libraries facilitate the development of *infovis* applications by providing the components frequently used. There are four libraries in DaisyViz: Data Access Lib, Visual Representation Lib, Render Lib, and Control Lib, as illustrated in Fig. 1.

Data Access Lib. To support data access and to define the unified underlying data structures, DaisyViz includes two sub-libraries in *Data Access Lib*: *Access Lib* and *Data Lib*. There are a variety of components, e.g., *DataTXTReader*, *DataXMLReader*, and *DataSQLReader*, used for access to formatted text files, XML, and relational database in *Access Lib*. Still, *DataXMLWriter* is used by UIMI builder for construction of XML profiles, and *DataTypeAdapter* is used for the transformation from the data types in UIMI (i.e., nominal, ordinal and quantity) to the variable types in program language (i.e., string, float, etc.). *Data Lib* defines unified data structures for tree, graph, multi-dimensional, and temporal data by providing the components of *InfoFacet*, *InfoFacetRelation*, *DataItem*, *DataNodeRelation*, *AttributeColumn*, etc. Since visual mappings often map a column of data items to a value range of retinal variables, *AttributeColumn* can be very helpful to all kinds of layout algorithms.

Visual Representation Lib. To aid visual mappings and to provide generic data structures for visual representations, *Visual Representation Lib* includes two sub-libraries: *MappingLib* and *RepresentationLib*. The component *VisualStructureLaout*, which is extensible, includes a host of well-known layout algorithms, e.g., TreeMaps [20], DOITrees [24], CirclePacking [26], Force-Directed Graph [28], Radial Graph [29], Scatterplots [30], Parallel coordinates [31], etc. *AxisMap*, used for generating spatial substrate, encapsulates the mapping functions for different types of axis. *RetinalVariableContinuousMap* and *RetinalVariableDiscreteMap* are used for assigning color, shape, size, and other retinal variables to graphical marks based on a collection of mapping functions. *RepresentationLib* organizes graphical elements to the generic data structures by providing components for defining views, visual structure, spatial substrate, graphical marks, etc.

Render Lib. This library is to simplify the drawing of all kinds of graphical elements displayed in interface. *ViewContainerRender* and *ViewContainerRelationRender* are used to draw the views and the links between related views. *VisualStructureRender*, *AxisRender*, *NodeRender*, *EdgeRender*, and *LabelRender* mainly serve for the visualization in a view, where axis, labels, graphical marks such as nodes and edges are drawn. *DynamicQuderyRender* can be used for dynamic query sliders drawing. *LegendRender* can be used to draw legends of visualization. *GUIRender* includes some traditional GUI components, e.g., text box, dropdown box, etc. Factories [39] are used in this library, which are meant to be extended and modified by users.

Control Lib. To simplify the customization of the interaction tasks of *infovis*, *Control Lib* provides a definition of some interaction events frequently used in *infovis*, and encapsulates some well-known *infovis* tasks into components. *InteractionEventListener* gives a list of usual events for user to choose, e.g., *OnItemLeftClick()* is an event that means user left clicks on a graphical item in visualizations. Current provided events include the operations, e.g., left or right click, left or right double-click, hover, left or right drag-and-drop, on the graphical elements, e.g., graphical marks and view. The components for task control, e.g., *OverviewControl*, *PanControl*, *ZoomControl*, *DynamicQueryControl*, *LegendFilterControl*, *KeywordSearchControl*, *DetailTooltipControl*, *DistortionControl*, *Brushing-and-LinkingCoordinationControl*, and *DrillDownCoordinationControl*, can support the *infovis* tasks mentioned above. *InteractionContextControl* is used for management of the interaction states, e.g., currently selected items and search results, which offers input parameters for the encapsulated components for task control.

5 Evaluation

5.1 Application Examples

We have built an interactive *infovis* application in a manufacturing enterprise to test the expressiveness, effectiveness, flexibility and extensibility of this toolkit.

Table 1 illustrates the requirements of the manufacturing enterprise application. The target information for analysis is "Manufacture". Since "Manufacture" is such an abstract conception that it needs to be divided into four related facets for user's analysis from different perspectives, as shown in the column "InfoFacet" in Table 1. We can find relationships between two facets through the common attribute in the column "DataAttribute". For example, there is a common attribute "ManufactoryID" between the facets "Manufactory" and "ProductOrder", which means each factory has many orders and every order belongs to a factory. We can find that, as Table 1 shows, this application should meet the demands as follows.

- Provide support for different data types, e.g., tree, graph, and multi-dimensional, as shown in the column "Data Type" in Table 1.

- Provide support for specific layout algorithms, e.g., Radial Graph, Force-Directed Graph, DOITrees, TreeMaps, and Scatter Plot, for tree, graph, and multi-dimensional data, as shown in the column "Layout" in Table 1.
- Provide interaction techniques, e.g., dynamic query, overview+detail, panning+zooming, focus+context, and multiple coordinated views, for the *infovis* tasks, e.g., overview, zoom, filter by data attributes, filter by legends, keyword search, detail-on-demand, and coordination.

Table 1. Requirement of an interactive *infovis* application in a manufacturing enterprise.

Target Information	InfoFacet	Data Attributes	Data Type	Layout	Interaction Task
Manufacture	Manufactory	ManufactoryID, ManufactoryName, OverallProductRate, Address, Manager, AlertStatus	Graph	Radial Graph, Force-Directed Graph	Overview,Pan,Zoom, DynamicQuery, KeywordSearch, Detail, Brushing-and-linking Coordination
	Product Order	ProductOrderID, Customer, ProductID, OrderNumber, Priority, ManufactureID	Tree	DOITrees,	Overview,Pan,Zoom, DynamicQuery, FilterByLegends, KeywordSearch, Detail, FocusPlusContext, Brushing-and-linking Coordination
	Manu Plan	PlanID, ProductOrderID, PlanNumber, FinishDate, ProductGroup	Tree	TreeMaps	Overview, Zoom, KeywordSearch, Detail, Brushing-and-linking Coordination
	Plan Execution	ExecID, PlanID, ProductID, Date, FinishNumber, IsExpire, Quality	Multi-dimensional	Scatter Plot	Overview,Pan,Zoom, DynamicQuery, FilterByLegends, KeywordSearch, Detail, Drill-down Coordination

According to the requirements, we have used DaisyViz Modeler to create the profile of UIMI. As illustrated in Fig. 3, DaisyViz Modeler comes with three panels to configure the data model, the visualization model, and the control model of UIMI. Since the data source is a shared relational database in the manufacturing enterprise, user should specify the connection strings and SQL to generate two tables for each facet of "Manufactory", "ProductOrder" and "ManuPlan", and one table for the facet "PlanExecution", respectively. Fig. 3a shows the results of two tables for the facet "Manufactory". One table is used to hold all the factories, and the other is used to represent the logistics relationships among the factories. The key attributes for each facet can be explicitly specified in this panel, otherwise the common attribute among the facets would by default support coordination mechanisms. Fig. 3b shows configurations of layout algorithm, spatial substrate and retinal variables of graphical marks for the facet "PlanExecution", which uses ScatterPlot with the data attributes

"Date" and "ProductID" as two axises. Users can configure multiple axises for those axis-based layout algorithms such as parallel coordinates. The data attributes "Quality" and "IsDelay" are specified for the shape and color mappings. Users can explicitly configure that which views would be the coordinated ones, otherwise the relationships among facets would support coordination mechanisms. Fig. 3c shows the customization of interaction tasks for the view of facet "Manufactory". For example, users specified "OnItemRightClick" as the *DirectManipulationEvent* for the task *Brushing-and-LinkingCoordination*, which means users can achieve the brushing-and-linking coordination by a right-click on nodes in the graph of "Manufactory". Users also configured the data attributes, such as "Manager" and "OverallProductRate", for the *KeywordSearchControl* and the *DynamicQueryControl*. The XML profile of UIMI constructed by DaisyViz Modeler is shown in Fig. 4.

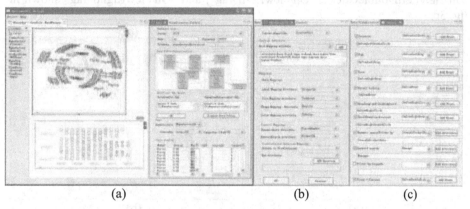

| (a) | (b) | (c) |

Fig. 3. Modeling the UIMI with DaisyViz Modeler which provides a GUI editor with three panels: (a), (b), and (c), for the customization of data model, visualization model and control model of UIMI. (a) The configuration of data model for the facet "Manufactory". (b) The configuration of visualization model for the facet "PlanExecution". (c) The configuration of control model for the view of facet "Manufactory".

Fig. 4. The XML profile of UIMI generated by DaisyViz Modeler.

Based on the XML profile of UIMI, DasiyViz Runner has generated a prototype system. As illustrated in Fig. 5a, there is a list of facet names on the left panel, and users can drag a facet to the blank area on the right panel to create a view. Each view contains two parts: visualization and control panel. Keyword search boxes, legends dropdown boxes, and dynamic query sliders are generated in control panels, which can be hidden so as to save display area. There are four coordinated views connected with red links, and each red link represents an underlying relationship between the two views of facets. Fig. 5b shows the results of coordination in four views when users perform a right-click on a node in the Force-Directed Graph, which have triggered the brushing-and-linking coordination in DOITrees and TreeMaps, and drill-down coordination in Scatter Plot. Fig. 5 also illustrates some other interaction techniques such as the detail tooltip and keyword search in the Force-Directed Graph, dynamic query and filter by legends in the Scatter Plot. Users can carry out the tasks of overview, pan and zoom by the *DirectManipulationEvent* definitions, such as "OnViewLeftDoubleClick", "OnViewLeftDrag", and "OnViewRightDrag" shown in Fig. 3c.

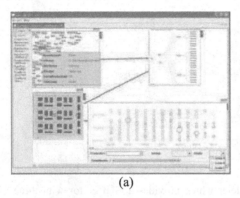 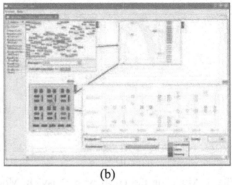

(a)   (b)

Fig. 5. (a) A prototype system generated by DaisyViz Runner. It includes four views connected with red links representing the relationships. Each view contains two parts: visualization and control panel which can be hidden. The visualizations in the views include Force-Directed Graph, DOITrees, TreeMaps, and Scatter Plot. (b) The results of multiple views coordination when users perform a right-click on an item in the Force-Directed Graph, which have triggered the brushing-and-linking coordination in DOITrees and TreeMaps, and drill-down coordination in Scatter Plot.

To test the flexibility and extensibility of DaisyViz, we extended the layout algorithms in *VisualStructureLaout* of *Mapping Lib* by adding a novel nested circle fisheye [40] based on CirclePacking [26] and a bar chart. Another prototype system, including Radial Graph, Nested Circle Fisheye, TreeMaps, and Bar hart, is illustrated in Fig. 6, which shows the results of brushing-and-linking coordination in TreeMaps and drill-down coordination in the nested circle fisheye and the bar chart.

Throughout the application development we can conclude that:
- DaisyViz can provide a unified data structure for tree, graph, and multi-dimensional data as the application examples shown. Since temporal, 1D, 2D, and 3D data is specific types of multi-dimensional data, DaisyViz still can cover them.
- DaisyViz can implement a variety of specific layout algorithms, including Radial Graph, Force-Directed Graph, DOITrees, TreeMaps, Scatter Plot,

Nested Circle Fisheye, and Bar chart in the application examples. And layout algorithms are extensible.

- DaisyViz can support a wide range of *infovis* tasks, e.g., overview, pan, zoom, filter by data attributes (i.e., dynamic query), filter by legends, keyword search, detail tooltip (i.e., detail-on-demand), coordination (e.g., brushing-and-linking, drill-down, etc.), by providing the interaction techniques, e.g., dynamic query, overview+detail, panning+zooming, focus+context, and multiple coordinated views, as the application examples shown.

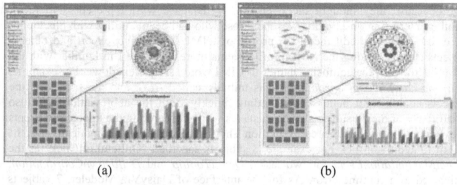

(a)   (b)

Fig. 6. Another prototype system generated by DaisyViz Runner. The visualizations in the views include Radial Graph, Nested Circle Fisheye, TreeMaps, and Bar chart.

5.2 Qualitative Usability Study

Although the expressiveness, effectiveness, flexibility and extensibility of DaisyViz are demonstrated in the application examples above, we still need to evaluate the usability of DaisyViz especially for non-expert users. To identify these usability issues, we conducted a qualitative usability study of DaisyViz, observing the development of applications by 10 non-expert users in the manufacturing enterprise and then interviewing them about the development process.

The 10 subjects had different backgrounds, including 4 computer programmers, 3 user interface designers, 2 data analysts, and 1 *infovis* expert. All lacked expertise on *infovis* techniques except that *infovis* expert. They all required *infovis* applications for data analysis in their work. The subjects were first given a tutorial for about 45 minutes, including the meaning of the concepts in UIMI, the XML schema of UIMI, some sample applications developed by DaisyViz. Then the subjects were asked to perform three tasks using a SQLServer database in the manufacturing enterprise. The first task was to create an application with three views, covering graph, tree, and multi-dimensional data. The subjects were asked to refine their views by using color, size, or shape to represent information about one or more data attributes. The second task was to add interaction controls to implement the functions including overview, pan, zoom, dynamic query, filter by legends, keyword search, and detail tooltip. Finally, the subjects were asked to add two coordination techniques among the three views, including brushing-and-linking coordination and drill-down coordination respectively. The tasks were carried out in a client-server environment and each subject was on a Windows PC client (2.6GHz Pentium 4 with 2GB RAM). The time limit was 150 minutes and the subjects' performance was recorded for further analysis. Then, an interview was performed to discuss the subjects' experiences during the three tasks.

Results showed that all subjects developed runnable applications. Eight of the ten subjects completed all tasks, and four subjects finished in 100 minutes. The most common difficulty the subjects encountered was that they had to switch frequently between the data model configuration panel and the SQLServer database to write SQL, because they thought the overview of database wasn't presented to them. Another interesting observation was that those who had been familiar with this toolkit preferred to directly edit the XML profile of UIMI. The *infovis* expert and other 5 subjects stated "Editing the XML profile seems more fast once I'm familiar with the UIMI." However, the confusing names in UIMI would slow them down. For example, *Brushing-and-LinkingCoordination* was initially called *BLC*, and most notably, the subjects couldn't get better understanding quickly from the abbreviation. We also found that 8 of the 10 subjects made mistakes while configuring the interaction events. They complained that the configuration should be detected automatically by the toolkit to avoid conflict. For example, 3 subjects specified "OnItemLeftClick" as the *DirectManipulationEvent* for two tasks, *DetailTooltip* and *DrillDownCoordination*, which led to a runtime error. As for the interface of DaisyViz Modeler, 7 subjects suggested that the controls for the mapping attributes configuration in the panel of control model, such as the dropdown box of the mapping attributes for dynamic query and keyword search, should be placed in the panel of visualization, because they thought these configurations all belonged to the mapping problems.

In response to these issues, we made some changes to DaisyViz to improve usability including: 1) An visualization of data schema for database was added to the DaisyViz Modeler interface (see Fig. 3a); 2) Some names in UIMI were changed for better understanding; 3) A conflict detection module for interaction events was added to the DaisyViz Modeler, and 4) Some mapping configurations for control model were also added to the panel of visualization model configuration in the DaisyViz Modeler interface. Therefore, the toolkit has made improvement through the usability study.

In addition, the interview showed most subjects appreciated the toolkit. Many non-expert users said "I'm surprised such complex applications can be created so easily and need little code as I did." The *infovis* expert, who had used many *infovis* toolkits, stated "It's unbelievable that the only thing I need to do is editing a simple XML." Eight of the ten subjects decided to use DaisyViz in their own work, and some applications are now using for data analysis in the manufacturing enterprise.

Both the application development examples and the user study have validated the goals of DaisyViz. The reaction from the subjects has been encouraging, and non-expert users or end-users can use the toolkit to quickly build their own *infovis* applications.

6 Conclusions and Future Work

This paper presented DaisyViz, a model-based user interfaces toolkit for development of interactive *infovis* system with multiple coordinated views. UIMI, a declarative interface model composed of data model, visualization model, and control model, serves as the core of the development process. The task of end-users is to build UIMI according domain-specific requirements, and then the prototype system would be generated automatically by DaisyViz. DaisyViz can support unified data structures and a lot of specific layout algorithms that are extensible. Besides, DaisyViz can support an extended taxonomy of *infovis* tasks by providing well-known interaction techniques. An application example for manufacturing enterprise has been developed to show the expressiveness, effectiveness, flexibility and extensibility of DaisyViz. Qualitative usability study validated the goals of DaisyViz, that is, it can support non-expert users or end-users to quickly build their domain-specific *infovis* applications without traditional programming. Future work is to improve the scalability of DaisyViz.

Acknowledgments. This research is supported by the National High-Tech Research and Development Plan of China under Grant NO. 2007AA04Z153, the National Grand Fundamental Research 973 Program of China under Grant No. 2007CB310900, 2006CB303105, and the National Natural Science Foundation of China under Grant No. U0735004.

References

1. Card S.K., Mackinlay J.D., Shneiderman B.: Readings in Information Visualization:Using Vision to Think. Morgan Kaufmann, San Francisco (1999)
2. Shneiderman B.: Dynamic queries for visual information seeking. IEEE Software. 11, 70--77 (1994)
3. Hornbæk K., Bederson B.B., Plaisant C.: Navigation patterns and usability of zoomable user interfaces with and without an overview. ACM Transactions on Computer-Human Interaction(TOCHI). 9, 362--389 (2006)
4. Furnas G.W.: A fisheye follow-up: further reflections on focus+context. In: Proceedings of the SIGCHI conference on Human Factors in computing systems, pp. 999--1008. ACM Press, New York (2006)
5. Baldonado M.Q., Woodruff A., Kuchinsky A.: Guidelines for using multiple views in information visualization. In: Proceedings of the working conference on Advanced Visual Interfaces(AVI'00), pp. 111--119. ACM Press, New York (2000)
6. Shneiderman B.: The eyes have it: A task by data type taxonomy for information visualizations. In: Proceedings of IEEE Workshop Visual Languages, pp. 336--343. IEEE Computer Science Press, Los Alamitos (1996)
7. Heer J., Card S.K., Landy J.A.: Prefuse: A toolkit for interactive information visualization. In: Proceedings of the SIGCHI conference on Human Factors in computing systems(CHI'05), pp. 421--430. ACM Press, New York (2005)
8. Bederson B.B., Hollan J.D., Perlin K., Meyer J., Bacon D., Furnas G.W.: Pad++: A zoomable graphical sketchpad for exploring alternate interface physics. Journal of Visual Language and Computing. 7, 7--31 (1996)

9. Bederson B.B., Meyer J., Good L.: Jazz: An extensible zoomable user interface graphics toolkit in Java. In: Proceedings of ACM Symposium on User Interface Software and Technology(UIST'00), pp. 171--180. ACM Press, New York (2000)
10. Bederson B.B., Grosjean J., Meyer J.: Toolkit Design for Interactive Structured Graphics. IEEE Transactions on Software Engineering. 30, 535--546 (2004)
11. North C., Shneiderman B.: Snap-Together Visualization: A user Interface for coordinating visualizations via relational schemata. In: Proceedings of the working conference on Advanced Visual Interfaces(AVI'00), pp.128--135. ACM Press, New York (2000)
12. Takatsuka M., Gahegan M.: GeoVISTA studio: a codeless visual programming environment for geoscientific data analysis and visualization. Computers and Geosciences. 28, 1131--1144 (2002)
13. Godinho P.I., Meiguins B.S., Meiguins A.S,, Carmo R.M., Carcia M.B., Almeida L.H., Lourenco R.: PRISMA-A multidimensional information visualization tool using multiple coordinated views. In: Proceedings of 11th International Conference on Information Visualization(IV'07), pp. 23--32. IEEE Computer Science Press, Washington (2007)
14. Stolte C., Tang D., Hanrahan P.: Polaris: A system for query, analysis and visualization of multi-dimensional relational databases. IEEE Transactions on Visualization and Computer Graphics. 8, 1--14 (2002)
15. Borner K., Zhou Y.: A software repository for education and research in information visualization. In: Proceedings of Fifth International Conference on Information Visualisation (IV'01), pp. 257--262. IEEE Computer Society Press, Los Alamitos (2001)
16. Fekete J.D.: The InfoVis Toolkit. In: Proceedings of IEEE Symposium on Information Visualization(InfoVis'04), pp. 167--174. IEEE Computer Society Press, Washington (2004)
17. Viegas F.B., Wattenberg M., van Ham F., Kriss J., McKeon M.: Many eyes: A site for visualization at internet scale. IEEE Transactions and Computer Graphics. 13, 1121--1128 (2007)
18. Matkovic K., Freiler W., Gracanin D., Hauser H.: ComVis: A coordinated multiple views system for prototyping new visualization technology. In: Proceedings of 12th International Information Visualization, pp. 215--220. IEEE Computer Society Press, Washington (2008)
19. Paterno F.: Model-based design and evaluation of interactive applications. Springer, Heidelberg (2000)
20. Bederson B.B., Shneiderman B.: Ordered and Quantum Treemaps:Making Effective Use of 2D Space to Display Hierarchies. ACM Transactions on Graphics. 21, 833--854 (2002)
21. Robertson G.G., Mackinlay J.D., Card S.K.: Cone Trees: Animated 3D Visualizations of Hierarchical Information. In: Proceedings of the SIGCHI conference on Human Factors in computing systems, pp. 189--194. ACM Press, New York (1991)
22. Lamping J., Rao R.: The Hyperbolic Browser: A Focus + Context Technique for Visualizing Large Hierarchies. Journal of Visual Languages and Computing. 7, 33--55 (1996)
23. Plaisant C., Grosjean J., Bederson B.: Spacetree: Supporting Exploration in Large Node Link Tree, Design Evolution and Empirical Evaluation. In: Proceedings of IEEE Symposium on Information Visualization (InfoVis'02), pp. 57--64. IEEE Press, Boston (2002)
24. Heer J., Card S.K.: DOITrees revisited: scalable, space-constrained visualization of hierarchical data. In: Proceedings of the working conference on Advanced visual interfaces(AVI'04), pp. 421--424. ACM Press, New York (2004)
25. Yang J., Ward M.O., Rundensteiner E.A.: InterRing: An Interactive Tool for Visually Navigating and Manipulating Hierarchical Structures. In: Proceedings of IEEE Symposium on Information Visualization (InfoVis'02), Boston, pp. 77-84. IEEE Press, Boston (2002)
26. Wang W.X., Wang H., Dai G.Z., Wang H.: Visualization of Large Hierarchical Data by Circle Packing. In: Proceedings of the SIGCHI conference on Human Factors in computing systems(CHI'06), pp. 517--520. ACM Press, New York (2006)

27. Eades P., Feng Q.W.: Multilevel Visualization of Clustered Graphs. In: Proceedings of the 4th Intl. Symposium on Graph Drawing, pp. 101--112. Springer, Heidelberg (1996)
28. Eades P., Huang M.L.: Navigating Clustered Graphs using Force-Directed Methods. Journal of Graph Algorithms and Applications. 4, 157--181 (2000)
29. Yee K.P., Fisher D., Dhamija R., Hearst M.S.: Animated exploration of dynamic graphs with radial layout. In: Proceedings of IEEE Symposium on Information(InfoVis'01), pp. 43--50. IEEE Computer Science Press, Los Alamitos (2001)
30. Becker R.A., Cleveland W.S.: Brushing scatterplots. Technometrics. 29, 127--142 (1987)
31. Inselberg A., Dimsdale B.: Parallel coordinates: a tool for visualizing multi-dimensional geometry. In: 1st conference on Visualization , pp. 23--26. IEEE Press, Washington (1990)
32. Havre S., Hetzler B., Nowell L.: ThemeRiver: visualizing theme changes over time. In: IEEE Symposium on Information Visualization(InfoVis'00). pp. 115--123. IEEE Press, Washington (2000)
33. Keim D.A., Schneidewind J., Sips M.: CircleView-A new approach for visualizing time-related multidimensional data sets. In: Proceedings of the working conference on Advanced visual interfaces (AVI'04), pp. 179--182. ACM Press, New York (2004)
34. Tominski C., Abello J., Schumann H.: Axes-Based Visualizations with Radial Layouts. In: ACM Symposium on Applied Computing, pp. 1242--1247. ACM Press, New York (2004)
35. Graphviz, http://www.research.att.com/sw/tools/graphviz
36. Marshall M.S., Herman I., Melancon G.: An object-oriented design for graph visualization. Software. Practice and Experience. 31, 739--756 (2001)
37. Thomsen E.: OLAP Solutions: Building Multidimensional Information Systems. Wiley Computer Publishing, New York (1997)
38. Krentzer W., Mckenzie B.: Programming for Artificial Intelligence, Method, Tools and Applications. Addison-Wesley, New Jersey (1991)
39. Jeffrey H., Maneesh A.: Software Design Patterns for Information Visualization. IEEE Transactions on Visualization and Computer Graphics. 12, 853--860 (2006)
40. Ren L., Wang W.X., Teng D.X., Ma C.X., Dai G.Z., Wang H.A.: A Focus+Context Technique for Interactive Visualization of Large Hierarchies (in Chiese). Journal of Software. 19, 3073--3082 (2008)
41. Chris W.: Metavisual Exploration and Analysis of DEVise Coordination in Improvise. In: Fourth International Conference on Coordinated & Multiple Views in Exploratory Visualization (CMV'06), pp.79--90. IEEE Computer Science Press, Washington (2006)

A New Interactive Platform for Visual Analytics of Social Networks

Quang Vinh Nguyen[1] and Mao Lin Huang[2]

[1]School of Computing & Mathematics, University of Western Sydney
[2]Faculty of Engineering & Information Technology, University of Technology, Sydney
vinh@scm.uws.edu.au, maolin@it.uts.edu.au

Abstract. This paper presents a new interactive platform for visual analytics of large networks and graphs. The platform integrates multiple graph layouts, interactive navigations and clustering algorithms into an effective and flexible analytical visual environment for better understanding of the nature of variety of different networks. This could lead to the discovery and revealing of hidden structures and relationships among the network items as well as the attributes associated with particular focused elements. We provide a number of interactive navigation and exploration methods so that it can provide a flexible and controllable way to archive the preferable view for analytics. We are extending our visual analytics platform into a large and high-resolution display.

Keywords: Information Visualisation, Graph Visualisation, Interaction, Visual Analytics, Network, Visualisation Framework.

1 Introduction

Our knowledge-driven technology-mediated environments generate more than 5 exabytes ($5x10^{18}$ bytes) of new information each year [1]. Much of this information reflects the complex interconnected processes and systems that operate in these environments that span across ecological micro- and macro-systems to interconnected financial markets. A network, such as a social network, can be defined as the information associated with and the relationships between actors which are elements in the network, such as people, groups, corporate organisations, business partners, and others. Considering such systems in isolation is not longer feasible. For the last decade, there has been a rapidly increasing interest in modelling and understanding such systems and processes through network models [2]. Real world networks are often very large with thousands or even millions of elements and relationships. Examples of such networks range from biological and ecological networks through to socio-technological networks, such as telephone call graphs and the underlying interaction graphs on the Internet [3]. These heterogeneous networks present big challenges on how to discover reliable and significant patterns and irregularities within them? How do we holistically make sense of these discoveries and their network models? How do we harness these data at different levels of granularity in collective decision making processes? The challenge - and the fundamental focus of this research - resides in creating a fast and effective platform in which analysts quickly analyse huge amount of data as well as share their insights and knowledge.

Network analysis brings a lot of benefits in a wide range of application domains, such as economics/finance analysis [4], homeland defence [5], and knowledge management, organisation development, social science, health informatics (see [6]). For example, analysing a terrorism network can help to understand the roles and relational structures among terrorists, their organisations, the associated events and other information that could reveal the potential vulnerabilities and identify any potential attack before it occurs. Another example is that the social network analysis for large cooperate organisations could identify the unofficial organisational roles, such as central connector, boundary spanner, information broker and peripheral specialists. The analysis of social network in organisations can provide business benefits including 1) identify and retention with vital knowledge and connections, 2) improvement of innovation, productivity and responsiveness, 3) lead to better decisions about organisational changes and establishment of key knowledge roles, and 4) insight into challenges of knowledge transfer and integration following restructuring, merges or acquisitions.

Many projects target the analysis of large information spaces, in which data sets are originated from many sources and they can contain millions of items, relations and attributes. Therefore, the scalability, efficiency and speed are the key issues in ensuring the effectiveness of analysis tools. Data is usually available from different sources, different formats and dimensions, the underlying system should provide the ability to access data seamlessly across data sources and formats and ingest the merged data into analysis tools. The seamless data access and data ingest processes should be seamless so that an analyst can perform his/her analysis tasks without concern about the underline data. The visual representation needs to be efficient enough for implementation in interactive large high resolution display systems. It is also a challenge to ensure the quality of large scale automated data analysis.

2 Large Network Visual Analytics

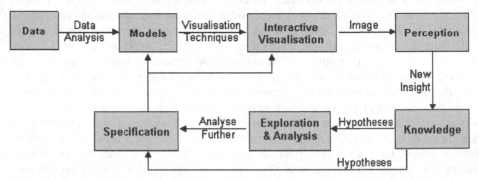

Figure 1. The process sequence of Visual Analytics based on sense-making loop (Adapted from [11])

Large network visualization has been considered as an advanced approach for data analysis that has attracted many research works and projects that attempted to use visualization tp enhance the data analysis process. There are a number of good techniques that are quite capable for visual analytics of large graphs or networks of thousands to hundred thousands of nodes and edges, such as *Tulip* [7] and *ASK-GraphView* [8]. A comprehensive classification of analytical network visualisation tools or methods can also be found from the report written by A. Gort and J. Gort [9]. Although there are quite number of available tools for network and graph analysis, research for answering how to effectively integrating interactive visualisations with sense-making sequence (see Figure 1) is still one of the challenges in data analysis.

Visual analytics systems have been introduced to bridge the gap between human visual analysis and automated analysis. Visual analytics is formally defined as the science of analytical reasoning facilitated by the interaction with visual representation of abstract data [10]. Technically, it combines automated analysis techniques (such as data mining, statistical analysis, compression and filtering) with interactive visualisations, analytical reasoning and other related disciplines to achieve effective understanding, reasoning and decision making. Visual analytics can also be seen as an integral approach to decision making by combining interactive visualisation, human-factors and data analysis. Therefore, it is particular suitable for the analysis of large and complex networks and data sets in general. our goal is for creating a platform to enable people to 1) synthesise information and derive insight from massive, dynamic, ambiguous, and often conflicting data, 2) detect the expected and discover the unexpected, 3) provide timely, defensible, and understandable assessments, and 4) communicate assessment effectively for action [11]. As a result, visual analytics has been applied into a number of application domains, such as Homeland Security [12], Visual Analytics at the Boeing Company [13], Foreign Animal and Zoonotic Diseases [14], Finance [15], and many others.

Although some available frameworks, such as *Have Green* [16] and *Universal Visualization Platform* [17], can be used effectively for visual analytics with normal displays, these models or frameworks are insufficient to be extended for large high-resolutions displays. We are looking for an visual platform that ensures the effectiveness of visual analytics process with a large high-resolution display. This platform serves a central medium for data analysis, knowledge discovery and decision making through a combination of automated analysis techniques, interactive visualisation, and analytical reasoning that is based the human sense-making loop (see Figure 1). The future analysis will be a strong connection between central analysts with remote analysts in which the knowledge and insight are concurrently shared and updated among them for better knowledge discovery.

This paper presents a visual analytics platform that combines of different graph layouts, interactive navigations and automated analysis algorithms. This integration of these components makes it flexible for handling a variety of networks and hierarchical structures. The paper is organised as follow. Section 3 presents the architecture of visual analytics tool. Section 4 provides technical details of the interactive navigation and exploration methods. The following section discusses about our current and future work for large and high-resolution displays. The final section summarises and concludes our work.

3 The Architecture

The architecture of our network analysis platform includes three main components: 1) data collection and conversion, 2) automated analysis, 3) visualization and interaction. These components are briefly described as below.

3.1 Collection and conversion

Raw data is collected from a variety of sources, such as email networks, protein networks, citation networks, and others. This process is responsible for converting the raw data of different formats into uniform XML format for automated data analysis and visualisation. This process is independent to other processes and is operated prior the automated analysis and visualization.

3.2 Automated analysis

This process analyses the structure of networks and finds out the clusters of similarity and connection based on the chosen algorithms. Network analysis includes concepts and data mining techniques based on degree distributions, centrality measures, clustering, network correlations, random graph models, and models of network evolution (see a summary at [18]). The automated analysis has a tight integration of interactive visualisation and related disciplines.

At this stage, graph clustering algorithms are used to discover the community structures embedded in a large graph and then divide them into densely connected sub-graphs. We use a fast graph clustering algorithm in which algorithm 1 can also achieve a consistent partitioning result in which a graph is divided into a set of clusters of the similar size [19], and algorithm 2 is used to discover communities with various size [20]. The clustering process works independently with the visualisation so that the findings can be updated as well as receiving feedback from visualisation.

3.3 Visualisation and Interaction

The interactive visualisation is more than just an interface. It provides users with an intelligent and appropriate display and users can also view, interact, and select different layout methods through the visualization. Interactive visualisation techniques usually perform well on particular application domains with similar data sets. Therefore, no particular technique is always superior to another. Intelligent interactive visualisation is one of the important approaches that takes the advantage of optimized algorithms by providing appropriate layouts and interactions based on the nature of applications, data sets and analysts' preferences.

A combination of several layout algorithms is employed to draw different clusters. We aim to optimize the utilization of geometrical space and so that a large network with multiple clusters can be drawn in a normal screen size. This interactive interface is able to not only show the abstract view of the entire network with its clustering property and relational structures but also display the detail of any particular group, item and their associate connections and properties. We use rich graphic attributes to assist viewers to quickly identify the domain specific properties associated with data items.

The visualisation consists of a collection of multiple modified layout algorithms, such as *Enccon* [20], *Spring Embedder* [21], *Circular Drawing*, and the combination of multiple algorithms on one layout [22]. These algorithms are employed automatically or are selected manually by user to provide the optimal layout for the large network. Refining processes, including layout adjustment and node overlapping remove, are also applied onto the display to enhance the clarity, aesthetical niceness and cluster properties of drawings. At any stage, user can switch between different layouts and vice versa to obtain the optimal and/or preferable displays. Figure 2 shows the layout of the same network using different algorithms in our system. Figure 3 shows a multi-scale layout and display using *Enccon* and *Spring Embedder* algorithms.

In the future, we aim to provide an intelligent visualization that can produce the most suitable displays with corresponding layouts and interaction mechanism based on the nature of applications, data sets, analyst preferences and underline sense-making rules. The visualisation can be manually adjusted via user's feedbacks during the interaction.

The challenge lays on the creation an effective mechanism to integrate different interactive visualisation techniques together so that the visualization can provide a best-possible display to satisfy analysts' preference and observation styles. During the navigation, we allow users to interactively adjust views and layouts to reach an optimized representation of the network; from which users can obtain the best understanding of the data and structures they are observing. The visualization consists of real time human-computer interactions, fast graph layout and navigation algorithms for visual processing of hundred thousands of items within minutes or seconds using a personal computer with limited display space and computational power.

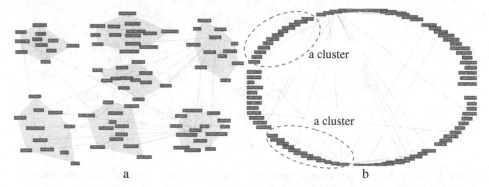

a   b

Figure 2. An example of two graph layouts of the same network in which a) using a Spring Embedder with Enccon partitionning, and b) using a circular layout algorithm.

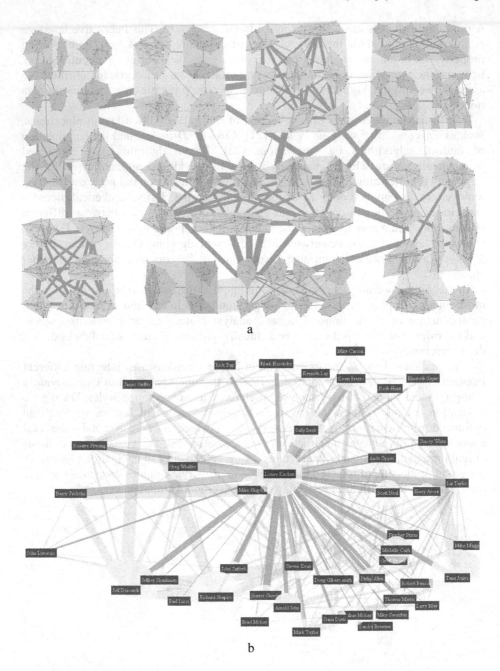

Figure 3. An example of the visualizations of different networks where a) shows the abstract view of a hierarchical graph and b) shows the detail view associate with an item.

4 Interactive Navigation and Exploration

There is no pure layout technique that could assist data retrieval without providing users with an associate interactive navigation mechanism in graphic user interface design. In our visualisation, during the navigation user can interactively adjust the views to reach an optimised representation of the graph; from which user can obtain the best understanding of the data and its relational structures he/she are currently interesting in. The navigation is an integration of various viewing and interaction techniques so that it can provide a flexible and controllable solution to archive the preferable view. Details of these techniques are further described.

4.1 Chain-Context View

We applied an efficient interaction method, Chain-Context View [23] for the navigation of large networks. Instead of displaying a single or small number of context views as in traditional approaches, we provide users with a display of a progressive sequence of context views attempting to maximize the displayed contextual information. The display of rich context information produced in the exploration path could greatly increase the accuracy of user decisions and reduce the unsuccessful trips and unnecessary views during visual exploration of the large structures.

Conceptually, Chain-Context View allows users to trace each step of their interaction and makes it easy for them to jump or return to any level of the hierarchy they have already visited. This method maintains user's orientation during exploration by providing multiple navigational views. This also enables users to explore large graphs by arbitrary paths while moving towards the target view. In comparison with traditional approaches which only allow sequential navigation; our proposed navigation scheme is believed to be more efficient.

Technically, the entire display area is initially divided into two regions: 1) a small area in the left-hand-side for displaying all context-views and 2) a large area in the right-hand-side for the main-view (or focus view).

The main-view - displays a current focus sub-structure or the complete structure. This view occupies the main portion of the entire display. By showing the detail of the focusing structure, users can inspect particular data items, analyse the structure for taking further actions.

The context-views - display inside a small rectangular region with an efficient partitioning. The display of an intermediate chain of context views during the navigation also enables users to choose an arbitrary path for reaching the target quickly and efficiently. While the chain of context views is responsible to display contextual information, it should not occupy the major portion of display space. Some details of the substructures displayed in the context views are filtered through visual abstraction. Only the main structures remain for guiding navigation. The abstracted context views aim to maintain users' orientation of where they are, where they came from, and where they have been during visual exploration.

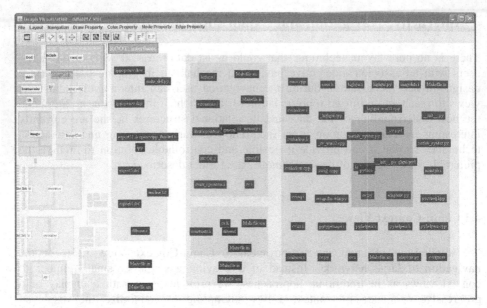

Figure 4. An example of the chain-context views when browsing a large file system. The context views are displayed on the small left-hand-side and the main-view is displayed a current navigation point on the large right-hand-side. The current mode is *highlight-and-select* method in which the first context view is highlight.

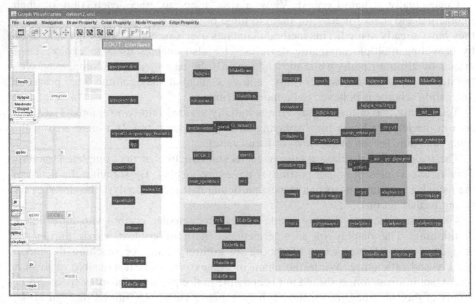

Figure 5. An example of *fisheye-browsing* of chain-context views using the same data set as Figure 4. This indicate the focus point is at the context view whose root is "NODE 1".

At any stage, users can interact with context views either using highlight-and-select or fisheye-browsing modes. Highlight-and-select includes two steps: 1) highlight and enlarge a context view in which more information can be displayed and 2) select the context to transform to the main-view. The highlight and enlarge step is aimed to provide a quick analysis at context views without showing these views at the focus panel (see Figure 4).

Fisheye-browsing enables the enlargement of context views dynamically using a modified fisheye distortion. In contrast to the highlight-and-select approach, in which the size of view boxes is decreased in order, the size of context views is now dependant on the position of the mouse pointer. The focus view is first defined at a current mouse pointer and than users can scroll down and up to change the focus point, and the position and size of all context views in the chain are then adjusted accordingly. We eliminate the distortion by making the uniform size at a particular context view (see Figure 5).

4.2   Group Selection

Group selection is the ability that a user can select a group of nodes for a quick analysis without retrieving all sub-networks that associating with these selected nodes. This technique is useful when the user want to inspect or analyse just a group of nodes. When a number of nodes in the *main-view* are selected, the program will recalculate the new layout of selected nodes and then display the main-view as a new structure (see Figure 6).

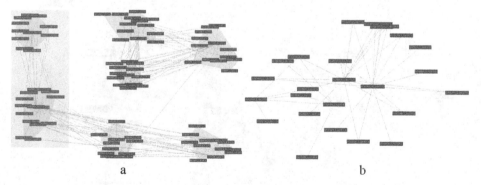

| a | b |

Figure 6. An example of group selection interaction. a) shows the network when the user is selecting a group of nodes at the left side and b) shows the corresponding visualisation for those selected nodes.

4.3   Node Centralised Selection

Node centralised selection is the ability that allows users to select one or more nodes for further analysis on sub-networks that are associated with these selected nodes.

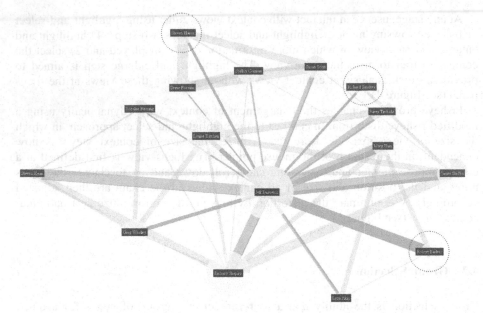

Figure 7. An example of node centralized selection for a particular node. The visualisation of the sub-network associated with the focus node "Jeff Dasovich" is selected from the larger network for deep analysis.

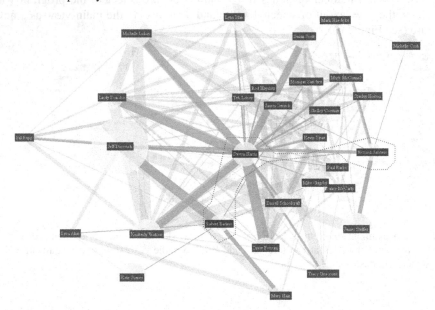

Figure 8. Another example of node centralized selection of a group of nodes. The visualization of the sub-network associated with three focused nodes: "Steven Harris", "Richard Sanders" and "Robert Badeer". These three nodes are red-circled that are selected from Figure 8.

This technique is particular useful when the user want to have a deep analysis on one or more particular nodes. Technically, when a number of nodes at the *main-view* are selected, the program will first find out the nodes from the entire network that link with the selected nodes. A layout algorithm is then applied to calculate the new layout of the sub-network. Rich graphics are also used to enhance to representation in which emphasised focus nodes and edges are highlighted while unfocused nodes and edges are less highlighted. For example, the selected nodes are drawn with brighter colours and the edges among un-selected nodes are painted with dimmer and transparent colours. Edges that are not associated with selected nodes are also painted in de-emphasised manner. Figure 7 and Figure 8 show examples of node centralised selection of one or multiple persons respectively of an email network.

4.3   Interactive Visual Clustering

Interactive Visual Clustering is a process that enable users to create and delete clusters and reform the clustering trees in the whole network.

In the clustering process, the whole visualization is fully animated. Every change at one of the lower layers, whether triggered by the user or by another agent, is animated at the picture layer. The use of multiple animations may reduce the cognitive effort of the user in recognizing change of the clustering structures. This preserves the user's "mental map" [24]. There are six types of animation that are implemented in our system. These are detailed below.

- *Force animation* - The force model above is used in the animation of all changes to picture. The forces move the nodes toward a minimum energy state, and this movement gives the sequence $D_1;D_2;\ \dots\ ;\ D_k$ of drawings to smoothly change the layout from abridgment to the next. Overall, the animation driven by the forces is the most important mechanism for the smooth transition between changes at the layers lower than the picture layer.
- *Animated addition and deletion* of nodes and edges - When a node is deleted or added to the abridgment, we use animated *shrinking* or *growing* to help the user identify nodes that are disappearing or appearing. Disappearing nodes lose their connecting edges, then shrink until they disappear. Appearing nodes are displayed in a reduced size with their edges, then grow to be full-sized nodes. This avoids the sudden disappearing/appearing of node images on the screen, which can disturb the user's mental map.
- *Animated cluster regions* - Nodes move according to the force model, and the rectangular regions representing clusters follow the nodes. At all times, each cluster is the minimum enclosing rectangle of its children. These rectangles move smoothly as the positions of the children change. This is especially important for the gathering operation; the clusters separate smoothly.
- *Animated scaling* - Animated shrinking scales down a picture if it gets too large for the screen. Further, animated enlarging is used to increase the size of the picture; this enables the user to see details and makes direct

manipulation operations of the picture easier. In fact, animated scaling is implemented by simply changing the forces in the springs; for example, to shrink the whole picture, every spring is increased in strength.

- *Animated cluster closing/opening* - When closing a cluster, we firstly use animation to reduce the size of closed region of this cluster. As soon as the size reaches a certain threshold layer we smoothly replace the representation of the cluster from its opened form (a red line bounded rectangle) to its closed form (a small black line bounded rectangle). When opening a cluster, we firstly smoothly replace the representation of the cluster from its closed form to its opened form. The children and relevant links of the cluster are smoothly added into the layout. Then we smoothly enlarge the size of this cluster to its normal size.
- *Camera animation* - Camera animation moves the whole drawing. It is optional. It can be used, for example, to move specific nodes of interest to the center of the screen.

All these animations operate in parallel.

5   Future Work - Large and High-Resolution Displays

With technological advances, large high-resolution (or wall-size) displays are becoming more and more available in many fields. From multi-monitor configuration to tiled LCD panels to projection-based seamless displays, researchers have been constructing large displays with various hardware configurations. A large scientific system is able to produce a high resolution display of ten million pixels to even hundreds of million pixels, such as the near 287 million pixels display of *HIPerSpace* [25]. Two common features of such displays are increasing physical size and higher resolution in which a wall-size display can display easily large contextual and detail information. Therefore, it is particularly suitable for serving as a medium for presenting, capturing, exchanging ideas and interaction in supporting visual analytics of very large and complex information spaces (see an example at Figure 9).

We are currently extending our visual analytics system for large and high-resolution displays. This adoption of our future work aims to provide 1) a more effective visual analytics framework, 2) more intelligent visualisations and 3) tight integration of automated analysis and interactive visualisations.

The new framework required to ensure the effectiveness of the use of large-high resolution displays so that it can handle a vast amount of information in a fast speed. This platform serves a central medium for data analysis, knowledge discovery and decision making through a combination of automated analysis techniques, interactive visualisation, analytical reasoning based our human sense-making loop (see Figure 1). There should be a strong connection between central analysts with remote analysts in which the knowledge and insight are concurrently shared and updated among them for better knowledge discovery. We will also investigate a more effective integration of automated analysis and interactive visualisations. The integration is not only at intelligent visualisation but also at general context of automated analysis and interactive visualisations.

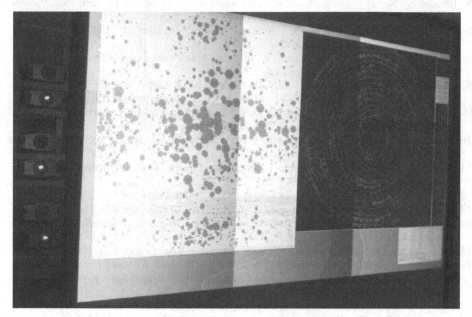

Figure 9. An example of multiple visualizations shown with large and high-resolution displays.

6 Conclusion

We have presented a new visual analytics tool for large networks and/or graphs analysis. Our system is a tight integration of different modules: data conversion, automated analysis and interactive visualisation. Each module is a combination of multiple algorithms so that an algorithm (or combination) can be selected to archive the optimal result. Although the work is still on progress, we believe that our work will be a valuable tool for the visual analytics of large networks and/or graphs. We will next extend our tool for large and high-resolution displays.

References

1. Lyman, P., Varian H.R.: How Much Information? University of California at Berkeley, http://www2.sims.berkeley.edu/research/projects/how-much-info-2003/
2. Newman, M. Watts, D., Barabási A.L.: The Structure and Dynamics of Networks, Princeton University Press (2006).
3. Almaas, E. and Barabási A.L.: The Architecture of Complexity: From the WWW to Cellular Metabolism. In: Dynamics of Complex Interconnected Systems: Networks and Bioprocesses, NATO Sciences Series (2006).
4. Malhotra, Y.: Enabling Knowledge Exchanges for E-Business Communities. Information Strategy: The Executive's Journal, pp. 26-31 (2005).

5. Ressler, S.: Social Network Analysis as an Approach to Combat Terrorism: Past, Present, and Future Research. Homeland Security Affairs, 2(2) (2006).
6. Patton, S.: Social Network Analysis Helps Maximize Collective Smarts. http://www.cio.com/article/print/6956.
7. Auber D.: Tulip: a Huge Graph Visualization Framework, Graph Drawing Software. Mathematics and Visualization, pp. 105-126 (2003).
8. Abello J., van Ham F., Krishnan N.: ASK-GraphView: A Large Scale Graph Visualization System. IEEE Transactions on Visualization and Computer Graphics, 12(5), 2006.
9. Gort, A., Gort, James.: Survey of Network Visualization Tools. Contract Report, DRDC Ottawa CR 2007-280, Defence R&D Canada, (2007).
10. Thomas, J.J., Cook, K.A.: Illuminating the Path. IEEE Computer Society Press, Los Alamitos (2005).
11. Keim D. et al: Visual Analytics: Definition, Process, and Challenges Information Visualization. LNCS 4950, pp. 154–175 (2008).
12. National Visualization and Analytics Center (NVAC), http://nvac.pnl.gov.
13. Kao, A.: Visual Analytics at the Boeing Company. VAC Consortium, (2008).
14. Clarke, N. and Nipp T.: Foreign Animal and Zoonotic Diseases: An Information Analysis Framework. VAC Consortium (2007).
15. Ribarsky, W.: Discovery Suspicious Financial Activity. VAC Consortium (2007).
16. Wong, P. C., Chin Jr, G., Foote, H., Mackey, P., Thomas J.: Have Green – A Visual Analytics Framework for Large Semantic Graphs. In: IEEE Symposium on Visual Analytics Science and Technology (VAST2006), pp. 67-74 (2006).
17. Gee, A. G. et al. Universal visualization platform. In: SPIE (2005).
18. Newman, M.E.J.: The Structure and Function of Complex Networks. SIAM Review, 45, pp. 167-256 (2003).
18. Huang M.L. and Nguyen Q.V.: A Fast Algorithm for Balanced Graph Clustering. In: 11th Int'l. Conf. on Information Visualisation (IV'07), IEEE, pp. 46-52 (2007).
19. Newman M.E.J., Girvan M.: Finding and Evaluating Community Structure in Networks. Physical Review E, 69:026113 (2004).
20. Nguyen, Q. V. and Huang, M. L.: EncCon: An Approach to Constructing Interactive Visualization of Large Hierarchical Data. Information Visualization Journal, Palgrave, 4(1), pp. 1-21 (2005).
21. Eades, P.: A Heuristic for Graph Drawing. Congressus Numerantium, 42, pp. 149-60 (1984).
22. Huang, M. L. and Nguyen, Q. V.: Large Graph Visualization by Hierarchical Clustering. Journal of Software, 19(8), pp. 1933-1946 (2008).
23. Huang, M. L., Nguyen, Q. V.: Space-Filling Interaction with Chain-Context View. In: *IEEE Symposium on Information Visualization 2008 (InfoVis 2008) - Poster Section*, IEEE, Columbus, Ohio (2008).
24. Eades, P., Lai, W., Misue, K. and Sugiyama, K.: Preserving the mental map of a diagram. In: Compugraphics 91, pp. 24-33 (1991).
25. Ramsey, D. Highest-Resolution Scientific Display System. http://www.spafi.org.

Strategic paths and memory map: Exploring a building and memorizing knowledge

Sandro Varano[1], Jean-Claude Bignon[2]

MAP CRAI UMR n°694/CNRS/CULTURE
[1] Ecole Nationale Supérieure d'Architecture de Strasbourg, 8 Boulevard du Président
Wilson, 67000 Strasbourg, France
[2] Ecole Nationale Supérieure d'Architecture de Nancy, 2 rue Bastien Lepage, BP 40435,
54001 Nancy, France
{varano, bignon}@crai.archi.fr

Abstract. Restoring archaeology and architecture, we propose a 3D navigation mode based on topographic and cognitive paths. During the exploration of a 3D model, the learner can create his own memory map facilitating the appropriation and memorization of knowledge. In this article, we will correlate the exploration and creation activities. The Great Pyramid of Giza is a support to this work.

Keywords: Archaeology and architecture, strategic path, memory map, learning.

1 Introduction

This work deals with archaeological and architectural restoration. The aim is to teach the public by facilitating the appropriation and memorization of new knowledge of cultural heritage. The system presented proposes a 3D navigation mode based on strategic paths dedicated to learning.

In our system, the real-time visit of an archeological site or an architectural monument leads to two activities that the learner performs in parallel:

- the exploration of the 3D model
- the creation of the memory map

These activities belong to a real educational project: the exploration based on clues discovery and riddles resolution incites the learner to participate; the creation helps the learner to organize and visualize information. Both processes allow him to structure and construct knowledge.

During the exploration activity, the learner is guided and motivated in sequenced and superimposed routes, while allowing a lot of freedom. This structure in double layers is composed of the topographical path and the cognitive path. During the creation activity, the learner materializes his mental map. The memory map evolves according to the progress of the learner on these paths.

M.L. Huang et al. (eds.), *Visual Information Communication*,
DOI 10.1007/978-1-4419-0312-9_16, © Springer Science+Business Media, LLC 2010

In this research work, we will correlate the creation of the memory map with the kind of narrative proposed during the exploration. In our study, we will choose the Great Pyramid of Giza in Egypt. With the help of Tristan Truchot, we created a prototype of an extract of the scenario to estimate and experiment our work.

2 Strategic paths

2.1 The topographical path

To be able to structure the movements, we introduce the notion of the topographical path by identifying critical points and secondary points in the path and by putting them in concordance. It is necessary to choose in the studied building the interesting critical points according to the message that we want to communicate to the learner. Each crossing point suggests specific actions that we wish to represent in the topographical path. The crossing points of the path consist of two types of points:

- the information points, defining the information route
- the knowledge points, defining the knowledge route

The data on the information route are reinvested in the knowledge points where the learner transforms the information into knowledge. The knowledge point is a critical point structuring the path in sequences.

The successive sequences define a quest. The number of information points in each sequence is defined in relation to the riddle proposed and the number of knowledge points in a quest is defined by the message (religious, structural aspect, etc.) to be taught (fig. 1).

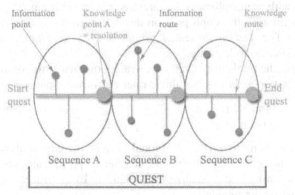

Fig. 1. Successive sequences of the path defining a quest.

2.2 The cognitive path

Research and cognitive experiments have shown that the learner must be constantly alerted and motivated to be interested in the studied topic. The acquisition of new knowledge depends on his willingness to achieve the objectives defined at the beginning.

To motivate the learner by avoiding a "cognitive overload" [1], we define a ludic aspect of the path in relation to the diversity of spaces that can be visited and in relation to the possible interactions in these spaces by manipulating multimodal information.

We decide to create some extensions of the path in the 3D base model. These spaces voluntarily added, fictitious or depending on the historical context of the building, belong to the information route and hold the clues for solving the riddle at the knowledge point and for moving to the next sequence. The knowledge points would thus be existing spaces in a building to be communicated. The transition between the existing spaces and added spaces is possible by crossing portals.

Imagine a path in the Cheops Pyramid in Egypt. The learner moves in real time in the existing spaces in the monument. He can take at any time inserted exterior spaces. By leaving the "King's Chamber", he could go for example to a mummification room of the second empire, to the Louvre Museum in Paris, to an invented virtual space allowing an interaction between the learner and his environment.

3 The memory map

During the creation activity, the learner outlines his path. Like a cartographer, he reveals his discoveries in order to establish a journal telling the story of his journey.

3.1 A multimedia notebook

According to David Cohen, multimedia has three components: Audiovisual, Interactivity and Network [2].

The memory map is a support crossing various graphic and sound representations: it allows the learner to store images, take notes, sketch drawings and play audio or video: multimodal information found during the 3D exploration or created by the learner. Information contained on the map is manipulated. Actions such as moving, connecting, correcting, removing, etc, maintain an interaction between information and the user.

The memory map is not a closed system with its own data library. Connections are possible with Internet. This concept of network extends the notions of space and distance between consulted information and the learner.

3.2 A locating tool

Outlining a path to explain where we have come from but also where we are going. In this context, a rapid movement system is thus established to navigate between the memory map and the 3D model. This feedback system is possible using sensitive areas. Teleportation provides a transfer between two points of view: an internal or subjective focus on the building and a zero focus around the memory map.

3.3 A memory tool

The memory map transmits messages. Its capacity to produce meanings allows the learner to build his own reasoning. According to Jean Piaget [3], knowledge results from the interaction between the person and the environment, compared to the constructivist hypothesis: we appropriate knowledge that we build ourselves.

The possible links between the information allow the learner to create associations between elements. This process is similar to the mnemonic method. This activity is a learning process by organizing information and by encouraging memorization.

4 A scenario in the Cheops Pyramid

A prototype is realized using the *Java* language in order to create the memory map and the level editor *Unreal Ed 4.0* (with the video game *Unreal Tournament 3* [4]) in order to create a 3D model of the pyramid (fig.2). The method consists in using the Internet protocols (*TCP* and *HTTP*) to put in relation the 3D model and the memory map.

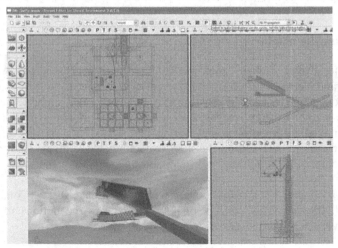

Fig. 2. The Cheops Pyramid in the level editor *Unreal Ed 4.0*.

The Great Pyramid contains many mysteries. Its architectural, symbolic or historic complexity, allows us to define several quests. In our study, we approach the religion of the pyramid.

4.1 Story of a journey into the afterlife

The pyramid is the funeral monument allowing the pharaoh to live eternally. The purpose of the quest is to reveal the journey of the pharaoh to reach the afterlife.

The learner will discover through the pyramid a considerable universe of symbols and religious practices assuring the rebirth of the deceased.

He will move in the monument with a subjective point of view embodying the soul of the pharaoh Cheops.

The quest possesses four riddles or four knowledge points (fig. 3):

- the entrance: the cosmos perceived from the Nile
- the Great Gallery
- the "Queen's Chamber": a path of obstacles
- the "King's Chamber": return to his sarcophagus without mistakes

Each solved riddle delivers a canopic jar to the learner. The four canopic jars collected allow him to reach the objective of the quest.

As an example, we will develop the knowledge point C.

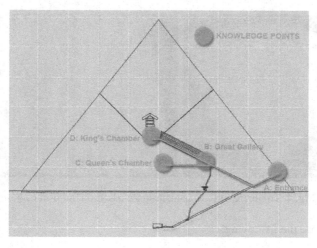

Fig. 3. The route of knowledge in the Cheops Pyramid.

4.2 The riddle of the "Queen's Chamber"

The "Queen's Chamber" has its name by mistake. In fact, the King's wives had their tombs near the Great Pyramid. This chamber, and in particular the North and South ducts, question researchers. These ducts are blocked by limestone doors possessing two copper handles.

The riddle is to discover the ducts and their astronomical and religious functions.

4.3 The information spaces

The number of information spaces results from the riddle of the chamber. We report three spaces and we will develop one to study the possible actions:

- Reading space: the invisible and immaterial entities of human being
- Immersion space: a journey by solar bark
- Logic and mechanism space: the weighing of the heart

This space informs about the ritual obstacles that the pharaoh must pass for his resurrection in the afterlife, materialized by the doors blocking the ducts.

In reference to the film *Cube* [5], the logic and mechanism space is constituted by attached boxes in three dimensions (fig. 4). These rooms and the passages assuring their communication are a labyrinth. They are a metaphor of traps and doors that the pharaoh must face.

The deceased must prove his purity by finding and reciting magic words. In the judgment room possessing scales, his weighed heart is then lighter than the feather of Maât.

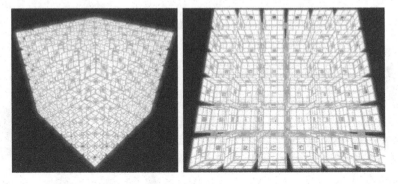

Fig. 4. The logic and mechanism space based on the film *Cube*.

The events are the following:

- The portal located in the horizontal corridor of the pyramid (fig. 5) teleports the learner to the first room. This room possesses an extract of the Egyptian *Book of the Dead* (Papyrus of Hunefer, British Museum, London) illustrating the weighing of the heart and the judgment.

Fig. 5. Teleportation portal located in the horizontal corridor.

- Each room possesses six doors with symbols based on the *Book of the dead*. The doors are present to guide the learner (fig. 6). There are the doors guarded by the hostile creatures Ammout and Apophis (crocodile, snake, insect, etc) and by passing through them, the learner is blocked in a room and is forced to come back.
- There are also the doors indicating the route of confession (feather, jar, etc). By passing through them, the learner discovers a fragment of papyrus mentioning a magic word to be recited ("I didn't incite to cry", "I didn't ordain to kill", etc).

Fig. 6. A room and its doors in the logic and mechanism space.

- The route of confession leads to the judgment room. It possesses scales in its center, a feather and a jar. Forty two judges and five gods Anubis, Maât, Thot, Horus and Osiris (frescoes on walls) attend the weighing done by the learner.
- A portal allows the learner to return into the pyramid. Then, he explores the other information spaces or goes to the "Queen's Chamber" to resolve the riddle.

5   Correlation between the memory map and the strategic path

Each knowledge point allows the realization of a screenshot. It is a page of the memory map as a support of representation. When the learner visits the knowledge point, he initializes automatically the screenshot illustrating the space where he is (fig. 7). Thus, the number of knowledge point determines the number of pages of the memory map.

Fig. 7. A screenshot in the « Queen's Chamber ».

Then, the learner builds his relation to the spaces using words and images related with the information spaces: he clicks on the information to display on a page; he writes key sentences; he draws details or plans.

In the information space *Cube*, the learner first stores the papyrus discovered in the first room. Thereafter, he can relate the symbols perceived on the doors to those of the papyrus, he then sketches the plan of the labyrinth to find his way and he writes magic words to remember (Fig. 8).

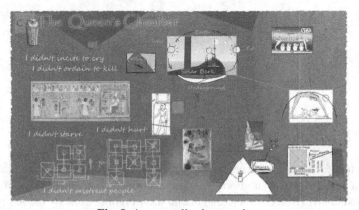

Fig. 8. A personalized screenshot.

Two types of links are managed in the system:

- The automatic links connect the information of the same space (2D links on a page) and the various knowledge points (3D links between pages).
- The personalized links created by the learner to connect similar elements.

When the riddle is solved, a canopic jar appears on the page.

The learner then begins the following sequence. He discovers the new riddle in the knowledge space and generates a new page of the memory map. The pages are added until the end of the quest (fig. 9).

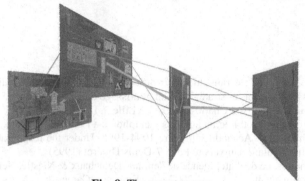

Fig. 9. The memory map.

A teleportation script (fig. 10) manages the transfers between the pages and knowledge spaces of the 3D model by clicking sensitive areas.

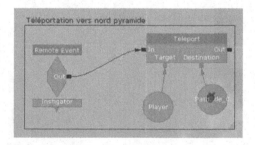

Fig. 10. A teleportation script in the level editor *Unreal Ed 4.0.*

6 Conclusion

During the visit of a 3D model, the exploration and creation activities allow us to elaborate a learning system supervising the navigation of the learner: by managing his movements and by taking into account his cognitive capacities.

We have seen how the creation of the memory map is based on the structure of the topographic and cognitive paths. The map accompanies the learner's exploration.

On the one hand, the paths manage movements and possible interactions in the spaces; on the other hand, the memory map retains traces as evidence of an exploration.

By producing meaning and by evoking his limits, the learner tries to master the unknown by his own representation.

Finally, the realization of the prototype shows some technical or screenplay problems. This prototype will allow us to validate or revise our work. An experiment is planned with students.

References

1. Jacquinot, G.: Les NTIC : écrans du savoir ou écrans au savoir. In: Chevalier, Y., Ateliers 9/1996, Outils multimédias et stratégies d'apprentissage du FLE, Cahiers de la Maison de la recherche, tome 1, Université Charles-de-Gaulle Lille 3, Lille (1996)
2. Cohen, D.: Interfactives ou l'écran agi. Les métaphores à l'écran. In: Écrits. Images. Oral et Nouvelles technologies. Actes du séminaire 1994-1995. Under the responsability of Marie-Claude Vettraino-Soulard, Université Paris 7-Denis Diderot (1995)
3. Piaget, J.: La naissance de l'intelligence de l'enfant. Delachaux & Niestlé, Neuchâtel (1936)
4. Unreal Tournament 3, 2007, Epic Games, Midway Games: http://www.unrealtournament3.com/
5. Natali, V.: Cube. Metropolitan FilmExport (1999)

Information visualization Approach on the University Examination Timetabling Problem

J. Joshua Thomas[1], Ahamad Tajudin Khader[2], Bahari Belaton[3]

[1,2,3] School of Computer Sciences Level 7, Room 720, Block G31,
11800 University Sains Malaysia Penang, Malaysia
http://www.cs.usm.my

Abstract. The university examination timetabling is known to be a highly constrained combinatorial optimization problem. We classify the examination timetabling into pre-processing, during the processing, and post-processing stages. In each of the processes the data places a crucial role to engross into the stages to generate timetables. Major research work on timetabling is to tune the algorithms or focused on the optimal timetable generations and its performance. In this paper, we propose an interactive system based on visualization techniques to guide the optimization process with constraint satisfaction algorithms. Visualization assists the user to learn the data (pre-processing) with that to make a medium between the scheduler and the timetable designers to improve the obtained solutions. To show the usefulness of our ideas, we apply graph visualization (*Prefuse)* on the pre-processing data that could effectively support a human timetable designer in the analysis of complex timetable generations.

Keywords: Examination timetabling, Graph visualization, Information visualization

1 Introduction

Timetabling problems arise in a wide variety of domains; education, transport, healthcare institutions Burke et al. 2001. The university timetabling problems have attracted the attention of scientists from a number of differing disciplines, including operations research and artificial intelligence, since the 1950s. *University examination timetabling problem* (UETP) is a specific case of the more general timetabling problem and known to *be* highly constrained combinatorial optimization problem.

The construction of an examination timetable is a common problem for all institutions of higher education. Given a set of exams, a set of students, a set of timeslots, a set of rooms, and a set of student enrolments, the problem is to assign exams to timeslots and rooms subject to a set of *hard* and *soft* constraints. The main difficulty is to obtain a *conflict free* schedule within a limited number of timeslots and rooms. Conflicting objectives and the changing set of constraints in different institutions makes the examination timetabling problem (ETP) very challenging. As a corollary a visual representation will be created and show the "conflicts-less" assignment before preparing the examination timetable which is constrain to the research.

---

[1],J. Joshua Thomas, [2], Ahamad Tajudin Khader, [3], Bahari Belaton
joshopever@yahoo.com , tajudin@cs.usm.my, bahari@cs.usm.my University Sains Malaysia

M.L. Huang et al. (eds.), *Visual Information Communication*,
DOI 10.1007/978-1-4419-0312-9_17, © Springer Science+Business Media, LLC 2010

Problems of this type occur in many complex real world applications. The communication problems between humans and computers may result from an internal representation of the problem which is difficult to understand from the user preconditions of the algorithm which are unknown to the user insufficient means for communicate, alternatives and algorithms that are not designed to learn the user's needs but deal with the user in an input-output fashion instead of a dialog. We need a shift of interaction through visualization to understand the processes. Our solution to this problem is to use visual interaction to improve the contact between the representation of the problem in the computer and the users and their goals.

The paper is organized in the following manner. A more details explanation on the background study and related work is at section 2. Section 3 explains an ideal examination timetabling problem. Section 4 contributes the Visual framework on Exam timetabling. In section 5 depict the Info-vis techniques used on the data and section 6 restrains the visualization of scheduler and how the visualization is helpful. An initial development of the pre-processing phase, during the processing with the venture of graph algorithms to visualize the examination timetabling schedules and how the information visualization techniques are useful for the timetablers are discussed.

2 Related Work

Our approach firmly combines research solutions from these areas: automated optimization, visualization, and interaction. In the area of automated optimization, there exist a large number of optimization algorithms such as simulated annealing Aarts and Korts, 1989, greedy and genetic algorithms Goldberg, 1989 as well as constraint programming Bartak, 1999. In the area of visualization, there are a large number of relevant approaches which allow the visualization of abstract information. Examples for information visualization (Info-Vis) techniques include geometric projection techniques, iconic techniques, hierarchical techniques, graph-based techniques, pixel oriented techniques, and combinations hereof. For an overview of information visualization techniques the interested reader is referred to Keim, 2000. The Info-Vis approach proposed in this paper uses multiple visualization paradigms to visualize the raw data (dataset) and to allow the user to interact and learn which leads to the optimization process. The new interactive timetabling system has the possibility to the user to arrange accordingly directly in planning of intervening the time table conceptions. The integration of automatic algorithms into the interactive systems makes it possible to use the strong ones of the computer with the dissolution of possible conflicts in the timetable. An approach on solving complex optimization problem Alexander Hinnderburg et. Al. 2003 had the visualization aspects on pixel plots on the timetabling system with user interaction on the conflicts.

3 Examination Timetabling Problem

The sets of constraints differ significantly from institution to institution. Different categories of people have different priorities in the timetabling process and are affected differently by its outcome Burke et al.2001. In the examination timetabling process, there are three main groups of people who are affected by the results of the process; administration, departments, and students. Consequently, the quality of a timetable can be accessed from various points of view and the importance of a particular constraint can very much depend upon the priorities of the three categories.

In Burke et al. 1995, from the survey conducted on 95 British Universities, the following constraints are observed, sorted in ascending order according to their importance: There must not *be* more students scheduled to a room than there are seats. Exams with questions in common must be scheduled in the same timeslot. Some exams may only be scheduled within a particular set of timeslots. Only exams of the same length may be scheduled in the same room. Exams with the most students must be scheduled early in the timetable. The basic hard constraint in an ETP is 'no student should have two exams in the same timeslot', i.e. no student conflicts. Burke et al. 2001 and Cote et al. 2004 considered this as the only hard constraint in their ETPs.

4 Visual Framework

Most visualization systems merge visualization and interaction techniques, assortment from simple slider and drag & drop interfaces to more advanced techniques such as Fish Eye Views. These techniques have in common that the visualizations transform data from an internal representation into an easily recognizable visual representation. The visual representation, however, does not contain more information about the data or problem than the internal representation.

Visual representations translate data into a visible form that highlights important features, including commonalities and irregularity. These visual representations make it easy for users to distinguish prominent aspects of their data quickly and involve the user to explore the data JJ.Thomas et al 2006. This exploration requires the user be able to interact with the data and understand trends and patterns and engage in the analytical reasoning process. It is a challenge Keim 2006 to create well-constructed visual representations. However, most visualization problems deal with abstract information so the researcher is left to select the best representation for the information.

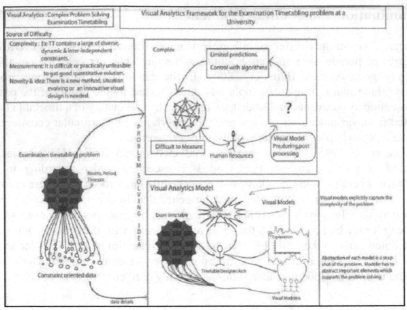

Fig. 1. Problem solving idea on the constraint data on complexity, measurement and the novelty of idea. Visual framework model with exploration together with visual modelers.

In some cases, the timetabling problem consists of finding any timetable that satisfies all constraints. In these cases, the problem is formulated as a search problem. In other cases, the problem is formulated as an optimization problem. In a timetable it satisfies majority of hard constraints and minimizes (or maximizes) a given objective function which embeds the soft constraints. Some approaches, the optimization formulation is just a means to apply optimization techniques to a search problem. In this case, what is minimized is the distance to feasibility. In both cases (search and optimization), the complexity is based on the decision of the problem. These are to be visualized whilst during the processing phase (scheduler).

The visual framework J.Joshua et al 2008 can be used to get out of situations, where the contact of constraints is hardly possible, or very time and space consuming. In the case of time tabling, the communication using visual interaction outwit very costly specifications, which are not realistic to be performed in practical applications. The visualization model contributes the combination with information visualization and exploration of data analysis which supports during processing and after processing of the examination timetabling phase to assist the visual modelers to make decision making.

In our approach, we use visualization to represent the time table data and to point out the conflicts. By interacting with the system, the user gets an impression of what is possible with the available resources and how conflicts may be resolved. By directly interacting with the time table data, the user can learn and incorporate additional knowledge into the time table. It is also possible that a group instead of a single user guides the time table modification.

5 Visualization approach (Info-Vis)

This graph view will provide the user with the ability to mark data values of interest. When too many data values are presented we can change the view of representation. The main idea is to making the values of interest visually distinct, and each to track.

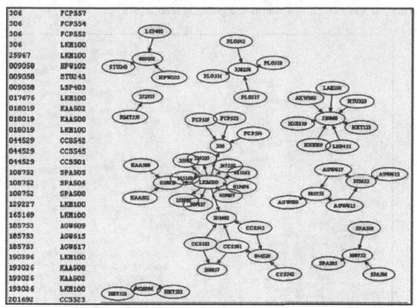

Fig.2. Time tabling data of student register for the subjects, the data has been clustered based on student registered for the subjects: Cluster Graph view. (*Graph-Viz*)

In Fig.2. Shows the order between the enrolled candidates with the course registered for a particular semester. The arrow head indicates the link between enrolled candidates with a course. For example, Student number 306 registered for FCP537, FCP554, FCP552, LKM100, 25967 registered for LKM100 and so on. The diagram illustrates the courses verses the student number for the same semester or current semester which is one of the significance of visualization on this pre-processing stage. This will be one of the visual explorations to the end-user on the raw-data which depict in Fig.1 visual analytics model on exploration to visual modelers and time table designers.

5.1 Graph visualization on a portion of dataset

Using *Prefuse*, we visualize the raw data, converted to the required GraphML structures. We aim to study course-data with respective of offered subjects by the schools This kind of analysis can help in enhancing the scheduler to identify the complex cluster among the department dataset, earlier and assist "user" constraints to better assigning of exams over the limited rooms, before the dataset is fed into the timetable scheduler or automated timetable systems. Here we use *Prefuse* a visualization toolkit to explore the sample data items. We identified graph visualization as it displays the subset of data values. The most common explore interaction technique is panning. It works like a camera across the viewpoint. Many Information Visualization systems use panning techniques.

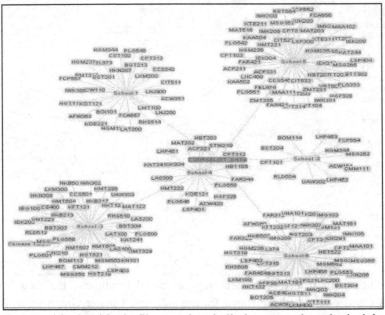

Fig.3. Dataset with algorithmic filters and node limiter to explore the insight of data with user interactions on Graph visualization on the Course data (user interaction)

In Fig.3. shows interaction is toward on the subject offered by the schools. We have identified six schools and the subject is offered in current semester. Course data as a root node which has linked with other subjects offered. The user or timetable designers identified and learn the information of subject offered from the visualization. The user can interact with the course data from various schools what are the subjects are offered for the current semester. The algorithmic filters are being used on the data; it has been populated with an undirected graph layout algorithm and spring algorithm to get the stability on the data with-in the visualization area. The user interaction is on the algorithmic filters and node limiter to get the insight of the data. The merits on this type of visualization is the end-user are able to zoom, panning, and highlight the clustering subject with the students enrollment for the course. In figure 3 it emphasize on the course data from various schools. This can be extended to various levels such to show the hard and soft constraints, concurrent room allocation, and so on.

6 Visualizing the Scheduler

Timetable scheduler that we used for our prototype is of constraint satisfaction. Here we do the optimization over examination schedules and make a relationship over Fig.2. cluster graph view. On every view of a timetable, two axes are represented: the day axis and the timeslot axis. It should be noted that there are no restrictions concerning the resources which appear on the day axis. In other words, it is possible to visualize on one screen the timetables of several groups, teachers, rooms and elements of equipment. This has two major advantages.

In Fig.4. the day of view retained here versus the timeslot view (exams, subject code), the teaching module point of view and a specific point of view in which the user chooses the information he/she wishes to see. However the options are not enabled at this stage. We highlight the earlier cluster graph view (refer Fig 2) assist the scheduler for cluster of highly registered subject. In Fig. 4 the user can see, for example the studentid's, subjects, cluster subjects with student id's before we run the optimization over the dataset. A button enables the user to switch from one point of view to another whilst keeping the general appearance of his/her view along with the same orders (addition, removal, etc)

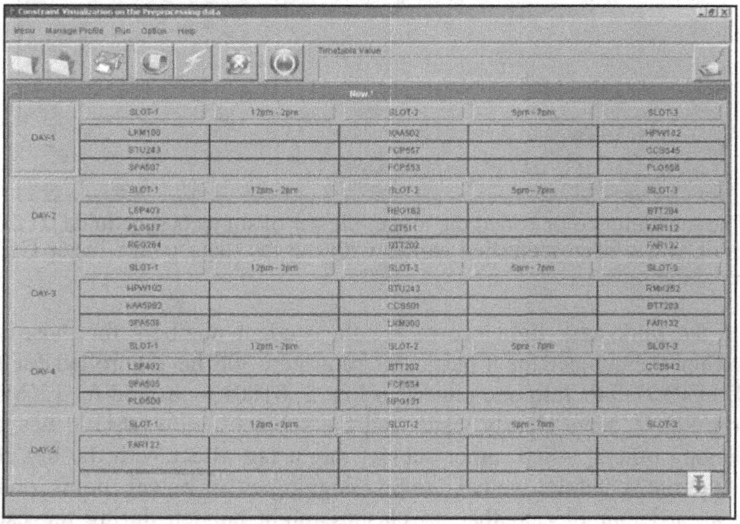

Fig.4. The scheduler has the weekly schedule of the examination with hard constraints no examination are allowed during a particular timeslot, Day, time slot view (automated Exam timetabling)

In Fig 4 the constraints to be respected can be classified in two groups: user constraints (also called hard constraints) and educational constraints (or soft constraints) which are linked to the academic quality of the timetables. User constraints cannot be violated otherwise clashing would arise. The above output illustrates the raw data are fed into the scheduler without producing any optimal solution. Here is the role of visualization we identified at Fig.2 cluster graph view, assists the scheduler in this aspect to identify which data from which school and which subject will make the clashes. This can be identified far before to execute the scheduler. These significance or value of visualization is over the examination timetabling systems at this stage of our work. Academic/educational constraints may be violated in this case; the timetable obtained is of a lower quality. Typically, these constraints are used to express what a "good" timetable should be for the students to attend exams and for the invigilators. In this work the academic constraints are used to visualize and the movement of dataset are being identified assisted with cluster graph view. However these are static view on the data, which can be overcome in Fig.3 as user can view the data and interactive with it.

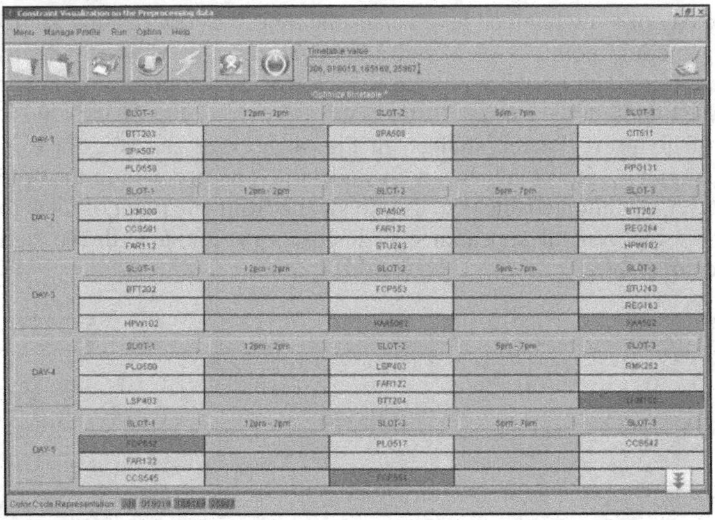

Fig.5. The scheduler color coded the longer cluster of subjects scheduled on the day with the timeslot, it has been identified earlier with the raw data with Cluster Graph versus Scheduler assignment

In Fig. 5 the pink, red, light brown are the student numbers for those who have registered for the subject for a particular semester. 306 have enrolled for LKM100, FCP554, FCP557 falls into one cluster in Fig. 2, 018019 enrolled for LKM100 alone and so on. Fig. 2, have clearly visualized the subject code LKM100 has the bigger cluster among others, where other subject might not affect with the big cluster. To give input to the scheduler we have to be assigning either bigger rooms, or spread the exam is a particular day so that no clashes might happen during the examination week. Usually this can be identified once the scheduler gave the output. Our work symbolize that visualization place a role on the preprocessing data itself and we learn the conflicts/ clashes might be happen because of this huge cluster of students enrolled for a subject e.g LKM100.

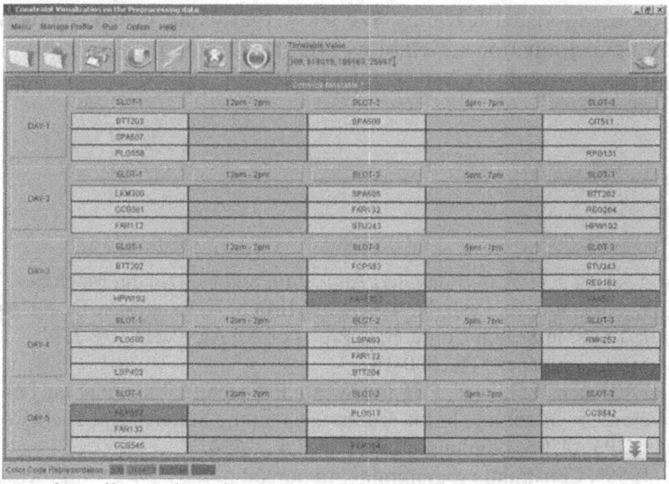

Fig.6. The course data allocated on the day are highlighted with color where the conflicts are happened it has been identified earlier with graph visualization as multiple Clusters from the raw data

In Fig. 6 the timetable designers can interact with the output and rearrange the assignment of rooms by clicking the optimization run timetable button. The timetable value has shown once the student number is entered or particular school identification has given as inputs the color coded information will be highlighted to show the clusters are there and it can be identified earlier before generating the examination schedule. Like in Fig. 5 here we can identified multiple clusters from the raw data. Preprocessing phase, the hypothesis/approach consists of developing graph visualization techniques and tools to effectively analysis the dimensions values within nominal raw data. The techniques enable the users to visualize the information in a graphical pattern to interact with the information spaces in a sensitive way, these visual representations make it easy for users to distinguish prominent aspects of their data quickly and involve the user to explore the data.

The exploration requires the timetable be able to interact with the data and understand trends and patterns and engage in the analytical reasoning process. It is a challenge to create well-constructed visual representations. However, most visual problems, deal with abstract information so the researcher is left to select the best representation for the information. We believe that this will help the visual modelers to understand the nature of data then apply into the timetable scheduler for producing time tables involving visualization as good interaction medium.

7 Conclusion

There are a considerable number of optimization problems where the optimization goal is varying depending on the user and the task. In most of the cases, the optimization goal cannot be achieved and is therefore not amenable to an automated solution using algorithms. Our work makes the user an integral part of the optimization by using visual learning. We show that using visual interaction leads to better solution of examination timetabling which is an optimization problem. We do hope this approach might simulate the research direction on the benchmark timetabling problem.

References

1. Aarts, E. and Korts, J. (1989). Simulated Annealing and Boltzmann Machines. Wiley.
2. Anderson, D, Anderson, E., Lesh, N. Marks, J. Mirtich, B. Ratajczak, D, and Ryall.K(2000) Human-guided Simple Search Conference Proc., of AAAI, pages 209-216. http://www.merl.com/papers/TR2000-16.
3. Burke, E. K., Elliman D.G. Ford, P.H and Weare R.F.(1995), Examination Timetabling in British universities – A survey. In Int. Conference on the Practice and Theory of Automated Timetabling ICPTAT'95, Edinburgh, UK, Pages 423-434.
4. Bartak, R. (1999). Constraint programming: In pursuit of the holy grail. Proc. of WDS99
5. Cote, P., Wong, T., Sabourin, R. (2004) Application of a Hybrid Multi-objective EvolutionaryAlgorithm to the Uncapacitated Exam Proximity Problem. *Proceedings of the 5th International Conference on the Practice and Theory of Automated Timetabling* (PATAT2004), Pittsburgh, pp: 151-168.
6. J.J. Thomas and K.A.Cook (2006) *Illuminating the path: The R & D agenda for visual analytics*
7. Keim, D. A. (2000). An introduction to information visualization techniques for exploring large databases. In Tutorial Notes of the IEEE Int. Conference on Visualization. IEEE CS
8. Keim D.A(2006), Florian Mansmann, Jorn Schneidewind, Hartmut Ziegler(2006) *Challenges in Visual Data Analysis* Tenth International Conference on Information Visualization (IV'06) pp. 9-16
9. Sims, K. (1993). Interactive evolution of equations for procedural models. The Visual Computer, 9:466-476.
10.J. Joshua Thomas, Ahamad Tajudin, Bahari Belaton, A Visual Analytics Framework for the Examination timetabling problem. *Proc. 5th International Conference on Computer Graphics, Imaging and Visualization.* CGIV, ISBN: 978-0-7695-3359-9 on page(s) pp, 305-310 IEEE Computer Society.
11.Alexander Hinnderburg, D.A. Keim(2003) Visual interaction to solving complex optimization problems. Data visualization: The state-of-the-art Kluwer academic publishers London.
12. R.Qu, E.K.Burke, B.McCollum, L.T.G.Merlot and S.Y.Lee (2009), A Survey of Search Methodologies and Automated System Development for Examination Timetabling, Journal of Scheduling 12(1), pp 55-89.

Making Traffic Safety Personal: Visualization and Customization of National Traffic Fatalities

Brian N. Hilton [1], Thomas A. Horan [1], Benjamin Schooley [1]

[1] Claremont Graduate University, School of Information Systems and Technology
130 East Ninth Street, Claremont, CA 91711, U.S.A.
{ Brian.Hilton, Tom.Horan, Benjamin.Schooley }@cgu.edu

Abstract. Communicating public health issues related to rural and urban road transportation safety is a challenging task. The approach to this task was to utilize an action-design research methodology to design and evaluate several innovative GIS-mashups that visually communicate traffic fatality information from the national to the local level. These web-based mashups (www.saferoadmaps.org) integrate a range of spatial data regarding motor vehicle crashes, transportation policy legislation, and driver behavioral data and present a visual representation of traffic safety across the United States. It was anticipated that these mashups, and related website, would help raise awareness and change fundamental perceptions regarding the magnitude, risk factors, and impacts of motor vehicle crashes and bring both increased safety and awareness to transportation policy makers and private citizens. Preliminary findings from around the world suggest that there is a strong interest in this type of information, particularly as users can customize it to local queries.

Keywords: Visualization Interface, GIS, Mashup, Public Health, Traffic Fatalities, Web 2.0, XML

1 Introduction

Road traffic injuries are a major but neglected public health challenge that requires concerted efforts for effective and sustainable prevention [1]. In the United States, the total economic cost of motor vehicle crashes is estimated to be 2 percent of Gross Domestic Product [1, 2], or approximately $275 billion for 2007. Medical and emergency services costs are roughly 15 percent of this total.

In 2007, in the United States, there were 41,059 fatalities; the result of 37,248 motor vehicle crashes – roughly 60 percent of these motor vehicle crashes occurred on rural, two-lane roads. Moreover, these crash victims are five to seven times more likely to die if arrival to a hospital exceeds 30 minutes. The average time between a crash and hospital arrival is 52 minutes in rural areas [3].

Clearly, there is an urgent need for governmental agencies, and other key institutions, to increase and sustain action to prevent motor vehicle injuries. Yet, while there is widespread use of visual-consumer systems for traffic congestion (both online and by media outlets such as local television stations), there has been very little

M.L. Huang et al. (eds.), *Visual Information Communication*,
DOI 10.1007/978-1-4419-0312-9_18, © Springer Science+Business Media, LLC 2010

if any attention to using such systems for traffic safety. The policy need is clearly present, as recent U.S. federal transportation legislation (Safe, Accountable, Flexible, and Efficient Transportation Equity Act: A Legacy for Users (SAFETEA-LU)) mandates that the pubic must be involved in the creation of a Transportation Improvement Program during both the planning and programming phases [4, 5].

At a general level, there is widespread acknowledgement to how public participation geographic information systems (PP-GIS) can be used to broaden public involvement in policymaking as well as to the value of GIS to promote the goals of non-governmental organizations, grassroots groups, and community-based organizations [6]. PP-GIS helps to empower these groups, as well as others, through the use of various spatial and visual technologies to increase awareness and participation in decision-making processes. As such, PP-GIS provides a unique approach for engaging the public in decision-making through its goal to incorporate local knowledge, integrate and contextualize complex spatial information, allow participants to dynamically interact with input, analyze alternatives, and empower individuals and groups [6].

Accordingly, this paper reports on the development and utilization of several innovative GIS-mashups that visually communicate traffic fatality information from the national to the local level. These web-based mashups (www.saferoadmaps.org) integrate a range of spatial data regarding motor vehicle crashes, transportation policy legislation, and driver behavioral data and present a visual representation of traffic safety across the United States. To that end, it is expected that these GIS-based mashups will be utilized in a variety of settings to:

- Inform – raise awareness of the general public as well as public representatives
- Educate – instruct through Driver Education Programs and organizations such as Mothers Against Drunk Driving
- Support Decision-Making – inform policy-making legislation and various governmental agencies charged with transportation system maintenance and development

Thus, it was anticipated that these mashups, and related website, would help raise awareness and change fundamental perceptions regarding the magnitude, risk factors, and impacts of motor vehicle crashes and bring both increased safety and awareness to transportation policy makers and private citizens. As will be noted below, the overwhelming success of the launch of the SafeRoadMaps website on 28 July 2008, and utilization thereafter, suggests that there is a strong demand for this type of visual information.

1.1 Action-Design Approach

The research approach is an action-design methodology; this methodology has emerged as a transdisciplinary approach to studying socio-technical systems in a manner that gives attention to both analysis and design aspects of the research endeavor [7]. As such, it is dedicated to the development of knowledge useful to both research and practice [8]. The goal of this action-design research is to communicate public health issues related to rural and urban road transportation safety while extending scientific knowledge [9]. This action-design research approach features multiple methods, including a systematic analysis of the problem, design-research and development of tools to understand and potentially affect the problem, and a quantitative assessment of the value and feasibility of implementing such tools to raise awareness of an important public health issue. In doing so, the authors aspire to create a data-driven understanding, as well as tools, to contribute to the body of knowledge underlying rural and urban road transportation safety research and evaluation [10, 11]. This specific action-design methodology entailed the iterative development of a multi-layer dynamic website, SafeRoadMaps, which was followed by a national launch and utilization analysis.

2 SafeRoadMaps Development

Internet-based information system development is well suited to Agile Development methodologies where close collaboration between developers and domain experts facilitate the frequent delivery of new and/or enhanced functionality. In this manner, incremental units of functionality may be made available to users instantly rather than being bundled with other functionalities subject to an arbitrary release schedule. As opposed to desktop applications that may have release cycles of several months or even years, it is not unusual for Internet-based information systems to be updated several times a day [12]. Agile methods were utilized during the development of these mashups, in particular, short, iterative, development cycles.

Through a series of iterative design and Agile Development sessions, the following functional requirements were defined:

- Map – visually display spatial data for analysis and decision support
- Safety Policy – map layers indicating areas of legislative policies
- Safety Profile – pre-defined queries of fatality events
- Safety Statistics – drill-down (query/filter) through various data sets to extract the specific information the end-user wants to display
- KML File – download KML files, both static and query-based, for display in Google Earth (or other KML reader)

These key requirements were identified as part of a larger, ongoing research effort, of which this website and mashups are a part. In particular, the following themes were identified as key to communicating public health issues related to rural and urban road transportation safety:

- Behavior – A fundamental requirement for improving rural transportation safety and health is to understand the human behaviors that affect rural travel. Behavior can involve driving patterns by specific driving groups (e.g., teenagers) or can be more general transportation attitudes and predispositions, including citizen attitudes about rural safety, rural roads, and health issues.

• Legislative – Specific to the legislative mandate to examine rural safety and economic development, there are pressing issues regarding the changing social demographics of rural areas and its implications for transportation investments, performance, and safety.

• Visual Display – It is critical to portray rural safety issues in a manner that is both comprehendible to a broad audience and at the same time brings together a range of related disparate data.

• Human – It is critical to humanize the tragedy behind road crash statistics. This might be accomplished via a link to a website for each tragic event.

• Policy – Policy related to rural traffic fatality reduction has focused on seat belt laws, impaired driving laws, graduated driver's license programs, and speeding enforcement laws. These policies were identified as having significant legislative and safety impact.

• Integrated Analysis – Allow for a profile of rural driving behavior, accidents, and fatalities. This will lay the groundwork for developing a regional vision and action plan with regional policy leaders and transportation and safety professionals.

In addition to the themes above, an investigation of several health-related, GIS-based, websites (HealthMap, a Harvard-MIT Division of Health Sciences and Technology website (http://www.healthmap.org/en), chicagocrime.org, a database of crimes reported in Chicago (http://www.chicagocrime.org), and the Los Angeles Times Homicide Map (http://www.latimes.com/news/local/crime/homicidemap)) further informed the design of this system, in particular their dynamic filtering and drill-down functionalities.

2.1 Data

The mission of the Fatality Analysis Reporting System (FARS) is to make vehicle crash information accessible and useful so that traffic safety can be improved. Fatality information derived from FARS includes motor vehicle traffic crashes that result in the death of an occupant of a vehicle or a non-motorist within 30 days of the crash. FARS contains data on all fatal traffic crashes within the 50 states, the District of Columbia, and Puerto Rico.

The National Highway Traffic Safety Administration contracts with an agency in each state to provide information on fatal crashes [13]. FARS analysts are state employees who extract the information and enter it into a standard format. Data on fatal motor vehicle traffic crashes are gathered from each state's source documents and are coded on standard FARS forms. Analysts obtain the documents needed to complete the FARS forms, which generally include the following:

• Police Accident Reports
• State vehicle registration files
• State driver licensing files
• State Highway Department data
• Vital Statistics

- Death certificates
- Coroner/Medical examiner reports
- Hospital medical records
- Emergency medical service reports

To be included in FARS, a crash must involve a motor vehicle traveling on a traffic way customarily open to the public, and result in the death of a person (either an occupant of a vehicle or a non-motorist) within 30 days of the crash. Each case has more than 100 coded data elements that characterize the crash, the vehicles, and the people involved. All data elements are contained in three major files – Accident, Vehicle, and Person.

These mashups are currently utilizing FARS data from 2001-2007; the most currently available [14]. A subset of the data contained in the Person table (Demographic and Behavioral attributes) was selected for use and then location information from the Accident table (Latitude and Longitude) was appended to this file. Unfortunately, due to missing and/or incomplete location information, approximately 8.47% of the fatality cases are not represented in the database (Table 1).

Table 1. FARS Data Geocoding Results.

Year	Fatalities	Not Geocoded	Geocoded	Percent Not Geocoded
2001	37,862	6,965	30,897	18.40%
2002	38,491	3,036	35,455	7.89%
2003	38,477	2,767	35,710	7.19%
2004	38,444	1,876	36,568	4.88%
2005	39,252	1,433	37,819	3.65%
2006	38,648	1,301	37,347	3.37%
2007	37,248	5,363	31,885	14.40%
	268,422	**22,741**	**245,681**	**8.47%**

It is anticipated that additional FARS data sets, as well as state-specific data, Emergency Management System data, Automatic Crash Notification data (e.g., General Motors OnStar data), and Trauma System data will be added to the system in incremental steps as they become available.

2.2 Web 2.0 Mashups and Renderings

One defining characteristic of Web 2.0 [15] application development is the use of mashups to integrate content from multiple sources through the use of an Application Programming Interface (API) or Web Service. Mashups are an exciting genre of interactive Web applications that draw upon content retrieved from external data sources to create entirely new and innovative services [16]. From a system development point-of-view, Web 2.0 brings with it new opportunities for deploying highly interactive web pages [17] and allows developers to leverage existing applications without the need to build a system from the "ground-up".

The website reported on in this paper contains several GIS-based mashups that were developed utilizing Google's "Google Maps" API and Microsoft's "Virtual Earth" API. Early design discussions identified the need for wide-ranging functionality and customization, hence, it was decided that the use of a mapping API would be required rather than a simple developer's tool.

When utilizing these APIs, developers have access to various predefined functions that allow them to create their own applications and perform operations on local and remote data. For example, the Google Maps API is essentially a collection of JavaScript classes that can be called from a web page in order to build various elements of an interactive map. As a result, the Google Maps API has encouraged a very considerable number of users with intermediate and advanced programming knowledge to build their own applications, using Google Maps data as a visualization interface [18].

Consequently, as the use of mashups has grown, so has the number of tools to ease their deployment. These mashup tools generally fall into two groups: those which are easy to use, but can only create a limited family of mashups; and those which are relatively difficult to use, but can create a wide range of mashups [19].

Specific to GIS, Google's "MyMaps", Microsoft's "MapCruncher", and the recently released GMap Creator tool [18] allow developers to easily create mashups involving maps. Unfortunately, while each of these tools is easy to use, they provide limited functionality in terms of application customization. Accordingly, Google, Microsoft, and Yahoo provide application developers with an API or Software Development Kit (SDK) (http://code.google.com/apis/maps/, http://dev.live.com/virtualearth/, http://developer.yahoo.com/maps/, respectively) to access their mapping products. ESRI, one of the largest GIS technology companies, provides access to more sophisticated GIS tools through e.g., ArcWeb Services, for integrating mapping functionality (http://www.esri.com/software/arcwebservices/).

The GIS-based mashups discussed in this paper utilize a mixed-source web platform – Windows 2003 Server, IIS, MySQL, and PHP (Figure 1). However, these mashups could have been easily implemented on an open source software platform, or with minimal effort, on a closed source platform.

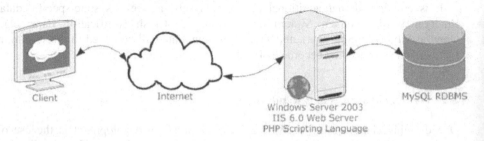

Client   Internet   Windows Server 2003   MySQL RDBMS
                                            IIS 6.0 Web Server
                                            PHP Scripting Language

Fig. 1. SafeRoadMaps Mashup Platform.

For this project, attribute data from FARS were loaded into the MySQL database. When a query is performed, utilizing the visualization interface, several PHP scripts are utilized to extract data from the database. These scripts retrieve the data and generate an XML file that contains basic event information as well as latitude and longitude location information. This information is brought together (mashed-up) in the form of a browser-based map that identifies the location of each event with an icon. This AJAX [20] approach to data transfer and GIS visualization brings with it improved performance and provides a more interactive user experience [21, 22]. The user may also display this information in a geo-browser (e.g., Google Earth or ArcGIS Explorer) by clicking on a link in the web page interface; a KML file is generated, the application is launched, and the data is displayed.

2.3 SafeRoadMaps User Design: Two Renderings

The resulting saferoadmaps.org website, as with most websites, has a number of pages, specifically – Home, Maps (where the user can set search criteria and view spatial data by state or street, view traffic fatality videos, or view area maps to learn where certain laws are in effect), Tutorials (where the user can view a video demonstration on how the SafeRoadMaps mashups work or can watch a video on how Google Earth can be used to dynamically create interactive maps), Data (where the user can learn more about the data utilized – Fatality Analysis Reporting System data – and how the National Highway Traffic Safety Administration manages this data repository), Resources (contains reference materials and U.S. Highway Safety policy legislation maps), Videos (contains informative videos on the importance of safe driving), Press Room (contains the latest videos and articles about SafeRoadMaps), and Contact Us.

The Maps page has a number of tabs for accessing various GIS-based information, these are: Safe State Maps, Safe Street Maps, Congressional District Maps, Traffic Fatality Videos, and Printable Maps. A concise description of two of these mashups follows. The first of these, Safe State Maps, is a GIS-based mashup, and is depicted in Figure 2.

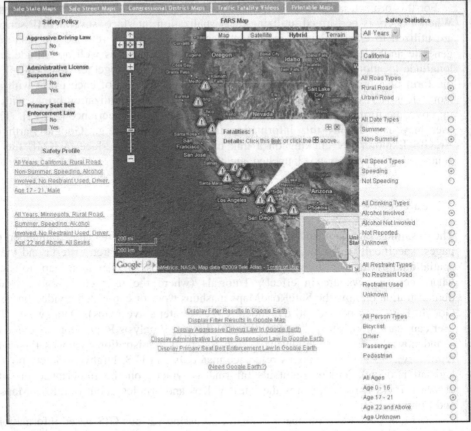

Fig. 2. SafeRoadMaps – Safe State Maps Mashup (Query result – "All Years, California, Rural Road, Non-Summer, Speeding, Alcohol Involved, No Restraint Used, Driver, Age 17 - 21, Male").

Safe State Maps interface elements include:

- Map – functionalities include: zoom-in and zoom-out, panning, geocoding, toggling various basemap layers, and an overview map
- Safety Policy – functionalities include: toggling various safety policy layers currently Aggressive Driving Law, Administrative License Suspension Law (i.e., driving under the influence of alcohol), and Primary Seat Belt Enforcement Law
- Safety Profile – predefined, illustrative, queries such as: "All Years, Minnesota, Rural Road, Summer, Speeding, Alcohol Involved, No Restraint Used, Driver, Age 22 and Above, All Sexes"
- Safety Statistics – ad-hoc queries utilizing:
  - Year
  - State
  - Road Types (Rural, Urban)

- o   Date (Summer, Non-Summer)
- o   Speed Types (Speeding, Not Speeding)
- o   Drinking Types (Alcohol Involved, Alcohol Not Involved, Not Reported, Unknown)
- o   Restraint Types (No Restraint Used, Restraint Used, Unknown)
- o   Person Types (Driver, Not a Driver)
- o   Ages (Age 0 - 16, Age 17 - 21, Age 22 and Above, Age Unknown)
- o   Sex (Male, Female, Unknown)
- • KML Files – download static safety policy layers and/or dynamically generated layers from Safety Profile or Safety Statistics queries for display in Google Maps, Google Earth, or other KML file reader

Figure 2 also depicts the result of the query – "All Years, California, Rural Road, Non-Summer, Speeding, Alcohol Involved, No Restraint Used, Driver, Age 17 - 21, Male". Here, when the user clicks on one of the traffic fatality location icons, they are presented with an "Information Bubble" that contains a link to a "drill-down" query for that specific event.

Figure 3 depicts the result of a drill-down query. The resultant web page contains general information regarding the event (Number of Fatalities and Date), as well as specific information for each person involved (SRM_ID, Road Type, Speeding, Drinking, Restraint Type, Person Type, Age, Sex, and Deceased). This web page also contains three additional elements: a "zoomed-in" map from Microsoft's Virtual Earth map service containing a "Bird's Eye" view, a "zoomed-in" map from Google's map service, and a "Street Level" 360 degree panoramic image also provided by Google's map service.

Fatalities	Month	Day	Hour	Minute	Year		
1	11	6	2	29	2002		

SRM_ID	Road Type	Speeding	Drinking	Restraint Type	Person Type	Age	Sex	Deceased
631582002	Rural Local Road or Street	Yes (Speeding Involved)	Yes (Alcohol Involved)	None Used	Driver	21	Male	Yes
631582002	Rural Local Road or Street	Yes (Speeding Involved)	Yes (Alcohol Involved)	Lap and Shoulder Belt	Passenger of a Motor Vehicle in Transport	22	Male	No
631582002	Rural Local Road or Street	Yes (Speeding Involved)	Yes (Alcohol Involved)	Lap Belt	Passenger of a Motor Vehicle in Transport	22	Male	No

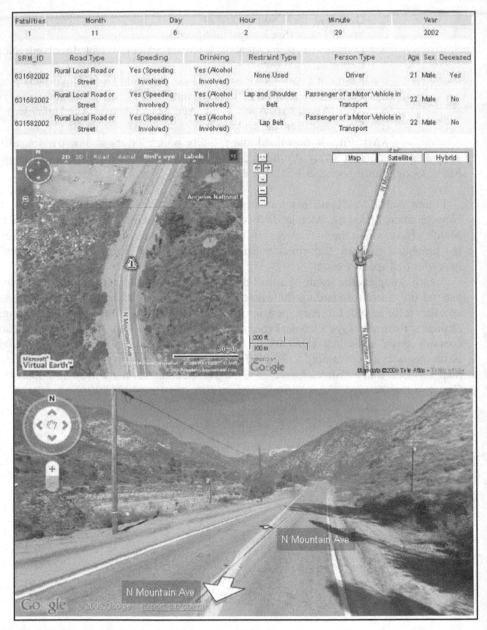

Fig. 3. SafeRoadMaps Mashup – Drill-down Result (Obtained by clicking-on the "Link" or "+" in the pop-up Info Window).

The second GIS-based mashup, "Safe Street Maps", also utilizes FARS data, but rather than make use of ad-hoc queries with filtering, this mashup allows the user to enter an address and discover all fatalities within a given distance of that address.

This is accomplished utilizing Google's geocoding engine and a specialized query in the MySQL database. As with the "Safe State Maps" mashup, the results of a drill-down query are also available. Figure 4 illustrates the "Safe Street Maps" mashup.

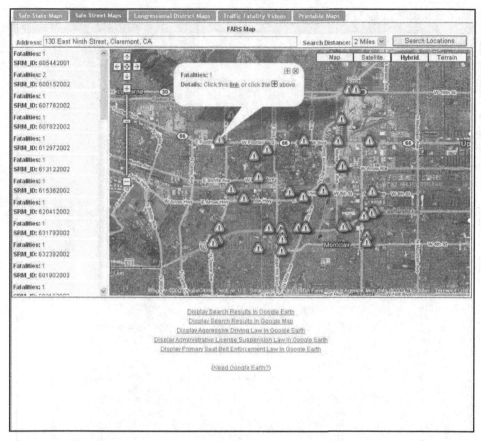

Fig. 4. SafeRoadMaps – Safe Street Maps Mashup (Query result – "130 East Ninth Street, Claremont, CA" – Search Distance = 2 Miles").

3 Launch and Utilization Analysis

The launch, on 28 July 2008, of the SafeRoadMaps website was publicly announced to coincide with the Center for Excellence in Rural Safety (CERS) 2008 Summer Institute. The initial response was overwhelming. During the first three days of its public debut, the site received over three million hits, had nearly one million page views, and 126,000 visits from the United States and around the world. This usage paralleled the media coverage, which included over 150 reports in newspapers, television news, radio, and related new-media outlets. While usage rates have subsided from this initial success, continued high attention over the past nine months (28 July 2008 – 30 April 2009) suggests that there is strong traveler (and analyst) demand for this type of visual, customizable information (Figures 5 and 6).

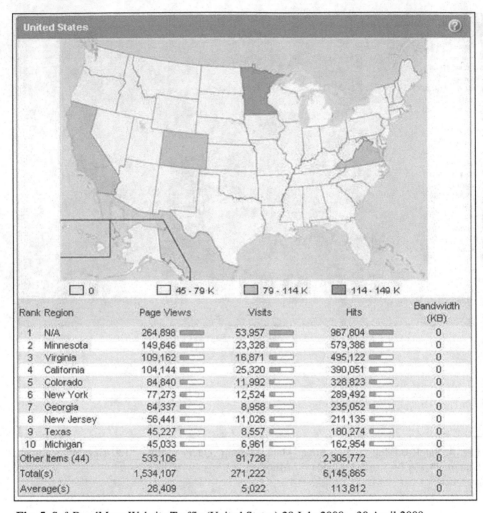

Fig. 5. SafeRoadMaps Website Traffic (United States) 28 July 2008 – 30 April 2009.

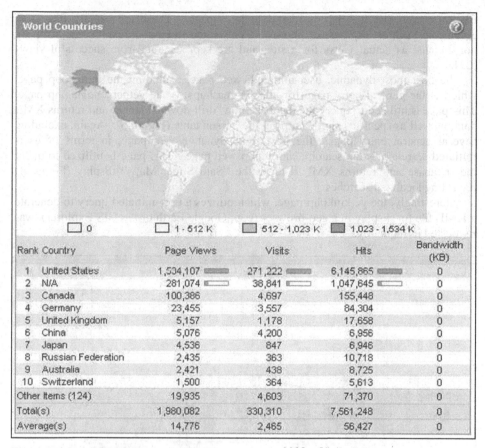

Rank	Country	Page Views	Visits	Hits	Bandwidth (KB)
1	United States	1,534,107	271,222	6,145,865	0
2	N/A	281,074	38,841	1,047,645	0
3	Canada	100,386	4,697	155,448	0
4	Germany	23,455	3,557	84,304	0
5	United Kingdom	5,157	1,178	17,658	0
6	China	5,076	4,200	6,956	0
7	Japan	4,536	847	6,946	0
8	Russian Federation	2,435	363	10,718	0
9	Australia	2,421	438	8,725	0
10	Switzerland	1,500	364	5,613	0
Other Items (124)		19,935	4,603	71,370	0
Total(s)		1,980,082	330,310	7,561,248	0
Average(s)		14,776	2,465	56,427	0

Fig. 6. SafeRoadMaps Website Traffic (World) 28 July 2008 – 30 April 2009.

3.1 General Versus Customized SafeRoadMaps Utilization

Figure 7 illustrates the "Top Dynamic Pages" (most often viewed dynamic web pages on the server) for the period 28 July 2008 - 30 April 2009. Dynamic web sites contain content that is stored in a database that is placed on a web page when requested. This content (text, images, etc.) may change in response to different contexts or conditions. Some content, though dynamically generated, is more general and is requested from the database as part of the normal functioning of the web site, e.g., a "Home Page" and requires no action on the part of the user. Other content, also dynamically generated, is more customized and is based on the results of a user-initiated search.

The most dynamic, user-initiated, SafeRoadMaps web page, in terms of "Page Views", is the getxml.php page. This page is utilized to query the database and returns XML data to the "Safe State Maps" display (Figure 2) and contains location information and pop-up window content. A "Page View" is a successful request for a file on a web site that is considered to be a page. These are usually files with extensions such as .asp, .aspx, .php, etc. Views generated as a result of an error are not counted as actual views for a site, and are kept separate from successful views [23].

The next most dynamic, user-initiated, web page, excluding the index.php page, which is the general entry page for all GIS mashups, is the getpersondata.php page. This page is utilized to query the database in a "drill-down" manner and returns XML data, as well as specific event data from the Person table (Figure 3). Again, excluding several general entry pages, the next most dynamic web page, in terms of user-initiated searches, is the searchlocation.php web page. This page is utilized to query the database and returns XML data to the "Safe Street Maps" display (Figure 4) regarding localized searches.

Interestingly, the getkml.php page, which utilizes a user-initiated query to generate a KML file for display in a geo-browser (e.g., Google Earth or ArcGIS Explorer), was requested infrequently.

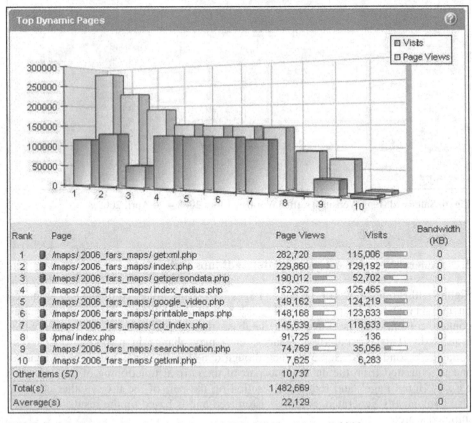

Fig. 7. SafeRoadMaps Top Dynamic Pages 28 July 2008 – 30 April 2009.

4 Discussion

Over the past year, a series of discussions have been held with national safety experts, government career professionals, and elected officials regarding the consumer value of SafeRoadMaps. In general, there has been widespread support to the use of innovative visually based technologies to raise awareness and improve traffic safety. Interestingly, there was also some initial reservation about how the public would react to the website (including fears about increasing complaints to local departments of transportation). These concerns have not been borne out; rather, transportation professionals have indicated interest in extending the national version of SafeRoadMaps into localized editions.

SafeRoadMaps (Version 2) is building on its initial success by incorporating website feedback from users and suggestions from the CERS 2008 Summer Institute findings, several state Department of Transportation offices, the United States Department of Transportation Office of the Secretary, the Federal Highway Administration, and the National Highway Traffic Safety Administration. In addition, SafeRoadMaps (Version 2) will utilize additional Web 2.0 technologies to reach a wider user and organizational audience. For example, it will include many new basic and advanced querying capabilities, expanded visual and user interface elements, and web services access.

Specifically, the following objectives are planned for the upcoming release of SafeRoadMaps:

- Provide Multi-year Fatality and Crash Data – There is a need and interest in upgrading and expanding data availability to include multiyear FARS and State-level severe crash data. Particularly for rural areas, it is important to have multiyear data in order to detect spatial patterns in crashes.

- Expand User-Friendly Interface Options – A major value of SafeRoadMaps is its intuitive approach to accessing traffic safety data. There is a continuing need to refine the interface to allow for a greater range of inquiries (e.g. pedestrian fatalities) and to provide an easier means for stakeholders to contribute content to, and receive safety data feeds from, SafeRoadMaps in a Web 2.0 manner.

- Provide Local and Regional Connections – There have been several expressions of interest to create state and regional level SafeRoadMaps as a means to interact with various state planning and community processes. Localized SafeRoadMaps sites will be explored and tested.

- Enhance Visual Representations – Heat maps represent an innovative means for communicating the spatial density of traffic fatalities. In order to create national and local heat maps, a series of spatial analysis techniques will be conducted to identify safety advisory zones in both urban and rural areas and allow for national as well as local visualization and analysis.

It is expected that the new version of SafeRoadMaps will be received with the same enthusiasm and interest as the initial version. The goal is to become a website and service of choice for those looking for readily accessible visually based information and research on traffic safety.

5 Conclusion

Communicating public health issues related to rural and urban road transportation safety is a challenging task. This paper summarizes the action-design approach taken to design, launch, and develop a GIS-based visualization system to understand and improve traffic safety. These mashups integrate a range of spatial data regarding motor vehicle crashes, transportation policy legislation, and driver behavioral data. They contain a map to visually display spatial data, several additional map layers indicating areas of specific legislative policy, and a drill-down capability that allows end-users to query/filter these data sets to extract information related to specific fatality events. The ability to dynamically create KML files to display query-based results, as well as static maps, in Google Earth or similar KML reader is also available.

As stated by the World Health Organization (WHO), the level of road traffic injury is unacceptable and is largely avoidable. Furthermore, a reduction in motor vehicle crashes, and corresponding injuries and fatalities, can be accomplished by:

• Creating greater levels of awareness, commitment, and informed decision making at all organizational levels,

• Contributing to a change in thinking about the nature of the problem of road traffic injuries and what constitutes successful prevention, and

• Strengthening institutions and creating effective partnerships to deliver safer road traffic systems [1].

It is expected that GIS-based mashups, such as those provided on the SafeRoadMaps website, will help in meeting these objectives. Over the next year, several new functionalities will be explored and it is hoped that this will further drive interest and awareness in traffic safety issues. Based on the feedback and use of SafeRoadMaps, we expect to further enhance not only the visualization options (e.g., heat maps), but to do so in a manner that builds on the strong interest in local customizable queries that transform traffic safety from a global concept to something quite local and personal.

Acknowledgements

This project was supported by the Center for Excellence in Rural Safety (CERS), which facilitates citizen-centered research, training, and outreach activities related to rural transportation safety. CERS is a joint program between the University of Minnesota's Hubert H. Humphrey Institute of Public Affairs State and Local Policy Program and the Center for Transportation Studies, and sponsored by the Federal Highway Administration.

6 References

1. Peden, M., et al., World report on road traffic injury prevention. 2004, World Health Organization: Geneva, Switzerland.
2. Blincoe, L.J., et al., The Economic Impact of Motor Vehicle Crashes, 2000. 2002, National Highway Traffic safety Administration: Washington, D.C.
3. Center for Excellence in Rural Safety, Rural Transportation Safety Research - Summary Report. 2007, Center for Excellence in Rural Safety: Minneapolis, MN.
4. Tang, K.X. and N.M. Waters, The internet, GIS and public participation in transportation planning. Progress in Planning, 2005. 64(1): p. 7–62.
5. Zhong, T., et al., A model for public involvement in transportation improvement programming using participatory Geographic Information Systems. Computers, Environment and Urban Systems, 2008. Volume 32(Issue 2): p. 123–133.
6. Sieber, R., Public Participation Geographic Information Systems: A Literature Review and Framework. Annals of the Association of American Geographers, 2006. 96(3): p. 491–507.
7. Hevner, A., et al., Design Science in Information Systems Research. MIS Quarterly, 2004. 28(1): p. 75-105.
8. Baskerville, R. and A.T. Wood-Harper, Diversity in information systems action research methods. European Journal of Information Systems, 1998. 7(2): p. 90-107.
9. Baskerville, R. and M.D. Myers, Special Issue on Action Research in Information Systems: Making IS Research Relevant to Practice - Foreword. MIS Quarterly, 2004. 28(3): p. 329-335.
10. Hilton, B., T. Horan, and B. Schooley. SafeRoadMaps: A GIS-based Mashup. in 2008 ESRI Business GIS Summit - University of Redlands Academic Track. 2008. Chicago, IL.
11. Schooley, B., et al. Integrated Patient Health Information Systems to Improve Traffic Crash Emergency Response and Treatment. in Hawaii International Conference on Systems Sciences (HICSS-42). 2009. Waikoloa, Big Island, HI.
12. Jazayeri, M., Some Trends in Web Application Development http://dx.doi.org/10.1109/FOSE.2007.26, in 2007 Future of Software Engineering. 2007, IEEE Computer Society. p. 199-213.
13. National Highway Traffic Safety Administration, FARS Overview. 2007, National Highway Traffic Safety Administration.
14. National Center for Statistics and Analysis, FARS Encyclopedia. 2007, National Center for Statistics and Analysis.
15. O'Reilly, T., What Is Web 2.0: Design Patterns and Business Models for the Next Generation of Software. 2005, O'Reilly Media, Inc.
16. Merrill, D., Mashups: The new breed of Web app. 2006, IBM developerWorks.
17. Stamey, J., et al., Client-side dynamic metadata in web 2.0 http://doi.acm.org/10.1145/1297144.1297176 in Proceedings of the 25th annual ACM international conference on Design of communication 2007 ACM: El Paso, Texas, USA p. 155-161
18. Gibin, M., et al., An Exploratory Cartographic Visualisation of London through the Google Maps API. Applied Spatial Analysis and Policy, 2008.
19. Ennals, R. and D. Gay, User-friendly functional programming for web mashups http://doi.acm.org/10.1145/1291151.1291187, in Proceedings of the 2007 ACM SIGPLAN international conference on Functional programming. 2007, ACM: Freiburg, Germany. p. 223-234.
20. Garrett, J.J., Ajax: A New Approach to Web Applications. 2005, Adaptive Path Inc.
21. Kei-Hoi Cheung, et al., HCLS 2.0/3.0: Health care and life sciences data mashup using Web 2.0/3.0. Journal of Biomedical Informatics, 2008. In Press, Corrected Proof.

22.Seung-Jun Cha, et al., Integrating Ajax into GIS Web Services for Performance Enhancement, in Lecture Notes in Computer Science. 2007, Springer: Berlin / Heidelberg. p. 562-568.
23.SmarterTools, I., SmarterStats Glossary. 2009, SmarterTools, Inc.

Visualizing Table Dependency Relations to Reveal Network Characters in Database Applications

Chengying Mao

School of Software,
Jiangxi University of Finance and Economics,
330013 Nanchang, China
maochy@yeah.net

Abstract. With the rapid growth of software size and complexity, how to understand and maintain a software system has become a great challenge in its life-cycle, especially from the global perspective. The paper mainly focuses on the comprehension problem of database-based software systems. A framework for visualizing and analyzing table dependency structure of a DB-based application is proposed, and its corresponding prototype tool named DBViewer is implemented. It mainly includes two main functions, i.e., table dependency visualization in database and structure feature metrics. The key methods of building this tool are proposed and some characters of table dependency relations in database are also found via metrics in this paper. Some experiments are performed on five DB-based software systems, and some preliminary rules have been found: (1) the degree distribution of table dependency graph roughly conforms to power law, (2) the average path length of the max connected sub-graph is small, and (3) the clustering effect is not so evident and the coefficients are all less than 0.05 in the max connected sub-graph of all table dependency relations.

Keywords: Software Visualization, Complex Network, Pareto Law, Graphviz

1 Introduction

With the rapid growth of software size and complexity, software developers, maintainers and users are confronted with great obstacles in understanding or digesting so huge information. Nowadays, the program code lines, data structures and the levels of abstract hierarchy in modern software systems become more complex than they used to be. Moreover, the volume of intermediate results or final output is too huge to be handled in the manual way. Fortunately, software visualization [1] and data mining-based software comprehension [2,3] provide a possible way to cope with this trouble.

In the past, most software quality checkers paid their attentions to the local details of software such as module interface, algorithm implementation and data structure. However, more prevalent way is to check the system from the global perspective to improve its holistic performance. The visualization and measurement results can

M.L. Huang et al. (eds.), *Visual Information Communication*,
DOI 10.1007/978-1-4419-0312-9_19, © Springer Science+Business Media, LLC 2010

provide two important functions for software development and maintenance. One is to help developers or maintainers to understand the internal constructs of software system. The other is to help them to reveal useful information through deeply mining the software structure network. Here, we adopt these techniques to assist the construction or maintenance of database-based software system.

Since the business logic becomes more and more complicated, the backend database in information system is usually characterized by large size and complex dependency relations between tables. The traditional data modeling techniques such as ER graph mainly treat the partial or local view, which have difficulty in dealing with the global structure display. Moreover, the ER graph-based modeling technique doesn't provide the ability of measuring the structure feature of dependency relation graph. The paper considers the table dependency graph as a complex network [4], and adopts the related metric items to describe the notable characters of database. It is not hard to find that, this metric value is quite useful for developers or maintainers to optimize or refactor database constructs. Based on the above consideration, a database analysis tool named DBViewer [5] is built to display the global structure of database and provide the feature value of table dependency graph (also called network). Furthermore, we employ experimental study on several real-applied database-based applications and find some interesting results about table dependency graph.

The rest of the paper is organized as follows: In the following section, it is a brief overview of software visualization and the basic concepts of complex network. In Section 3, the architecture and working principle of the prototype tool DBViewer are addressed in details. Based on such tool, several real database applications are used in experimental study, and some characters about table dependency network are revealed and discussed in Section 4. Section 5 presents the conclusion and future work in this area.

2 Background

2.1 Software Visualization

Software visualization is concerned with the static visualization as well as the animation of software artifacts, such as source code, executable programs, and the data they manipulate, and their attributes, such as size, complexity, or dependencies [6]. This topic has been deeply discussed by world-wide researchers in past decades, and some mature techniques have been introduced into programming tools. The practical feedback shows that these techniques (or tools) can help software system developers or maintainers to understand their systems better.

In general, most existing work about software visualization can be classified into four aspects: (1) *Program code visualization*. It assists programmers to read or understand their code easily, and the typical style is the keyword highlight display. It can help programmers to distinguish keywords from common variables, even facilitate them to know the structures such as branch and cycle. Another advanced style is to extract the summary information from a code segment (e.g., the methods and variables of a class) in some integrated development environments (IDEs). (2)

System dependency visualization. To visualize the dependencies between programs elements is the main task in this direction. The representative dependency relations are the control dependency, data dependency and information flow, and usually to be described in the graphs such as CFG, call graph, PDG/SDG and program slicing [7]. Such information is especially useful for maintainers to understand the legacy system during the activities of software maintenance, reverse engineering and re-engineering. For instance, the UML diagrams extracted from Java source code in the tool Together [8] make maintainers know the classes and their interactions in software. Moreover, the dependency between source files and external files (or APIs) also need to be depicted in the graph style. (3) *Software process visualization.* Software development takes place in a dynamic context of frequently changing technologies, and limited resources. Therefore, the effective process management can improve software quality and reduce development cost. How to represent, analyze and simulate the complicated software process is a hot but difficult research issue today. Fortunately, software visualization provides a possible way to handle this difficulty. Through monitoring and sampling the character data at the key checkpoints of all development activities, the process is usually modeled via workflow diagram [9]. Most of the prevalent software process management tools provide the modeling and visualization functions for high-level mangers in current software industry. Moreover, process mining [10] techniques are applied to these tools to find some potential knowledge. (4) *Organization relation visualization.* The before-mentioned system dependency reflects the interaction of software modules, but the communication and infection between stakeholders are also very important for the success of software development, especially for the large-scale, distributed co-working software project. Therefore, visualizing the social network among analyst, designer, coder, tester and manager is necessary and meaningful [11]. It can find some communication and schedule problems in development teams. Conway's law [12] states that the structure of the system mirrors the structure of the designers' organization. So C. Amrit et al. [13,14] try to reveal the interaction principle between those two kinds of structures, another work [15] wants to detect the community of developers to facilitate the subsystem partition.

Besides the above four important aspects, software visualization also include the following points: algorithm visualization, evolvement history visualization, dynamic behavior visualization, and so on [1]. Previous research mainly focuses on the graphical representations of program code and documents, and scantily considers the case of database applications. In the paper, we try to visualize the dependency relations between tables in the backend large-scale database. Such dependency graph can help developers to check the integrality, consistency and interaction of whole database. Furthermore, we attempt to find some common network features of table dependency graph so as to optimize or refactor the concept structure of database.

2.2 Complex Network and Its Metrics

Complex network [4] is an active research topic in the field of systems science, which inspires large amount of empirical studies of real-world networks such as computer networks and social networks. Most social, biological, and technological networks display substantial non-trivial topological features, including a heavy tail in the degree distribution, a high clustering coefficient, community structure, and hierarchical structure. Here, we mainly discuss three key issues of network as below.

(1) *Average path length*. The distance d_{ij} between two nodes (i and j) is defined as the number of edges along the shortest path connecting them. The diameter D of a network G is the maximum length of shortest paths between two nodes in the network, i.e.

$$D = \max_{i,j} d_{ij} \tag{1}$$

Then, average path length L of a network is defined as the average distance of each node pair:

$$L = \frac{1}{N(N+1)/2} \sum_{i \leq j} d_{ij} \tag{2}$$

where N is the node number of network.

(2) *Clustering coefficient*. Suppose a selected node i in the network, which connects k_i other nodes by k_i edges. If the first neighbours of the original node were part of a clique, there would be $k_i(k_i - 1)/2$ edges between them. The ratio between the number E_i of edges that actually exist between these k_i nodes and the total number $k_i(k_i - 1)/2$ gives the value of the clustering coefficient of node i.

$$C_i = \frac{2E_i}{k_i(k_i - 1)} \tag{3}$$

Obviously, the clustering coefficient of the whole network is the average of all individual C_i's.

(3) *Degree distribution*. Not all nodes in a network have the same number of edges. The spread in the number of edges a node has, or node degree, is characterized by a distribution function $P(k)$. Recent empirical results show that, for a large number of networks, including the World-Wide Web, Internet or metabolic networks, the degree distribution has a power-law tail (refer to formula 3) [16]. Such networks are called scale-free, implying that the degree distribution of these networks has no characteristic scale.

$$P(k) \sim k^{-\gamma} \tag{4}$$

While considering the table dependency graph, the above structure features can give developers a more in-depth understanding on the backend database. Specifically, the average path length of a table dependency network can reflect the propagation effects of some item change produced in a specific table. The larger average path length means that a small change can cause large range side effects, so programmer should pay attention to the consistency problem while performing modification operations on some specific tables. For the factor of clustering coefficient, the table dependency graph manifests the clustering phenomenon if it has high clustering coefficient. Then managers can detect the community structure with direction of such data, and further manage tables in the way of division and conquering so as to improve efficiency and parallelism. The clue about the degree distribution can reflect the significance of tables in database. According to the distribution spectrum, programmers should pay much attention to the modification of the tables with high degree. Because a little change in that table can lead to the update of quite a few connected tables.

3   Framework of Table Dependency Viewer

In order to facilitate developers or maintainers to manipulate and manage database, it is necessary to construct a visualization tool to display connection relations from the global perspective. That is to say, we are not concerned about the details such as attribute, prime key, and foreign key of one specific table, but the network characters of whole dependency relations. It is the particular point different from the visualization function of traditional database management tool.

The prototype tool DBViewer has two functions: dependency relation visualization and structure feature metrics. In the visualization module, the tables and their reference relations are automatically analyzed, and then the relations are stored in adjacent matrix. In order to display such relations in a legible style, we convert the relation matrix into a dot file [17], and then adopt the third-part component Graphviz [18] to display the relation graph in tool's viewer interface. Therefore, the visualization subsystem mainly consists of the following function points: DB connection management, dependency relation analysis, dot file generation and storage, dependency graph display, and dependency graph storage.

On the other hand, some basic structure (or network) features are calculated using the relation matrix. These features can be classified into following four kinds: basic metric value, degree distribution, average path length and clustering coefficient. Of course, the measurement subsystem also needs to provide the functions of displaying and storing metric results.

3.1   Technical Roadmap of DBViewer

Based on the descriptions of the static architecture of the tool DBViewer, its working principle and technical roadmap can be addressed as Figure 1. First, connect to the target database (used in the software under analysis), and then acquire the list of all tables in that database. Consequently, the dependency relations can be recognized by analyzing the prime and foreign keys of each table. In general, there are several ways to express such dependency relations. One way of exploring dependency relations is to check table's attribute item one by one. For each foreign key in this table, it is necessary to search the corresponding prime key in other tables. The other way is to read this information from system table in the target database directly. Obviously, the second way is much simpler but requires the database is integral. The key code segment of this style can be illustrated here.

```
select so1.name, so2.name, count(constid) as weight
from sysforeignkeys sf, sysobjects so1, sysobjects so2
where sf.fkeyid = so1.id and sf.rkeyid = so2.id
group by so1.name, so2.name
order by so1.name asc, so2.name asc
```

For the purpose of simplicity and facility, we adopt the adjacent matrix to represent relations between tables. The matrix is only the dynamic form in memory, so it should be converted into external file so as to facilitate the reuse of dependency relations. For the purpose of visualization, the tool adopts the third-part component, i.e. Graphviz [18], to draw the dependency relation graph. In order to avoid the repeated generation of table dependency graph, the prototype also provides the function of graph storage and management.

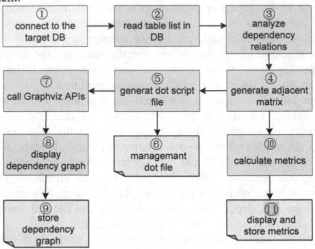

Fig. 1. The technical roadmap of the prototype tool DBViewer

On the other side, we presume that the table dependency graph can be viewed as complex network. Then, the measurement system is adopted to calculate the feature value of that graph. As a consequence, we verify whether the calculation results satisfy the properties of complex network. Then we can judge whether dependency relation graph is a specific complex network or not. It is not hard to find that the metrics value is also very useful for developers or maintainers to optimize the database design.

At present, we only implemented the above basic function in the tool DBViewer. Based on the visualization of table dependency graph, slicing, change impact analysis and dynamic evolvement measurement can be employed in next step.

3.2   Dependency Relation Visualization and Metrics

Graph representation is the core function of a software visualization tool. Here, we integrate the third-part open source component into our prototype system. The Graphviz is a graph layout engine developed via AT&T lab, and **grappa** is a Java package of it. Since grappa is an independent program package, the visualization tool based on it is characterized by powerful portability and extendibility.

The dependency relations between tables are obtained in the following two steps: The first is to get the table list in database, which can be implemented via scanning the target database or accessing the system table. It should be noted that we don't extract all tables in database but only those with `type='U'`. The results are stored in a hash table `<String, Integer>`. Then, we can use the two methods which are addressed in the former subsection to analyze the interaction relations between these tables. After all table dependency relations are calculated, they can be stored in a triple `RecordSet` as below.

< table name, referenced table name, weight>

Based on the above records, an adjacent matrix can be used to represent the dependency relations between tables, and can be further converted into a dot file. In this file, the dependency edge can be expressed in the following form.

```
graph G {
......
table name -> referenced table name [label=weight]
......
}
```

The weight in the `RecordSet` and dot file represents the number of foreign keys of the current table. Then the tool can invoke the third-part package grappa to draw the dependency graph in a panel according to the achieved dot file. Figure 2 is a snapshot of the tool displaying the table dependency relations in an example database.

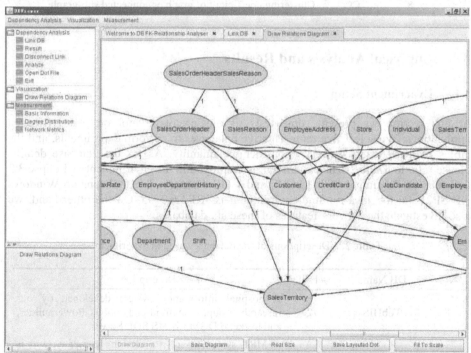

Fig. 2. The snapshot of displaying dependency graph in tool DBViewer

As mentioned in the former section, dependency graph visualization in this paper is used to handle the large-scale database. However, ER graph is mainly used to tackle the situation of the partial view of whole database. Therefore we need to measure the dependency graph to reveal some key properties of database system. Besides of some basic metrics, we adopt three attribute items which are widely used in complex network research field to measure the dependency relation graph. Therefore, all metric items can be listed in Table 1.

Table 1.   Metric items of the table dependency graph

No.	Abbr.	Description
1	NN	Node number, i.e. number of tables in database
2	EN	Edge number, i.e. number of relations in database
3	MD	Max degree in undirected graph, i.e. number of bidirectional cited relations in DB
4	MID	Max in-degree in directed graph, i.e. number of cited relations in DB
5	MOD	Max out-degree in directed graph, i.e. number of citing relations in DB
6	DD	Degree distribution, or in(out)-degree distribution
7	APL	Average path length
8	CC	Clustering coefficient of graph or connected sub-graph

4   Empirical Analysis and Results

4.1   Experiment Setup

In this section we present some tests of our prototype tool on real DB-based applications. We select five representative databases to perform experiments, and the tables of these databases reach considerable quantity. As for the database details, please refer to Table 2. The experiment is employed in the environment of Eclipse 3.2 and runs on Pentium 4 with 1.8GHz and 1 GB memory. The tool runs on Windows XP SP2, and the Java runtime environment is JRE1.6.0_05. On the other hand, we also investigate the network features of these six databases.

Table 2.   Descriptions of the databases used in experiment

No.	DB Name	#Table	Description
1	TobHIS	725	A hospital information system developed by our research group. The front-end tool is Powerbuilder, and backend DBMS is MS SQL Server.
2	ClothingMRP	138	A MRP system used in a clothing company, and is developed by Delphi6. It's downloaded from http://code.ddvip.com/view/11339712006387.html
3	SE2000	327	An ERP system used in manufacturing industry, and is developed by VisualBasic. Downloaded from http://code.ddvip.com/result.php

| 4 | MRPII | 199 | A general MRP system, which can be used in Enterprises such as machining, electronics etc., downloaded from http://www.winu.cn/attachment.php?aid=64377 |
| 5 | AdventureWorks | 71 | An example database system in Microsoft SQL Server 2005, it also can be downloaded from Microsoft corporation Web site. |

For each database, the tool DBViewer displays the dependency relation as a graph. So it is necessary to understand the database structure by reading the basic features of such dependency graph. In Table 3, the basic parameters of table dependency including NN, EN, MD, MID and MOD graph are listed for facilitating to know the general view. The other features about network structure are detailedly discussed in following subsection.

Table 3.   The basic parameters of each table dependency graph

No.	DB Name	NN	EN	MD	MID	MOD
1	TobHIS	725	266	13	13	5
2	ClothingMRP	138	114	27	25	3
3	SE2000	327	199	45	42	7
4	MRPII	199	146	31	30	6
5	AdventureWorks	71	88	18	14	9

4.2   Degree Distribution

The degree distribution is a key issue for revealing interaction features of tables in database. If database designer complies with 3NF rule, the dependency relation seems likely to be flat, that is, the distribution approximately obeys uniform function. However, most designers do not adhere to database design principle so strictly. They usually take convenience and usability as the first-line aims in the real environment. Although the database design theory about 3NF is perfect, we have to accept the practical phenomena. Therefore, it's necessary to find the real status of degree distribution of table dependency in database.

For the five real applied databases, we calculated the degree distribution so as to find some rules. As shown in Figure 3, the degree distribution obeys the "80-20" principle or pareto law [19], that is, most nodes have very low degree and the nodes with high degree generally account for small proportion in table dependency graph. While considering the database TobHIS, the nodes with zero degree occupy 50.07%, and 1-degree nodes account for 28.69% of all nodes. That is to say, eighty percent of tables have merely one or even no connection with other tables in database. For the second database ClothingMRP, 34.78 percentages of tables have not any relation with other tables, and 1-degree nodes (or tables) account for 22.46% of all nodes. On the whole, the nodes with degree less than 2 reach the proportion of 78.25 percentages.

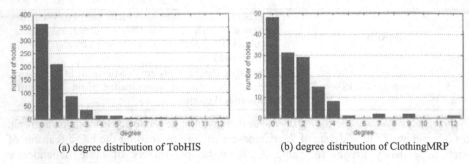

(a) degree distribution of TobHIS   (b) degree distribution of ClothingMRP

Fig. 3. The degree distribution (histogram representation) of two DB-based applications

In fact, the reference relation in table dependency graph is a directed edge. So it's necessary to consider the distribution according to edge's direction, i.e. primal key or foreign key. As seen from Figure 4, the in-degree distribution and out-degree distribution all approximately follow the "80-20" principle.

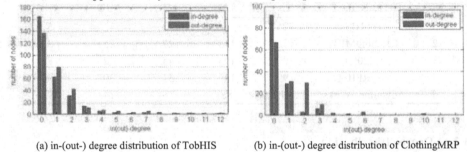

(a) in-(out-) degree distribution of TobHIS   (b) in-(out-) degree distribution of ClothingMRP

Fig. 4. The in-(out) degree distribution of two examples

In order to answer the question "whether the degree distribution obeys power law", we analyzed other three DB-based applications in the logarithm reference frame. For the sake of convenient expression, we utilized the value $log(degree+1)$ on X-axis in Figure 5. For the application SE2000 and MRPII, the distributions of their degree and out-degree are obviously obeys the power law, but the in-degree distribution is not so evident. While considering the fifth application AdventureWorks, its degree and in-degree distribution conform to the power law, however the out-degree feature isn't clear. In the Figure 5(d), we consider the degree distributions of three applications together. It's not hard to find that the degree distributions of them are all in line with the power law. Comprehensively consider the five application examples, we can draw a conclusion that the degree distribution of table dependency graph (or network) in database-based application roughly obeys the power law. This character means that the table dependency graph is a scale-free network, and the achieved results in the field of complex network can be introduced to direct the maintenance activities of database system, especially for analyzing its evolvement character. When a table or a attribute in table is changed, we can adopt the dynamic analysis technology to predict its corresponding change impact [20].

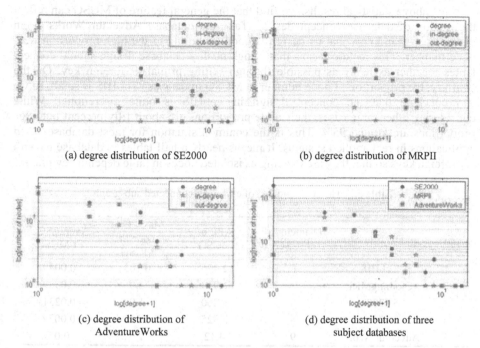

(a) degree distribution of SE2000

(b) degree distribution of MRPII

(c) degree distribution of
AdventureWorks

(d) degree distribution of three
subject databases

Fig. 5. The degree distribution in the logarithm reference frame

4.3 Average Path Length and Clustering Coefficient

For each dependency graph of the above five DB-based applications, it is an unconnected graph. However, the network features such as average path length (APL for short) and clustering coefficient (CC) are usually used for a connected graph. Due to this reason, we firstly identify the max connected sub-graph (MCSG) from each table dependency, and then compute the feature value according to the deduced sub-graph. The basic feature of each max connected sub-graph is shown in the following table.

Table 4. The basic features of each max connected sub-graph in experiment

No.	DB Name	Node number of MCSG	Proportion w.r.t node number	Edge number of MCSG	Proportion w.r.t edge number
1	TobHIS	21	2.90%	24	9.02%
2	ClothingMRP	72	52.17%	99	86.84%
3	SE2000	117	35.78%	193	96.98%
4	MRPII	84	42.21%	139	95.21%
5	AdventureWorks	66	92.96%	87	98.86%

From above statistical results, we find that the general feature of MCSG can reflect the quality of database concept design. Take the database AdventureWorks as an example, we can know that its design is good according to the high proportion w.r.t node number. This feature means that a high quality database design should connect tables together as many as possible through setting primal or foreign key. On the contrary, the proportion of node number in MCSG in database TobHIS is small, so we can conclude that the concept design in TobHIS is quite discretional. While considering other three cases, their node proportions are about fifty percent but edge proportions are around 95%. This is the common situation for most database-based applications in real applied systems. It means nearly a half tables in database haven't set foreign keys so that they are existing as isolated nodes in table dependency graph.

Table 5.   The APL and CC of each max connected sub-graph

No.	DB Name	Diameter of MCSG	APL of MCSG	Max CC of node in MCSG	Average CC of MCSG
1	TobHIS	6	2.476	0.103	0.0049
2	ClothingMRP	11	3.919	1.0	0.0350
3	SE2000	8	3.260	1.0	0.0231
4	MRPII	8	3.325	0.333	0.0072
5	AdventureWorks	9	4.12	1.0	0.05

As shown from the above table, the diameter of each max connected sub-graph is small although it holds quite a few nodes or edges. As a consequence, the average path length is also small, that is, they are all less than 4.2. The result is in line with the actual situation: When a database designer constructs the concept structure of DB, he/she should consider the query efficiency. In other words, he/she should ensure that DB user can search valuable results by using as few as possible table connection operations. From this point, the APL of the table dependency graph should be controlled within a reasonable range. While considering the clustering coefficient of MCSG, the value of most nodes is zero although some node can reach the max value (i.e. 1.0 for the database ClothingMRP and SE2000). Therefore, the average CCs of all five MCSGs in experiment are quite little, that is, they are all less than 0.05. From this result, we can know that the clustering phenomenon in table dependency graph is not so clear. The table dependency graph is more likely to be random graph from the perspective of low clustering coefficient.

4.4   Discussions

With the help of prototype tool DBViewer, the table dependency graphs of real applications are vividly displayed in the global perspective, and some practical phenomena of the applied databases' design are also revealed via the structure metrics of dependency graph. In theory, the table dependency graph should be a connected graph so as to ensure database's consistency and integrality. However, there are quite a few isolated tables in most real applied databases in industry. This symptom tells us that we should strengthen the training for database designers to construct high quality database system in the filed of software industry. The degree distribution implies that there exists the "hub" nodes in table dependency graph, and such tables should be noticed in maintenance activities.

Although the table number in database is large and the size of table dependency graph is huge, the average path length of the max connected sub-graph is small and less than 4.2 in general. Therefore, we can guess that the "small world" phenomenon also exists in dependency graph of database. This is also quite in line with the actual situation, the joint (or connection) times should be very limited when the programmer implements a query, otherwise, the concept structure needs to be re-designed. However, the metric about clustering coefficient is not so coincidental with our expectation. The clustering coefficient is very small, so it implies table dependency graph seems to be "random graph".

Based on the above empirical results, we can know that the table dependency graph reflects complex network's characters such as power law and small APL, but some other items (e.g., low clustering coefficient) can't provide further support. Although we can't provide consistent conclusion, the feature value about table dependency graph can help database maintainers to employ continuous improvement. For an instance, they can concentrate on those critical tables according to degree distribution. On the other hand, the indicator of average path length can facilitate maintainers to optimize the concept view of database.

5   Concluding Remarks

The rapid development of software technology and its wide application bring great pressure to maintainers in latter stage. At present, most researches address maintenance problem from the perspective of programming language, but lack consideration on system's construction. The paper mainly treats the comprehension problem for the database-based software systems. The main contributions lie in two aspects, that is, table dependency visualization in database and structure feature metrics. Based on the third-part component Graphviz, a prototype tool called DBViewer is built for DB-based system maintenance and reconstruction. With the help of measurement function of the prototype tool, the experiment is performed on five DB-based software systems. Some preliminary rules have been found: (1) Because most DB designers don't obey the 3NF demand, table dependency graph has so many 0-degree nodes, and the degree distribution roughly conforms to power law. (2) In the max connected sub-graph of table dependency graph, the average path length is small and less than 4.0 in general. (3) While considering the clustering coefficient of the max connected sub-graph, the clustering effect is not so evident and the coefficients are all less than 0.05. From this feature, the sub-graph is more likely to be a random graph.

The paper proposed a framework for visualizing and analyzing table dependency structure of a DB-based application. This study provides an important starting point, but much remains to be done. For example, the visualization tool can be built as plug-in and migrated into integrated development environment for database-base applications. If some continues versions of applied database can be achieved, the dynamic evolution of structure metrics of such database can be deeply analyzed. Furthermore, the relevance between structure feature values (especially for APL and CC) and query efficiency also need to be further explored.

Acknowledgements

This work was supported in part by the National Natural Science Foundation of China (NSFC) under Grant No. 60803046, China Postdoctoral Science Foundation under Grant No.20070410946, the Science Foundation of Jiangxi Educational Committee under Grant No.GJJZ-2007-267, and the Youth Foundation of Jiangxi University of Finance and Economics. We are also grateful for the great help from Qiong Zhang, Chunxu Huang, Shengbiao Huang, Qiang Liu and Wenjia Ouyang.

References

1. Stasko, J. T., Domingue, J. B., Brown, M. H., Price, B. A.: Software Visualization, MIT Press (1998)
2. Kanellopoulos, Y., Tjortjis, C.: Data Mining Source Code to Facilitate Program Comprehension: Experiments on Clustering Data Retrieved from C++ Programs. In: Proc. of the 12th International Workshop on Program Comprehension, Bari, Italy, pp. 214-225. IEEE CS Press (2004)
3. Zaidman, A., Calders, T., Demeyer, S., Paredaens, J.: Applying Web Mining Techniques to Execution Traces to Support the Program Comprehension Process. In: Proc. of the 9th European Conference on Software Maintenance and Reengineering, Manchester, UK, pp. 134-142. IEEE CS Press, (2005)
4. Newman, M. E. J.: The Structure and Function of Complex Networks. SIAM Review 45, 167-256 (2003)
5. Mao, C.: DBViewer: A Tool for Visualizing and Measuring Dependency Relations between Tables in Database. In: Proc. of the 2009 World Congress on Software Engineering (WCSE 2009), Xiamen, China, pp. 13-17. IEEE CS Press (2009)
6. Koschke, R.: Software Visualization in Software Maintenance, Reverse Engineering, and Re-engineering: A Research Survey. Journal of Software Maintenance and Evolution: Research and Practice, 15, pp. 87-109, John Wiley & Sons (2003)
7. Tip, F.: A Survey of Program Slicing Techniques. Journal of Programming Languages, Vol.3, No. 3, pp. 121-189 (1995)
8. Together, Borland, 2009. http://www.borland.com/together
9. Fuggetta, A.: Software Process: A Roadmap. In: Proc. of the Conference on the Future of Software Engineering, Limerick, Ireland, pp. 25-34. ACM Press (2000)
10. Rubin, V., Günther, C. W., Aalst, W. M. P., Kindler, E., Dongen, B. F., Schäfer, W.: Process Mining Framework for Software Processes. In: Wang Q., Pfahl D., Raffo D. M. (eds.): Software Process Dynamics and Agility, International Conference on Software Process, LNCS, vol. 4470, pp. 169-181, Springer, Heidelberg (2007)
11. Souza, C. R. B., Quirk, S., Trainer, E., Redmiles, D.F.: Supporting Collaborative Software Development through the Visualization of Socio-Technical Dependencies. In: Proc. of the 2007 International ACM Conference on Supporting Group Work, pp. 147-156. ACM Press, New York (2007)
12. Conway, M.: How Do Committees Invent. Datamation, 14, pp. 28-31 (1968)

13. Amrit, C : Coordination in Software Development: The Problem of Task Allocation. ACM SIGSOFT Software Engineering Notes, vol. 30, no. 4, pp. 1-7, ACM Press (2005)
14. Amrit, C., Hillegersberg, J.: Matrix Based Problem Detection in the Application of Software Process Patterns. In: Proc. of the 9th International Conference on Enterprise Information Systems, Funchal, Madeira, Portugal, June 12-16, vol. 3, pp. 316-320 (2007)
15. Valetto G., Helander M., Ehrlich K., Chulani S., Wegman M., Williams C.: Using Software Repositories to Investigate Socio-technical Congruence in Development Projects. In: Proc. of the Fourth International Workshop on Mining Software Repositories, pp. 25-25. IEEE CS Press (2007)
16. Faloutsos, M., Faloutsos, P., Faloutsos, C.: On Power-law Relationships of the Internet Topology. ACM SIGCOMM Computer Communication Review, vol. 29, no. 4, pp. 251-262 (1999)
17. The DOT language, http://www.graphviz.org/doc/info/lang.html
18. Graphviz, http://www.graphviz.org
19. Bookstein, A.: Informetric Distributions, Part I: Unified Overview. Journal of the American Society for Information Science, 41, pp. 368-375 (1990)
20. Pastor-Satorras, R., Vespingnani, A.: Epidemic Spreading in Scale-free Networks. Physical Review Letters, vol.86, no. 4, pp. 3200-3203 (2001)

Visualized Feature Modeling in Software Product Line

Li Zheng[1], Chao Zhang[1], Zhanwei Wu[1] ,Yixin Yan[1]

[1] Department of Computer Science and Technology, Tsinghua University
{zhengli.ts, mnchaoster, vincent.ng.thu}@gmail.com, yanyx06@163.com

Abstract. In the research of commonalities and variations of domain modeling, feature modeling is proved to be an effective and widely used method. But how to visualize the feature models in user interfaces remains to be a problem. In studying the data processing domain, we design rendering rules to combine features to user visible engines in GUI XML and UML based Architecture Description Language (ADL). Furthermore, we visualize the process in our IDE tool based on Eclipse.

Keywords: Software Product Line, Feature Modeling, Visualization

1 Introduction

In Software Product Line (SPL), how to manage commonalities and variations is the main concern. Feature modeling is an effective and popular method to solve the problem. It is mainly used in requirements engineering in domain engineering process, and product configuration in product engineering. One of the challenging issues within SPL engineering is that there is a gap from features of feature models to the realization of the features by specific software artifacts [10].

To bridge this gap, Czarnecki et al. proposed a template based approach [11, 12] where features from feature models are connected with UML model elements by Presence Conditions. Presence Conditions are expressions that are directly annotated to the UML model elements by using XPath expressions or UML stereotypes. By introducing this connection between features and model artifacts, an initial step towards automatic product derivation is done. However, As the realization models grow in size and complexity, it becomes even harder to understand and visualize connections.

This paper mainly proposes a method to visualize the transformation and configuration of feature model. We use an ADL transformation method to map the feature model and the product line, and visualize the process by a GUI XML. Finally, we implement this idea in a data processing system.

M.L. Huang et al. (eds.), *Visual Information Communication*,
DOI 10.1007/978-1-4419-0312-9_20, © Springer Science+Business Media, LLC 2010

2   Data Processing Domain

Data Processing is an important computer application domain. In the information era, huge amount of data emerge every day, which are closely related to the national economy, society, defense and scientific research. Therefore, using information technology to handle data is necessary. Data processing is related to many other areas including data warehousing, data mining, decision supporting system, business intelligence, data report, ETL and OLAP. Many similar systems sharing common functions exist in the Data Processing Domain (DPD). Building a data oriented SPL can largely reduce the effort of developing a product. So far, there are no researchers who have analyzed the domain of data processing. It is thus of great importance to bring the concept of the product line into data processing software development and analyze the domain. And it helps to improve the productivity and quality of the software.

Data processing system is usually categorized into data-operational system and data-analytical system. Data-operational system, which is transaction driven, manipulates data directly, and stores the processed data into database. Data-analytical system obtains data from isomeric data sources, analysis data in data warehouse to meet users' demands, and present the analysis results. Data analytical system provides the historical, present and future data. Generally, it restores data in a data warehouse or data marts. Data analytical system usually doesn't modify data in the data source which is called operational data.

A typical analytical data processing system includes Extract, Transformation, Analysis and Presentation (ETAP). Operational system and analytical system differ mainly in whether it follows the ETAP process. Analytical system can be further categorized into generalized analytical system and specialized analytical system. The former is designed for general data processing, which has every fundamental analytical function, while the latter is designed for special areas, and it can provide complex specialized high-level analytical results [6]. Our objective is to build a generalized analytical SPL.

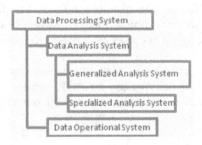

Fig. 1. Taxonomy of Data Processing System

We selected representative data processing software from the domain, including data-operational system like information system in Tsinghua University, Datum print media processing system, specialized analytical system including Excel, SPSS, SAS, TM1, and specialized analytical system including wind resource analytical system, medical information analytical system, football manager genie scout etc. For operational systems, we ignore the workflow, only focus on the functional modules, and categorize them into the corresponding ETAP group. Besides, we take the output of operational systems as the data source of the data processing system, which means the data to be processed. For specialized analytical system, we divide the professional data processing functions into basic functions without specialized knowledge, and then extract them as features. It is not so complicated to analyze generalized analytical systems because they are more similar to our objective system. We can directly divide them into functional features following ETAP process and extract them into layered architecture.

Through the research and analysis of DPD, we propose a typical general data processing system functional model shown in Figure 2.

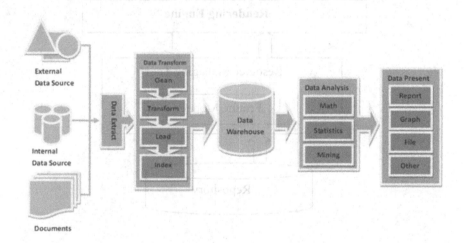

Fig. 2. Typical General Data Processing System Functional Model

3   Feature Oriented Product Line

3.1   Overview of the Product Line

There are three important parts in data processing oriented SPL. The resource repository where resources are stored in conformance to the specification is not allowed to be accessed directly by users. Users manage resources through the resource managing tool. The managing tool organizes resources in the form of a feature model, which dramatically enhances the convenience of store and query. At the configuration stage of the product line, a resource composing IDE helps developers to fetch and compose resources into a final product. Developers may as well create new resource which is originally not in the repository. The composing IDE includes three engines. Application engine and process engine deal with functional composing and workflow composing respectively, and they are visible to users. There is a gap between feature model and user visible engines which needs the rendering engine to fill. The rendering engine used to visualize the feature model is the main focus of this paper. Fig 3 presents the overview of the product line and connections between different parts.

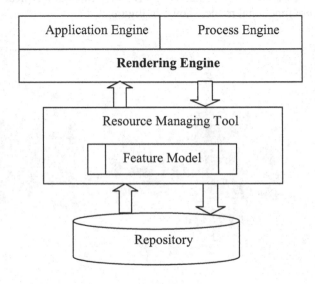

Fig. 3. Overview of the Product Line

3.2   Feature Analysis

In SPL, how to manage commonalities and variations is the major concern. Feature modeling is a very effective and popular method to solve the problem. It is mainly used in requirements engineering in domain engineering process, and product configuration in product engineering. The earliest feature modeling method is FODA proposed by Kang et al in 1990 [2]. Later on, researchers modify FODA and make various extensions to it. However, these extensions differ in symbols, feature decompositions, feature constraints and formal semantics. But so far, none of them is widely accepted to be an established method. [1]. Prominent extensions of feature modeling methods include FORM [3], cardinality based feature models, propositional logical feature modeling method [4] [5].

In 1998, Kang et al proposed FORM method based on FODA. FORM has made two significant improvements to FODA. The first is changing the tree structure into Direct Acyclic Graph (DAG) which can support more complex structure. The second is to bring in new architecture, including layers, implemention relation and integrated/generalized relation.

Cardinality based feature models are proposed by Czarnecki K et al in 2005, whose main idea is to reuse features in the product. Its feature diagram can have references and attributes. There is even a corresponding context free grammar which can mutually transform with feature diagram. Besides, this method has a staged configuration in the product engineering process, eliminating unnecessary features in each stage. Staged configuration can meet different requirements of software supply chains, optimization, policy standards, time, targets and roles etc.

Batory and Czarnecki K et al transform feature model and propositional logic mutually. On one hand, feature model can be changed to propositional formulas so that researchers may use the strict theory to implicate and validate feature modeling, such as SAT solvers and Binary-Decision Diagram (BDD) libraries; On the other hand, propositional formulas can be translated back into feature model.

Feature model is usually expressed by feature diagram which can manage variations at larger granularity. The main contents in a feature diagram include the commonalities and variations of features, the dependency relationship of features and legal constraints of combination of features.

Feature diagram is a tree of features or a directed acyclic graph. To reduce complexity, we show our feature model in a tree form. Every node of the tree represents a feature and every feature originates from the root feature. A feature is either grouped or solitary. Solitary feature can be mandatory or optional while grouped features are decomposed in XOR relationship or OR relationship. These basic categories and relations are always abundant to organize a complex model. To describe the relationship between any features, additional constraints of features specified in propositional logic are added to the feature diagram. Features can be reused by introducing the concept of cardinality, which means the times a feature may repeatedly appear under the parent feature [5].

Feature diagram needs prescriptive symbols to explain semantics. Since there is not a unified symbol standard, we use our own symbols.

The following are examples to illustrate this issue.

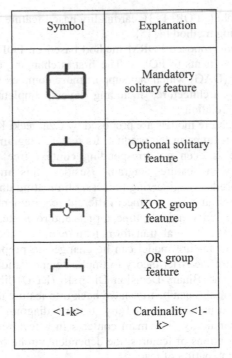

Symbol	Explanation
	Mandatory solitary feature
	Optional solitary feature
	XOR group feature
	OR group feature
<1-k>	Cardinality <1-k>

Fig. 4. Symbols of Feature Diagram

According to the symbols shown in Figure 4, we present our feature diagram in DPD in Figure 5.

There are specialized requirements in DPD. The Procedure which follows ETAP process is usually clear. Data processing functions are extremely large in number and types and layers. Resources with generalized function may be modified and configured differently. Current methods can not satisfy the requirements of DPD. Then we use FODA as a basic model, adding the main ideas mentioned above, and making necessary changes accordingly to meet the domain needs.

Fig. 5. Feature Diagram in DPD

3.3   Feature Configuration

A feature model represents a set of configurations. Each configuration is a set of features selected from a feature model according to its semantics.

In application engineering, feature model obtained in domain engineering is configured to concrete product under logical constraints. The configuration is composed of two activities, tailoring the feature model and extending the feature model [7].

Tailoring takes place when it is reused. Requirements analysts determine features needed and remove the unnecessary, getting a sub tree of the feature tree diagram. The sub tree is a concrete application model if it satisfies the logical validation.

Sometimes requirements cannot be fully covered by a feature model. New functions will be added to feature model. The extending process is similar to modifying a feature tree, the only difference is that the new feature doesn't have to be reusable.

Extending the feature tree takes much more efforts than the tailoring. To avoid the cost, we need to do further researches in the specific domains, make the repository as complete as possible to cover more functions. Nevertheless, requirements are always changing, extending features is necessary.

4   Visualizing the product line

There are various method of presenting a feature model. Among them, Ontology based method, XML based method, UML based method and Architecture Description Language (ADL) based method are the most popular.

Each method has its advantages and disadvantages. The Ontology can express very complex properties and relations compared to other methods, but developing the parsing, inducing and presenting tools is also an exhausting job, the cost of establishing the information repository is also high. On the contrary, XML based method is limited in semantics; however, the corresponding visualizing tools are abundant and strong, especially in Java environment. The data processing domain has relatively clear procedures so XML based method is more fit for the scenario.

UML and ADL perform better in detail design and code generation. UML is outstanding in its standard visualization and popularity, but it's also too complex, and it doesn't support architecture design and code generation well. ADL has better adaptability because it's designed by us according to actual DPD requirements. An ADL may also comply with UML and exchange mutually.

In our product line, Application engine focuses on the component presentation while process engine focuses on workflow design. So in the rendering engine, we adopt XML and ADL based method to meet those requirements.

4.1   XML GUI

GUI components are described with a script language named GUI XML which is independent of programming languages, platforms and environments. Many tags, attributes and enumeration values are defined to supports a rich set of GUIs. And the rendering of GUI components is implemented in application and process engines. In this way, the foreground applications can be easily transferred from one platform to another. E.g. if the rendering engine is design to generating Java foreground applications, the GUI XML description will be translated to java GUIs running on the Java Runtime Environment (JRE). Another rendering engine which is design to generating html web pages can translate the same GUI XML copy to foreground pages which are viewed in a web browser. The Java rendering engine is now available on the web site [9] along with a "News Item Management System".

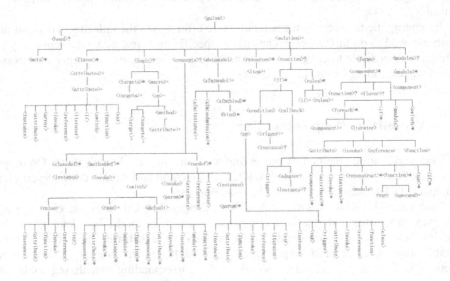

Fig. 6. Syntax Tree of GUI XML

GUI XML syntax specifies all elements for rendering engine. It can render a single feature or a combination of features. All the elements are predefined as empty values to reduce the XML construction effort.

4.2   ADL Transformation

A SPL architecture model is commonly based on domain analysis whose output is a domain model. In this research, it is a feature model, which represents the standard features and their relationships within a product line. [2]

Feature model inspires architecture model in the architecture-modeling phase, or maps automatically with tools supported. Thus, the architecture model variability will reflect the feature model variability, which requires the ADL to support variability description. Most of the traditional ADLs do not support product line modeling [8]. It means that they can only model the commonality of product line architecture but not the variability. It is expected that the ADL can model products of a whole software family, and in it there will be some meta concepts which reflect the variability.

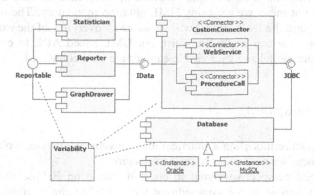

Fig. 7. A DPD product line architecture

Figure 7 shows a DPD product line architecture. This product family provides an interface Reportable to the external. And three components provide the interface. There may be one of the components Statistician, Reporter or GraphDrawer, which is named an assembly variability of the product line. There is an internal architecture of the connector CustomConnector, which can delegate the external interfaces to WebService or ProcedureCall. That is the composition variability. Component Database has two instances: Oracle and MySQL. And a product in a product line will only use one of them, which is an implementation variability. It is evident that architecture variability will be reflected in assembly, composition and implementation. An ADL supporting all of these variability descriptions will be applied to a product line description language.

The consideration of the meta model of our ADL above fulfills data processing domain requirements and is inspired by traditional ADLs. Figure 8 shows the major part of the meta concepts.

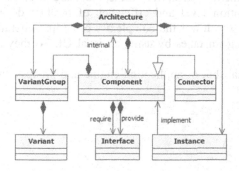

Fig. 8. Meta concepts of our ADL

All of meta concepts are domain independent. The major job of our ADL is to describe architecture which includes components and their implementations, connectors and interfaces. A description of architecture represents a single system or a SPL.

Each part will attach an example modeled in UML notation and described in the ADL. It does not mean we are using UML notation mandatory. The description may be incomplete and the UML model will visualize an overview of the examples.

Furthermore, we can easily transform our UML based ADL to code framework. Thus the feature model and user visible engines are well connected.

5   Tools Snapshot

To make feature modeling a practical and convenient method, tools for designing and development are necessities to the architecture.

We designed perspective layout in our IDE based on Eclipse Forms technique. Different data appear in the same editing UI view. We can configure properties of components.

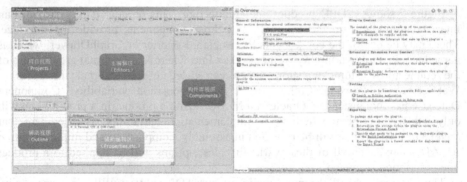

Fig. 9. Overview of the IDE Layout and Configuration

Tools make it easier to design foreground GUIs, processes as well as the linkage of them. Any tool can be extended as long as uniform description and interface standard is determined. As mentioned above, these tools are used as assistant methods to improve the automation level and efficiency of product design and development. These tools also help to lower the complexity of script generation and eliminate the probability of making mistakes by using a visual UI. So they are usually integrated into the SPL.

Fig 10 gives a snapshot of application engine and process engine, which are main user visible engines.

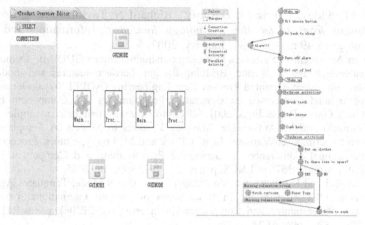

Fig. 10. Application and Process Engine

5   Acknowledgement

This research is Supported by National High-tech R&D Program (863 Program) under grant No 2007AA010306.

References

1. P. Heymans P. Y. Schobbens J.C. Trigaux Y. Bontemps R. Matulevicius A. Classen, Evaluating formal properties of feature diagram languages, Software, IET, Volume 2, Issue 3, June 2008 Page(s):281 - 302
2. KANG K., COHEN S., HESS J., NOVAK W., PETERSON S., Feature oriented domain analysis (FODA) feasibility study, Technical Report CMU/SEI-90-TR-21, Software Engineering Institute, Carnegie Mellon University, November 1990
3. KANG K.C., KIM S., LEE J., KIM K., SHIN E., HUH M., FORM: a feature-oriented reuse method with domain-specific reference architectures, Ann. Softw. Eng., 1998, 5, pp. 143–168
4. BATORY D.S., Feature models, grammars, and propositional formulas. Proc. 9th Int. Conf. Software Product Lines (SPLC' 05), 2005, pp. 7 - 20
5. Czarnecki, K.; Wasowski, A., Feature Diagrams and Logics: There and Back Again, Software Product Line Conference, 2007. SPLC 2007. 11th International 10-14 Sept. 2007 Page(s):23 - 34
6. Power, D.J. A Brief History of Decision Support Systems. DSSResources.COM, World Wide Web, http://DSSResources.COM/history/dsshistory.html, version 4.0, March 10, 2007.
7. P. Heymans P. Y. Schobbens J.C. Trigaux Y. Bontemps R. Matulevicius A. Classen, Evaluating formal properties of feature diagram languages, Software, IET, Volume 2, Issue 3, June 2008 Page(s):281 - 302

8. Nenad Medvidovic , Eric M. Dashofy , Richard N. Taylor, *Moving architectural description from under the technology lamppost*, Information and Software Technology, v.49 n.1, p.12-31, January, 2007

9. News Item Management System in http://keg.cs.tsinghua.edu.cn/GUIXML_Demo.zip

10. F. Heidenreich and C. Wende. Bridging the gap between features and models. In 2nd Workshop on Aspect-Oriented Product Line Engineering (AOPLE'07) co-located with the 6th International Conference on Generative Programming and Component Engineering (GPCE'07). Online Proceedings, 2007. URL http://www.softeng.ox.ac.uk/aople/.

11. K. Czarnecki and M. Antkiewicz. Mapping Features to Models: A Template Approach Based on Superimposed Variants. In R. Gl'uck and M. Lowry, editors, Proceedings of the 4th International Conference on Generative Programming and Component Engineering (GPCE'05), volume 3676 of LNCS, pages 422–437. Springer, 2005.

12. K. Czarnecki and K. Pietroszek. Verifying Feature-Based Model Templates Against Well-Formedness OCL Constraints. In Proceedings of the 5th International Conference on Generative Programming and Component Engineering (GPCE'06), pages 211–220, New York, NY, USA, 2006. ACM.

A Useful Visualization Technique: A Literature Review for Augmented Reality and its Application, limitation & future direction

Donggang Yu[1] , Jesse Sheng Jin[1] , Suhuai Luo[1], Wei Lai[2] , andQingming Huang[3],

[1] School of Design, Communication and Information Technology, The University of Newcastle, Callaghan, NSW 2308, Australia
[2] Faculty of Information and Communication Technologies, Swinburne University of Technology, Hawthorn, VIC3122, Australia
[3] Graduate University, China Academy of Sciences, China

Abstract. Augmented reality (AR), a useful visualization technique, is reviewed based literatures. The AR research methods and applications are surveyed since AR was first developed over forty years ago. Recent and future AR researches are proposed which could help researchers of decide which topics should be developed when they are beginning their own researches in the field.

1 Introduction

Augmented reality (AR), a useful visualization technique, is a field of computer research which deal with the combination of real-world and computer-generated data (virtual reality) [129]. Basically AR is that the virtual images made by computer arc merged with the real view to create the augmented display [171]. The basic idea of AR is to mix reality with virtual reality. In general not only virtual reality but also more information data such as graphics, audio, senses, touch, smell and taste which are superimposed over a real world environment to produce an AR environment. AR can make the user to interact with the virtual images. Typically computer generated graphics are overlaid into the user's field-of-view to provide extra information about their surroundings, or to provide visual guidance for the completion of a task [170]. AR is an advanced visualization technology. Therefore, as a useful visualization technique it is possible that AR technology can be used in many domains such as engineering, medical, robot, military, mobile, traveling, education, entertainment and so on. The AR technology was developed in [130]. The first Videoplace allows users to interact with virtual objects [131]. Since then AR has become an important research direction which combine computer vision, computer graphics and image processing. More and more research papers are published in some international conferences and journals. The first International Workshop on AR (IWAR'98) in San Francisco, October 1998. The first International Symposium on Mixed Reality (ISMR'99), Yokohama, Japan, March 1999. The first International Symposium on AR (ISAR 2000), Munich, Oct. 2000. The first International Symposium on Mixed

M.L. Huang et al. (eds.), *Visual Information Communication*,
DOI 10.1007/978-1-4419-0312-9_21, © Springer Science+Business Media, LLC 2010

and AR (ISMAR 2002), Darmstadt, Oct. 2002. The AR world is coming closer and industry will increase awareness. The first Workshop on Computer Aided Medical Procedures & AR (AMIARCS 2004), held in Rennes, France, Sept. 2004. AR was introduced in [177-181]. Some related AR surveys and reviews can be found in [182, 5, 114, 25, 86, 128].

2008 was a great year for AR. This emerging technology is on a 15-plus-year-long journey from the lab and into the mainstream. With too many events to list, 2008 marks an important year in that quest.

Some important AR research results have been developed in 2008 [132]: the year started with the largest consumer electronics show (CES); video game gurus recognize AR as the future of gaming; high end mobile AR devices hit the market; native mobile tracking engines released; the AR market picked up steam in 2008 with high visibility deals such as Total Immersions products.

Approaches and applications of AR are described in Section 2. The limitation and future research of AR is discussed in Section 3. Finally a conclusion is given in Section 4.

2 Approach and method of AR

AR is the research field in which the computer-generated data are overlay on the real world. Basically, the virtual objects is involved in a real environment. Typically the graphics made by computer are overlaid on into the users field-of-view to provide extra information about their surroundings, or to provide visual guidance for the completion of a task [170]. Therefore, the computer graphics, computer vision and image processing with regard to AR need to be approached. AR has been used on robotic navigation, mobile, computer assisted surgery, education, entertainment, gaming, advertisement, market shopping, tourism, military device, manufacturing, product assembly and repair, architecture etc. Many subject researches with regard to AR have been developed. It is clear that these subjects concern of many researches such as computer graphics, computer vision, image processing, multiple view geometry and hardware and software development (interface, display and view device).

2.1 Visualization and AR

AR is a useful visualization technique to overlay computer graphics on the real world. AR can combine visualization method to apply to many applications [183]. A vision-based AR system was presented for visualization interaction in [200]. A device, GeoScope, was developed to support some applications such as city, landscape and architectural visualization in [201]. AR visualization for laparoscopic surgery was approached in [24, 27]. An integrated visualization system based AR was developed for surgical planning and guidance [33]. Robot visualising was described in [126]. Two examples of education AR visualization can be found in [282, 187].

Sales, advisement based AR

AR technique can be used in sales, advisement of market where customer could get a lot of product information and services. In 1996, an approach, agent AR, was proposed to support shopping and walking with navigational aids and information [189]. In 1999, augmented commerce based AR was described for shopping in a physical retail store [190]. E-commerce based AR was developed to provide shopping assistance and personalized advertising [191]. The design of an automated AR shopping assistance was approached in [192]. Another AR e-commerce assistance system was developed based on user-centered design principles to provide more direct information about products, and the study (called the future of shopping) found out that tomorrow's customer expects a lot of product information and numerous services at the point of sale based AR in [193]. MINI AR advisements were created by Germany agencies Buzzin Monkey and Die Agentour GmbH in 2008 [195]. Fantas virtual tennis was one of the first real examples to advertise their products based on MAR to give consumers some thing fun that they can play with [64] in 2009. World's first MAR Ad was made in 2009 [67]. The first instance of using AR technique in a consumer communication situation for car sale was shown in [194] in 2009.

Geovisualization based AR

Hardware and software were described for collaborative geographic data visualization using two interfaces based AR [197]. AR can be used for planning of military training in urban terrain [196]. How to demonstrate ecological barrier and show their locations in the landscape was discussed based on AR technology in [203]. An approach was proposed for realistic landscape visualisation based on integration of AR and GIS [204] where using AR to represent GIS-model-based landscape changes in an immersive environment. AR interface paradigms were addressed to provide enhanced location based services for urban navigation and way finding in [202]. A tangible augmented street map (TASM) based AR was developed in [198]. One system based MAR techniques was developed for building and presenting geographical information in [199]. An approach, smart point clouds in virtual globes, was proposed in 3D city modeling in 2009 [205].

Architecture and construction based AR

AR is a decision support way of in architecture and interior design. A system was presented for constructing collaborative design applications based on distributed AR in [210]. AR technique was developed to explore relationships between perceived architectural space and the structural systems in [211]. It was developed for using AR systems to improve methods for the construction, inspection, and renovation of architectural structures in [212]. An approach is using AR to visualize architecture designs in an outdoor environment in [213]. A prototype system was developed to use AR for an architectural application in facility management and maintenance [214]. In [215] calibration-free AR based affine representation was described for urban planning. It was approached for using a tangible interface and a projection-based AR tabletop interface to research urban simulation and the luminous planning table [216, 218]. A System based on AR with a tangible interface was demonstrated for city planning in [11]. AR user interaction techniques were developed to support the capture and creation of 3D geometry of large outdoor construction structures in [219]. A co-operative AR design system, A4D, for AEC (architectural, engineering and construction) was approached in [220]. It was presented that a system with human computer interaction, AR visualization and building simulation can interact with buildings [230, 221]. AR as tool was approached to be used in architecture, building performance visualization, retrieving information of building equipment and construction management in [229--232,228] respectively. In [222], one system based AR was designed to support complex design and planning decisions for architects. 3D animation of simulated construction operations based AR was investigated in [223]. The research spatially AR design environment can be used in urban design [224]. How to use AR technique to aid construction management was described in [225]. Using AR and GIS in architecture was discussed in [226]. Technologies and theories of using AR in architecture were described in [227].

Military training based AR
AR can be used to display the real battlefield scene and augment it with annotation information [206]. Some HMD's were researched and built by company Liteye for military usage [208]. In [173] hybrid optical and inertial tracker that used miniature MEMS (micro electro-mechanical systems) sensors was developed for cockpit helmet tracking. In [196] it was described how to use AR technique for planning of military training in urban terrain. Using AR technique to display an animated terrain, which could be used for military intervention planning, was developed by company Arcane [207]. The helicopter night vision system was developed by Canada's Institute for Aerospace Research (NRC-IAR) using AR to expand the operational envelope of rotor craft and enhance pilots' ability to navigate in degraded visual conditions [209]. HMD was developed to a display that can be coupled with a portable information system in military [185].

2.2 Mobile and AR

Development of mobile hardware and software have made mobile augmented reality (MAR) possible [5, 113, 114].

More MAR research is outdoor tracking with GPS (Global Positioning System), GSM (global system for mobile communications) and UMTS (universal mobile telecommunications system) [97, 77, 98, 100, 78, 84, 152, 82, 91, 115]. An ubiquitous tracking system was described where the gyroscope worn by a mobile user is automatically fused with an insideout marker tracking in [116]. Other mark tracking research and development for MAR were approached [90, 88, 85, 72, 119].

It was designed that MAR mark tracking was used in cultural heritage onsite guide [79, 96]. Optical tracking based mark with ARToolkit and video see through for MAR was approached in [111, 107] respectively. Human Pacman, a mobile entertainment system, was developed for MAR respectively in [117, 93].

Two approaches on MAR game were described in [95, 94]. It is potential that MAR systems can integrate virtual information with the real world to provide it to users for collaborative work. Some researches of collaborative interface and system of MAR were described in [99, 103, 89, 83, 275]. A design review of collaborative MAR can be found in [86].

A MAR system, the SitePack, based feature tracking techniques can help architects making decisions on site concerning visual impact assessment in [62]. Many MAR systems are developed with related to information filtering, industrial environments, writing complex AR applications maintenance of power-plants, geometrical model, virtual reality service, PDA (personal digital assistance), teleoperation system in unstructured environment, construction sentor, pervasive computing environments and industrial maintenance applications [101, 104, 109, 102, 76, 92, 108, 70, 68, 71, 110, 120, 121].

Some MAR research and development are further made. An MAR, Zenitum, was developed not only to detect certain features in incoming video but also to build 3D maps based on a depth perception algorithm engine [69].

Simplified Spatial Target Tracker (SSTT) is a computer vision based tracking library for AMR applications which runs at approx. 1-5fps with tracking and 15fps without on this Samsung Omnia phone [65]. A MAR game, Kweekies, by Int13 can be used in iPhone, Windows Mobile and Smartphones [66].

3D model is overlaid in the mobile phone's display, and user can interactively change the perspective to see them from different angles. The 2D tracking allows the mobile to display photographs from different rooms [72].

Some techniques of MAR were developed in company Zenitum [63]. The first true AR application running on the iPhone was reported based ARToolKit v4.4 in [106].

2.3 Medical applications and AR

AR method can be used in wind range of the medical applications deal with image guided surgery, pre-operative imaging training and education because AR can provide the surgeon with the necessary view of the internal anatomy. Video see-through systems, head-mounted display or Helmet mounted display (HMD) can make precise and reliable augmentation of video.

Surgeries are a prime example of using AR. For example, surgeries can be performed based on pre-gathered information, volume rendered images of physical implants, tumors, the procedure and state of the patient, which is imposed over the view of the subject. The surgeon can take full advantage of x-rays and other knowledge about the patient on the spot in this way. AR application in the operating room was described in [163]. Automated registration methods for frameless stereotaxy, image guided surgery, and AR visualization are approached in [164]. AR visualization in a surgical environment was described in [165]. Evaluating and validating an automated registration system in surgery was discussed in [166]. AR was used in some medical surgeries such as radio frequency ablation [36, 21], laparoscopic liver resection [32, 13, 38, 9, 23], cardiac surgery and needle biopsy [39, 12, 37]. Research in these areas focuses primarily on tracking and registration quality as well as specific visualizations in support of the medical procedure. An AR application for minimally invasive surgery is described in [52].

Rendering, registration and occlusion of AR are important in medical application. A volumetric rendered ultrasound image of the fetus overlaid on the abdomen of the pregnant woman can be viewed with an optical see-through display [167]. Object registration can be used to superimpose registered images onto a video image of a patient's body [168]. A framework for fusing stereo images with volumetric medical images was developed in [169]. A method to perform registration in markerless AR systems was approached using MRI data sets to build up the 3D model for the medical case [40]. In [41] occlusion handling for medical AR was researched using volumetric phantom model. An AR environment was developed which consists of hardware and software system to provide 3D visualization and support direct 3D user intervention for medical application [28].

Tracking methods for medical AR are critical research topics. Three tracking methods were discussed for medical AR with using infrared camera, precise robot arm and camera calibration processing based pattern recognition [42]. Deformation of 3D lung models was described for AR based medical visualization [57, 58]. A hybrid tracking scheme is developed for medical AR based on a certified medical tracking system [43]. In [60] AR was used for minimally invasive therapy. Realtime organ tracking was approached for endoscopic AR visualization using miniature wireless magnetic tracker [44].

AR method provided a useful tool for medical guidance, training, education, procedure and workflow. AR was approached in computer aided liver surgery planning [31]. It was introduced that the results of a randomized, controlled trial to compare the accuracy of standard ultrasound-guided needle biopsy to biopsies performed using a 3D AR guidance system [45]. An interface based AR was developed for a puncture guidance system on an abdominal phantom [48]. An AR system of guiding radio-frequency tumor ablation is described in [36]. In [59] an AR system was approached for therapy guidance. A system for microscope assisted guided interventions was developed to provide stereo AR navigation for ENT (ear, nose and throat) and neurosurgery [47]. Some computer aided surgery planning based AR was approached in [31, 34]. AR for computer-aided medical procedures was researched in [56]. AR in surgical procedures is presented in [51]. Integrated medical workflow based AR was discussed in [49, 50]. AR was used in a laparoscopic simulation system for laparoscopic skills training [55]. AR delivery simulator for medical training was presented in [46]. An AR training kit was developed to offer novel teaching solution for future cardiac surgery and other medical professionals [53]. AR was used to improve training for keyhole surgery [54].

AR was used in modeling 3-D lung dynamics as a planning tool in [268]. AR is described how to understand anatomical relationships to a patient or coworker and learn the interior of the Human Body in [299, 30] respectively.

2.4 Industry and AR

Many researches with AR are approached in industries. Industry and medical AR based real-time was described in [26]. Robot AR approach in design was reviewed in [184]. One AR application was presented for tracking of industrial objects in [269].

One method was addressed to use AR technique for perform real-time flexible augmentation on cloth in [276].

Robotics based AR

AR is an ideal platform for human-robot collaboration [184]. Medical robotics and image guided surgery based AR was discussed in [29, 236, 241]. Predictive displays for telerobotics were designed based on AR [123]. Remote manipulation of using AR for robot was researched in [124, 125]. Robots can present complex information by using AR technique for communicating information to humans [233]. AR technique was described for robot development and experimentation in [234]. In [235] it was researched to combine AR technique with surgical robot system for head-surgery. An AR approach was proposed to visualizing robot input, output and state information [126]. Using AR tools for the teleoperation of robotic systems was described in [239]. It was developed how to improve robotic operator performance using AR in [240]. It was explored for AR technique to improve immersive robot programming in unknown environments in [238]. Robot gaming and learning based AR were approached in [237].

3D AR display during robot assisted laparoscopic partial nephrectomy (LPN) was studied in [246]. It was researched to use markerless AR techniques in the visualization of robotic helicopter related tasks [244] and robots in unprepared environments [243] respectively. AR technique can be used in the operation of robot, which was developed in the company, KUKA Roboter GmbH [245]. A vision system with AR was proposed to used in network based mobile robot [242].

An interface with AR support was designed for the simulation and teleoperation of a robotic arm in [247]. Using AR environment to improve intuitive robot programming was discussed in [248]. The Matrix method (also known as "CyberCode") is a new technique for AR that identifies real world objects and estimates their coordinate systems simultaneously [186].

Design, maintenance and training based AR

AR can be used for design, maintenance and training in some areas such as industries. It was presented to use AR techniques for guiding maintenance of complex mechanical elements in [251]. It was reported that a mobile device offers a multimodal user interface which can synchronize a 3D AR view with a location-sensitive 3D speech-driven interface for industrial maintenance [254]. Nuclear power plant maintenance work based AR was studied in [270, 272]. Aviation maintenance and construction training was approached based on AR support in [264, 266] respectively.

Industry task analysis, planning and training based AR was discussed in [122]. Using AR system for training and assisting in maintaining equipment was presented in [252]. Using an AR system to make additional information into the view of a user for training and assisting in maintaining equipment was presented in [253, 256, 261]. A distributed medical training prototype with AR system was designed to train medical practitioners' hand-eye coordination when performing endotracheal intubations (ETI) in [255].

Interactive tools were approached for evaluating assembly sequences and guidance based AR technique in [249, 263, 274] respectively. Product design, design process tool, assembly feature and architectural design with related to AR were approached in [10, 265, 262, 267, 273] respectively. 3D reconstruction system for modeling urban scenes was presented in [271]. Using AR for improving the efficiency of mechanical design was explored in [257]. VR/AR-supported simulation of manufacturing system was approached in [259]. AR interfaces were developed in waste water treatment work with personal digital assistant (PDA) in [250]. Ten AR projects from automotive and aerospace industry (space station filter change, engine maintenance, tram diagnosis, airplane cabin design, collaborative design review, cockpit layout, fuse placement, picking, wiring and driver safety training) were introduced in [258]. Boeing used AR for wire harness assembly, space flight, decision support, and technical communication [260].

2.5 Edutainment and AR

Education and training based AR How to use AR in education, training, game and tourism is reviewed in this section. Some medical, industry and military education and training based AR are reviewed in the above related sections respectively. One system AR based was presented to be served as an interactive virtual laboratory in educational processes [283].

Mathematics and geometry education with AR technique was approached in [282, 284-288, 328, 291] respectively. Using AR technique to study in chemistry education was researched in [290, 294, 295, 302] respectively. Physical Experiments and teaching with AR were presented in [297, 298] respectively. Remote Experimentation of using AR technology was designed in [277].

AR technique was developed to help students to study geography in [281]. AR technologies can be applied to higher education such as engineering by using engineering multimedia contents with authoring AR tools[292]. An interactive multimedia AR interface for E-Learning was presented in [280]. A support on the remote interaction was approached for utilization in AR systems based on ARToolkit in [296].

MagicBook, an AR interface, was approached to be used in some areas such as book reading of education [278]. The future classroom was described to enhance education with AR technique in [279]. AR system, a visualization tool, was used for computer-aided design (CAD) classes [187]. In one book [300] mobile educational games was described for mobile learning's design, development, and implementation in recent years based AR technology.

A literature review was presented to investigate for training spatial ability with AR technologies in a wide range of studies [289]. It was discussed for AR technology to influence pupils knowledge about human digestive system in [301].

Game based AR
The computer games with AR technologies are not only used for amusement but also used for various fields such as education, tourism and medical treatment. ARQuake, an AR game, was developed to be used for outdoor/indoor mobile AR application in

[78]. Human Pacman, an interactive role-playing game, was developed using AR techniques in [117]. Neon Racer, a multi-user AR racing game which includes the physical reality as part of the game, was developed in [320].

A mathematical education game was developed using AR technology in [328]. Virtools system (www.virtools.com), a 3D Authoring System, was extended to develop an AR game [322]. A location-aware AR game was designed to help fire emergency response students learn embodied team coordination skills in [323]. Battleship, an interactive AR game, was approached in [324]. Ghost Hunter, a handheld AR game system with dynamic environment, was developed in [325]. An AR racing game was created using an AR infrastructure with a game development platform in [327]. In [326] AR in computer games was introduced: computer games using AR components; a game, ARQuake. The techniques of games and technological challenges of AR games were discussed in [317, 329, 78, 319] respectively. An adaptive approach was introduced for augmenting the players satisfaction of a AR games in real-time in [330, 331]. The feasibility of handheld AR games was demonstrated by using marker-based embodied interaction in [321]. The useful tools, MAR (mobile AR) Toolkit components, were presented for building mobile AR games in [318]. AR was approached to enhance the player's gaming experience in mobile in 2009 [61]. ARf, an AR virtual pet on the iPhone has been developed in 2009 [106].

Tourism based AR

The ARCHEOGUIDE, a project AR based cultural heritage on-site guide, was described to provide cultural-heritage sites with archaeological information to visitors [217]. An interactive visualization system based AR technologies was developed to enhance cultural tourism experiences in [309]. AR technique was investigated for historical tourism on mobile devices in [315].

One design, Augmented City, with information sharing and filtering was proposed for tourist guide based on AR technology in [305]. The design of AR interfaces was approached for guided tours (visiting cultural heritage places) using multimedia sketches in [307]. An accessible and collaborative platform was provided for tourist guide based on AR technology and mobile devices in [313]. AR technologies were used to enhance tourists's knowledge exploration experience, exhibitions, mobile multimedia museum guide and viewing in museum in [303, 306, 311, 312] respectively.

In thesis [308] AR technology was described to be used in museum tour in detail. AR techniques were used for museum wandering by recognizing markers with CCD camera in [310].

A tour system with 3D AR technique and mobile computing was developed in [304]. Augmented museum tour system was approached for museum wandering by using AR techniques in [314].

2.6 The Tracking techniques and AR

The most mature AR research development is focusing on tracking the position and motions of the user in virtual reality systems. The primary AR tracking technologies are sensor-based, vision-based, and hybrid tracking techniques [128]. Position tracking is needed in virtual reality to instruct the graphics system to render a view of the world from the user's new position. The type of display used by the AR system will determine the accuracy needed for registration of the real and virtual images. In addition, measurement delays have been found in the 40 to 100 msec range for typical position sensors [137]. AR researchers are looking at hybrid techniques for tracking [135, 136].

The real-time system was development has developed in [172] and it is marker-less model-based real time 3D visual tracking system. The similar work has done in [138, 139] and improved in [140, 141, 15]. The tracking system has further improved in [142--144]. The visual tracking need emerge visual serving which has approached in [145], and the work applied to AR systems in [146--148]. Camera pose computation and estimation vision-based AR tracking systems were studied in [18, 16, 17, 14, 149]. The model-based tracking was demonstrated in [150-152, 155, 156] where features such as points, lines, edges or textures are used. A hybrid visual tracking system was presented in [133], which is based on a computer-aided design (CAD) model of edge and a serving system. A marker-less camera tracking approach and user interaction methodology for AR on unprepared tabletop environments was done in [21], and in which distinctive image features of the scene are detected and tracked frame-to-frame by computing optical flow. A natural feature-based 3D object tracking method was described in [153] for wearable AR. The pose tracking from natural feature is demonstrated in [118]. Robust 2D tracking for real-time AR is a vision-based corner tracker [20]. A vision and inertial pose estimation system was used for real-time hand-held AR [154]. Fiducial tracking and visual marker based tracking were approached in [19, 2, 3] respectively. Outdoor/Indoor tracking is described in [78, 84, 4]. Some video motion tracking approaches can be found in [157--162]. A marker-less tracking technique with the windows (mobile pocket PC platform) allows the development of standalone AR applications for handheld devices based on natural feature tracking [22].

2.7 Hardware, toolkit and AR

Hardware and toolkit development of AR is important. Some user interfaces were developed in [6--8, 48]. Exploring MARS, indoor and outdoor user interfaces to a MAR was developed in [75]. An autonomous mobile platform was designed based on AR in [127].

AR through wearable computing was described in [74]. One AR device, NaviCam, a magnifying glass was approached in [73]. The fundamental communication and navigation platform based AR was described in [80, 81] respectively. Volumetric medical intervention aiding AR device was designed in [28]. AR testbed, feature and HMD systems were designed and developed at Siemens Corporate Research in [174--176], which can allow the physician to see CT, MR or Ultrasound images overlaid on patient during operation. A review of display hardware with medical AR can be found in [25].

It was described that a platform based on field programmable gate array was to help developers on the construction of embedded AR applications [1]. An open source software toolkit was developed based AR for image-guided surgery [33]. An AR toolkit for designers was developed in [35]. ARToolKit, one useful open source AR toolkit, was introduced in [293]. The distributed wearable AR framework (DWARF) was developed in [105]. Field programmable gate array (FPGA) device based AR was developed for image processing of visually impaired people [188].

3 Limitation and future directions of AR

Despite the considerable advances made in each of these areas, there are still limitations with the technology that needs to be overcome. AR system has to deal with vast amount of information in reality. Therefore the hardware used should be small, light, and easily portable and fast enough to display graphics. Also the battery life used by these complicated AR devices is another limitation for AR's uses. Also, AR tracking needs some system hardware such as GPS to provide accurate marker, ask them to be both accurate and reliable enough. These hardware obstacles need to be resolved for practical AR use.

AR systems usually obtain a lot of information, and need software to filter the information, retain useful information, discard useless data and display it in a convenient way.

Several possible future directions are speculated for further research. Many HMDs created specifically with AR in mind need to be developed. HMDs are still too clumsy and have limited field of vision, contrast and resolution. HMDs and other wearable equipments, such as data-gloves and data-suits, is a limitation for the user. All wearable equipments need be developed to be lighter, smaller and easier to work with the user. Also the AR system researchers need consider other challenges such as response time delays, hardware or software failures from AR systems.

One limitation of AR systems is registration error. Occlusion detection is an active area of study of AR systems. Analyzing various tracking methods, possible tracking research directions are identified that allow researchers to effectively capitalize on knowledge in video frames, or integrate vision-based methods with other sensors in a novel way.

It is important to incorporate a recognition system to acquire a reference representation of the real world. Further research on this direction could provide promising results, but it is mostly a top-down process and hard to deal with object dynamics, and evaluation of different hypotheses. The challenge is to construct a pervasive middle ware to support the AR system.

4 Conclusion

This paper has reviewed the development in AR research which related to tracking, medical, mobile, visualization, edutainment, industry and hardware. Other related research areas such as computer vision, image processing, computer graphics and multiple view geometry are also included in these researches. Currently, to bring AR research from laboratories to industry and widespread use is still challenging, but both academia and industry believe that there is huge potential for AR technology in a wide range of areas. Fortunately, more researchers are paying attention to these areas, and it is becoming easier than ever before to be involved in AR research.

References

1. G. F. Guimaraes et al., FPGA infrastructure for the development of augmented reality applications, Proceedings of the 20th annual conference on Integrated circuits and systems design, Copacabana, Rio de Janeiro, pp. 336-341, 2007.
2. M. Maidi et al., Robust fiducials tracking in augmented reality, In IWSSIP '06: The 13th International Conference on Systems, Signals and Image Processing, Budapest (Hungary), pp. 423-426, 2006.
3. M. Maidi et al., A performance study for camera pose estimation using visual marker based tracking, Machine Vision and Applications, Springer-Verlag, 2008.
4. I. Zendjebil et al., Outdoor augmented reality: State of the art and issues, VRIC'2008, pp. 177-187, 2008.
5. R. Azuma et al., Recent advances in augmented reality, IEEE Computer Graphics and Applications, 21(6), pp. 34-47, 2001.
6. B. Bell et al., An annotated situation awareness aid for augmented reality, Proc. of the 15th annual ACM symposium on User interface software and technology, New York, NY, USA, pp. 213-216, 2002.
7. M. Dias et al., Usability evaluation of tangible user interfaces for augmented reality, IEEE International Augmented Reality Toolkit Workshop, Tokyo, Japan, pp. 54-61, 2003.
8. H. Kato and M. Billinghurst, Marker tracking and HMD calibration for a video-based augmented reality conferencing system, Proc. of the 2nd IEEE and ACM International Workshop on Augmented Reality, Washington, DC, USA, 1999.
9. H. Kato et al., Virtual object manipulation on a table-top ar environment, Proc. of the International Symposium on Augmented Reality, Munich, Germany, pp. 111-119, 2000.
10. G. Klinker et al., ``Fata morgana'' a presentation system for product design, Proc. of the 1st International Symposium on Mixed and Augmented Reality, Washington, DC, USA, 2002.
11. H. Kato et al., A city-planning system based on augmented reality with a tangible interface, Proc. of the 2nd IEEE/ACM International Symposium on Mixed and Augmented Reality, Washington, DC, USA, 2003.
12. G. A. Lee et al., Occlusion based interaction methods for tangible augmented reality environments, Proc. of the 2004 ACM SIGGRAPH international conference on Virtual Reality continuum and its applications in industry, New York, NY, USA, pp. 419-426, 2004.
13. B. E. Shelton and N. E. Hedley, Using augmented reality for teaching earthsun relationships to undergraduate geography students, ART '02: The First IEEE International Augmented Reality Toolkit Workshop, Darmstadt, Germany, 2002.
14. F. Ababsa and M. Mallem, Robust camera pose estimation using 2d fiducials tracking for real-time augmented reality systems, Proc. of the 2004 ACM SIGGRAPH international conference on Virtual Reality continuum and its applications in industry, Singapore, 2004.
15. R. Koch et al., Markerless image-based 3D tracking for real-time augmented reality applications, Proc. WIAMIS 2005, Montreux, Switzerland, 2005.
16. J. Park et al., Vision-based pose computation: robust and accurate augmented reality tracking, Proc. Augmented Reality 1999 (IWAR '99), pp. 3-12, 1999.
17. B. Jiang et al., Camera Tracking for Augmented Reality Media, Proc. IEEE Int'l Conf. Multimedia Expo 2000, Los Alamitos, Calif., pp. 1637-1640, 2000.
18. U. Neumann and Y. Cho, A Self-Tracking Augmented Reality System, Proc. of ACM Virtual Reality Software and Technology 96, pp. 109-115, 1996.

19. Y. Cho, Scalable Fiducial-Tracking Augmented Reality, Ph.D. Dissertation, Computer Science Department, University of Southern California, 1999.
20. S. Malik et al., Robust 2d tracking for real-time augmented reality, Proc. Vision Interface, 2002.
21. T. Lee and T. Hollerer, Multithreaded Hybrid Feature Tracking for Markerless Augmented Reality, IEEE Trans. on Visualization and Computer Graphics, vol. 15, no. 3, pp. 355-368, 2009.
22. J. P. Lima et al., A Standalone Markerless 3D Tracker for Handheld Augmented Reality, arXiv:0902.2187, 2009.
23. T. M. Peters et al., Towards a Medical Virtual Reality Environment for Minimally Invasive Cardiac Surgery, LNCS 5128, pp. 1-11, 2008.
24. F. Henry et al., Augmented Reality Visualization for Laparoscopic Surgery, Proc. of First International Conference on Medical Image Computing and Computer-Assisted Intervention, MA, USA, pp. 11-13, 1998.
25. T. Sielhorst et al., Advanced Medical Displays: A Literature Review of Augmented Reality, Journal of Display Technology, Vol. 4, Issue 4, pp. 451-467, 2008.
26. N. Navab, Medical and Industrial Augmented Reality: Challenges for Real-Time Vision, Computer Graphics and Mobile Computing, LNCS 2191, 2001.
27. J. Marescaux, Augmented-RealityAssisted Laparoscopic Adrenalectomy, JAMA, Vol. 292 No. 18, pp. 2214-2215, 2004.
28. D. Balazs and E. Attila, Volumetric Medical Intervention Aiding Augmented Reality Device, Information and Communication Technologies, ICTTA'06, pp. 1091-1096, 2006.
29. M. Blackwell et al., Augmented reality and its future in orthopaedics : Computer assisted orthopaedic surgery: Medical robotics and image guided surgery, Clinical orthopaedics and related research, No. 354, pp. 111-122, 1998.
30. Medgadget, How About Augmented Reality in Clinical Applications?, http://blogs.nature.com/stories/893, 2009.
31. A. Bornik et al., Computer aided liver surgery planning: An augmented reality approach, SPIE Medical Imaging'03, pp. 395-405, 2003.
32. H. Fuchs et al., Augmented reality visualization for laparoscopic surgery, Proc. of the First International Conference on Medical Image Computing and Computer-Assisted Intervention, London, UK, pp. 934-943, 1998.
33. K. Gary et al., Igstk: An open source software toolkit for image-guided surgery. Computer, 39(4), pp. 46-53, 2006.
34. D. Gering et al., An integrated visualization system for surgical planning and guidance using image fusion and an open mr., Journal of Magnetic Resonance Imaging, volume 13, pp. 967-975, 2001.
35. B. MacIntyre et al., Dart: The designer's augmented reality toolkit, ISMAR, pp. 329-330, 2003.
36. S. Nicolau et al., An augmented reality system to guide radio-frequency tumour ablation, Computer Animation and Virtual World, 16(1), pp. 1-10, 2005.
37. M. Rosenthal et al., Augmented reality guidance for needle biopsies: An initial randomized, controlled trial in phantoms, Medical Image Analysis, volume 6, pp. 313-320, 2002.
38. C. Paloc et al., Computer-aided surgery based on auto-stereoscopic augmented reality, Proc. of Information Visualisation, volume 13, Eighth, pp. 189-193, 2004.
39. F.K. Wacker et al, An augmented reality system for mr image-guided needle biopsy: initial results in a swine model, Radiology, 2 (238), pp. 497-504, 2006.
40. D. Trevisan et al., Augmented Medical Visualization, AMI-ARCS'04, pp. 57-66, 2004.
41. J. Fischer et al, Occlusion Handling for Medical Augmented Reality using a Volumetric Phantom Model, VRST04, Hong Kong, 2004.
42. A. Pandya et al., Tracking Methods for Medical Augmented Reality, MICCAI 2001, LNCS 2208, pp. 1404-1405, 2001.

43. J. Fischer et al., A hybrid tracking method for surgical augmented reality, Computers and Graphics, 31, pp. 39-52, 2007.
44. M. Nakamoto et al., Realtime Organ Tracking for Endoscopic Augmented Reality Visualization Using Miniature Wireless Magnetic Tracker, MIAR 2008, LNCS 5128, pp. 359-366, 2008.
45. M. Rosenthal et al., Augmented Reality Guidance for Needle Biopsies: A Randomized, Controlled Trial in Phantoms, LNCS 2208, pp. 240-248, 2001.
46. T. Sielhorst et al., An Augmented Reality Delivery Simulator for Medical Training, AMI-ARCS'04, pp. 11-20, 2004.
47. P. J. Edwards et al, Clinical Experience and Perception in Stereo Augmented Reality Surgical Navigation, LNCS 3150, pp. 369-376, 2004.
48. S. Nicolau et al., An Augmented Reality and Virtuality Interface for a Puncture Guidance System: Design and Validation on an Abdominal Phantom, MIAR 2004, LNCS 3150, pp. 302-310, 2004.
49. D. Kalkofen et al., Integrated Medical Workflow for Augmented Reality Applications, Proc. AMI-ARCS, Copenhagen, Oct 2006.
50. D. Kalkofen et al., Interactive Focus and Context Visualization in Augmented Reality, Proc. 6th IEEE International Symposium on Mixed and Augmented Reality, Nara, Japan, pp. 191-200, 2007.
51. E. Samseta, et al., Augmented Reality in Surgical Procedures, Proc. of SPIE 2008.
52. L. T. De Paolis, An Augmented Reality Application for Minimally Invasive Surgery, Proc. 14th Nordic-Baltic Conference on Biomedical Engineering and Medical Physics, pp. 489-492, 2008.
53. R. C. Shetty : Augmented Reality Training Kit Can Offer Novel Teaching Solution For Future Cardiac Surgery And Other Medical Professionals, The Internet Journal of Medical Simulation, 2(1), 2006.
54. Augmented reality improves training for keyhole surgery, http://www.news-medical.net/print article.asp?id=47683, 2009.
55. M.B.I. Sanne et al., Augmented versus Virtual Reality Laparoscopic Simulation: What Is the Difference? A Comparison of the ProMIS Augmented Reality Laparoscopic Simulator versus LapSim Virtual Reality Laparoscopic Simulator, World J Surg 31, pp. 764-772, 2007.
56. N. Navab et al., Action- and Workflow-Driven Augmented Reality for Computer-Aided Medical Procedures, IEEE Computer Graphics and Applications, 27(5), pp.10-14, 2007.
57. A. Santhanam et al., Physically-based deformation of high-resolution 3D lung models for augmented reality based medical visualization, Proc. AMIARCS, Rennes, St. Malo, pp. 21-32, 2004.
58. A. P. Santhanam et al., Modeling Real-Time 3-D Lung Deformations for Medical Visualization, IEEE Trans. on Information Technology in Biomedicine, 12(2), pp. 257-270, 2008.
59. S. Nicolau t al., An accuracy certified augmented reality system for therapy guidance, ECCV'04, LNCS 3023, pp. 79-91, 2004.
60. T. Studeli et al., Assessing Quality of Computer Systems and User Interfaces of Future Medical Workplaces Augmented Reality for Minimally Invasive Therapy, Proc. of the UITQ 2007 Workshop, Stockholm, Sweden, 2007.
61. http://www.mobile-augmented-reality.com/, 2009.
62. M. Bang Nielsen et al., G Mobile Augmented Reality Support for Architects Based on Feature Tracking Techniques, ICCS 2004, LNCS 3038, pp. 921-928, 2004.
63. http://www.zenitum.com/mobile-augmented-reality.
64. http://thefutureofads.com/2009/01/28/fanta-uses-mobile-augmented-reality-to-play-virtual-tennis/.
65. http://technotecture.com/content/mobile-augmented-reality-sstt-mobile.

66. http://www.youtube.com/watch?v=RsZTbIjLHNA&feature=related.
67. http://cb.nowan.net/blog/2009/02/17/kweekies-mobile-augmented-reality-game-by-int13/.
68. J. L. Izkara et al., Mobile augmented reality, an advanced tool for the construction sector, 24th W78 Conference, Maribor, 2007.
69. A. H. Behzadan, and V. R. Kamat, Animation of Construction Activities in Out-door Augmented Reality, Proc. of the Joint International Conference on Computing and Decision Making in Civil and Building Engineer-ing, Reston, VA. 2006.
70. X. Wang and P. S. Dunston, Mixed Reality Enhanced Operator Interface for Teleoperation Systems in Unstructured Environment, CD Proc. of the 10th Biennial ASCE Aerospace Division International Confer-ence on Engineering, Construction and Operations in Chal-lenging Environments (Earth and Space 2006), League City/Houston, Texas, 2006.
71. H. Kimura et al., System support for mobile augmented reality services, SAC07, Seoul, Korea, 2007.
72. A. Olwal and A. Henrysson, LUMAR: A Hybrid Spatial Display System for 2D and 3D Handheld Augmented Reality, 17th International Conference on Artificial Reality and Telexistence, pp. 63-70, 2007.
73. J. Rekimoto, NaviCam: A Magnifying Glass Approach to Augmented Reality, Presence: Teleoperators and Virtual Environments, vol. 6, no. 4, pp. 399-412, 1997.
74. T. Starner et al., Augmented Reality through Wearable Computing, Presence: Teleoperators and Virtual Environments, 6(4), pp. 386-398, 1997.
75. T. Hollerer et al., Exploring MARS: Developing Indoor and Outdoor User Interfaces to a Mobile Augmented Reality System, Computers and Graphics, 23(6), pp. 779-785, 1999.
76. Y. Baillot et al., Authoring of Physical Models Using Mobile Computers, Proc. Intl Symp. Wearable Computers, IEEE CS Press, Los Alamitos, Calif., 2001.
77. W. Piekarski et al., Integrating Virtual and Augmented Realities in an Outdoor Application, Proc. 2nd Intl Workshop Augmented Reality (IWAR 99), IEEE CS Press, Los Alamitos, Calif., pp. 45-54, 1999.
78. B. Thomas et al., ARQuake: An Outdoor/Indoor Augmented Augmented Reality First Person Application, Proc. 4th Intl Symp. Wearable Computers (ISWC 2000), pp. 139-146, 2000.
79. D. Stricker et al., Design and Development Issues for Archeoguide: An Augmented Reality based Cultural Heritage On-Site Guide, Proc. Intl Conf. Augmented Virtual Environments and 3D Imaging, Greece, pp. 1-5, 2001.
80. J. Rekimoto et al., Augmentable Reality: Situated Communication through Physical and Digital Spaces, Proc. 2nd Intl Symp. Wearable Computers, IEEE CS Press, Los Alamitos, Calif., pp. 68-75, 1998.
81. R. Behringer et al., A Wearable Augmented Reality Testbed for Navigation and Control, Built Solely with Commercial- off-the-Shelf (COTS) Hardware, Proc. Intl Symp. Augmented Reality 2000, Calif., pp. 12-19, 2000.
82. R. Azuma, J. Leonard, Performance Analysis of an Outdoor Augmented Reality Tracking System that Relies Upon a Few Mobile Beacons, Proc. of ISMAR 2006, Santa Barbara, CA, pp. 119-122, 2006.
83. A. Henrysson et al., Face to Face Collaborative AR on Mobile Phones, Proc. of ISMAR 2005, 2005.
84. W. Piekarski et al., Designing Backpacks for High Fidelity Mobile Outdoor Augmented Reality, Proc. of ISMAR'04, Arlington, 2004.
85. D. Wagner and D.Schmalstieg, ARToolKitPlus for Pose Tracking on Mobile Devices, Computer Vision Winter Workshop 2007, Austria, 2007.
86. A. Stork et al., IMPROVE: An innovative application for collaborative mobile mixed reality design review, Proc. of Virtual Concept 06, 2006.

87. A. Cheok et al., Human Pacman: A Mobile Entertainment System with Ubiquitous Computing and Tangible Interaction over a Wide Outdoor Area, Human-Computer Interaction with Mobile Devices and Services, LNCS 2795, pp. 209-223, 2003.

88. J., Zauner and M. Haller, Authoring of Mixed Reality Applications including Multi-Marker calibration for Mobile Devices, Proc. of 10th Eurographics Symposium on Virtual Environments, pp. 87-90, 2004.

89. P. Renevier et al., Generic Interaction Techniques for Mobile Collaborative Mixed Systems, Fifth International Conference on Computer-Aided Design of User Interfaces CADUI'2004, ACM, Funchal, pp. 307-320, 2004.

90. J. Gausemeier et al., Development of a Real Time Image Based Object Recognition Method for Mobile AR-Devices, Proc. of the ACM SIGGRAPH AFRIGRAPH 2003: 2nd International Conference on Computer Graphics, Virtual Reality, Visualisation and Interaction in Africa, Cape Town, 2003.

91. S. DiVerdi and T. Hollerer, GroundCam: A Tracking Modality for Mobile Mixed Reality, IEEE Virtual Reality, Charlotte, North Carolina, USA, pp. 75-82, 2007.

92. M. Torabi, Mobile Virtual Reality Services, Bell Labs Technical Journal. 7(2), pp. 185-193, 2002.

93. A.D. Cheok, et al., Human Pacman: A Mobile Entertainment System with Ubiquitous Computing and Tangible Interaction over a Wide Outdoor Area, Proc. Mobile HCI 2004 6th International Symposium, Glasgow, UK, pp.209-223, 2004.

94. D.J. McCaffery, and J. Finney, The need for real time consistency management in P2P mobile gaming environments, Proc. 2004 ACM SIGCHI International Conf of Advances in Computer Entertainment Technology, pp. 203-211, 2004.

95. K. Mitchell, et al., Six in the City: Introducing Real Tournament A Mobile IPv6 based Context-Aware Multiplayer Game, Proc. 2nd Workshop on Network and System Support for Games, pp. 91-100, 2003.

96. G. Papagiannakis and N. Magnenat-Thalmann, Mobile Augmented Heritage: Enabling Human Life in ancient Pompeii, International Journal of Architectural Computing, Multi-Science Publishing, 5(2), pp. 395-415, 2007.

97. S. Feiner, The importance of being mobile: Some social consequences of wearable augmented reality systems, Proc. IWAR'99 (IEEE and ACM Int. Workshop on Augmented Reality), San Francisco, CA, pp. 145-148, 1999.

98. S. Feiner et al., Wearing it out: First steps toward mobile augmented reality systems, Mixed Reality: Merging Real and Virtual Worlds, Berlin, pp. 363-377, 1999.

99. T. Hollerer et al., User interface management techniques for collaborative mobile augmented reality, Computers and Graphics, 25(5), pp. 799-810, 2001.

100. T. Hollerer et al., Steps toward accommodating variable position tracking accuracy in a mobile augmented reality system, Proc. 2nd Int. Workshop on Artificial Intelligence in Mobile Systems, pp. 31-37, 2001.

101. S. Julier et al., Information filtering for mobile augmented reality, Proc. ISAR'00 (IEEE and ACM Int. Symposium on Augmented Reality), pp. 3-11, Munich, Germany, 2000.

102. G. Klinker et al., Augmented maintenance of powerplants: a prototyping case study of a mobile AR system, Proc. ISAR '01 (IEEE and ACM Int. Symposium on Augmented Reality), New York, NY, pp. 124-133, 2001.

103. G. Reitmayr, and D. Schmalstieg, Mobile collaborative augmented reality, Proc. ISAR '01 (Int. Symposium on Augmented Reality), pp. 114-123, New York, NY, 2001.

104. X. Zhang et al., Taking AR into large scale industrial environments: Navigation and information access with mobile computers, In Proc. ISAR '01 (Int. Symposium on Augmented Reality), New York, NY, pp. 179-180, 2001. 105. DWARF Project, http://ar.in.tum.de/Chair/ProjectDwarf.

106. iPhone Apple, http://www.apple.com/iphone/.

107. M. Mohring et al., Optical Tracking and Video Seethrough AR on Consumer Cell-Phones, Proc. International Symposium in Mixed and Aug-mented Reality, Arlington, USA, pp. 252-253, 2004.

108. W. Pasman et al., Augmented Reality with Large 3D Models on a PDA, Implementation, Performance and Use Experiences, Int. Conf. on Virtual-Reality Continuum and Its Applications in Industry, Singapore, pp. 344-351, 2004.

109. W. Piekarski, and B. Thomas, Tinmith evo5 An Architecture for Supporting Mobile Augmented Reality Environments, Proc. of the International Symposium on Augmented Reality, New York, USA., 2001.

110. ULTRA Project ULTRA light Augmented Reality Mobile System, http://ist-ultra.org/publications.shtml, Feb 2007.

111. D. Wagner and D. Schamalstieg, ARToolKit on the PocketPC platform, Proc. of the 2nd IEEE In-ternational Augmented Reality Toolkit Workshop, Tokyo, Japan, 2003.

112. Zune Microsoft, www.zune.net, 2007.

113. H. T. Hllerer and S. K. Feiner, Telegeoinformatics: Location-Based Computing and Services, Taylor and Francis Books Ltd., 2004.

114. G. Papagiannakis et al., A survey of mobile and wireless technologies for augmented reality systems, Computer Animation and Virtual Worlds, 19(1), pp. 3-22, 2008.

115. W. T. Fong et al., A Differential GPS Carrier Phase Technique for Precision Outdoor AR Tracking, IEEE International Symposium on Mixed and Augmented Reality 2008, pp. 25-28, 2008.

116. D. Pustka and G. Klinker, Dynamic Gyroscope Fusion in Ubiquitous Tracking Environments, IEEE International Symposium on Mixed and Augmented Reality 2008, pp. 13-20, 2008.

117. A. D. Cheok et al., Hunman Pacman: A Sensing-based entertainment System with Ubiquitous Computing and Tangible, Proc. of NetGame'03, pp. 106-117, 2003.

118. D. Wagner et al., Pose Tracking from Natural Features on Mobile Phones, IEEE International Symposium on Mixed and Augmented Reality 2008, pp. 125-134, 2008.

119. D. Wagner et al., Robust and Unobtrusive Marker Tracking on Mobile Phones, IEEE International Symposium on Mixed and Augmented Reality 2008, pp. 121-124, 2008.

120. J. Tumler et al., Mobile Augmented Reality in Industrial Applications: Approaches for Solution of User-Related Issues, IEEE International Symposium on Mixed and Augmented Reality 2008, pp. 87-90, 2008.

121. M. Hakkarainen et al., Augmented Assembly using a Mobile Phone, IEEE International Symposium on Mixed and Augmented Reality 2008, pp. 167-168, 2008.

122. Kim and S. Won, Advanced Teleoperation, Graphics Aids, and Application to Time Delay Environments, Proc. of the 1st Industrial Virtual Reality Show and Conference (IVR'93), Makuhari Meese, Japan, pp. 202-207, 1993.

123. Kim and S. Won, Virtual Reality Calibration and Preview / Predictive Displays for Telerobotics, Presence: Teleoperators and Virtual Environments 5(2), pp. 173-190, 1996.

124. E. Oyama et al., Experimental Study on Remote Manipulation Using Virtual Reality, Presence: Teleoperators and Virtual Environments, pp. 112-124, 1993.

125. G. Tharp et al., Virtual Window Telepresence System for Telerobotic Inspection, SPIE Proc. volume 2351, Telemanipulator and Telepresence Technologies, Boston, MA, pp. 366-373, 1994.

126. T. H. J. Collett and B. A. MacDonald, Developer Oriented Visualisation of a Robot Program, Proc. 2006 ACM Conference on Human-Robot Interaction, pp. 49-56, 2006.

127. B. Giesler et al., Using augmented reality to interact with an autonomous mobile platform. Proc. 2004 IEEE International Conference on Robotics and Automation, Piscataway, United States, pp. 1009-1014, 2004.

128. F. Zhou et al., Trends in Augmented Reality Tracking, Interaction and Display: A Review of Ten Years of ISMAR, IEEE International Symposium on Mixed and Augmented Reality 2008, pp. 193-202, 2008.

129. http://en.wikipedia.org/wiki/Augmented reality.

130. I. Sutheland, The ultimate display, In IFIP'65, pp. 506-508, 1965.

131. M. Krueger, Artificial Reality, Addison-Wesley Professional, 1991.

132.http://gamesalfresco.com/2008/12/14/2008-wrap-up-top-10-milestones-in-augmented-realit y

133. G. Klein and T. Drummond, Robust visual tracking for noninstrumented aug-mented reality, Proc. ISMAR'03, pp. 113-122, 2003.

134. P. Corporation, Polhemus Trackers, http://www.together.com/trackres/ourprod.html.

135. R. Azuma, Tracking Requirements for Augmented Reality, Communications of the ACM 36(7), pp. 50-51, 1993.

136. K. Zikan et al., A note on dynamics of human head motions and on predictive filtering of head-set orientations, Proc. of SPIE, 2351, pp. 328-336, 1994.

137. B.D. Adelstein et al., A Testbed for Characterizing Dynamic Response of Virtual Environment Spatial Sensors, Proc. of 5th Annual Symposium on User Interface Software and Technology, Monterey, CA, pp. 15-21, 1992.

138. B. Donald, Gennery: Visual tracking of known three-dimensional objects, International Journal of Computer Vision, 7(3), pp. 243-270, 1992.

139. D. Lowe, Robust model-based motion tracking through the integration of search and estimation, Intl. Journal of Computer Vision, 8, pp. 113-122, 1992.

140. M. Armstrong and A. Zisserman, Robust object tracking, In Proc. Asian conference on Computer Vision, vol. I, pp. 58-61, 1995.

141. L. Hohl and T. Quack, Markerless 3D Augmented Reality, Semester Thesis, CVL, ETH, 2003.

142. T. Drummond and R. Cipolla, Real-time tracking of complex structureswith on-line camera calibration, Proc. British Machine Vision Conference (BMVC'99), vol. 2, BMVA, Nottingham, pp. 574-583, 1999.

143. E. Marchand et al., Robust real-time visual tracking using a 2D-3D model-based approach, Proc. 7th IEEE International Conference on Computer Vision (ICCV'99), vol. 1, Kerkyra, Greece, pp. 262-268, 1999.

144. G. Simon and M.O. Berger, A two-stage robust statistical method for temporal registration from features of various type, In Proc. 6th IEEE International Conference on Computer Vision (ICCV'98), Bombay, pp. 261-266, 1998.

145. B. Espiau and F. Chaumette, A new approach to visual servoing, IEEE Trans. on Robotics and Automation, 8, pp. 313-326, 1992.

146. V. Sundareswaran and R. Behringer, Visual servoing-based augmented reality, Proc. First IEEE Workshop on Augmented Reality (IWAR'98), San Francisco, pp. 193-200, 1999.

147. R. Behringer et al., Model-based visual tracking for outdoor augmented reality, Proc. IEEE and ACM International Symposium on Mixed and Augmented Reality (ISMAR'02), Darmstadt, Germany, 2002.

148. E. Marchand and F. Chaumette, Virtual visual servoing: a framework for realtime augmented reality, Proc. Eurographics 2002, 21(3), Saarbrcken, Germany, pp. 289-298, 2002.

149. Z. BIAN et al., Real-Time Tracking Error Estimation for Augmented Reality for Registration with Linecode Markers, IEICE TRANS. INF. and SYST., VOL.E91D, NO.7, pp. 2041-2050, 2008.

150. A. Comport et al., A real-time tracker for markerless augmented reality, Proc. ISMAR'03, pp. 36-45, 2003.

151. H. Wuest et al., Adaptive line tracking with multiple hypotheses for augmented reality, Proc. ISMAR'05, pp. 62-69, 2005.

152. G. Reitmayr and T. Drummond, Going out: robust model-based tracking for outdoor augmented reality, Proc. ISMAR'06, pp. 109-118, 2006.
153. T. Okuma et al., A Natural Feature-Based 3D Object Tracking Method for Wearable Augmented Reality, AMC'04, Kawasaki, Japan, pp.451-456, 2004.
154. J. Steinbis et al., 3D Fiducials for Scalable AR Visual Tracking, IEEE International Symposium on Mixed and Augmented Reality 2008, pp. 183-184, 2008.
155. L. Vacchetti et al., Combining edge and texture information for real-time accurate 3d camera tracking, Proc. ISMAR '04, pp. 48-57, 2004.
156. E. Rosten and T. Drummond, Fusing points and lines for high performance tracking, Proc. 10th IEEE International Conference on Computer Vision (ICCV'05), vol. 2, Beijing, pp. 1508-1515, 2005.
157. J.S. Jin et al., A Stable Vision System for Moving Vehicles, IEEE Trans. on Intelligent Transportation Systems, 1(1), pp. 32-39 2000.
158. R.D Xu, J. G. Allen and J. S. Jin, Robust Mean-shift Tracking with Extended Fast Colour Thresholding, Proc. of 2004 International Symposium on Intelligent Multimedia, Video and Speech Processing, Hong Kong, pp. 542-545, 2004.
159. L. Duan et al., A Unified Framework for Semantic Shot Classification in Sports Video, IEEE Trans. on Multimedia, 7(6), pp. 1066-1083, 2005.
160. X. Tong et al., Periodicity Detection of Local Motion, Multimedia and Expo, ICME 2005, pp. 650-653, 2005.
161. L. Duan and J.S. Jin et al., Nonparametric Motion Characterization for Robust Classification of Camera Motion Patterns, IEEE Trans. on Multimedia, 8(2), pp. 323-324, 2006.
162. R.Y.D. Xu and J.S. Jin, Camera Control and Multimedia Interaction using Individual Object Recognition, JOURNAL OF MULTIMEDIA, 2(3), pp. 77-85, 2007.
163. W. Lorensen et al., Enhancing Reality in the Operating Room, In Proc. of the 1993 IEEE Visualization Conference, pp. 410-415, 1993.
164. W.E.L. Grimson et al., An Automated Registration Method for Frameless Stereotaxy, Image Guided Surgery, and Enhanced Reality Visulatization, Proc. IEEE Conference on Computer Vision and Pattern Recognition, pp. 430-436, 1994.
165. J.P. Mellor, Enhanced Reality Visualization in a Surgical Environment, Masters thesis, AI Lab, Massachusetts Institute of Technology, 1995.
166. W F.L. Grimson et al., Evaluating and Validating an Automated Registration System for Enhanced Reality Visualization in Surgery, Proc. of Computer Vision, Virtual Reality, and Robotics in Medicine '95, pp. 3-12, 1995.
167. A. State et al., Case Study: Observing a Volume Rendered Fetus within a Pregnant Patient, Proc. of the 1994 IEEE Visualization Conference, pp. 364-368, 1994.
168. M. Uenohara, and T. Kanade, Vision-Based Object Registration for Real-Time Image Overlay, Computer Vision, Virtual Reality and Robotics in Medicine: CVRMed '95, pp. 14-22, 1995.
169. F. Betting et al., A New Framework for Fusing Stereo Images with Volumetric Medical Images, Proc. of Computer Vision, Virtual Reality, and Robotics in Medicine '95, pp. 30-39, 1995.
170. G. Klein, Visual Tracking for Augmented Reality, PhD thesis, University of Cambridge, 2006.
171. J. R. Vallino, Interactive Augmented Reality, PhD thesis, University of Rochester, 1998.
172. C. Harris, Tracking with rigid models, A. Blake, ed., Active Vision, chap. 4, pp. 59-73, MIT Press, 1992.
173. E. Foxlin et al., Flight Tracker: A novel optical/inertial tracker for cockpit enhanced vision, ISMAR'04, pp. 212-221, 2004.

174. F. Sauer et al., Augmented reality visualization of ultrasound images: System description, calibration, and featur, Proc. International Symposium for Augmented Reality, New York, USA, 2001.
175. F. Sauer et al., Augmented workspace: Designing an AR testbed, Proc. International Symposium for Augmented Reality, pp. 165-174, Munich, Germany, October 2000.
176. F. Sauer et al., A head-mounted display system for augmented reality image guidance: Towards clinical evaluation for imriguided neurosurgery, Proc. MICCAI, Utrecht, The Netherlands, 2001.
177. C. Ludwig and C. Reimann, Augmented Reality:Information at Focus, C-LAB Report, 4(1), Cooperative Computing & Communication Laboratory, 2005.
178. K. Bonsor, How Augmented Reality Will Work, http://www.howstuffworks.com/augmented-reality.htm, 2009.
179. R. Silva et al., Introduction to Augmented Reality, Technical Report: 25/2003, LNCC, Brazil, 2003.
180. J.R. Vallino, Introduction to Augmented Reality, http://www.se.rit.edu/ ~ jrv/research/ar/introduction.html, 2002.
181. M. Sairio, Augmented Reality, Helsinki University of Technology, 2002.
182. R. Azuma. A survey of augmented reality, Teleoperators and Virtual Environments 6(4), pp. 355-385, 1997.
183. R.L.S. SILVA et al., Augmented Reality for Scientific Visualization: Bringing Data Sets inside the Real World, Proc. SCSC'04, pp. 520-525, 2004.
184. A. Scott et al., Human-Robot Collaboration: A Literature Review and Augmented Reality Approach in Design, International Journal of Advanced Robotic Systems, 5(1), pp. 1-18, 2008.
185. E. Ethrigde, Head Mounted Displays (HMD), The Defense Advanced Research Projects Agency, http://www.darpa.mil/mto/displays/hmd/, Referenced 2001.
186. MATRIX: visual-marker based Augmented Reality, http://www.sonycsl.co.jp/person/rekimoto/matrix/Matrix.html, 2009.
187. B.C.A. Fernandes and J. F. Sanchez, Acceptance of an Augmented Reality system as a visualization tool for Computer-Aided Design classes, Interactive Educational Multimedia, 16, pp. 1-8, 2008.
188. F.J. Toledo et al., Image Processing with CNN in a FPGA-Based Augmented Reality System for Visually Impaired People, IWANN 2005, LNCS 3512, pp. 906-912, 2005.
189. K. Nagao and J. Rekimoto, Agent Augmented Reality: A Software Agent Meets the Real World, Proc. ICMAS-96, pp. 228-235, 1996.
190. A.B. Brody and E. J. Gottsman, Pocket BargainFinder: A Handheld Device for Augmented Commerce, Proc. International Symposium on Handheld and Ubiquitous Computing (HUC'99), 1999.
191. W. Zhu, et al., Personalized In-store E-Commerce with the PromoPad: an Augmented Reality Shopping Assistant, The Electronic Journal for E-Commerce Tools & Applications, 2004. 1(3).
192. W. Zhu et al., Design of the PromoPad: an Automated Augmented Reality Shopping Assistant, 12th Americas Conference on Information Systems, Acapulco, Mexico, 2006.
193. Yuzhu Lu and Shana Smith, Augmented Reality E-Commerce Assistant System: Trying While Shopping, Human-Computer Interaction, Part II, HCII 2007, LNCS 4551, pp. 643-652, 2007.
194. Augmented Reality with Ford Ka campaign in Europe's cities, http://www.everysingleoneofus.com/no-way-back-from-here/1--lay-of-the-land/case-studies/augmentedrealitywithfordkacampaignineuropescities, 2009.
195. New MINI augmented reality ad is a creative masterpiece, http://www.automotto.org/entry/new-mini-augmented-reality-ad-is-a-creative-masterpiece/, 2009.

196. M.A. Livingston et al., An augmented reality system for military operations in urban terrain, Proc. Interservice/Industry Training, Simulation, and Education Conference, (I/ITSEC '02), Orlando, Florida, pp. 1-8, 2002.

197. N.R. Hedley et al., Explorations in the use of augmented reality for geographic visualization, Presence: Teleoperators and Virtual Environments, 11(2), pp.119-133, 2002.

198. A. Moore, Cubes, shadows and comic strips - a.k.a. interfaces, metaphors and maps?, In: 16th Annual Colloquium of the Spatial Information Research Centre, Dunedin, New Zealand, pp. 97-102, 2004.

199. F. Liarokapis et al., Mobile Augmented Reality Techniques for GeoVisualisation, Proc. Ninth International Conference on Information Visualisation, pp. 745-751, 2005.

200. W. Qi, A Vision-Based Augmented Reality System for Visualization Interaction, iv, Proc. Ninth International Conference on Information Visualisation, pp.404-409, 2005.

201. C. Brenner, The Geoscope a Mixed- Reality System for Planning and Public Participation, UDMS 2006, 2006.

202. F. Liarokapis et al., Exploring Urban Environments Using Virtual and Augmented Reality, Journal of Virtual Reality and Broadcasting, 3(5), pp. 1-13, 2007.

203. J.M. Krisp, Geovisualization and knowledge discovery for decision making in ecological network planning, doctoral dissertation, Helsinki University of Technology, 2006.

204. P. Ghadirian and I. D. Bishop, Integration of augmented reality and GIS: A new approach to realistic landscape visualisation, Landscape and Urban Planning, 86, pp. 226-232, 2008.

205. S. Nebiker et al., Smart Point Clouds in Virtual Globes a New Paradigm in CityIModeling?, http://www.geovisualisierung.net/geoviz hamburg/papers/092Nebiker.pdf, 2009.

206. E. C. Urban, The Information Warrior, IEEE Spectrum, 32(11), pp. 66-70, 1995.

207. Demo: Military Application : Operational contents manipulation on a virtual topographic map, http://www.arcane-technologies.com/?page id=19, 2008.

208. C. E. Howard, Department of Defense invests in delivering augmented reality technology to foot soldiers, http://mae.pennnet.com/display article/291411/32/ARTCL/none/none/1/Department-of-Defense-invests-in-delivering-augmented-reality-technology-to-foot-soldiers/, 2007.

209. Canadian helicopter verifies night vision system with Ascension's laserBIRD, http://iar-ira.nrc-cnrc.gc.ca/press/news 1 15 e.html, 2004.

210. K. Ahlers et al, Distributed Augmented Reality for Collaborative Design Applications, ECRC-95-03, 1995.

211. S. Feiner et al., Architectural anatomy, In Presence, 4(3), pp. 318-325, 1995.

212. A. Webster et al., Augmented reality in architectural construction, inspection and renovation, Proc. ASCE Third Congress on Computing in Civil Engineering, Anaheim, CA, pp. 913-919, 1996.

213. B. Thomas, Using Augmented Reality to Visualize Architecture Designs in an Outdoor Environment, Design Computing on the Net November, 1999.

214. K. Kensek et al., Augmented Reality: an application for architecture, Proc. 8th International Conference on Computing in Civil and Building Engineering, ASCE, Stanford, CA, pp. 294-301, 2000.

215. J. Shen et al., Urban Planning Using Augmrnted Reslity, Journal of Urban Planning and Development, pp. 118-125, SEPTEMBER 2001.

216. E. Ben-Joseph, Urban Simulation and the Luminous Planning Table: Bridging the Gap between the Digital and the Tangible, Journal of Planning and Education Research, Vol. 21, pp. 196-203, 2001.

217. T. Gleue and P. Dahne, Design and Implementation of a Mobile Device for Outdoor Augmented Reality in the ARCHEOGUIDE Project, Proc. of the ACM Conference on Virtual reality, Archeology, and Cultural Heritage, pp. 161-168, 2002.

218. H. Ishii et al., Augmented urban planning workbench: overlaying drawings, physical models and digital simulation, Proc. of the International Symposium on Mixed and Augmented Reality (ISMAR 2002), pp. 203-211, 2002.
219. W. Piekarski and B. H. Thomas, Interactive Augmented Reality Techniques for Construction at a Distance of 3D Geometry, IPT/EGVE 2003, Zurich, Switzerland, 2003.
220. J.M.S. Dias et al., A4D: Augmented Reality 4D System for Architecture and Building Construction, CONVR 2003, Virginia Tech, 2003.
221. A. Malkawi et al., Interactive, Immersive Visualization for Indoor Environments: Use of Augmented Reality, Human-Computer Interaction and Building Simulation, Proc. of the Eighth International Conference on Information Visualization, pp. 833-838, 2004.
222. W. Broll et al., ARTHUR: A Collaborative Augmented Environment for Architectural Design and Urban Planning, Proc. of Seventh International Conference on Humans and Computers, pp. 102-109, 2004.
223. A.H. Behzadan and V.R. Kamat, Visualization of construction graphics in outdoor augmented reality, Proc. of the 2005 Winter Simulation Conference, pp. 1914-1920, 2005.
224. C.T. Chen and T.W. Chang, Spatially Augmented Reality Design Environment, Innovations in Design & Decision Support Systems in Architecture and Urban Planning, Van Leeuwen, Dordrecht: Springer, pp. 487-499, 2006.
225. A. Sa et al., Augmented reality to Aid Construction Management, CMNE/CILAMCE 2007, Portugal, 2007.
226. Y. Guo et al., Application of Augmented Reality GIS in Architecture, Proc. The International Archives of the Photogrammetry, Remote Sensing and Spatial Information Sciences, Beijing, pp. 331-336, 2008.
227. D.A. Belcher, Augmented Reality, Architecture and Ubiquity: Technologies, Theories and Frontiers, thesis, University of Washington, 2008.
228. J. Lertlakkhanakul et al, Using the Mobile Augmented Reality Techniques for Construction Management, Proc. of the 10th International Conference on Computer Aided Architectural Design Research in Asia (CAADRIA 2005), pp. 396-403, 2005.
229. W. Lonsing, Augmented Reality as Tool in Architecture, Proc. of the 22nd eCAADe Conference: Architecture in the Network Society, pp. 495-499, 2004.
230. Malkawi, A. and R. Srinivasan, Building Performance Visualization Using Augmented Reality, Proc. of the Fourteenth International Conference on Computer Graphics and Vision, pp. 122-127, 2004.
231. S. Park and J. Choi, Retrieving and Browsing Information of Building Equipment Using Augmented Reality Techniques, Proc. of the 9th International Conference on Computer Aided Architectural Design Research in Asia (CAADRIA 2004), pp. 911-926, 2004.
232. H. Seichter and M.A. Schnabel, Digital and Tangible Sensation: An Augmented Reality Urban Design Studio, Proc. of the 10th International Conference on Computer Aided Architectural Design Research in Asia (CAADRIA 2005), pp. 193-202, 2005.
233. M. Daily et al., World Embedded Interfaces for Human-Robot Interaction, Proc. of the 36th Hawaii International Conference on System Sciences (HICSS03), 2003.
234. M. Stilman, Augmented Reality for Robot Development and Experimentation, report, Robotics Institute, Carnegie Mellon University, 2005.
235. H. Worn et al., New augmented reality and robotic based methods for head-surgery, Int. J. Medical Robotics and Computer Assisted Surgery, 1(3), pp. 49-56, 2005.
236. T. Akinbiyi et al., Dynamic Augmented Reality for Sensory Substitution in Robot-Assisted Surgical Systems, EMBS '06, pp. 567-570, 2006.
237. M. Kostandov et al., Robot gaming and learning using augmented reality, In ACM SIGGRAPH Technical Posters, San Diego, CA, USA, Aug 2007.
238. J.W.S. Chong et al., Methodologies for Immersive Robot Programming in an Augmented Reality Environment, The International Journal of Virtual Reality, 6(1), pp. 69-79, 2007.

239. H. Portilla and L. Basanez, Augmented Reality Tools for Enhanced Robotics Teleoperation Systems, Proc. 3DTV Conference 2007, pp. 1-4, 2007.

240. J.C. Maida et al., Improving Robotic Operator Performance Using Augmented Reality, Proc. of the Human Factors and Ergonomics SocietyO 51st ANNUAL MEETING, pp. 1635-1639, 2007.

241. N. Suzuki, Benefits of augmented reality function for laparoscopic and endoscopic surgical robot systems, Proc. MICCAI 2008, New York City, USA, 2008.

242. H. Lee et al., Augmented Reality Based Vision System for Network Based Mobile Robot, APCHI 2008, LNCS 5068, pp. 123-130, 2008.

243. I. Y. Chen at al., Markerless Augmented Reality for Robots in Unprepared Environments, Australian Conference on Robotics and Automation 2008, 2008.

244. I. Y. Chen at al., Markerless Augmented Reality for Robotic Helicoptor Applications, RobVis 2008, LNCS 4931, pp. 125-138, 2008.

245. J. Schulze-Ferebee, KUKA Roboter enhances perception of reality in robotics, KUKA Roboter GmbH, 2008.

246. L. Su et al., Augmented Reality During Robot-assisted Laparoscopic Partial Nephrectomy: Toward Real-Time 3D-CT to Stereoscopic Video Registration, UROLOGY 73 (4), pp. 896-900, 2009.

247. C. Java et al, An augmented reality interface for training robotics through the web, Proc. of the 40th International Symposium on Robotics, Barcelona, pp. 189-194, 2009.

248. J. W. S. Chong et al., Robot programming using augmented reality: An interactive method for planning collision-free paths, Robotics and Computer-Integrated Manufacturing, 25(3), pp. 689-701, 2009.

249. V. Raghavan et al., Interactive Evaluation of Assembly Sequences Using Augmented Reality, IEEE Trans. on Robotics and Automation, 15(3), pp. 435-449, 1999.

250. O.W. Bertelsen and C. Nielsen, Augmented reality as a design tool for mobile interfaces, Proc. of the Third Conference on Designing Interactive Systems (DIS 2000), pp. 185-192, 2000.

251. B. Schwald et al., Starmate: Using augmented reality technology for computer guided maintenance of complex mechanical elements, E-work and ECommerce, pp. 196-202, 2001.

252. F. Fruend et al., AR-based Product Design in Automobile Industry, The First IEEE International Augmented Reality Toolkit Workshop, 2002.

253. B. Schwald and B. Laval, An augmented reality system for training and assistance to maintenance in the industrial context, 11th International Conference in Central Europe on Computer Graphics, Visualization and Computer Vision'2003, 2003.

254. S. Goose et al., Speech-Enabled Augmented Reality Supporting Mobile Industrial Maintenance, Pervasive Computing, pp. 65-70, JANUARYMARCH 2003.

255. F.G. Hamza-Lup et al., Distributed training system with high-resolution deformable virtual models, Proc. of the 43rd Annu. ACM Southeast Conf., Kennesaw, GA, 2005.

256. C. Ke et al., An Augmented reality-based Application for Equipment Maintenance, LNCS, 3784, pp. 836-841, 2005.

257. Y.L. Poh et al., Facilitating Mechanical Design with Augmented Reality, Singapore-MIT Alliance Symposium, Singapore, 2005.

258. H. Regenbrecht et al., Augmented Reality Projects in Automotive and Aerospace Industry, IEEE Computer Graphics and Applications, pp. 48-56, November/December 2005.

259. W. Dangelmaier et al., Virtual and augmented reality support for discrete manufacturing system simulation, Computers in Industry, 56, pp. 371-383, 2005.

260. A. E. Majoros and W. R. Jackson, Technology Augmented Reality for Space Flight Training and Mission Support American, American Astronautical Society National Conference and 52'nd Annual Meeting ``Building Bridges to Exploration: The Role of the International Space Station", Houston, Texas, 2005.

261. B. Kang et al., An Augmented Reality System for Computer Maintenance, ICAT 2006, LNCS 4282, pp. 284-291, 2006.
262. Y. Pang et al., Assembly feature design in an augmented reality environment, Assembly Automation, 26(1), pp. 34-43, 2006.
263. M.L. Yuan et al., Augmented reality for assembly guidance using a virtual interactive tool, International Journal of Production Research, 46(7), pp. 1745-1767, 2006.
264. J. Christian, Augmented Reality in Corporate Pervasive e-Education: Novel ways to support aviation maintenance training, Innovation North Research Conference 2006, Leeds Metropolitance University, 2006.
265. M. Haller et al., Shared Design Space: Sketching ideas using digital pens and a large augmented tabletop setup, Proc. of the 16th International Conference on Artificial Reality and Telexistence, ICAT 2006, China, 2006.
266. X. Wang and P. S. Dunston, Design, Strategies, and Issues towards an Augmented Reality-based Construction Training Platform, Journal of Information Technology in Construction, International Council for Research and Innovation in Building and Construction (CIB), 12, pp. 363-380, 2007.
267. X. Wang et al., Perceptions of Augmented Reality in the Design Sector, 7th International Conference on Construction Applications of Virtual Reality, pp. 132-138, 2007.
268. F.G. Hamza-Lup et al., Distributed Augmented Reality With 3-D Lung Dynamics-A Planning Tool Concept, IEEE Trans. on Information Technology in Biomedicine, 11(1), pp. 40-46, 2007.
269. H. Wuest and D. Stricker, Tracking of industrial objects by using CAD models, Journal of Virtual Reality and Broadcasting, 4(1), 2007.
270. Z. Bian et al., Development of a Tracking Method for Augmented Reality Applied to NPP Maintenance Work and its Experimental Evaluation, IEICE Trans. on Information and Systems, E90-D(6), pp. 963-974, 2007.
271. B. Reitinger et al., Augmented reality scouting for interactive 3d reconstruction, in Proc. of IEEE Virtual Reality, pp.219-222, 2007.
272. H. Ishii, Augmented Reality Applications for Nuclear Power Plant Maintenance Work, International Symposoum on Symbiotic Nuclear Power System for 21 Century (IAANP2008), pp. 262-268, 2008.
273. X. Wang et al., An Empirical Study on Designers' Perceptions of Augmented Reality within an Architectural FIRM, Information Technologies in Construction (ITcon), 13, pp. 536-551, 2008.
274. J. Saaski et al, Integration of design and assembly using augmented reality, In Proc. IPAS'2008, Chamonix, France, 2008.
275. A.H. Behzadan et al., General-purpose modular hardware and software frame-work for mobile outdoor augmented reality applications in engineering, Advanced Engineering Informatics, 22, pp. 90-105, 2008.
276. D. Bradley et al., Augmented Reality on Cloth with Realistic Illumination, Machine Vision and Applications, 20(2), 2009.
277. C. Salzmann et al., Remote Experimentation: Improving User Perception Using Augmented Reality, NIWeek 2000, Austin, TX, pp. 17-20, 2000.
278. M. Billinghurst et al., The MagicBookMoving Seamlessly between Reality and Virtuality, IEEE Comput. Graph, 21(3), pp. 6-8, 2001.
279. J.R. Cooperstock, The classroom of the future: enhancing education through augmented reality, Proc. HCI Inter. 2001 Conf. on Human-Computer Interaction, New Orleans, USA, pp. 688-692, 2001.
280. F. Liarokapis, Multimedia Augmented Reality Interface for E-learning (MARIE), World Trans. on Engineering and Technology Education, 1(2), pp. 173-176, 2002.

281. B.E. Shelton and N.R. Hedley, Using augmented reality for teaching earth-sun relationships to undergraduate geography students, Proc. of the First IEEE International Augmented Reality Toolkit Workshop, Darmstadt, Germany, 2002.
282. H. Kaufmann and D. Schmalstieg, Mathematics and geometry education with collaborative augmented reality, Computers and Graphics, vol. 27, pp. 339-345, 2003.
283. S. Zagoranski and S. Divjak, Use of Augmented Reality in Education, Proc. EU-ROCON 2003 Ljubljana, Slovenia, pp. 339-342, 2003.
284. H. Kaufmann, Geometry Education with Augmented Reality, Ph.D. Thesis. Vienna: Vienna University of Technology, 2004.
285. H. Kaufmann et al., Improving Spatial Abilities by Geometry Education in Augmented Reality - Application and Evaluation Design, First International VR-Learning Seminar at Virtual Reality International Conference (VRIC), Laval, 2005.
286. H. Kaufmann et al., General Training of Spatial Abilities by Geometry Education in Augmented Reality, Annual Review of CyberTherapy and Telemedicine: A Decade of VR, 3, pp. 65-76, 2005.
287. H. Kaufmann, The Potential of Augmented Reality in Dynamic Geometry Education, 12th International Conference on Geometry and Graphics, Salvador, Brazil, 2006.
288. H. Kaufmann and M. Papp, Learning Objects for Education with Augmented Reality, Proc. of EDEN 2006 (European Distance and E-Learning Network) Conference, Vienna 2006, pp. 160-165, 2006.
289. A. Dnser et al., Virtual and Augmented Reality as Spatial Ability Training Tools, Proc. of the 7th ACM SIGCHI, Christchurch, New Zealand, pp. 125-132, 2006.
290. Y.C. Chen, A study of comparing the use of augmented reality and physical models in chemistry education, Proc. of the 2006 ACM international conference on virtual reality continuum and its applications, pp. 369-372, 2006.
291. H. Kaufmann and A. Dunser, Summary of Usability Evaluations of an Educational Augmented Reality Application, LNCS 4563, pp. 660-669, 2007.
292. M. Olabe et al., Engineering Multimedia Contents with Authoring Tools of Augmented Reality, http://158.227.75.138/Joomla/images/pdf/inted 2007 rasmap 2.pdf, 2007.
293. M. Said and N. Ismail, Overview of Open Source Augmented Reality Toolkit, 1st International Malaysian Educational Technology Convention, 2007.
294. E. Medina and S. Weghorst, Understanding biochemistry with Augmented Reality, Proc. of World Conference on Educational Multimedia, Hypermedia and Telecommunications 2007, pp. 4235-4239, 2007.
295. M. Fjeld, Tangible User Interface for Chemistry Education: Comparative Evaluation and Re-Design, Proc. CHI 2007, San Jose, CA, USA, pp. 805-808, 2007.
296. E.P. Affonso1 and A.C. Sementille, Support on the Remote Interaction for Augmented Reality System, 17th International Conference on Artificial Reality and Telexistence 2007, pp. 190-196, 2007.
297. H. Kaufmann and B. Meyer, Simulating educational physical experiments in augmented reality, In Siggraph asia 08: Acm siggraph asia 2008 educators programme, pp.1-8, 2008.
298. P. Buchanan et al., Augmented Reality and Rigid Body Simulation for Edutainment, Proc. Advanced in Computer Entertainment Technology 2008, pp. 17-20, 2008.
299. C. Juan et al., An Augmented Reality System for Learning the Interior of the Human Body, Proc. of the 2008 Eighth IEEE International Conference on Advanced Learning, pp. 186-188, 2008.
300. E. Klopfer, Augmented learning: Research and Design of Mobile Educational Games, The MIT Press, 2008.
301. M. Vilkoniene, Influence of augmented reality technology upon pupils' knowledge about human digestive system: The results of the experiment, US-China Education Review, 6(1), pp. 36-43, 2009.

302. P. Maier et al., Augmented Reality for teaching spatial relations, Conference of the International Journal of Arts & Sciences 2009, Toronto, 2009.
303. K. Mase et al., Meta-Museum: A Supportive Augmented-Reality Environment by For Knowledge Sharing, International Conference on Virtual Systems and Multimedia 1996, pp. 107-110, 1996.
304. S. Feineret al., A Touring Machine: Prototyping 3D Mobile Augmented Reality Systems for Exploring the Urban Environment, In Proc. ISWC'97, Cambridge, MA, pp. 74-81, 1997.
305. D. Ingram, Trust-based Filtering for Augmented Reality, Proc. of the First International Conference on Trust Management, LNCS 2692, 2003.
306. R. Wojciechowski et al., Building Virtual and Augmented Reality Museum Exhibitions, Proc. of the ninth international conference on 3D Web technology (2004), pp. 135-144, 2004.
307. M. Martinez and G. Munoz, Designing augmented interfaces for guided tours using multimedia sketches, In Proc. of the Workshop MIXER'04, Funchal, Madeira, 2004.
308. P.A.S. Sinclair, Integrating Hypermedia Techniques Integrating Hypermedia Techniques, Ph.D thesis, University of Southampton, 2004.
309. F. Fritz et al., Enhancing Cultural Tourism experiences with Augmented Reality Technologies, The 6th International Symposium on Virtual Reality, Archaeology and Cultural Heritage VAST, 2005.
310. F. Liarokapis and M. White, Augmented Reality Techniques for Museum Environments, The Mediterranean Journal of Computers and Networks, 1(2), pp. 90-96, 2005.
311. A. Damala et al., Merging Augmented Reality Based Features in Mobile Multimedia Museum Guides, XXI International CIPA Symposium, Athens, Greece, 2006.
312. D.H. Lee and J. Park, Augmented Reality Based Museum Guidance System for Selective Viewings, Second Workshop on Digital Media and its Application in Museum and Heritages, pp. 379-382, 2007.
313. F. Diez-Diaz et al., An Accesible and Collaborative Tourist Guide Based on Augmented Reality and Mobile Devices, Universal Access in HCI 2007, LNCS 4555, pp. 353-362, 2007.
314. H. Su et al., Research and Implementation of Hybrid Tracking Techniques in Augmented Museum Tour System, Edutainment 2008, LNCS 5093, pp. 636-643, 2008.
315. S. Bres and B. Tellez, Localisation and Augmented Reality for Mobile Applications in Culture Heritage, http://www.commission5.isprs.org/3darch09/pdf/bres tellez.pdf.
316. B. Thomas, Challenges of Making Outdoor Augmented Reality Games Playable, In 2nd CREST Workshop on Advanced Computing and Communicating Techniques for Wearable Information Playing, 2003.
317. D. Schmalstieg, Augmented reality techniques in games, Proc. Fourth IEEE and ACM International Symposium on Mixed and Augmented Reality, 2005.
318. K. Kuikkaniemi et al., Toolkit for User-created Augmented Reality Games, MUM06, Stanford, CA, USA, 2006.
319. W. Broll et al., Meeting Technology Challenges of Pervasive Augmented Reality Games, Netgames'06, Singapore, 2006.
320. W. Litzlbauer et al., Neon Racer: Augmented Gaming, In 10th Central European Seminar on Computer Graphics, CESCG 2006, Slovakia, 2006.
321. M. Rohs, Marker-Based Embodied Interaction for Handheld Augmented Reality Games, Journal of Virtual Reality and Broadcasting, 4(5), 2007.
322. C. Geiger et al., Development of an Augmented Reality Game by Extending a 3D Authoring System, Proc. of the 2007 ACM SIGCHI international conference on Advances in computer entertainment technology, Salzburg, Austria, 2007.
323. Z.O. Toups and A. Kerne, Location-Aware Augmented Reality Gaming for Emergency Response Education: Concepts and Development, CHI 2007, San Jose, USA, 2007.

324. D.C. Silva and V. Vinhas, An Interactive Augmented Reality Battleship Game Implementation, Proc. Learning with Games, pp. 213-219, 2007.
325. K. Cho et al., Ghost Hunter: A Handheld Augmented Reality Game System with Dynamic Environment, Entertainment Computing ICEC 2007, LNCS 4740, pp. 10-15, 2007.
326. J. Schulz, Augmented Reality in Computer Games, http://campar.in.tum.de/Chair/TeachingSs07ArProseminar, 2007. 327. Ohan Oda et al., Developing an Augmented Reality Racing Game, The Second International Conference on Intelligent Technologies for Interactive Entertainment (ICST INTETAIN '08), 2008.
328. H.S. Lee and J.W. Lee, Mathematical Education Game Based on Augmented Reality, Edutainment 2008, LNCS 5093, pp. 442-450, 2008.
329. F.C. Luz et al., Augmented Reality for Games, DIMEA'08, Athens, Greece, 2008.
330. G. N. Yannakakis and J. Hallam, Real-time Adaptation of Augmented-Reality Games for Optimizing Player Satisfaction, In Proc. of the IEEE Symposium on Computational Intelligence and Games, Perth, Australia, 2008.
331. G. N. Yannakakis, How to Model and Augment Player Satisfaction: A Review, in Proc. of the 1st Workshop on Child, Computer and Interaction, ICMI'08, Chania, Crete, 2008.

Novel Blind Steganalysis for JPEG Images

Li Zhuo[1,1], Chen Jian[1], Jiang Xiaoning[1], Zeng Xianting[1], Pan Xuezeng[1],

[1] College of Computer Science, Zhejiang University, Hangzhou, China
Lizhuo84@gmail.com

Abstract. A new blind steganalytic scheme is proposed in this paper for JPEG images. Based on the DCT domain and the decompressed spatial domain, nine statistical models are constructed for a JPEG image. By using the center of mass (COM) of histogram characteristic function (HCF), we calculate the energy distribution for each statistical model in the frequency domain as a part of the feature set. Besides, we select suitable individual elements which hold main information of the statistical models based on DCT domain as the other part of the feature set. Then a 194-dimensional feature vector is obtained for each image. Support vector machines (SVM) are utilized to construct the classifiers. Experimental results show that the proposed scheme provides good detection accuracy on five popular JPEG steganographic algorithms, and outperforms several recently reported similar steganalytic methods, especially when the embedded messages are small.

Keywords: Steganalysis; Blind detection; Statistical model; Feature vector; Support vector machine.

1 Introduction

Steganography, which is sometimes referred to as information hiding, is used to conceal secret messages into the cover medium such as digital images imperceptibly. Opposite to the steganography, steganalysis focuses on discovering the presence of the hidden data, recognizing what the embedding algorithm is, and estimating the ratio of hidden data eventually. In general, steganalytic techniques can be divided into two categories — targeted approaches and blind steganalysis. The former can also be called as specific steganalysis [1-3], which is designed to attack a known specific embedding algorithm. While the latter, blind steganalysis, is designed independent of specific hiding schemes. The biggest advantage of blind steganalysis is that there is no need to develop a new specific targeted approach each time a new steganography appears. In comparison with the targeted approaches, blind steganalysis has much better extensibility.

---

[1] Project supported by the Science and Technology Project of Zhejiang Province, China (No. 2008C21077), the Key Science and Technology Special Project of Zhejiang Province, China (No. 2007C11088, No. 2007C11068)

M.L. Huang et al. (eds.), *Visual Information Communication*,
DOI 10.1007/978-1-4419-0312-9_22, © Springer Science+Business Media, LLC 2010

For blind steganalysis, machine learning techniques are often used to train a classifier capable of classifying cover and stego feature sets in the feature space. It has been proved that natural images can be characterized using some numerical features, and the distributions of the features for cover images are likely different from those for their corresponding stego images. Therefore, by using methods of artificial intelligence or pattern recognition, a classifier can be built to discriminate between images with and without hidden data in the feature space.

The idea using the trained classifier to detect steganography was first proposed by Avcibas et al. [4]. The authors used image quality metrics as the features and tested their scheme on several watermarking algorithms. Later in their work [5], they proposed a different set of features base on binary similarity measures between the lowest bit planes to classify the cover and stego images. Lyu et al. [6] presented a universal steganalyzer based on first-and high-order wavelet statistics for gray scale images. The first four statistical moments of wavelet coefficients and their local linear prediction errors of several high frequency subbands were used to form a 72-dimensional (72-D) feature vector for steganalysis. Harmsen et al. [7] proposed a novel method to detect additive noise steganography in the spatial domain by using the center of mass (COM) of the histogram characteristic function (HCF). It exploited the COM changes of HCF between cover and stego images. However, the capability of these blind steganalyzers in defeating JPEG steganography is rather limited, because the features of those are selected from the spatial or wavelet transform domains.

Generally, the JPEG steganographic schemes [13-19] always embed the secret messages by manipulating the quantized DCT coefficients. As a result, the feature set constructed in DCT domain may lead to be more sensitive to classify cover and stego images. Many steganalytic methods in which the features are constructed mainly in DCT domain have been presented recently [8-12].

In [8], Fridrich developed a steganalytic scheme designed for JPEG steganography. The author claimed to estimate the statistics of the original image by a calibrated image, which was obtained by decompressing the given JPEG image, cropping four rows and columns on the boundary and then recompressing the cropped image using the original quantization table of the given image. A 23-dimensional feature vector was generated for steganalysis. This scheme achieved a good performance on some popular JPEG steganography, such as F5 [13] and Jsteg [14]. Fu et al. [9] presented a universal JPEG steganalytic scheme with 200 features basically based on quantized DCT coefficients. The Markov empirical transition matrices were used to exploit the correlations between quantized DCT coefficients in both intra-block and row scanning inter-block sense. A new steganalytic scheme based on Markov process was presented by Shi et al. [10] to effectively detect modern JPEG steganography. At first, a JPEG 2-D array was formed from the magnitudes of quantized block DCT coefficients. Difference JPEG 2-D arrays along horizontal, vertical and diagonal directions were then calculated and Markov process was applied to modeling these difference 2-D arrays. Elements of transition probability matrices of those Markov processes were selected as features for steganalysis. Chen et al. [11] extended Shi et al.'s scheme [10] and presented another effective JPEG steganalysis based on Markov process. Mode 2-D arrays of the given JPEG image were used to generate difference mode 2-D arrays along different directions. These difference mode 2-D arrays were then modeled by Markov process to construct inter-block features. Combined with the intra-block features collected in [10], a 486-D feature set was constructed. The detection accuracy of these universal steganalyzers [8-12] in defeating JPEG steganographic schemes is much higher that of [4-7].

In our work, we combine the idea of COM of HCF [7] and image calibration [8] with the feature-based classification to construct a new blind steganalyzer capable of detecting JPEG steganography effectively. Statistical models are constructed in the DCT domain and the decompressed spatial domain, and 194 features are extracted from these models for an image. In addition, we utilize the support vector machine (SVM) to construct classifiers in our experiments. To evaluate the proposed scheme, we detect stego images embedded with five popular steganography — JPHide [15], Outguess2 [16], Steghide [17], MB1 [18] and MB2 [19]. In comparison with several previous known blind approaches, our scheme provides better performance in terms of detection accuracy.

The rest of this paper is organized as follows. In the next section, we describe the details of statistical models constructed from the DCT domain and the decompressed spatial domain. Section 3 describes how the features are calculated. In Section 4, we illustrate the experimental details to evaluate our proposed scheme. At last, the paper is concluded in Section 5.

2   Statistical Models

In principle, the features for steganalysis should be sensitive to the embedding changes of the stego image while not care about the image content. Since most steganography for JPEG images manipulate the quantized DCT coefficients to embed messages, statistics constructed in the same domain are likely more sensitive to the changes. Besides, if we decompress JPEG images to the raw format, we can observe some statistical differences of the pixels value between the images with and without hidden data. Hence, statistical models constructed from the decompressed spatial domain can also reveal changes partly. To describe the formulas presented later in this section conveniently, we first introduce a function $\varphi(x, y)$ as below.

$$\varphi(x, y) = \begin{cases} 1, & if\ x == y \\ 0, & elsewise \end{cases}. \tag{1}$$

2.1   DCT Domain Statistics

Suppose the processed file is a JPEG image with size M×N. Let $dct(i, j)$ denote the DCT coefficient at location (i, j) in an 8×8 DCT block, where $1 \leq i \leq 8$ and $1 \leq j \leq 8$. In each block, $dct(1,1)$ is called the DC coefficient, which contains a significant fraction of the image energy. Generally little changes occur to DC coefficients during the embedding procedure, so we mainly consider the remaining 63 AC coefficients in each DCT block.

Histogram of Global AC Coefficients

The first statistic is the histogram of all AC coefficients. Suppose the JPEG image is represented with a DCT block matrix $dct_{r,c}(i,j)$, where (r,c) denotes the index of the DCT block, and $r \in [1, M/8]$, $c \in [1, N/8]$. Then the histogram of all AC coefficients can be computed as following.

$$H_1(d) = \sum_{r=1}^{M/8} \sum_{c=1}^{N/8} (\sum_{i=1}^{8} \sum_{j=1}^{8} \varphi(d, dct_{r,c}(i,j))). \tag{2}$$

where $(i,j) \neq (1,1)$, $d \in [L,R]$, $L = \min(dct_{r,c}(i,j))$ and $R = \max(dct_{r,c}(i,j))$.

Histograms of AC coefficients in specific locations

Some steganographic schemes may preserve the global histogram $H(d)$. So we add individual histograms for low-frequency AC coefficients to our set of functional. Equation (3) describes the histograms at the special location (i,j).

$$H_2(d) = \sum_{r=1}^{M/8} \sum_{c=1}^{N/8} \varphi(d, dct_{r,c}(i,j)) \tag{3}$$

where $ij \in \{12,13,21,22,23,31,32,33\}$.

Histograms of AC coefficients with specific values

For a fixed coefficient value d, we calculate the distribution of all AC coefficients in the 63 locations separately among all DCT blocks. In fact, $H^d(i,j)$ is an 8×8 matrix.

$$H_3(i,j) = \sum_{r=1}^{M/8} \sum_{c=1}^{N/8} \varphi(d, dct_{r,c}(i,j)) \tag{4}$$

Histogram of AC coefficient differences between adjacent DCT blocks

Many steganography may preserve the statistics between adjacent DCT coefficients, but the dependency of the DCT coefficients in the same location between adjacent DCT blocks may hardly be preserved. So we can describe this dependency as (5). All DC coefficients are still not considered.

$$H_4(v) = \sum_{r=1}^{M/8} \sum_{c=1}^{N/8-1} \sum_{i,j=1}^{8} (\varphi(v, dct_{r,c}(i,j)) - dct_{r,c+1}(i,j)) +$$
$$\sum_{r=1}^{M/8-1} \sum_{c=1}^{N/8} \sum_{i,j=1}^{8} (\varphi(v, dct_{r,c}(i,j)) - dct_{r\_1,c}(i,j)) \tag{5}$$

where $v \in [L - R, R - L]$.

Co-occurrence matrix is a very important second order statistic to describe the alteration of luminance for an image. It can not only inspect the distributional characteristics of luminance, but also reflect the positional distribution of pixels with the same or similar luminance. Therefore, we utilize co-occurrence matrix to construct two statistical models.

Co-occurrence Matrix of coefficients in adjacent DCT blocks

Co-occurrence matrix of DCT coefficients in the same location between adjacent blocks is calculated as following.

$$C_5(d1, d2) = \sum_{r=1}^{M/8} \sum_{c=1}^{N/8-1} \sum_{i,j=1}^{8} (\varphi(d1, dct_{r,c}(i,j)) \cdot \varphi(d2, dct_{r,c+1}(i,j)) +$$
$$\sum_{r=1}^{M/8-1} \sum_{c=1}^{N/8} \sum_{i,j=1}^{8} (\varphi(d1, dct_{r,c}(i,j)) \cdot \varphi(d2, dct_{r+1,c}(i,j)) \tag{6}$$

where $d_1, d_2 \in [L, R]$.

Co-occurrence Matrix of coefficient differences between adjacent DCT blocks

Co-occurrence matrix of DCT coefficients differences in the same location between adjacent blocks is calculated as following.

$$C_6(v_1, v_2) = \sum_{r=1}^{M/8} \sum_{c=1}^{N/8-2} (\sum_{i,j=1}^{8} \varphi(v_1, dct_{r,c}(i,j) - dct_{r,c+1}(i,j)) \cdot \varphi(v_2, dct_{r,c+1}(i,j) - dct_{r,c+2}(i,j)) +$$
$$\sum_{r=1}^{M/8-2} \sum_{c=1}^{N/8} (\sum_{i,j=1}^{8} \varphi(v_1, dct_{r,c}(i,j) - dct_{r+1,c}(i,j)) \cdot \varphi(v_2, dct_{r+1,c}(i,j) - dct_{r+2,c}(i,j)) \tag{7}$$

where $v_1, v_2 \in [L-R, R-L]$.

2.2   Spatial Domain Statistics

Although steganography for JPEG images usually embed messages into the DCT domain, the embedding operation would also cause some alterations to the decompressed pixels value. Hence, we would propose some significant statistical models from the spatial domain in this section.

Histogram of Adjacent pixel Differences

The distribution of adjacent pixel differences can also reveal some information when embedding happens. And many steganographic schemes do not preserve its distributional characteristics, so we can utilize the histogram of pixel differences as a feature.

$$H_7(e) = \sum_{i=1}^{M} \sum_{j=1}^{N-1} (\varphi(e, b(i,j) - b(i, j+1))) + \\ \sum_{i=1}^{M-1} \sum_{j=1}^{N} (\varphi(e, b(i,j) - b(i+1, j))) \tag{8}$$

Obviously we can find that e is in range [-255,255].

Histogram of adjacent pixel differences along the DCT block boundaries

Embedding operations on modifying the DCT coefficients would make the boundaries of DCT blocks in the decompressed spatial domain more discontinuous. So, distributional characteristic of pixel differences at the side locations in the DCT blocks would help to capture the discontinuous property. We calculate it by (9) as following.

$$H_8(e) = \sum_{r=1}^{M/8} \sum_{c=1}^{N/8} (\sum_{j=1}^{8} \varphi(e, b_{r,c}(1, j) - b_{r,c}(2, j)) + \sum_{i=1}^{8} \varphi(e, b_{r,c}(i,1) - b_{r,c}(i, 2))) \tag{9}$$

where $b_{r,c}(i, j)$ is the pixel value in the decompressed spatial domain corresponding to $dct_{r,c}(i, j)$.

Co-occurrence Matrix of adjacent pixel differences

Similar to the feature extraction in DCT domain, we introduce co-occurrence matrix in the spatial domain. Adjacent pixel differences would enlarge the discontinuous property in stego images, so we can calculate the co-occurrence matrix of adjacent pixel differences to depict this characteristic.

$$C_9(e1, e2) = \sum_{i=1}^{M} \sum_{j=1}^{N-2} \varphi(e1, b(i,j) - b(i,j+1)) \cdot \varphi(e2, b(i,j+1) - b(i,j+2)) +$$
$$\sum_{i=1}^{M-2} \sum_{j=1}^{N} \varphi(e1, b(i,j) - b(i+1,j)) \cdot \varphi(e2, b(i+1,j) - b(i+2,j)) \tag{10}$$

As mentioned above, nine statistical models are constructed in either DCT domain or spatial domain.

3   Features Calculation

In this section, we calculate the feature vector from the statistical models presented in Section 2.

3.1   Image Calibration

Image calibration is used to accurate the obtained statistics. In [8], Fridrich has proposed the idea of image calibration to estimate the statistics of the original images. We can get the calibrated JPEG image from the given one by decompressing, cropping and recompressing processes. The author claimed that the statistics of the calibrated image is perceptually similar to the cover image. As a result, the difference between features collected from the calibrated image and its original version will more sensitive to the embedding changes. Features are calculated as below:

$$f = F(J_1) - F(J_2) \tag{11}$$

where F indicates the feature extraction functions, J1 and J2 correspond to the detected JPEG image and its calibrated version.

3.2   Global Features

Harmsen et al. [7] have proposed to use "histogram characteristic function (HCF)" and "center of mass (COM)" to estimate the embedding changes in frequency domain of statistical models. HCF is a representation of a histogram in the frequency domain, and COM can be introduced as a measure of the energy distribution in the HCF. We calculate the COM of all statistical models presented in Section 2 and call them "global features".

For each histogram, we can take its 1-dimensional Discrete Fourier Transform as its HCF. Then the COM can be calculated using (12). For each co-occurrence matrix, the 2-dimensional Discrete Fourier Transform can be considered as the HCF, and the COM in each dimension can be calculated by (13). DFT is central symmetric, so for a DFT sequence with length N, we only need to compute COM in range [1,N/2]. Finally, as shown in Table 2, there are 28 global features in total.

$$COM_1(HCF_1[k]) = \frac{\sum_{k=1}^{N/2} k \cdot |HCF_1[k]|}{\sum_{k=1}^{N/2} |HCF_1[k]|} \tag{12}$$

$$COM_2(HCF_2[k_1,k_2]) = \frac{\sum_{k_1=1}^{N_1/2}\sum_{k_2=1}^{N_2/2} (k_1,k_2) \cdot |HCF_2[k_1,k_2]|}{\sum_{k_1=1}^{N_1/2}\sum_{k_2=1}^{N_2/2} |HCF_2[k_1,k_2]|} \tag{13}$$

3.3   Individual Features

Besides the global features, every element in each statistical model can also be treated as a feature and reflect some statistical changes caused by data hiding, especially the statistical models based on DCT domain. We call them "individual features". Obviously, the number of these features is too large. In fact, most individual features hold little information and are useless. So, we should select a suitable set of elements as the individual features.

In our experimental works reported in this paper, an image set consisting of 1640 JPEG images downloading from Greespun [22] is used. The average of histograms of DCT coefficients is shown as Fig.1 (a). The average of histograms of DCT difference between adjacent DCT blocks is shown in Fig.1 (c). Fig.1 (b) and (d) are the respective histograms corresponding to a randomly selected image in the image set. It is observed that the distributions of the elements are Laplacian-like. The values of mean and standard deviation of percentage number of elements of DCT coefficients and coefficient differences falling into [-T, T] when T = 1, 2, 3, 4, 5, 6, and 7 are shown in Table 1. It is observed that more than 92% elements in the DCT coefficients histogram fall into the interval [-2, 2], and more than 92% elements in the difference histogram fall into the interval [-3, 3].

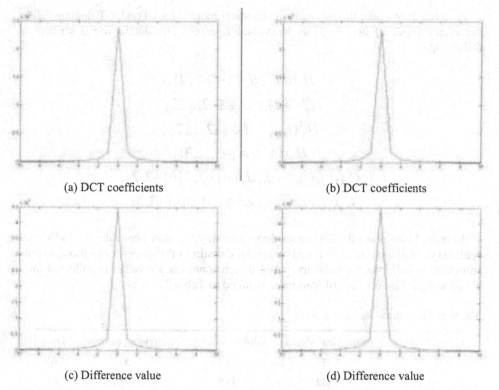

(a) DCT coefficients   (b) DCT coefficients

(c) Difference value   (d) Difference value

Fig. 1. Histogram plots. Part (a) displays average of histograms of DCT coefficients of the image set consisting of 1640 JPEG images. Part (b) displays the histogram of DCT coefficients of a randomly selected image named "aberdeen-boat-lady-85.4" in the image set. Part (c) displays average of histograms of differences of DCT coefficients at the same location between adjacent DCT blocks. Part (d) corresponds to the difference histogram of the selected image named "aberdeen-boat-lady-85.4".

Table 1. Mean and standard deviation of percentage numbers of elements of DCT coefficients and coefficients differences falling within [-T, T] for T = 1, 2, 3, 4, 5, 6 and 7

		[-1,1]	[-2,2][1]	[-3,3][2]	[-4,4]	[-5,5]	[-6,6]	[-7,7]
DCT coefficients	Mean (%)	88.81	92.15	93.88	94.96	95.69	96.22	96.62
	Deviation	4.57	3.27	2.52	2.03	1.68	1.42	1.22
coefficients differences	Mean (%)	85.76	90.23	92.56	94.04	95.08	95.84	96.43
	Deviation	5.93	4.50	3.64	3.04	2.60	2.26	1.99

[1] 92.15% of all elements of DCT coefficients fall into the interval [-2, 2], and the standard deviation is 3.27.

[2] 92.56% of all elements of coefficients differences fall into the interval [-3, 3], and the standard deviation is 3.64.

As a result, we take the elements of statistical models based on DCT domain fall in the interval [-2, 2] or [-3, 3] as individual features. The details are described as following.

$$H_1(d), \quad d \in \{-2,...,2\}.$$
$$H_2^{(i,j)}(d), \quad d \in \{-2,...,2\}.$$
$$H_3^d(i,j), \quad d \in \{-2,...,2\}.$$
$$H_4(v), \quad v \in \{-3,...,3\}.$$
$$C_5(d_1,d_2), \quad (d_1,d_2) \in [-2,2] \times [-2,2].$$
$$C_6(v_1,v_2), \quad (v_1,v_2) \in [-3,3] \times [-3,3].$$

In order to decrease the feature set dimensionality, we don't consider the individual features of statistical models based on spatial domain in this paper, even though some information will lose. In summary, a 194-dimensional feature vector is collected for a JPEG image. The final set of features is detailed in Table 2.

Table 2. All features used in our work

	Statistical Models	Global Features	Individual Features	Total
	H1	1	5	6
	H2	1×8	5×8	48
	H3	2×5	8×5	50
DCT Domain	H4	1	7	8
	C5	2	5×5	27
	C6	2	7×7	51
	H7	1	0	1
Spatial Domain	H8	1	0	1
	C9	2	0	2
Total		28	166	194

4   Experimental Results and Discussions

4.1   Image Set

As mentioned in Section 3, we create an image set consisting of 1640 natural color images which are downloaded from Greenspun [22]. These images span decades of digital and traditional photography and consist of a broad range of indoor and outdoor scenes. For each image, we crop it to a central 640×480 pixel area and compress it with a quality factor of 75 to generate the cover image.

Our experiments focus on attacking five popular JPEG steganographic methods: JPHide [15], Outguess2 [16], Steghide [17], MB1 [18] and MB2 [19]. A reasonable way to define embedding rate is to consider a ratio between message lengths to non-zero DCT coefficients. The ratio is often measured in the unit of bpnc (bits per non-zero JPEG DCT coefficients). In our experiments, we embed into each cover image with a random binary stream of different ratio — 0.05, 0.10, 0.20, 0.30bpnc for a given image.

4.2   SVM Classifier

The foundations of support vector machine (SVM) were developed by [20] and gained much popularity due to many attractive features and promising empirical performance. A classification task usually involves with training and testing data which consist of some data instances. Each instance in the training set contains one "target value" (class labels) and several "attributes" (features). The goal of SVM is to produce a model which predicts target value of data instances in the testing set which are given only the attributes.

In our work, we use LibSVM [21] to construct the classifiers. LibSVM is a publicly available library for SVM, and it provides some automatic model selection tools for classification. For convenience, we use the provided tools, such as *svm-scale*, *svm-train* and *svm-predict*, to construct classifiers in the following experiments. Prior to training, all elements for the feature vector are scaled to the interval [-1, 1] by using *svm-scale*. The scaling parameters are always derived from the training set and applied to the testing set. The tool *svm-trian* is used to generate the model, and *svm-predict* is used to predict target value of the testing data.

4.3   Experimental Results

In this subsection, experimental results are presented to evaluate the performance of our method. In this experiment, we construct SVM classifiers to distinguish cover images from stego images embedded with five popular steganographic methods (JPHide, Outguess2, Steghide, MB1 and MB2). We randomly select 500 cover images and their corresponding stego images to train the SVM classifier, and the remaining images to test the trained classifier. We also construct such classifiers with four known similar steganalytic methods (Fridrich's [8], Fu et al.'s [9], Shi et al.'s [10] and Chen et al.'s [11]) the same way. The results shown in Table 3 are the arithmetic average of 20 random experiments. TPR, TNR represent the true positive rate and the true negative rate, and AR is the final accuracy rate, calculated as AR= (TNR+TPR)/2.

Table 3. Performance comparison with other popular blind steganalysis (in the unit of %)

	bpnc	Fridrich's			Fu et al.'s			Shi et al.'s			Chen et al.'s			Our Proposed		
		TNR	TPR	AR	TNR	TPR	AR	TNR	TPR	AR	TNR	TPR	AR	TNR	TPR	AR
JPHide	0.05	88.28	60.44	74.36	85.51	14.55	50.03	36.68	63.61	50.14	37.69	62.56	50.13	97.09	60.86	**78.97**[*]
	0.10	87.91	66.66	77.28	81.79	26.23	54.01	40.71	63.89	52.30	34.18	71.97	53.08	96.96	71.95	**84.46**
	0.20	90.00	79.15	84.58	83.15	75.68	79.41	71.18	80.55	75.86	66.14	74.41	70.27	97.83	89.10	**93.47**
	0.30	96.19	88.11	92.15	94.27	92.81	93.54	95.08	94.93	95.01	92.68	92.90	92.79	99.40	96.39	**97.90**
Outguess2	0.05	63.10	68.68	65.89	85.69	25.61	55.65	65.05	60.43	62.74	85.09	77.91	81.50	95.69	93.46	**94.58**
	0.10	84.71	90.45	87.58	88.85	57.13	72.99	85.07	92.12	88.60	97.20	97.40	97.30	99.71	98.73	**99.22**
	0.20	98.94	98.70	98.82	98.05	96.95	97.50	98.44	99.49	98.96	99.40	99.45	99.43	99.99	99.01	**99.50**
	0.30	99.81	98.82	99.31	99.59	94.86	97.23	99.69	99.30	99.49	99.76	99.44	99.60	100.00	99.20	**99.64**
Steghide	0.05	38.80	73.12	55.96	85.17	20.70	52.93	62.89	49.62	56.26	67.74	63.51	65.62	69.88	72.25	**71.06**
	0.10	44.73	72.78	58.76	85.55	22.65	54.10	58.37	60.25	59.31	76.16	72.32	74.24	76.93	78.74	**77.83**
	0.20	55.39	73.75	64.57	83.43	34.28	58.86	66.84	68.54	67.69	90.23	84.61	87.42	86.67	88.88	**87.77**
	0.30	60.81	76.99	68.90	85.73	41.40	63.57	77.28	80.18	78.73	94.64	91.90	93.27	93.70	93.66	**93.68**
MB1	0.05	44.47	67.75	56.11	84.97	26.92	55.94	72.84	43.18	58.01	82.71	27.55	55.13	69.56	69.56	**69.56**
	0.10	53.98	73.63	63.80	90.14	57.75	73.94	83.20	72.07	77.63	82.17	71.11	76.64	85.89	86.55	**86.22**
	0.20	72.93	82.61	77.77	93.48	98.13	95.80	96.80	98.11	97.45	96.19	99.35	**97.77**	97.61	96.61	97.11
	0.30	85.96	88.56	87.26	97.16	99.62	98.39	99.46	99.68	99.57	99.59	99.99	**99.79**	99.65	99.18	99.41
MB2	0.05	42.67	69.73	56.20	81.63	31.62	56.63	71.18	52.32	61.75	76.68	41.23	58.95	73.65	72.25	**72.95**
	0.10	59.69	68.39	64.04	89.13	48.59	68.86	81.68	86.98	84.33	77.07	88.54	82.81	89.34	88.75	**89.05**
	0.20	75.21	74.96	75.08	92.47	95.70	94.09	98.05	99.00	98.53	97.68	99.66	**98.67**	99.04	97.45	98.25
	0.30	85.11	78.69	81.90	98.12	98.98	98.55	99.62	99.77	99.70	99.71	99.96	**99.84**	99.89	99.35	99.62

[*] The highest accuracy rate among the five universal steganalytic schemes are emphasized with bold.

Table 4. Detection accuracy with individual statistical model (in the unit of %)

	bpnc	H1 TNR	H1 TPR	H1 AR	H2 TNR	H2 TPR	H2 AR	H3 TNR	H3 TPR	H3 AR	H4 TNR	H4 TPR	H4 AR
JPHide	0.05	76.79	41.33	59.06	94.99	67.08	79.96	91.27	54.58	72.24	80.12	37.57	58.90
	0.10	74.31	47.72	61.02	94.82	77.73	87.02	89.89	68.14	78.29	78.87	39.81	59.56
Outguess2	0.05	59.93	57.47	58.70	78.05	73.06	75.88	79.77	75.89	77.15	71.27	66.52	69.34
	0.10	66.28	68.17	67.22	92.22	89.30	90.39	93.06	90.82	92.15	84.68	78.69	82.29
Steghide	0.05	52.21	57.53	54.87	58.28	54.43	56.49	59.69	54.48	57.46	60.05	62.18	60.92
	0.10	56.61	56.09	56.35	59.36	59.63	59.65	61.35	60.47	61.18	65.19	65.22	65.22
MB1	0.05	59.61	50.00	54.80	63.47	53.68	58.38	65.75	50.89	57.98	56.26	62.02	59.78
	0.10	65.09	53.24	59.17	72.19	57.58	64.25	71.04	57.17	64.61	66.58	70.21	68.42
MB2	0.05	52.05	58.05	55.05	64.45	54.08	59.08	66.97	50.66	58.82	60.48	62.38	61.58
	0.10	60.89	59.24	60.06	73.64	59.80	66.89	73.01	59.05	65.44	70.70	71.48	70.75

	bpnc	C5 TNR	C5 TPR	C5 AR	C6 TNR	C6 TPR	C6 AR	H7,H8,C9 TNR	H7,H8,C9 TPR	H7,H8,C9 AR
JPHide	0.05	79.48	48.87	63.68	82.14	36.80	58.55	54.75	56.82	55.79
	0.10	76.73	52.92	64.56	81.46	37.78	59.56	54.97	57.91	56.44
Outguess2	0.05	92.72	89.10	90.39	87.98	85.36	87.46	75.08	35.46	55.27
	0.10	99.14	97.63	98.47	98.17	95.84	96.93	63.69	57.99	60.84
Steghide	0.05	66.35	70.11	68.25	64.31	61.97	63.68	68.36	42.03	55.20
	0.10	72.74	77.45	75.39	69.10	67.53	68.55	70.17	45.27	57.52
MB1	0.05	69.75	70.43	71.27	61.35	61.41	61.36	63.61	37.36	50.49
	0.10	84.62	84.84	85.22	68.75	70.91	69.96	68.52	43.47	56.00
MB2	0.05	71.99	71.71	70.79	60.93	62.96	61.36	70.08	41.09	55.59
	0.10	86.82	86.71	86.45	74.09	74.63	74.39	66.00	50.05	58.03

As we can see, our proposed method provides the best detection accuracy among all in detecting JPHide, Outguess2 and Steghide, no matter whether the embedding rate is low (0.05, 0.10bpnc) or high (0.20, 0.30bpnc). In detecting MB1 and MB2, our method is much better than other four steganalytic methods when the embedding data is small (0.05, 0.10bpnc), and has a similar performance as Fu et al.'s, Shi et al.'s and Chen et al.'s when the embedding rate is high (0.20, 0.30bpnc) – the difference of the accuracy rate between our method's and the best scheme's is little than 1%. So we can conclude that our method provides the best detection performance on JPEG steganography among all.

We also conduct the experiments with each statistical model presented in Section 2. The number of features calculated from each statistical model based on decompressed spatial domain is small, so we consider them as integrity in this experiment. The results are shown in Table 4 and are the arithmetic average of 20 random experiments.

Comparing with Table 3 and Table 4, we can observe that combining all these statistical models has enhanced the detection rate in attacking JPEG steganography.

5   Conclusion

In this paper, we propose an effective universal steganalytic method for detecting JPEG steganography. The main contributions of this paper can be summarized as follows.

(1)   Statistical models are collected in both the DCT domain and the decompressed spatial domain for JPEG images. These statistics reflect the tiny differences between a cover image and its corresponding stego image.

(2)   The concepts of histogram characteristic function (HCF) and center of mass (COM) are used to calculate the energy distribution of each statistical model in frequency domain as the "global feature". Besides, some suitable elements which hold main information about the statistics of DCT coefficients are selected as the "individual feature". They formed the feature set for steganalysis.

(3)   By testing its performance on detecting some popular JPEG steganography: JPHide, Outguess2, Steghide, MB1 and MB2, our proposed method can achieve the best performance compared with the similar steganalytic schemes reported recently.

References

1. Fridrich, J., Goljan, M., Hogea, D.: Steganalysis of JPEG Images: Breaking the F5 Algorithm. In: Proceedings of the 5th Information Hiding Workshop, Lecture Notes in Computer Science, pp.310--323 (2002)
2. Fridrich, J., Goljan, M., Hogea, D.: Attacking the Outguess. In: ACM Multimedia 2002 Workshop W2 - Workshop on Multimedia and Security: Authentication, Secrecy, and Steganalysis, pp.3--6 (2002)
3. Zhang, T., Ping, X. J.: A new approach to reliable detection of LSB steganography in natural images. Signal Process, 83:2085—93 (2003)

4. Avcibas, I., Memon, N., Sankur, B.: Steganalysis Based on Image Quality Metrics. In: IEEE 4th Workshop on Multimedia Signal Processing, pp.517—522 (2001)

5. Avcibas, I., Khrrazi, M., Memon, N., Sankur, B.: Image steganalysis with binary similarity measures. EURASIP Journal on Applied Signal Processing, 17, pp.2749—2757 (2005)

6. Lyu, S., Farid, H.: Detecting Hidden Messages Using Higher-Order Statistics and Support Vector Machines. In: Proc. of 5th International Workshop on Information Hiding, pp.340—354 (2002)

7. Harmsen, J.J., Pearlman, W.A.: Steganalysis of Additive Noise Modelable Information Hiding. In: Proceedings of SPIE - The International Society for Optical Engineering, v.5020, pp.131—142 (2003)

8. Fridrich, J.: Feature-based Steganalysis for JPEG Images and Its Implications for Future Design of Steganographic Schemes. In: Proc. 6th Int. Information Hiding Workshop, pp.67—81 (2004)

9. Fu, D.D., Shi, Y.Q, Zou, D.K., Xuan, G.R.: JPEG steganalysis using empirical transition matrix in block DCT domain. In: IEEE 8th International Workshop on Multimedia Signal Processing, pp.310-313 (2006).

10. Shi, Y.Q., Chen, C.H., Chen, W.: A Markov process based approach to effective attacking JPEG steganography. In: Proc. of the 8th Information Hiding Workshop, pp.249-264 (2007).

11. Chen, C.H., Shi, Y.Q.: JPEG image steganalysis utilizing both intrablock and interblock correlations. In: IEEE International Symposium on Circuits and Systems, pp.3029-3032 (2008).

12. Shi, Y.Q., Chen, C., Chen, W.: A Markov process based approach to effective attacking JPEG steganography. In: Proc. of 8th International Workshop on Information Hiding, pp.249—264 (2006)

13. Westfeld, A.: F5-a steganographic algorithm: high capacity despite better steganalysis. In: Proc. of the 4th Information Hiding Workshop, pp.289-302 (2001).

14. Jsteg, http://ftp.funet.fi/pub/crypt/steganography/.

15. Jphide&Seek, http://linux01.gwdg.de/~alatham/stego.html.

16. Provos, N.: Defending against statistical steganalysis. In: Proc. of the 10th Usenix Security Symposium, pp.323-335 (2001).

17. Stefan, H., Petra, M.A.: graph-theoretic approach to steganography. In: Proc of the 9th IFIP TC-6 TC-11 International Conference, pp.119-128 (2005).

18. Sallee, P.: Model based steganography. In: Proc. of the 2nd International Workshop on Digital Watermarking, pp.154–167 (2004).

19. Sallee, P.: Model-based methods for steganography and steganalysis. International Journal of Image and Graphics, 5(1) pp.167-189 (2005).

20. Corteo, C., Vapnik, V.: Support-Vector Networks. Machine Learning, vol.20, pp. 273—297 (1995)

21. Chang, C.C., Lin, C.J.: LIBSVM: A Library for Support Vector Machines, http://www.csie.ntu.edu.tw/~cjlin/libsvm

22. Greenspun Image Library, http://philip.greenspun.com

A Polarization Restraint Based Fast Motion Estimation Approach to H.264 Stereoscopic Video Coding

Mingjing Ai[1], Lili Zhao[1], Yongmei Zhu[1], Qinping Zhao[1],

[1] State Key Laboratory of Virtual Reality Technology and Systems, Beihang University, Beijing, China
{amj@buaa.edu.cn, behe85@163.com, wczym@yahoo.com.cn, zhaoqp@moe.edu.cn}

Abstract. An efficient polarization restraint based fast motion estimation algorithm for H.264 stereoscopic video coding is proposed in this paper. For parallel binocular-camera systems, there exists a certain principle called polarization restraint, according to which, for the object in a 3D scene, there is no vertical disparity between its projection point on the left plane and that on the right plane. The Motion Estimation (ME) complexity in the right view channel can be greatly reduced by adopting the algorithm presented in this paper. Experimental results show that, compared with the Full Search Block Match Algorithm (FSBMA), the number of search candidates of the proposed algorithm are only 1/136 of that of the FSBMA with similar decoded video quality. Besides, the computation complexity of the proposed algorithm is lower than that of Diamond Search (DS) and of Three Step Search (TSS) with much better decoded pictures' quality.

Keywords: polarization restraint, stereoscopic video coding, H.264, parallel binocular-camera

1 Introduction

Compared with mono-view video, stereoscopic video can give users vivid information about the scene structure, since it can provide the users with a sense of depth perception by showing two frames to each eye simultaneously. However, stereoscopic video coding systems require much more computational complexity than mono-view video coding systems. Video coding standard H.264 was developed by the ITU-T SG16 Q.6 Video Coding Experts Group (VCEG) and the ISO/IEC JTC1/SC29/WG11 Moving Picture Experts Group (MPEG). H.264 saves nearly 50% bits compared with H.263 and MPEG-4, which contributes to reduce the video bit rates. However, computational complexity is still a crucial problem that needs to be solved for stereoscopic video coding.

There is strong correlation among pictures from the two channels of stereoscopic video system, in which motion estimation (ME) removes the temporal redundancy while disparity estimation (DE) removes the inter-view redundancy. H.264 adopts blocked based motion estimation (ME) while encoding a block [1]. To take coding efficiency into consideration as well as have better compatibility with the existing

M.L. Huang et al. (eds.), *Visual Information Communication*,
DOI 10.1007/978-1-4419-0312-9_23, © Springer Science+Business Media, LLC 2010

video coding standard, block-based DE, like ME, is adopted in H.264 based stereoscopic video coding systems. As a result, the prediction part, which consists of ME and DE, becomes the most computationally intensive part in a stereoscopic video coding system. Therefore, an efficient prediction scheme is necessary for stereoscopic video encoding.

Lots of fast motion estimation search algorithms, such as Three Step Search (TSS), Diamond Search (DS), Logarithm Search (LS) etc., have been presented to speed up mono-view video coding [2], which, however, can still not satisfy certain real-time application when they are used in stereoscopic video coding, what is more, the quality of the decoded pictures can not be guaranteed. For two parallel cameras, there is intensive relation between motion vectors (MVs) and disparity vectors (DVs) in neighboring frames. By utilizing the inter-view correlation, a fast motion estimation with inter-view motion vector prediction for stereoscopic and multi-view video coding scheme has been proposed to reduce computational redundancy [3], which, however, didn't fully remove the inter-view redundancy of a parallel binocular-camera system and to great extent needs improving.

For parallel binocular-camera systems, there exists a certain principle called polarization restraint, that is, the two epipolar lines on the left and the right projection planes are superposed, which makes them into a single straight line. According to polarization restraint, for the object in the 3D environment, there is no vertical disparity between its projection point on the left plane and that on the right plane.

In this paper, an efficient H.264 based fast motion estimation algorithm for right-view images of stereoscopic video is proposed after analyzing the polarization restraint of parallel binocular-camera system.

This paper is organized as follows: the H.264 based stereoscopic video coding systems are introduced in Section 2, the polarization restraint principle is introduced in Section 3, the details of the proposed algorithm is presented in Section 4, experimental results are shown in Section 5, and we conclude this paper in Section 6.

2   H.264 Based Stereoscopic Video Coding Schemes

There are mainly three schemes in H.264 based stereoscopic video coding system, as shown in **Fig. 1**, in which grey blocks and white blocks respectively represent the coding blocks in the left and the right channel [4].

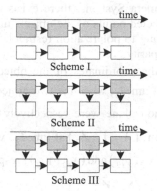

Fig. 1. H.264 based stereo video coding schemes

In scheme I, images in both the left and the right channels are encoded with motion compensation prediction (MCP) respectively by an H.264/AVC encoder, which does not utilize the correlation between the two channels at all, and thus has very low coding efficiency.

In scheme II, images in the left channel are encoded with MCP by an H.264/AVC encoder while images in the right channel are encoded with only disparity compensation prediction (DCP), which utilizes the spatial correlation between the two video channels, the temporal correlation among pictures in the same channel is not considered, however.

In scheme III, images in the left channel are encoded with MCP by an H.264/AVC encoder while images in the right channels are encoded both with MCP and DCP, which to a great extent removes both temporal redundancy among pictures in the same channel and spatial redundancy between pictures in the left and the right channel.

Based on the above analysis, scheme III is adopted to test the proposed algorithm in this paper.

3   Polarization Restraint in the Parallel Binocular-camera Systems

A point in the World Coordinate System and the two camera optical centers define a plane called the Epipolar Plane. The two intersection lines of the Epipolar plane and two projection planes are the Conjugate Epipolar Lines, on which there are projected points of an object in a 3D scene [4].

The proposed algorithm in this paper is based on a Parallel Binocular-Camera System, in which the optical axis of the left camera and that of the right camera are parallel, and the two cameras' projection centers have the same vertical offset. As a result, the two epipolar lines on the left and the right projection plane are superposed, making them into a single straight horizontal line which is called polarized line. For the Parallel Binocular-Camera Systems, there exists a principle called polarization restraint, namely, the projected points of the objects in a 3D scene are always on the polarized line [5]. According to polarization restraint, the two projected points of an object have no vertical disparity.

As shown in **Fig. 2**, the coordinates of the object W in the World Coordinate System was (X_1, Y_1, Z_1) at time t_1, when the two projected points' coordinates on the left and the right projection plane were respectively (x_{l1}, y_{l1}) and (x_{r1}, y_{r1}). Then object W moved to location (X_2, Y_2, Z_2) at time t_2, when the two projected points' coordinates changed into (x_{l2}, y_{l2}) and (x_{r2}, y_{r2}), respectively.

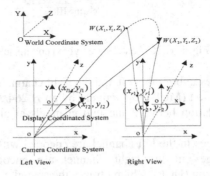

Fig. 2. Parallel binocular-camera system projection model

According to polarization restraint, the two projected points of object W have non-zero horizontal offset but zero vertical offset. Therefore, we have in **Fig. 2** the following set of equations:

$$y_{l1} = y_{r1} \tag{1}$$

$$y_{l2} = y_{r2} \tag{2}$$

Suppose Δy_l and Δy_r respectively represent the two projected points' vertical offset of object W on the two projection planes, namely:

$$\Delta y_l = y_{l1} - y_{l2} \tag{3}$$

$$\Delta y_r = y_{r1} - y_{r2} \tag{4}$$

Thus,

$$\Delta y_l = \Delta y_r \tag{5}$$

4   A Polarization Restraint Based Fast Motion Estimation for Stereoscopic Video Coding

Block based ME as well as DE is adopted in H.264 based stereoscopic video coding systems. H.264 adopts a tree-structure partition mode, in which a macroblock may be partitioned in 7 modes: 16×16,16×8,8×16,8×8,8×4,4×8 and 4×4 luma samples and associated chroma samples [1].

DE is done before a macroblock of a right-view image is encoded with ME. For example, a matched sub-macroblock $block_l$ of $block_r$ in the right-view image can be got by DE, as shown in**Fig. 3**, where the solid line blocks in the right and the left image represent the sub-macroblock to be encoded with ME and its matched sub-macroblcok after DE, respectively. The two black dotted line blocks in **Fig. 3** represent the optimal matched blocks of the current blocks in the previous frames, and $mv_l(x, y)$ and $mv_r(x, y)$ are the Motion Vectors (MVs) of the current sub-macroblocks $block_l$ and $block_r$, respectively.

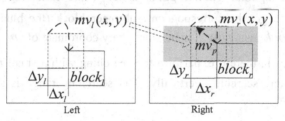

Fig. 3. Illustration of proposed MV prediction

According to equation (5) in section 3, the y coordinate of $mv_l(x, y)$ is equal to that of $mv_r(x, y)$ in **Fig. 3**.

Based on the above analysis, a polarization restraint based fast estimation approach to the right-view images is presented in this paper. The details of the proposed scheme are described as follows:

Step I. After DE for the sub-macroblock $block_r$ in current right-view frame, a matched block $block_l$ in the left-view frame was found, whose MV is proposed to provide an initial guess of MV for the $block_r$, which is to say, $mv_l(x, y)$ is assigned to variable mv_p, as illustrated in **Fig. 3**, where mv_p is an initial value of $mv_r(x, y)$.

Step II. The MVs of the left, top, and top-right neighboring blocks of $block_r$ are also used to predict an initial value of $mv_r(x, y)$ as in H.264. Namely, another 3 initial guesses, mv_{pl}, mv_{pt} and mv_{ptr}, might be assigned to $mv_r(x, y)$.

Step III. The optimum initial guess is chosen from mv_p, mv_{pl}, mv_{pt} and mv_{tr} by Lagrangian function.

$$J_{mv}(S_k, MV_p \mid \lambda_{mv}) = D(S_k, MV_p) + \lambda_{mv} \times R(S_k, MV_p) \tag{6}$$

Where, $MV_p \in (mv_p, mv_{pl}, mv_{pt}, mv_{ptr})$, S_k represents block samples to be encoded, $D(S_k, MV_p)$ is the rate distortion calculated using the predictor MV_p, and $R(S_k, MV_p)$ is the bit rates generated by encoding value MV_p. Finally, the MV_p that makes Lagrange value $J_{mv}(S_k, MV_p \mid \lambda_{mv})$ minimum is chosen as the optimum initial guess of $mv_r(x, y)$.

Step IV. If the optimum initial guess is one of those mv_{pl}, mv_{pt} and mv_{ptr}, the Full Search Block Match Algorithm (FSBMA) is adopted.

Else, if the optimum initial guess is mv_p, the following search scheme is performed: first, get the correspondent sub-macroblock (the blue dotted line block in**Fig. 3**) of $block_r$ using mv_p; then, since the y coordinate of $mv_r(x, y)$ is equal to that of $mv_l(x, y)$, therefore, perform the searching with a small range horizontally, and don't do any searching vertically. The searching range is shown as the grey region in **Fig. 3**.

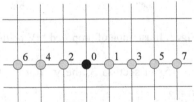

Fig. 4. Searching order of proposed algorithm

The horizontal searching order of the proposed scheme is illustrated in **Fig. 4**, where the black point is the initial search location and the grey points represent the search candidates within the search range. The numbers beside the samples illustrate the searching order.

5   Experimental Results and Analysis

The proposed algorithm in this paper is compared with FSBMA [6]. The illustrations of the coding structure are shown as scheme III in **Fig. 1**. It is implemented by modifying JM10.2 [7][8]. Rate-distortion performance of only right channel is compared because the ME parts in the left channel in both cases are implemented with FSBMA. The first 30 frames of sequences "Booksale", "Crowd" and "Soccer", with size 320×240 and encoding frame rate 30f/s, are tested. The search ranges of ME in the left channel as well as that of DE in the right channel in both cases are [-16, +16] in horizontal and vertical directions.

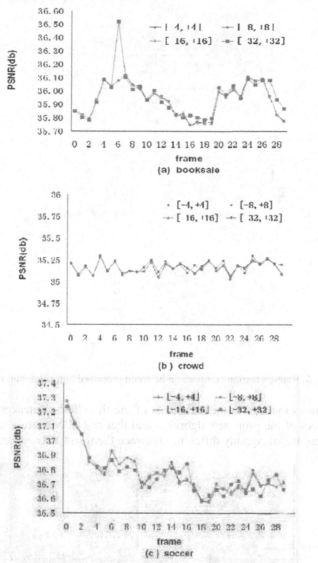

Fig. 5. Coding performance of the proposed scheme with different search ranges

Fig. 5 illustrates the proposed algorithm's coding performance curves of the three test sequences with different horizontal search ranges. It is shown that the performance curves with search ranges [-4, +4], [-8, +8] and [-16, +16] are almost superposed, and only very few frames show better coding performance with range [-32, +32], namely, there is no apparent higher performance when the horizontal search range is [-32, +32]. That is to say, the horizontal search range [-4, +4] is sufficient. Therefore, the search range of the proposed algorithm in this paper is set as [-4, +4].

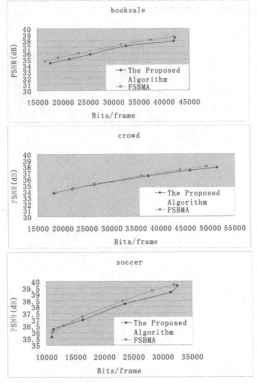

Fig. 6. Rate-distortion comparison between proposed algorithm and FSBMA

Fig. 6 shows the rate-distortion curves of the three test sequences. It is observed that the curves of the proposed algorithm and that of FSBMA are almost superposed meaning there is little quality difference between them and so our search range [-4, +4] is accurate.

(a)   (b)

Fig. 7. Reconstructed frames comparison.(a) FSBMA.(b) the proposed algorithm.

The reconstructed frames of the 25th frames in "Booksale" sequences with quantization step QP =28 is shown in **Fig. 7**, where, (a) is the result of FSBMA and (b) is that of the proposed algorithm. It can be seen that the two reconstructed frames are the same with each other with subjective visual standard.

Table 1. PSNR and number of search candidates

Number of search candidates / PSNR(dB)	Test Sequences		
	Booksale	Crowd	Soccer
The proposed algorithm	8/38.654	8/37.996	8/39.679
FSBMA	1089/38.681	1089/38.006	1089/39.727
DS	76/38.452	76/37.798	976/39.446
TSS	24/38.352	24/37.769	24/39.55

Table 1 shows the number of search candidates when pictures are coded respectively with four algorithms and the correspondent luma PSNR value.

Suppose λ (algorithm) $= \dfrac{N_{(algorithm)}}{N_{pa}}$, where, N_{pa} denotes the number of search candidates of the new algorithm presented in this paper while $N_{(algorithm)}$ represents that of the FSBMA, DS or TSS, and Δ (algorithm) is the result of the decoded pictures' PSNR encoded by FSBMA, DS or TSS minus by the PSNR of which are encoded with the proposed algorithm.

Table 2. ME complexity reduction and PSNR loss.

λ (algorithm)/ Δ (algorithm)	Test Sequences		
	Booksale	Crowd	Soccer
λ (FSBMA)/ Δ (FSBMA)	136/0.027	136/0.010	136/0.048
λ (DS)/ Δ (DS)	9.5/-0.202	9.5/-0.198	9.5/-0.233
λ (TSS)/ Δ (TSS)	3/-0.302	3/-0.227	3/-0.120

Table 2 shows ME complexity reduction and Luma PSNR loss. Compared with FSBMA, the proposed algorithm's ME complexity is greatly reduced as can be seen that the number of search candidates of the proposed algorithm is only 1/136 of that in FSBMA while the PSNR loss is only less than 0.05 dB meaning that the video quality can still be maintained. The search candidates number of the proposed is 1/9.5 and 1/3 of that in DS and in TSS respectively, but the decoded pictures quality with the proposed algorithm is much better than that with DS and TSS. Therefore, the proposed polarization based fast motion estimation algorithm in this paper is efficient.

6   Conclusion

A polarization restraint based fast motion estimation approach to H.264 stereoscopic video coding is proposed in this paper. Based on polarization restraint, the proposed algorithm can greatly reduce ME complexity by decrease the search candidates to

1/136 that of FSBMA with only 0.01-0.05 dB quality degradation. In the mean time, the computation complexity of the proposed algorithm is lower than that of DS and of TSS with much better coding performance. Therefore, the proposed algorithm is efficiently feasible.

References

1. Iain E.G. Richardson: H.264 and MPEG-4 Video Compression-Video Coding for Next-generation Multimedia, John Wiley & Sons Inc, England (2005)
2. Ki Beom Kim, Young Ghu Jeon, and Min-Cheol Hong: Variable Step Search Fast Motion Estimation for H.264/AVC Video Coder , IEEE Trans (2008)
3. Li-Fu Ding, Pei-Kuei Tsung, Wei-Yin Chen, Shao-Yi Chien, and Liang-Gee Chen: Fast Motion Estimation with Inter-view Motion Vector Prediction For Stereo and Multi-view Video Coding , IEEE Trans (2008)
4. Li-Shi Ping: Research on Network Faced Stereoscopic Video Coding and Transmission, Chinese Academic of Sciences (2006)
5. Xu Bin, Yu Mei, Ye Xi-en , and Jiang Gang-yi: A fast disparity estimation algorithm for stereo video coding based on H.264, Journal of Zhejiang University(Science Edition) (2006).
6. Chen Zhi-bo, Zhou Peng, and He Yun: Fast Integer Pixel and Fractional Pixel Motion Estimotion for JVT, JVT-F017, Japan (2002)
7. Keng-Pang Lim, Gary Sullivan, and Thomas Wiegand: Text Description of Joint Model Reference Encoding Methods and Decoding Concealment Methods, JVT-O079, Korea (2005)
8. ITU-T Rec. H.264| ISO/IEC 11496-10 AVC[S]. JM10.2

Multi-core Parallel of Photon Mapping

Huaiqing He [1], Tianbao Wang [2], Qing Xu [3], Yaoyu Xing [4]

[1,2,4] College of Computer Science and Technology,
Civil Aviation University of China, Tianjin 300300,China
[3] School of Computer Science and Technology, Tianjin University,Tianjin,China
{ huaiqinghe@yahoo.com.cn, violin_wang@yahoo.cn, qingxu@tju.edu.cn,
yaoyuxing@163.com}

Abstract. By analyzing the internal parallelism in the rendering stage of photon mapping and by learning the idea of ray tracing in parallel, this paper carries out the photon mapping in parallel in multi-core processors. It solves the problem of load balancing through dynamic scheduling the refined data blocks. The improved algorithm achieves good acceleration ratio using multi-threaded programming language of OpenMP. The experimental results show that the improved algorithm has better performance and improves the rendering speed of the photon map algorithm to a certain extent.

Keywords: multi-core, photon mapping, parallel rendering, dynamic scheduling

1   Introduction

In recent years, it is not only a slogan that the microprocessor will carry out "multi-core" style, and it has become the reality we have to face every day. The technology of multi-core system integrates more implementation core in a single integrated package, and every core has its own logic unit, control unit, computing unit, first cache, shared or unique secondary cache. The integrity of multi-core system components is exactly the same compared with the kernel of single-core processor, which offers material basis for really parallel realization. So it has become a matter of concern that how to design parallel algorithms and compile parallel applications to give full play to the advantages of resources in multi-core architecture.

As the development of graphics rendering such as video games, cartoon execution in movies, industrial modeling, science simulation and so on, it is a severe challenge to the methods on traditional graphics rendering that how to deal with the image detail and massive data processing better. One of the effective ways to solve this challenge is parallel drawing, and the photon mapping based on the framework of tracing algorithm is an important research component of rendering realistic images. This paper aims to discuss the parallel rendering stage of photon mapping under multi-core architecture, and make use of various means to deal with load balancing in order to enhance the algorithm performance.

M.L. Huang et al. (eds.), *Visual Information Communication*,   365
DOI 10.1007/978-1-4419-0312-9_24, © Springer Science+Business Media, LLC 2010

2   Related Work

In the field of realistic image rendering, global illumination is one of the key points to study. Ray-tracing [1] and radiosity [2] are two commonly used model of global illumination. Ray tracing is simple, powerful and easy to achieve, but it cannot deal with the effects such as bleeding, caustics commonly showed in realistic graphics, while radiosity algorithm is not very good to deal with the point light source and gloss surface in addition to the shortcomings of slow speed.

The theory of Photon Mapping is an extension of ray tracing algorithm brought forward by Henrik Wann Jensen in 1995 [3]. The global illumination based on photon mapping is a two-pass algorithm [4]. The first pass is to establish a photon map, it is to shoot photons to the scene through the light source, when the photons hit the surface of non-specula objects, they will be stored in a data structure called photon map. The second pass is the rendering stage, it is, using the classical method of ray tracing to launch light from the light point, to extract incident flux and reflected radiance and other information on the rendering point with statistical principle from the photon map.

Photon map is existing independently of scene geometry, it is the main feature of photon mapping technique which enables it to simulate the overall illumination of complexity scenes including hundreds of millions of triangular films, a lot of geometric objects and objects achieved by a large number of procedures. The advantage of photon mapping algorithm lies on that there is no need to structure any grid compared with the radiosity methods. Even, the calculating speed of photon mapping method does not slow down while the complexity of the scene increases. And the main advantage of photon mapping is the feature of good effectiveness compared with Monte Carlo's ray-tracing methods, the final rendering image is with less noise although it takes additional memory to store photonic information.

Parallel studies have been touched a lot, such as the parallel rendering of radiosity algorithm achieved in the GPU is proposed in literature [5], while literature [6] refers to a kind of new method of photon mapping based on MPI environment, a non-shared memory system, which aims to remove the disadvantages like large calculating and taking amount of memory space of normal photon mapping method. Literature [7] presents a new parallel method of the ray tracing compared with the ray tracing parallel rendering under mixed-mode. And literature [8] introduces a novel framework of photon map, it is the final integration phase to speed up the photon mapping technique using the parallel of a single instruction stream and multiple data stream (SIMD). Making use of MPI (Message Passing Interface), the parallel of photon mapping is studied and carried out mostly based on distributed memory environment of cluster system, but the study on photon mapping parallel appeared in recent years under the multi-core systems is rare. This paper aims to present an algorithm to realize and optimize the parallel of photon mapping using shared storage system environment based on multi-core structure of PC.

3   Analysis and Design of Parallel Mode

3.1   Mathematics base of rending stage

According to the global illumination algorithm of two-pass photon mapping proposed in literature [4], the second step-rendering stage is finished mainly through a way of Distributed Ray Tracing and the mathematics formula (1) for estimating light intensity.

$$L_r(x,\vec{\omega}) = \int_{\Omega_x} f_r(x,\vec{\omega}',\vec{\omega}) L_i(x,\vec{\omega}')(\vec{n}_x \bullet \vec{\omega}') d\vec{\omega}' + L_e(x,\vec{\omega}) \cdot \qquad (1)$$

L_r stands for the reflected light intensity of x point along $\vec{\omega}$ direction, Ω_x is the hemisphere surface along the incident direction while f_r is the Bidirectional Reflectance Distribution Function of x point (BRDF), and L_i is the incident light intensity. The reflected light intensity L_r is required above, and the unknown parameters are the incident light L_i and bidirectional reflectance function f_r at the right equation. We can handle it this way: f_r will be divided into two parts: specular reflection $f_{r,s}$ and diffuse reflection $f_{r,d}$.

$$f_r(x,\vec{\omega}',\vec{\omega}) = f_{r,s}(x,\vec{\omega}',\vec{\omega}) + f_{r,d}(x,\vec{\omega}',\vec{\omega}) \qquad (2)$$

The incident light intensity can be divided into three parts: the direct light $L_{i,l}$ from the light source, the indirect light $L_{i,d}$ through at least one diffuse reflection, and the indirect illumination $L_{i,c}$ after specula reflection or refraction.

$$L_i(x,\vec{\omega}') = L_{i,l}(x,\vec{\omega}') + L_{i,c}(x,\vec{\omega}') + L_{i,d}(x,\vec{\omega}') \qquad (3)$$

We can get formula (4) as follows by above (1), (2), (3).

We can believe that the calculation of the light intensity of a point that could be reflective to the human eye (camera) in a scene can be divided into five parts: direct illumination, specula reflection and specula strong light, caustics, as well as repeated diffuse reflectance, light intensity launched by the point itself, the five parts calculate respectively. The calculation of direct illumination part needs to estimate the light intensity of the photon in the global photon map in order not to track the light line shadow rather than to take the calculation of shadow line by ray tracing. Ray tracing simulates the illumination effect from specula reflection and specula strong light. And the simulation of the caustics phenomenon is obtained through the calculation of caustics photon map. The calculation of repeated diffuse reflectance is completed making use of photon information stored in the photon map while the last part launched by it is solved by photon map that is the same with direct light part. We can conclude the five light intensity parts reflected to the camera lens by some point in a calculation scene can be divided into two major categories: one is the kind through the calculation of photon map (including the global photon map and caustics photon map), and the other is the way of ray tracing (for the surface with non-diffuse reflection). But the two major categories can be taken in parallel design or in the serial style to be realized depending on the mode of task decomposability which is run unattached. This article takes serial design to achieve, mainly due to more synchronization requirements, bigger lock competition, which cause difficulty in optimizing the problem of severe load imbalance.

$$L_r(x,\vec{\omega}) = \int_{\Omega_x} f_r(x,\vec{\omega}',\vec{\omega})L_i(x,\vec{\omega}')\cos\theta_i \, d\omega'_i \qquad (4)$$

$$= \int_{\Omega_x} f_r(x,\vec{\omega}',\vec{\omega})L_{i,l}(x,\vec{\omega}')\cos\theta_i \, d\omega'_i +$$

$$\int_{\Omega_x} f_{r,s}(x,\vec{\omega}',\vec{\omega})(L_{i,c}(x,\vec{\omega}') + L_{i,d}(x,\vec{\omega}'))\cos\theta_i \, d\omega'_i +$$

$$\int_{\Omega_x} f_{r,d}(x,\vec{\omega}',\vec{\omega})L_{i,c}(x,\vec{\omega}')\cos\theta_i \, d\omega'_i +$$

$$\int_{\Omega_x} f_{r,d}(x,\vec{\omega}',\vec{\omega})L_{i,d}(x,\vec{\omega}')\cos\theta_i \, d\omega'_i + L_e(x,\vec{\omega})$$

3.2 Parallel Analysis

The basic idea used in the rendering stage of photon mapping (Phase II) is the theory of ray tracing. And there are two types of ideas to parallel algorithm of ray tracing: One way is to take a pixel point as a single unit and parallel the ray tracing of each pixel point in turn; the other way is to divide the being image into pieces, and carry out the ray tracing of different pixel point of a number of image pieces at the same time. The first method is with smaller parallel size and better load balancing, but it can access pixels only through serial algorithm, while the second method is with larger parallel size and it can access pixels in parallel, but it can't lead to a balanced load.

Our idea is based on the basis of the above first method, but the key factor is on how to access pixel through serial algorithm to improve the parallel efficiency of the rendering phase of photon mapping. During the whole rendering stage of Photon mapping algorithm, we observe, after repeated testing and comparison, that the serial operation with strong associated data flow [9] occupies relatively less time in the rendering stage of photon mapping, while those parallel operations which are able to reflect the theory of the ray-tracing (mainly exist based on a large number of cycles and recursive way) usually account for about 90% of the whole rendering stage time. That is the main reason to implement parallel to the rendering stage. Therefore, we take the derivative/connect (Fork/Join) mode to parallel the design space of "support structure" [10]. The so-called fork/join mode refers to that a main execution unit (UE) derives from a number of sub-execution units (UE), and these sub-execution units can complete a certain part of the whole work concurrently. Usually the main execution units are waiting until all the sub-execution units terminate and connect with each other. To the specific multi-core system of shared memory architecture, the execution unit usually is presented by thread, and the fork/join mode is transferred into the corresponding task of creating the main thread at the beginning of the task, it will derivative sub-thread to complete the corresponding tasks and return to the main thread in the final when the parallel parts need to be handled. The fork/join model is the standard programming model of OpenMP [9], so we can use the multi-threaded programming language of OpenMP to achieve the parallel of photon mapping.

3.3 Design of Parallel Module

Learning from the ideas of parallel ray tracing mentioned above, we combine the benefits of the above two basic parallel ideas to introduce the parallel algorithm which is suitable to rendering phase of photon map. In our designed algorithm, the being image generated by photon mapping is to be divided into n scts of sub-data, each sub-data set is corresponding to a task subset, then each sub-data set further is divided into m sub-blocks to form a kind of queue organization, so there are total n queues, each queue element is as an input data source of the implementation unit. The whole task is divided into $n \times m$ sub-task, we use symbols $T (i, j)$, $i = 1, ... N; j = 1, ... m$ stand for the sub-task of j in the queue of i.

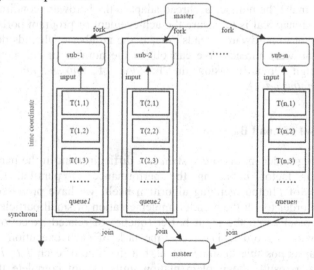

Fig. 1. Parallel implementation model

Fork/join mode is used between the main threads and the sub-threads. Main thread is responsible for importing a variety of photon maps generated in the first phase of photon mapping and carrying out serial operations to the screen division. It derives from n sub-threads after finishing setting the queue size. The main thread is in a state of waiting normally after the sub-threads are derived, but in OpenMP, the main thread transfers into one of many sub-threads and parallel together with other sub-threads. Each derived sub-thread will be destroyed when all sub-threads finish their task and transfer the data dealt with by them to the main thread, then the main thread continues to run to complete the later tasks such as data blocks.

We can note that although this form of multiple input queue can make the task of the various implementation units tend to be average, the processing time needed by each basic data block $T (i, j)$ is so different that each thread cannot complete the task at the same time, as a result, we establish a synchronization point before sub-thread outputs data and the sub-threads will wait until all the sub-threads complete their task to return the main thread synchronously. In OpenMP, the statement of # *pragma omp* provides a sync point, the sub-thread continue the implementation only when the sub-thread runs to this statement and waits until all the sub-threads reach this point.

The number of sub-thread n depends on the number of hardware threads of multi-core system. If n is larger than the number of hardware threads, the mapping relationship from the execution unit (UE) to the hardware threads is many-to-one style, which will lead to a phenomenon that more than one sub-thread compete for one hardware thread resource. In order to ensure that all sub-threads can be run in the hardware thread reasonably, the operating system will frequently involve the operation of sub-threads such as hanging, restoring of threads. Most of the threads system transfers are kernel operation due to the modern operating systems supporting multi-tasking are based on the core-objects, which will cause a lot of system overhead. And if the number of sub-threads is less than the one of hardware threads, the physical hardware resources cannot be fully taken advantage of to avoid wastage. Our solution is to make the number of thread adapt to the hardware conditions dynamical, the so-called dynamical is to ensure the achievement of program portability, and the so-called "adapt to hardware threads" means the number of threads does not exceed the one of hardware threads. We can obtain the number of actual threads and set threads through OpenMP using the function of *omp_get_num_threads ()* and *omp_set_num_threads ()*.

3.4   Disposal of Load Balance

Load balancing under multi-core system is a difficult point in the parallel study and also a major factor impacting the performance of parallel. Combining the characteristics of Photon mapping algorithm itself, we have proposed to refine the data block in order to get the parallel implementation of small particle, and place the refined data blocks into the input buffer (queue) of related execution unit (UE) in accordance with the order. Therefore, the task of each execution unit should be average as far as possible to some extent, but the time of each $T (i, j)$ calculation is not fixed, as a result, the implementation units cannot complete their respective mandates at the same period of time. According to the analysis above, we can add another scheduling module $T (i, j)$ to the main thread, whose main task is dynamic scheduling the remainder $T (i, j)$ to the input queue which is without sub-threads in the late running period of sub-threads. But this scheduling module is not always working; it only can be activated when a thread completes its sub-tasks in the sub-task-queue. The basic process of this scheduling algorithm is: When the input queue of I is an empty set by a sub-thread, the scheduling requests will be applied to the scheduling module which will find the remaining number of T (i, j) inputting the queue by other sub-threads and select appropriate number of T (i, j) of input queue with largest number of remaining to the I sub-thread to schedule. What we are worthy of concern is that it just needs lock competition with the scheduled two other threads, relatively less competition during the process of scheduling. This kind of parallel execution model ensures the higher efficiency and better load balancing between the threads.

3.5 Steps of Rendering Phase

The rendering stage of photon mapping algorithm after multi-threaded parallel can be divided into following interrelated steps: (1) it receives all kinds of data from the first stage of photon mapping, mainly various photon map, and defines the relevant information of image plane. (2) it defines sampler at the image plane and regulates hits as s for each pixels point. (3) it determines the number of sub-threads in accordance with the hardware condition and sets n queues at the same time. (4) it initializes the various sub-threads based on the above parameters, each T (i, j) stands for the light information of different pixel points after sampling for s times. The work of each sub-thread include: pixel sampling, sample tracking in scenario and the calculation of brightness. The thread will activate scheduling module to enter the scheduling when the task of a queue is empty. (5) all sub-threads will output the pixel brightness information to the image flat file.

4   Experimental Results and Analysis

The realization of entire photon mapping algorithm is based on the PBRT rendering system. PBRT is a classic rendering system completed by MattPharr, GregHum phreys and so on. And PBRT is a completely open-source rendering system used for non-commercial purpose. It is written entirely in C + + language, and its various parts are transferred into the main program in the form of type and plug-ins, which guarantees the changes of other parts will be minimized if the relevant parts need improvement. In this system with complex structure and complicated interface, although what we have improved are some of the photon mapping, just the parallel on a particular part cannot improve the overall efficiency of the system effectively. We need to get the parallel of the photon mapping part based on the optimization of the entire system. Therefore, these types provided in the form of plug-ins interface is relatively independent, but they call each other and are interdependent during work, which makes the system very complicated and will encounter unknown difficulties when it is improved.

The hardware environment of Algorithm realization is dual-CPU structure, and each CPU has a core. And Windows XP is the supported operating system while using 1.02 PBRT version. It is realized through the combination of programming language OpenMP and multi-threading programming Win32. And the Intel C + + compiler supporting the OpenMP environment is selected, so it not only can optimize the overall process better, but also is able to deal with and instruct the multi-core Intel processors better. Figure 2 shows the acceleration ratio at optimization when there is no load balancing, in serial and when n = 2,3 (the number of sub-thread).

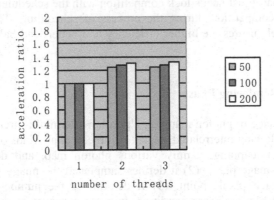

Fig. 2. The acceleration ratio at pre-optimization of load balancing and at after multi-threading

We should pay attention to the above figure, there are three symbols, namely, the experimental results when m = 50,100,200 (the number of T (i, j) input the queue). We can find the acceleration ratios of three legends have little increased with the increase of the number of threads, but the increase extent is limited. The main reason lies in the final stage when the thread deal with the data in queue, while the load imbalance makes a waste of CPU, the other threads still continue to process data.

In addition, we also can find from the previous figure when the number of thread reaches 3, the increase of acceleration ratio for each legend is slow, mainly because we have two hardware threads, when three threads are run, the situation of 3 software threads map 2 hardware threads is formed, it is not one-one mapping, the operating system can only make use of time slice rotating to schedule effectively, which results in a large number of CPU time is occupied on the system scheduling and performance degradation.

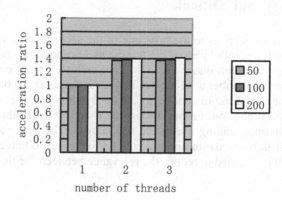

Fig. 3. Acceleration Ratios after Performance Optimization

The efficiency of algorithm is further enhanced after performance optimization (mainly load balancing). As shown in Figure 3, the acceleration ratio is improved to some extent compared former performance, and during all stages of thread increasing, acceleration ratio showed in the three legends is basically the same, the load is well balanced, the impact from the size of divided sub- blocks on the performance is weaken a lot.

Although the performance after Optimization is improved to a certain degree, it is not perfect for performance increase on the whole. The predicted possibilities of the problem are as follows: (1) the difference between hardware, the realization of multi-CPU system and multi-core system is in great distinction that is mainly reflected in the communication issue between the threads. (2) the nature of PBRT rendering platform of large system and complicated internal structure results in inefficiency in parallel. These two issues will be the focuses of the study follow-up. We will further transplant the system to quad-core SMP machine for the research in next stage.

We obtain a certain amount of acceleration ratio, and the performance of algorithm has been improved a lot, but the final rendering image quality gets little change compared with the serial algorithm, like Figure 4 and Figure 5 below, we observe almost no change in image quality with the naked eye.

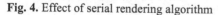

Fig. 4. Effect of serial rendering algorithm   Fig. 5. Effect of multi-thread rendering algorithm

5 Summary and Outlook

Through the further analysis to the principle of the second phase of photon mapping, this paper draws the parallel idea of ray tracing and proposes the parallel algorithm of photon mapping algorithm under the multi-core architecture. We refine the data and organize them into a number of block buffer queues that is as the basic parallel model, and we make use of fork/join mode to create dynamic parallel tasks to get better performance. But it does not further discuss the issues on multi-threaded performance such as false sharing, making use of the secondary cache better and so on. It needs more future research on how to optimize the performance so that the global variables photon map will be divided to reduce the relevance between the threads.

Acknowledgments

This work has been supported by the National Natural Science Foundation of China grant 60572169, Scientific Research Foundation for the Returned Overseas Chinese Scholars, State Education Ministry grant D4200407, Tianjin Natural Science Foundation grant 06YFJMJC00400, and Tianjin Natural Science Foundation grant 05YFJMJC09200. The authors are grateful to the anonymous reviewers for their helpful suggestions and comments.

References

1. Turner Whitted: An Improved Illumination Model for Shaded Display. J. Communications of the ACM. 23 (6) :3432349(1980)
2. Goral, C.M., Torrance, K.E., Greenberg, D.P., and Battaile, B.: Modeling the Interaction of Light between Diffuse Surfaces. Proceedings of the 11th annual conference on Computer Graphics and Interactive Techniques, pp. 213-222(1984)
3. Henrik Wann Jensen: Importance Driven Path tracing Using the Photon Map. J. In: Proceedings of the 6th Eurographics Workshop on Rendering, pp. 326-335(1995)
4. Henrik Wann Jensen: Global Illumination Using Photon Maps. In: Proceedings of the eurographics workshop on Rendering techniques, pp. 21-30(1996)
5. Wang Jing, Wang Lili, Li Shuai: An Algorithm of the Expected Radiometric Transmission with All-frequency Shadow Based on GPU. J. In: computer research and development, 43 (9),pp. 1505-1510(2006)
6. M.Tamura, H.Takizawa, and H.Kobayashi(Japan): A Parallel Image Generation Algorithm based on Photon Map Partitioning. In: Proceeding computer Graphics and Imaging(2008)
7. Erik Reinhard, Alan Chalmers, Frederik W.Jansen: Hybrid Scheduling for Parallel Rendering Using Coherent Ray Tasks. In: Proceedings of the IEEE symposium on Parallel visualization and graphics, pp. 21-28(1999)
8. Shawn Singh, Petros Faloutsos: SIMD Packet Techniques for Photon Mapping. In: IEEE/EG Symposium on Interactive Ray Tracing, pp. 87-94(2007)
9. Shameem Akhter, Jason Roberts: Multi-Core Programming: Increasing Performance through Software Multi-threading. Intel Press.,US (2006)
10. Mattson,T.G.,Sanders,B.A., Massingill,B.L.: Patterns for Parallel Programming. Addison-Wesley Professional, (2004)

Author Index

M.L. Huang et al. (eds.), *Visual Information Communication*,
DOI 10.1007/978-1-4419-0312-9, © Springer Science+Business Media, LLC 2010